ALL OF THE ABOVE

VOLUME I

**SECOND EDITION – 2009
WITH SUPPLEMENT**

ALL OF THE ABOVE
VOLUME I
GENEALOGY AND HISTORY
LINEAL ANCESTORS OF
ELIZABETH HUEY TAYLOR COOK

TAYLOR, HUEY, MOORE, CROUCH, MAYO, BALDWIN, SCOTT, DAWSON, PUTNAM (PUTTENHAM), PORTER, HA(W)THORNE, DOYNE, WHARTON, STONE, WINSTON, GAINES, WATTS, GOUGE, GRAVES, WILLIAMS, HUNT (HARP), JEWETT/JUETT, MASON, PENDLETON, GAMEWELL, SWAINE, PARSONS, BOOTH, WOODBURY, DWIGHT, WALTON, MAVERICK, HARRISON, LYTTLETON, VALLETTE, MARMADUKE, GYE, HEDGES (DE LACY), KENDRICK, NOBLE, BATTAILLE, BOWEN, FLEMING, DAVIS, DEVOTION, SHEPHERD, POND, LOWE, RICE, COTTON, MAINWARING, CURTIS, GREGORY, ELYOT, SMITH, CRUTTENDEN, PARSONS, STRONG, HINKSON, GREGSON, CHURCH, MARSH, POMEROY, MATHER, ABRAM(S), ROCKETT, BARBEE, WOODWARD, STEBBENS, WHITING, CROWE, REEDS, GODWIN, PARTRIDGE. LYMAN, DELAMARE, BREWER, THROCKMORTON, SCUDDER, DAWKINS, FRANKLIN, VAUGHN, JOHNSON, MORRILL, CRAIG, TALIAFERRO, HAWKINS, FAULCONER (FALKONER), JENKIN, GARLAND, COLLINS, WATSON, MEDFORD (MITFORD), HEPBOURNE, MACKALL, DOLAND (DOWLAND), BROWNE, POWELSON, MUNN, COOKE, WHITE, COEBOURNE, STALCOP

Richard Baldwin Cook

ALL OF THE ABOVE
Volume I
GENEALOGY AND HISTORY
LINEAL ANCESTORS OF
ELIZABETH HUEY TAYLOR COOK

By

Richard Baldwin Cook

ISBN – 13: 978-0-9791257-1-3
ISBN – 10:   0-9791257-1-5

Copyright Richard Baldwin Cook

Second Edition – 2009
with SUPPLEMENT

NATIVABOOKS.COM
Nativa Publishing
Cockeysville, Maryland

Available at on line book sellers and at bookstores

Introduction: Too Intrinsic for Renown	Page 5
Elizabeth Huey Taylor Cook (1918-2000)	Page 11
Nan Elizabeth Huey Taylor (1893-1993)	Page 29
John Oliver Taylor, Jr (1891-1960)	Page 41
James Addison Huey (1862-1961) Sara Crouch (1861-1956)	Page 53

Two Couples:
    Joseph Addison Huey (1819-1896)
    Amanda Watts Gaines (1821-1895)
&
    Virginia Watts (1803-1882)
    James Gaines (1798-1872)
	Page 89

John Oliver Taylor Sr (1862-1922) Mary Baldwin Moore (1863-1936)	Page 113
Charles Taylor (1819-1897) Charlotte Jane Gamewell (1828-1910)	Page 139
Catherine Gould Parsons (1791-1865) Oliver Swayne Taylor (1784-1885)	Page 179
John Maverick (1578-1635/6) Mary Gye (c. 1580-aft 1666)	Page 201
Marmaduke Moore (1808-1883) Jane Hedges Baldwin (1809-1893)	Page 213
Jonah Baldwin (1777-1864/5) Sarah Scott (1791-1817)	Page 225
William Moore (1780-1859) Elinor Vallette Dawson (1781-1834)	Page 251

Thomas Moore (1745 -1823)
Mary Harrison (1761-1835)   Page 257

Henry Hunt Mayo (1810-1877)
Louisa Winston (?-?)   Page 275

Daniel Mayo (1762-1838)
Mary Putnam (1773-1838)   Page 283

Esther Kendrick (?-?)
Joseph Mayo (1720-1776)   Page 323

Nicholas Dawson (1745-1789/90)
Vilette/Valette Ly(i)ttleton (1759-1842)   Page 337

Mary Stone (?-1683/86)
Robert Doyne (?-1689)   Page 357

William Stone (1603-1660)
Verlinda Cotton (?-c. 1675)   Page 363

Roster of Illustrations   Page 377

Index   Page 379

Supplement   Page 393

"TOO INTRINSIC FOR RENOWN"
Emily Dickinson
(Time and Eternity, LXXXII)

Members of our family have participated in both major events (the Indian Wars, the Battle of Bunker Hill, the American Revolution, the Civil War) and some of the mythic incidents, which have contributed to the character and self-understanding of the people of the United States. A number of the signal episodes were legal proceedings (Salem Witch Trials, Boston Massacre trials, a runaway slave trial).

A large number of male ancestors were clergy of one or another Christian variety. A vocational attachment to devout notions of destiny beyond this life runs deep and consistent across the centuries. Beginning in the late nineteenth century and into the twentieth, we find this same current of devotion present in female ancestors, who would have been debarred in an earlier age from any vocational expression of their religious inclinations and who, in some communions, still are. Beyond child rearing activities, the records of the doings of females, is scant, until we reach the twentieth century.

Our ancestors in America were adventurers and settlers from Europe. Their own anonymous, ancient ancestors had participated in the out-from-Africa clan migrations of past millennia. In successive and uncounted generations, they played their part in the formation of the tribes and tribal federations, which, long before the European occupation of America, had begun to coalesce into the familiar European nation states of today. Many *events* in history (such as the creation of nations) are better thought of as *movements* for they were large population shifts which occurred over decades and centuries. These mass migrations were marked by eviction, dislocation and absorption of resident populations, and thus, by considerable violence. The upheavals were rarely as well documented as the Norman invasion of England. (The French, whether in England after 1066 or in Louisiana, in the eighteenth and nineteenth centuries, always seem to keep good records. Thus we know that two of the twenty-five barons at Runnymede, who placed the Magna Carta before King John in 1216, are connected to Taylor ancestors.)

The creation of the distinct ethnic groupings of Europe can be seen as a prelude to the peopling of North America by Europeans. Their appearance in North America might be described (from this side of the Atlantic Ocean) as a relentless invasion by uninvited interlopers, arriving onto lands already occupied. Did it matter if these filthy, violent newcomers thought of themselves as pilgrims and pioneers? No known right, merely brutal conquest gave them any entitlement to settle and divide among themselves the territory they insisted upon calling, quite mistakenly, a "new" world. Was the arrival and expansion of European settlements merely an extension of the clan migrations of earlier eons?

Our direct ancestors were on only one side of the genocidal struggles against the *Indians* – a name given to them by others. The Indians were themselves members of migrating clans but of Asiatic rather than European origin. They had been in North America for thousands of years before the first European voyagers came across them.

Against the advance of European settlement, the Asians had no chance. Their lack of resistance to epidemic disease caused a population imbalance and social disintegration that undermined their every effort at survival. But that is the long view. It is not the perspective of a family terrified in the night, in its little cabin, listening to whispers and the near-silent foot fall, and wondering if the log door would hold, uncertain, even, of survival into the next day, when one must venture out to tend crops and care for animals.

Terror in the night was the experience of people in their outpost clearings in isolated Ohio and Kentucky forests towards the end of the eighteenth century and a century earlier in Massachusetts or Virginia woods and meadows. It was also the experience of families in Indian towns, petrified by advancing militiamen, who were coming to kill and enslave on the pretext that because native gods were different, the natives were therefore depraved. In fact, Indians would be driven to the brink of extinction because they were in the way of European occupiers, who quickly learned the purifying power of total annihilation. The resident peoples were exterminated by our people: Hawthorns, Swaynes, Moores, Harrisons and others of our Taylor line; Graves, Farmers, Dubois, Van Meters, Crocketts, Cooks and others of our Cook line.

The Huguenot ancestor often appears in our decendency. Because of this frequency, precious space is given in this book, and its companion volume, to the tracing of Huguenot origins to France and the absorption and ultimate loss of Huguenot identity within the family and perhaps generally.

The writing of biography, even the modest ancestral sketch, is a reversal of the Easter narrative, which moves forward from sacrificial death to miraculous life. But our stories move backward, from death to a glimpse of prior life. This writing is motivated by an attempt to comply with a duty to acknowledge, describe and so honor our ancestors. This obligation, as undertaken in this instance, extends beyond memory, and thus beyond the thin historical data we have. History is not all that happened or even all that was important. History is what is recorded and remembered. A story out of the past is what you have after connecting certain selected and arranged facts.

A facet of human life which surely separates us from all other life on this planet is our ancient insistence upon warehousing the bodies of our beloved dead. Many of the old cemeteries still exist and may be located by way of the Index, with directions to some of them.

The occasional redundant mention of names and dates is intended to permit the reader to take up a sketch here and there and not feel pressed to read from cover to cover.

ELIZABETH HUEY TAYLOR COOK – BETTY COOK

This book (in two volumes) is my attempt to honor the memory and the labors of my mother, Elizabeth Huey Taylor Cook (1918-2000). Betty Cook worked on a family genealogy for half a century. She did the necessary tasks: preserving documents, asking questions of her elders, writing and calling distant cousins, organizing her data and discussing it all with the next generation. Betty passed along her research in the form of a grand genealogical chart book in which she collected the facts and made the connections. Betty's effort is the basis of the present work, whose author hopes Betty's ancestors will become a presence to her descendents, as they were to her.

PROOFREADING & FACT CHECKING

Hearty thanks are offered for a thankless task, well done with tenacity and grace, by Rosemarie Coffman and Merry Toups, who proofread an early version and are not responsible for remaining faults. The writer, who continued to fool with the proofread manuscript, owes his gratitude to an observant granddaughter, Isabella Henderson Cook Mendez, for pointing out brand new, last-minute typos. Thanks, Isa. Thanks also to Jean Taylor, the writer's aunt, who checked and corrected Taylor and Huey facts, as did Dr. J.M. Huey, grandson of James Addison Huey and Sara Crouch Huey. The writer is of course responsible for any and all errors.

ERRORS CAN BE CORRECTED

Because of digital technology and print-on-demand capability, this book can be edited and re-printed with relative ease. If you spot factual or other errors, do not hesitate to let me know. To suggest a change, please contact me at cookrb1@gmail.com.

LEAH FANNING MEBANE – THE ARTIST –
www.fanningart.com

This book would miss much of its character and value but for the remarkable artistic gifts of Leah Fanning Mebane, who has taken our family's photos, ancient portraits, and the occasional precious but poorly preserved daguerreotype, and given nuance and character to our beloved ancestors. In both volumes, Leah's charcoal drawings are magnificent.

THE *AMATEUR* FAMILY HISTORIAN

A word of sincere appreciation is owed to each of those family historians and genealogists who have actively searched out the connections upon which this present work so much relies. These tenacious and single minded individuals are *amateur* in the original sense of that word: one who loves the subject.

THIS BOOK IS AVAILABLE ON THE INTERNET AND AT BOOKSTORES

This volume and its companion, **All of the Above II**, (the genealogy of Betty's husband, Cecil Virgil Cook Jr), are available at amazon.com and other internet book sellers as well as at bookstores.

Elizabeth Huey Taylor – Betty Cook

"A HIGH PARTICULAR"

Elizabeth Huey Taylor Cook

Elizabeth ("Betty") Huey Taylor (1918-2000) was born July 18, 1918, in Cincinnati, OH. By long tradition, she was given a family name; Elizabeth was Betty's mother's middle name. Her parents were **John Oliver Taylor Jr** (1891-1960) and **Nan Elizabeth Huey Taylor** (1893-1993). Betty was born in Bethesda Hospital in Cincinnati. Her Ohio birth was a bare formality to her; she always thought of herself as a native of Kentucky. Betty grew up in Union in Northern KY, and in Wheeler, AL (a brief 2-3 years), in Montgomery (a few months) and in Louisville, KY for elementary, junior high, high school and college. Betty's first home was her grandparents' farmhouse in Union, KY, and then "Sunnybrook Farm" in Wheeler, which belonged to Miss Annie Wheeler. Betty's father, John had moved his family there in order to work as a farmer and "overseer" of cotton and other operations.

The connection to Alabama had come about in France, during "the Great War" of 1914-18. Betty's uncles, Mayo and Dwight Taylor, had been called into service as ambulance drivers with MacArthur's "Rainbow Division." This division was the first American unit to have responsibility for a section of the allied front in France - the Baccarat sector. The division was composed of National Guard troops from different states (and so was described by its commander as a "rainbow" across the US). These soldiers saw action at Champagne, the Marne, the Offensive of St. Mihiel and the Meuse-Argonne Campaign. While in France, Mayo met the elderly Annie Wheeler, daughter of Confederate General "Fighting" Joe Wheeler. "Miss Annie" was working with the Red Cross. After serving as part of the occupying forces in Germany, the Rainbow Division was re-deployed to the US. Mayo Taylor was permitted to remain in France, delaying his return in order to work with Miss Wheeler. This relationship led to an invitation to Mayo to come to Alabama and work for

"Miss Annie" on her "Sunnybrook" Farm.

John Oliver Taylor shortly followed his brother Mayo to Wheeler, Alabama. John stayed at Sunnybrook while Mayo moved over to a neighboring plantation.

Betty's sister **Sara Katharine** was born at Sunnybrook on Jan 5, 1922. Baby sister **Jean Valette** was born July 16, 1929 in Montgomery, AL. Following tradition, each infant was given a family name. The second of John and Nan Elizabeth's daughters - always known as "Katharine" – was named for her mother's mother, Sara Crouch Huey (1861-1956). Baby Jean was named after her father's beloved older sister, Jean Valette (1888-1965).

Family lore maintains that Betty was named Elizabeth because her mother liked the name. However, in a video interview she gave to her son David in 1999, Betty offered another reason. Betty stated that her mother had told her, "I wanted to name my baby girl for myself." Thus Betty was named for her mother. There remains a complication. Her mother's first name was *Nanny* a name Nan Elizabeth never liked and declined to bestow on this or either one of her other girl babies. Her mother never understood, said Betty, why she was named *Nanny* at all, as her mother, Sara, told her she had been named for Sara's mother, **Nancy Williams Crouch** (1843-1923).

After the stint as an Alabama farmer in the twenties, Betty's dad, John Taylor became branch manager of B.F. Avery, selling farm equipment from his office in Montgomery Alabama. He was soon promoted to the home office in Louisville, where the family was located by January 1930. Six months later the company closed as the Great Depression completely ruined the chronically vapid economy of the South. Young Betty remembered discovering her father sitting alone at home one day about this time, crying.

After the move to Louisville and the closure of B.F. Avery, John Oliver - "Boba" ("Baba" to Cook grandsons) to his daughters, so named by the infant Betty - was soon employed. He took a traveling job, selling farm machinery and implements in a sales region extending from Louisville west to Nebraska and south to New Orleans. "Mother really raised us, for the most part," Betty has written. (Some of the details of Betty's life and much about her mother and father have been taken from a privately printed book, created by three grandchildren of Nan Elizabeth and John Oliver Taylor, ***Nan Elizabeth Huey Taylor "The Heirloom Seed"*** Editors: David Cook, Reade Taylor and Nancy Vonk [1993]).

Intense discussions marked the dinner table in the Taylor home. On more than one occasion, an adolescent girl made her point through tears, as her father would take a contrarian position or at least make a forceful argument requiring an equally forceful counterpoint. In later years, Betty and her two sisters confirmed all this to their children, nieces and nephews. A consensus, if not the unanimous opinion of Baba's grandchildren would be that his daughters Betty, Katharine and Jean thoroughly absorbed the lessons of this early training in argument and debate. The three sisters expected their own children to hold and to defend well considered opinions.

From an early age, Betty possessed a devout temperament. She maintained this disposition throughout her life, and expressed it as an active Baptist from start to finish. Her September 2000 funeral, in Louisville's Crescent Hill Baptist Church, the church both of her adolescence and her final forty years, was attended by friends from afar and most of the congregation. To her sons, Betty left well marked Bibles and other estimable tomes, which she had collected and studied; reading was a habit begun in her girlhood. Betty's religious nature was widely known among friends, as is shown by the frequency of gifts to her of a Bible or some other book of solemn or confessional content. These Bibles and other books, inscribed to "Betty Taylor" and later to "Betty Cook," are full of marginal comments, underlining, bookmarks, church bulletins, handwritten notes and other small items, which testify to regular church attendance, engaged reading and Bible study that only deepened across her many decades.

Betty is remembered as devout but not pious. She was faithful in her Christian convictions but not the least oppressive in insisting upon her own way. Betty combined her principles with a complete absence of condescension towards the views of others. This liberality towards dogma and doctrine seems to have been a Taylor as well as a Huey trait. Both lines demonstrate, down the generations, faithfulness and active involvement in Methodist and Baptist churches. Betty frequently remarked with warm approval her parents' acceptance of the expression of wide ranging opinions.

In contrast to observations she occasionally made about her Taylor grandparents, Betty always spoke affectionately of her mother's parents, the Hueys, **James Addison Huey** (1862-1961) and **Sara Crouch Huey** (1861-1956). The jovial and loving Hueys impressed Betty as unfailingly cordial towards her and accepting of the views of others. She attributed her special status in part to her rank as their only daughter's first child. She said she was doted on by her grandparents and other Huey relatives, especially her Uncle Gaines. "Oh, I was a high particular," she told son David in her video reminiscence in 1999.

Of Granny Taylor, Betty remarked to David, "I learned from my two sets of grandparents how to treat in-laws - and how not to." Where the Hueys were accepting and cordial, Granny Taylor was sarcastic and biting, or seemed so to a young granddaughter. Although Betty's grandfather, John Taylor Sr, had died in 1922, her Granny lived until 1937; the old lady's acerbic personality was well remembered by Betty, who did not judge her grandmother in wholly negative terms. Minnie Taylor, Betty recalled, was a bright woman who expected one to have her own views - and to express them. Betty remembers the extended conversations that were the rule in Granny's household, as they were to be in Betty's own parents' home. A long table, with room for ten, would be the scene for breakfast at Granny Taylor's. It was not unusual for many people, grandchildren included, to remain at table discussing various topics until lunchtime. Subsequent generations have sat and debated around that table, found today in the home of Granny's great grandson, David Huey Cook and his wife, Kathy (Kathleen).

Betty remembered a discussion at Granny's about Mary and Martha, two sisters mentioned in the Gospels. While Mary sat listening to Jesus, Martha was preparing a meal. Betty recalls stating her opinion that Mary had acted selfishly in letting Martha do all the kitchen chores while she herself sat in the front of the house enjoying the conversation. Granny Taylor corrected Betty. No. Mary knew what was most important and she also knew she had every right as a woman to be there taking part. Betty, in 1999, said she never forgot what Minnie had said, that a woman must insist on an equal place. Both granddaughter, Betty, and Minnie's daughter, Nancy Collier Taylor Johnson, spoke of local reporters and friends calling on Minnie in her home in Erlanger just to talk with her for a while.

Betty's uncle Mayo Taylor (1893-1982) (her father's brother) was a lifelong Methodist Sunday School teacher in Erlanger, KY. Betty often remarked upon Mayo as a guileless, open-hearted man of gentle spirit, whose views (see below, page 112, 178) about God and life's deeper meaning were grounded in the natural world. Mayo was tolerant to the point of universal inclusion and greatly influenced Betty. In 1975, at 82 years of age, Uncle Mayo wrote a statement about his values.

> *"[. . .] Jesus the Christ came to administer to all mankind, just not alone my peculiar ethnic group but to all mankind every where. And that He challenges me to take up the cross, the cross of service, of vicarious suffering daily and go out and be the channel of the flow of creativity that He gave Himself to establish in His brief physical experience here as the Word made flesh. [. . .] One of the greatest rewards that*

life has brought me is when some young person has come and said, under this condition, this circumstance with which he is confronted, 'what is the way to take?' The fact that they considered for a moment that I had something that would help them to make a right decision has been an inspiration for me to try and qualify my life as a channel through which these values can flow out of this experience into the life of another."

Young Betty wanted to experience formal educational opportunities and savor the wider world. She did so to a surprising degree in the very teeth of the economic straits, which plagued her parents' household in the thirties. In her genealogical records, Betty identifies herself as a 1939 graduate of the University of Louisville, of having attended summer school at New York University in 1938, and of taking courses at the Southern Baptist Theological Seminary, 1940-41. Betty also worked briefly after college for the Works Projects Administration in rural Kentucky. During college, she found a way to make at least one trip to the Chautauqua Institution near Buffalo, New York.

Betty married **Cecil V Cook, Jr** (1913-1970) on December 30, 1941. The wedding took place in his parents' home at 406 Altamont Circle, Charlottesville, VA. The wedding was a hurried event, brought on by Cecil's ultimatum that Betty must either marry him immediately or he might cease courting her. Betty herself placed this interpretation upon events in conversations with her sons during the long years after Cecil's death in 1970. As Betty told it, she and Cecil had been seeing each other a good deal in 1940 and '41. During this time there had been at least one other boyfriend. By the spring of '41, Cecil had graduated from the Southern Baptist Theological Seminary (Bachelor of Divinity) and had accepted the pastorate of Napoleon Avenue Baptist Church (at the corner of

Napoleon & South Claiborne) in New Orleans. Before Cecil left Louisville, an engagement had been proposed and agreed to by Betty, but she had then hesitated. Another young man may have had pride of place with Betty that summer. Cecil's ring may have been returned. But Cecil persisted. He came to Louisville in early December, 1941 and urged a decision from Betty. They must marry, he said, or he would trouble her no more.

Betty realized, she said, that she did not want Cecil out of her life. She agreed to marry him. But in giving this news to her parents, Betty recalled in 1999, her father spoke harshly to Cecil. Perhaps John believed Cecil was pressuring Betty against her own will. Or perhaps a severity was expressed by the father of three daughters, when the first of them announced her decision to leave his home forever, to live with a man. Or perhaps an asperity was not at all intended by John but nevertheless perceived by a daughter, who had hoped for an instant celebration of the most momentous decision of her young life. Perhaps she wished for a joy that might envelope both her father and her intended. In the event, Betty believed Cecil was wrongly and roughly treated. So, when he suggested privately to Betty, "why don't I come back for you at Christmas time and we'll just go away and get married?" she agreed.

In one of the few impetuous acts in a circumspect life, Betty eloped with Cecil just before Christmas, 1941. Without telling her parents, Betty and Cecil boarded a train in Louisville, KY and traveled to Washington, DC. Cecil called his parents, who wired him money for the rest of the trip to Charlottesville. The wedding took place promptly in the Cook family home, with the father of the groom presiding.

The newly wedded pastor and his bride traveled by train to New Orleans. He was twenty-eight. She was twenty-three. They lived in a house at 5415 Miro Street, a residence offered them by the Bristow family, members of their church, whose son, Louis Jr, did not then need the house as he was away in the navy.

In January 1942, Betty started a journal, which she would keep for the rest of her life. "On December 30, 1941, I began a new page in my life, a brand new page. . . . One of my greatest feelings has been that of Lot's wife: the backward looker, failing or virtue. I will look back for a few moments. . . On December 2, Cecil asked me to marry him . . . There was a sense of alrightness that filled my heart."

Of her wedding, Betty wrote, "I faced my husband and looked straight into his eyes as I made my vows before God to be a loving wife 'until death do us part.' It's rather strange how just saying those words and hearing the minister's prayers makes one grow from a girl to a woman." Death parted them much sooner than Betty could have imagined. She would live almost sixty years after penning these lines. Only half of those years would be with Cecil.

Cecil was so proud of his church! He drove Betty over to see it their first night in New Orleans. Betty wrote of her "fear and trembling" as she was introduced by Cecil to church members on Sunday morning, January 4, 1942. "It's funny the thrill it gives you to hear your husband say 'my wife' to someone else." To her journal, if not also to Cecil, Betty, from the first, maintained an independent critique of her circumstances, especially if she felt she was being put upon. When ushered to a Sunday School class that first Sunday and being asked if she had "something to say, because we haven't anything else to do," Betty writes, "I didn't know whether to wiggle my nose, or pull a rabbit out of a hat or run." She also wrote in this first journal entry, "Husbands are mighty sweet, even though they make you type lists of names when you are about dead." She also wrote, in her journal, of her first days as a wife. "The pattern was a glow with bright tints and shades. Later to be mingled with darker ones, which in my heart I believe has enriched and deepened the quality of our lives."

Forty-one years later (1982), looking back on Cecil's 1970 death, Betty would return to the metaphor of dark and bright colors. In a meditation she entitled "Death of a Husband," (**Women on Pilgrimage**, Broadman Press,

1982), Betty wrote, "*A lack of joy in the events of each day is a supreme waste. We have been created to live and to take the events over which we have no control and weave them into a tapestry. This tapestry of our lives is made up of bright and vivid colors as well as some which are muted and dark. All are woven together to make a pattern of beauty.*" (See Appendix, **All of the Above II**.)

Betty described her elopement as a hurtful shock to her parents, who were deprived of any role whatever in planning and celebrating the wedding of their eldest daughter. In 1999, Betty said that one good consequence of her elopement was that her two younger sisters had a very smooth experience, when the time came to introduce their prospective husbands to her father. Betty also recalled that Cecil's unfailing good cheer and respectability dissipated her father's anger at the elopement.

The Taylor family did a lot of reaching out to the newlyweds. Sisters Katharine and Jean visited in July of '42, if not sooner and their father went to see Betty and Cecil in September. Harmony in the family was probably helped along by the prompt advent of grandsons **William Dorland** (January 26, 1943) **Richard Baldwin** (January 13, 1944) **Cecil Virgil** (March 26, 1946), **David Huey** (January 22, 1948). Four infant boys in five years honored three hundred years of family planning - or the absence of it - among Taylors, Cooks and their lineal and collateral lines. Betty and Cecil hoped always for a girl. But this wish would not be granted. On September 19, 1953, there appeared **Charles Merritte** - five years after the fourth son. Charlie has stated that of all the sons, he was obviously the "love child."

Betty remarked in later life that the arrival of so many babies so quickly put her in a state of stress from which she emerged only in subsequent decades. With tots coming on one after another, Betty found herself pushing toilet training hard upon the little fellows. "I just could not have two babies in diapers at once," Betty confessed to her adult sons. Did anyone feel pushed out? Or pushed aside? Despite the stress of nurturing the next newborn, Betty found time to read Bible and bedtime stories, recite nursery rhymes and put on 78 rpm story-records for her squirmy, tow-headed toddlers. We sat in front of the gigantic record player for hours on end. (Who can forget the story of the math whiz, Hypotenuse Turtle and his trip to the moon? or the crow with the southern drawl, who made his home in the Cornfield? or the bird that was a combination of chicken, turkey, duck and goose: a *churkenduse*.) Betty introduced her young sons to poetry. "*Blessings on thee little man,*" she would recite, "*barefoot boy with cheeks of tan!*" She would bring out an ancient volume of **Pilgrim's Progress**, passed down from a century before, place it on her lap to read and direct a boy's gaze at the bold woodcuts, each a story in itself.

It was no surprise to hear Betty recall how she perceived her youthful self: a young mother, not as capable or confident as she would like. As was her own mother, **Nan Elizabeth**, Betty was self-deprecating. In the case of Nan Elizabeth, this may have been (as many a grandchild, or son-in-law perceived) a mostly benign stratagem for eliciting a compliment about, say, her cooking. In Betty, but not at all in her mother, there was a life-long note of self-doubt. This element may have been part of her father's Taylor-Moore heritage. One could identify in Betty a reserve not so pronounced in her as in her father, which might be identified in **John Oliver Taylor Jr** as a shadowy taciturnity. In Betty, there was a reticence about placing herself forward, which marked in her own mind, an honest self-appraisal of her capabilities, but which as a widow, she struggled hard to overthrow.

In truth, coping in the '40's and '50's with so many children while in the visible role of a young pastor's wife was a burden to Betty. It probably would have been to any woman. The children came first in her time and her preoccupations. As busy and stressed as Betty remembered herself to be as a mother, she always expressed interest in the doings of each small one in her care and worked to expand their interests and abilities. She was also good at stretching the food budget like a rubber band, to feed her brood on the modest salary of a Baptist pastor. No child ever got up hungry from Mother's table. With so much to attend to at home, Betty's public role suffered. Eva Easley, a church member from Betty and Cecil's West Virginia years (1944-1959) remarked in 2005 that Betty was not well known around the church during the forties, because she was hardly ever there.

Help was available. Betty's mother **Nan Elizabeth Taylor** (1893-1993) and her mother-in-law, **Blanche Dorland Cook** (1873-1967) were ready to make an appearance for a few days at the birth of the next baby. Betty's two younger sisters were present from time to time, as well, beginning even at the beginning, during the first months in New Orleans. Katharine married Paul Miller in 1946 and they began their own family of four by 1947, with the arrival of their John. In time, Betty's sister, Jean and her husband, Henry Taylor would have four children as well, naming the youngest one John. Did anyone ever ask Betty why she did not name a son after her own father? Perhaps after all, the rancor of the elopement ricocheted around the nursery.

Betty's sister Jean Taylor was twelve years old when Betty and Cecil married. Jean spent her final year of high school with Betty and Cecil, graduating as a "Beaver" from Bluefield High School in 1946-47. Jean's move to Bluefield relieved stress on her parents; John was working in Raleigh and Elizabeth, recovering from cancer, moved "up home" to her parents, in Union, KY. Jean was available then (and later) to help care for and tutor young, quizzical nephews. On one occasion, Jean explained the objective of the missionaries, Marquette and Joliet, who went forth from France, said Jean, "to mish the Indians."

Cecil, having done what he did to create this large family, did what he could for Betty. His sons recall going to the drive-in theater in August, 1953 to see "The African Queen," sitting all in a row on the back seat of a 1948 Packard, with an attentive father and a very pregnant mother in the front. One wonders if Betty might have identified too fully with iconic Katherine Hepburn in the role of the zealous spinster missionary, who was much-put upon by the coarse and slovenly Bogart riverboat captain. True - the entire adventure took place on a scow in a leech-infested river - but there was nary a crying baby or any squabbling toddlers in view.

Beginning in 1958, Betty became a single parent for nine months each year. This turn came after Cecil left the pastorate in Bluefield and went on the road as a fund raising professional. Betty and Cecil have left dozens of letters written during the decade of this separation (1959-1968), which proved to be the final years for Cecil. Interestingly, the letters which have been located are those Betty wrote to Cecil, but not many of Cecil's to Betty. Did Cecil write fewer letters? Did he save hers but she not his? Her letters invariably begin: "My Darling." (Note to self and progeny: writing 'My darling' lots of times is likely to strengthen conjugal ties.)

This is a 'My Darling' dated Sept 10 1959, which Betty marked on the envelope, "Charles' first day at school."

My Darling,

While the details are fresh in my mind, I want to tell you about Charles' venture out into the wide-wide world. He had given me instructions to wake him up early, had gone over his supplies dozens of times and had a hard time going to sleep.

I got him up and he bounded out of bed. Telling me he was going to brush his teeth "like Daddy" and with instructions about his clothes he began to get ready. He said the blessing and I too said a blessing asking God to take care of him and to be with him on this first day of school. After I finished, he asked, Why did you have to butt in with a blessing, Mother?

Here is a note from Charles:

> *Dear Daddy,*
>
> *This is a letter from Charles, you send me back one. If you have a calendar check the day it's the 10th. I am going to school today. Daddy I had a good lunch. You should have had some. We had a hot dog applesauce for dessert. That was all. I forgot we had milk. We had two recess time, one a big one and one a little one. You should have come there it is a real good school.*
> *Love, Charles Merritte Cook*

To go back to the first day of school. Charles wanted me to walk with him and I did. We stopped by and walked along with Carolyn Hall. Charles would skip along and then come back and quietly take my hand. He was willing for me to leave him at the door of the school, but kept waving and calling goodbye. I surely had a big lump in my throat as the school swallowed him up. I walked back for him this afternoon. I want him to get used to walking so I can just go and meet him at the corner of McCready and Lexington Road. He was happy when I picked him up this afternoon, but did seem tired.

The weather is delightful. Air conditioner hasn't been on all day!

All my love, Betty

In 1968, Cecil was made vice-president of his firm, Ward Dreshman & Reinhardt; Betty and Cecil moved from Louisville with Charles to the home office in Worthington, Ohio. At that time, Betty's mother, **Nan Elizabeth Taylor** (1893-1993) moved in with them. Widowed in 1960, "Mama" had remained in Union, KY to care for her father **James Addison Huey** (1862-1961) but she had been living in her own apartment in Louisville since 1962.

Cecil, Betty, Charles and Mama had no sooner unpacked their Kentucky possessions in Ohio when catastrophe struck them. At Christmas, 1968, Cecil was diagnosed with lung cancer. This horrific news came to them soon after Betty and Cecil sold their home on Trinity Road in Louisville and bought a house (her "dream house" she said) in Worthington, a Columbus suburb. Cecil promptly submitted to radical surgery, the removal of a lung. But terminal damage had been done by Dad's years of smoking "Lucky Strikes." Cecil did not give up smoking until after the cancer diagnosis, when he said he could no longer even look at a cigarette. Cecil died in July, 1970. He was fifty-seven.

In the forties, Betty began to pull together her history of the Cooks and Taylors. She worked intently on this project, checking dates and facts and covering both hers and Cecil's family with equal thoroughness. This activity charted numerous family lines through several centuries and seems to have come to an end by 1967. In her genealogical chart-book, Betty recorded her mother-in-law, **Blanche Dorland Cook**'s birth date but not the date of her death in '67, nor did Betty mark Cecil's death in July 1970. The family history project was renewed with vigor in the mid-70's, after Cecil's death and after Betty had relocated herself, Charles, and her mother, back to Louisville, where she continued to gather data but no longer made notations in the chart book.

In '71 Betty, Charles and Mama, settled into a Cape Cod Betty had picked out at 4023 Ormond Road in St. Matthews, a Louisville suburb. The next decade saw Charles grow up and Nan Elizabeth ("Mama") Taylor and Betty make a home together. Becoming increasingly frail of mind and body in the early '80's, Mama was moved into a residential care center in Winston-Salem, NC, near the home of her daughter Jean and Jean's husband, Henry Taylor. Not long after, Betty sold her home and moved into a townhouse in the same part of St. Matthews.

After the return to Louisville, Betty became more active in the church of her childhood, Crescent Hill Baptist.

She became a Sunday School teacher of a class of young women, a venue which forged strong and loving relationships that endured the rest of her life. Aware of the need to counter her taciturn nature, Betty willed herself forward into more public activities. Already in the sixties, she had found the inner strength to march for civil rights in Louisville. By the early seventies, she summoned the will not only to speak publicly, but even to permit herself to be elected a deacon and express her views in gatherings of mostly assertive and accomplished men. Increasingly, Betty spoke up at various church events. Discovering that she wrote well, and encouraged by some of the younger women who attended her Sunday School Class, it was at this time that Betty contributed her chapter, "Death of a Husband" to a book **Women On Pilgrimage.** (For this chapter, please see the Appendix to this book's companion volume.)

Living alone in Louisville after her mother was moved to Winston-Salem, Betty welcomed opportunities to spend time with her children and grandchildren as well as with her sisters and their husbands. In the eighties, Betty made regular car trips to Winston-Salem, NC to see her mother and sister Jean and husband, Henry Taylor and their family. Less often, she would travel to Millville, NJ to visit her sister Katharine and Paul Miller and their children. Distinctly uninterested in "babysitting" her grandsons, Betty preferred to see each grandchild individually, inviting first one and then another for a meal and a chat.

In the 1980s Betty became a great fan of the University of Louisville basketball team, getting season tickets for several years and attending home games with friends. Everybody wore Cardinal Red. She would occasionally go to an important "away" game and would more often follow the team on TV, positioning her 5'1" frame crosswise in an easy chair, with her short legs dangling over an armrest. She would sometimes put on her cardinal sweater to watch the televised games alone.

During the lengthening years of her widowhood

Betty cultivated and deepened her spirituality. Without imposing, she was quick to share her views and observations. She became increasingly candid about her joys, trials and experiences. In this way, Betty developed the gifts of listening and of sharing. In the sixties, Betty had begun reading the books of the Swiss physician and psychiatrist Paul Tournier and was also exposed to both the writings and the lectures of the well regarded pastoral counselor and teacher, Wayne Oates. Betty read deeply and reflectively and tried to put into practice what she understood to be the wisdom of relating empathetically to other persons. As a result, in conversation with Betty, one felt recognized and honored.

In Betty's presence one experienced a penetrating sense of acceptance. Betty's capacity for offering a spiritual embrace to The Other Person was noted by family members and many others. This welcoming quality was powerful within her, to the point where her appearance in a gathering could induce a change in mood in those who had experienced Betty in private conversation.

In her advancing years, the prospect of her body outliving her brain imposed a heavy anxiety upon Betty. She wished to avoid Alzheimer's and any similar diseases that might undermine her mental abilities. Thus she devoted considerable energy to an examination of her mortality. How to be released from life without a long and slow cerebral decline? Was it ironic, then, or merely responsible, that Betty always was quick to get medical attention at the first hint of any sort of ailment? Seeking advice from an attorney with special expertise in elder law, Betty secured a living will and selected a medical power of attorney. She took these steps more than once, as she tried to keep her documents current with changes in the law. Betty wanted an iron-clad written instrument that would enjoin any and all: no heroic medical measures! Betty joked with Barbara Cook, her physician daughter-in-law, that Betty ought to have "Do Not Resuscitate!" tattooed on her chest. Betty left instructions for her body to be cremated and the ashes buried beside Cecil's in the

Dorland plot at Cave Hill Cemetery in Louisville.

In the event, Betty was spared any kind of lingering. A year before her death, Betty incurred uterine cancer, which she elected to treat with radiation but without risking the debilitations of chemotherapy. On September 7, 2000, precious Betty flew away.

STRONG AT THE BROKEN PLACES

Life is difficult. This is a great truth. Once we see this truth, understand and accept it, we transcend it.

My Heavenly Father began to do good things for me before I was born, by giving me good parents and grandparents, whose faith and example undergirded my early days. I have seen them meet the deprivation of the depression times of the thirties without a whimper. I saw my grandparents [Sara and James Huey] meet the death of their youngest son [Gaines] through an accident at the age of thirty-five. My grandmother taught her Sunday School class the next Sunday.

"The world breaks every one and afterward many are strong at the broken places." (Hemingway, *A Farewell to Arms*, p. 249.)

Betty Cook, 1982

Elizabeth Huey Taylor Cook

"KNOWING WHAT TO DO WITH WHAT COMES"

Nan Elizabeth Huey Taylor

Mother of Betty Taylor Cook (1918-2000)

Nan Elizabeth Huey (1893-1993) was born in Union, KY on Sept 12, 1893. She died almost one hundred years later, on May 30, 1993 in Winston-Salem, North Carolina. The town of "Winston" before its merger with "Salem" had been named for Joseph Winston (1746-1815), for his prominent participation in the Battle of Kings

Mountain (Oct 7, 1879). Joseph was the brother of **John Winston** (1756-1830), third great grandfather of Nan's husband **John Oliver Taylor** (1891-1960). (Page 279.)

Nan Elizabeth grew up in the house in which she was born, the home of her parents, **James Huey** (1862-1961) and **Sara Huey Crouch Huey** (1861-1956). *Nanny* (her given name, which she disliked, preferring, *Elizabeth*) was the only daughter and middle child of parents who spread the births of three children over seventeen years. Following a strong tradition of naming infants for venerated relatives, Nan was named for her mother's mother, **Nancy Williams Crouch** (1843-1923). Nan's brothers were Joseph Addison Huey (1884-1963) and James Gaines Huey (1901-1935). Brother Joseph was the namesake of his father's father. The youngest child was given the name of a great grandfather, **James Gaines** (1798-1872), the father of **Amanda Watts Gaines Huey** (1821-1895), the mother of his own father. Elizabeth's younger brother was called "Gaines" for all of his brief life.

Gaines' death at age 34 was a devastating calamity to his parents and two siblings. "Boss" Huey was 72 and gave up farming as a result. (See page 57.) In later life, Elizabeth spoke of her little brother (to grandsons, at least) in melancholy tones. At Gaines' accidental death, she and husband **John Taylor** went immediately "up home" for the funeral but decided to leave their three daughters behind. Betty remembered this as a poor decision. Betty, Katharine and Jean loved Gaines as a favorite uncle, who always had time for them, and included them in activities that children would enjoy. Betty was hurt that she was not present and able to grieve with the rest of her family.

In fact, Elizabeth did know how to include children in funerals. Daughter Jean recalls attending the funeral "up home" of Nan's great aunt, Louisiana Castleman (June 8, 1834-August 4, 1934). What Jean (born: July 16, 1929) remembered was playing outside the church, with her mother.

Elizabeth recalled her childhood as a period of contentment and joy. She developed a life-long love of reading and absorbed into her adult life the thoughtful spirituality of her church-going, Baptist parents. The Hueys seem to have doted on their only daughter. In later life, Nan Elizabeth returned this favor to the cheerful, mirthful "Mama" and "Daddy" Huey. This pair was remembered by all as exuberantly happy together.

Throughout her long life, Elizabeth looked forward to her visits with her parents in their grand, white home on the hill in Union, KY. Although the parents no longer lived in the house where she had been born and raised, Nan Elizabeth took great pleasure in these extended tarriances, a pleasure matched by that of her young daughters, who were taken to Union for many a summer with the Hueys. Nothing could quite match going "up home" to Mama and Daddy Huey's.

As an adolescent, Elizabeth moved into nearby Covington, KY and lived with cousins Sam and Betty Shepherd so she could attend high school. The Shepherds were interested in politics; Betty was an aunt of Senator John Sherman Cooper. Nan Elizabeth recalled that Sam and Betty encouraged Nan to take her own interest as well.

After high school, Elizabeth went away to Stephens College in Columbia, Missouri. This school was selected for her because a relative, the husband of Aunt Lula Quisenberry, was college president. With her gift for friendships, Elizabeth maintained ties to a handful of college classmates throughout her long life. After two years at Stephens, she returned to her parents' home.

John Oliver Taylor Jr (1891-1960) must have captivated Elizabeth with his good looks and dashing manner. They were married on New Years Day, 1916. Everything reported and known of their marriage suggests it was a match marked by strong bonds of affection and contentment. "They delighted in being together," daughter Betty has written. The only somber resonance in their marriage would be caused by the many long months apart, as John worked for more than thirty years as a traveling salesman of agricultural implements and equipment. She and John began married life on the road on their honey-

Nan Elizabeth Huey

moon. They traveled throughout New York State, as John embarked on his career as a salesman.

Elizabeth and John were hard hit with blows of deprivation and uncertainty, caused by his unavoidable separations from the family. The stress of a scuffling salesman's life in the '20s was compounded by the Great Depression of the '30s. These years were well remembered by their oldest daughter **Betty Huey Taylor** (1918-2000), who has written that her mother met all circumstances with fortitude and good cheer. Betty has written: *"The depression of the late twenties and early thirties caught up with our family shortly after Boba was promoted from Branch Manager of B.F. Avery in Montgomery Alabama to a member of the sales force in the Louisville home office. We moved to Louisville in January 1930. In the summer Avery folded. Boba was not without work long and was employed by Brinly Hardy Farm Implement Company. His territory extended as far west as Nebraska and as far south as New Orleans. The size of his territory meant long months away. Mother never uttered a single word of complaint. No 'poor me.' ever crossed her lips. She met this as she met every experience in her life; with great courage. I remember she rode to town on the bus to pay our bills to save postage. When our hero Franklin Roosevelt took office he closed the banks to save a run on them. I remember Boba wired us money for groceries. Mother really raised us for the most part. She was a strong person in my opinion but never recognized this quality in herself."*

The family lived in a downstairs apartment at 333 South Peterson in the Crescent Hill section of Louisville, KY. "When the time came for Boba to leave," daughter Betty wrote, "the Yellow Cab pulled up to take him to the train - Mother began to busy herself, emptying his ashtrays, putting away the linens he had used."

Her husband's long absences must have been an unsettling echo of the life of his father, the oft-absent "traveling salesman," **John Taylor, Sr** (1861-1922). But the separations were not the only threats to Nan

Elizabeth's tranquility. She faced a menace to her very life at age 53. Daughter Betty told of it, "When cancer came to her in 1946, Boba was working in North Carolina. She faced the radiation and radium treatment with the same fortitude and Christian faith that had always sustained her. She made the most of the long trips to the hospital on the bus. She said sometimes she was so sick and weak she just sat down on the curb and waited for the bus." Nan survived her cancer and lived another 47 years. Reaching her hundredth year, Nan narrowly surpassed her parents; her mother, **Sara Crouch Huey**, lived to 95, and her father, **James Addison Huey** to 99.

By the nineteen-fifties, John's health was broken. Years of smoking had brought on crippling emphysema. He could no longer work but had not qualified for Social Security or for any kind of pension. Daughter Betty and her husband, Cecil, came to John and Elizabeth's aid. "We took a small inheritance of my husband's mother [**Blanche Dorland Cook,** (1873-1967)] and bought a book shop. And this provided income in the form of interest for her and jobs for my parents. This was a good time in our lives. It was good to see Mother blossom as she lived her life in the business world, a totally new experience for her." (A sketch of Blanche is in **All of the Above II.**)

By the late fifties. John at last had qualified for Social Security, which enabled him and Elizabeth to move to her beloved parents' home in Union, KY to care for her widowed father **James Addison Huey** (1862-1961). John Oliver Taylor Jr died in 1960.

With the death of her parents as well as John, and herself entering old age, Elizabeth sold the "home place" in Union and moved to nearby Louisville, which had been home to her and John when their girls were young. Betty and Cecil helped her find an apartment in "Seminary Village" off Frankfort Avenue, where Nan Elizabeth lived for eight years. Her apartment was near the home of Betty and Cecil and their five sons. Nan's life centered on family and Crescent Hill Baptist Church, just as it had thirty years before.

This was the momentous decade of the sixties and Elizabeth entered the fray. Living in Louisville, she encouraged daughter, Betty, who marched for civil rights for African Americans. Elizabeth also offered moral support to her near at hand Cook grandsons, in their varied activities. At one point in the mid-sixties, while one was involved in campus civil rights activities, another had joined the Marine Corps. Before the decade had passed, another Cook grandson was serving as a conscious objector and two had joined the Peace Corps. Born in the nineteenth century, Mama appeared to take it all in stride.

Nan Elizabeth was a great letter-writer and included not only her daughters but also her grandchildren in the circle of her correspondents. She would write you back if you would write to her. Through letters she would introduce a uniquely phrased note of levity and acceptance that melted the decades and breached generational divides. To grandson Reade Taylor, who saved her letters, Elizabeth thought she "might do you more good by sending you a stamp" than a letter. Again to Reade: ". . . and in KY it is a beautiful morning. Sun trying hard to shine. Thunder showers creeping up. Don't know why I said it was beautiful. Wasn't really thinking of the weather." She advised Reade, "I've found out long ago the important thing is knowing what to do with what comes."

In 1968, daughter Betty and her husband Cecil moved to Columbus, Ohio. This was a job-inspired move, as Cecil became vice-president of his firm, which relocated their corporate headquarters away from New York City. Cecil personally asked Nan Elizabeth to move with them and youngest son, Charles. She agreed, gave up her Louisville apartment, and moved into the Cook family home in Worthington, Ohio.

Within five months of the move to Ohio, Cecil was diagnosed with lung cancer and died in July, 1970. Cecil's death at 57 came just as he was entering into his powers as vice president of his company. This was an appalling blow to Betty and Charles, then 17. But Elizabeth seemed to know what to say and to do when life, which gives so much,

Nan Elizabeth Huey Taylor

also takes much away. Betty wrote, "*She walked with me as Cecil died. Words are inadequate to express what her presence meant. She had an innate sense of one's need for privacy. I came home from the hospital the night of December 30th 1968. This was the evening before Cecil was to have surgery for lung cancer and also our twenty-seventh wedding anniversary. She had placed the vase of red roses he had sent me in our bedroom and had not said a word about it. She knew my need to be alone.*"

Nan Elizabeth spoke clearly about life's great cruelties. She avoided the delusion that difficulties will disappear if you will just banish them from your conversation. In January, 1970, while her son-in-law was dying in a room nearby, Elizabeth wrote to daughters, Katharine and Jean. "Cecil's illness has made me more conscious of all of you that I love - how much you mean to me - how thankful I am for all of the good things in my life. As you can see I am counting my blessings."

Nan Elizabeth lived with Betty for twelve years after Cecil died: two widows, mother and daughter. This could have been a trying interval for both, had either Betty or Nan Elizabeth viewed life as overly-diminished or drained of value. But surrender to negativity was not in the make-up of these women. Betty's life became more enriched through her circle of church and community friends, and Nan Elizabeth continued her correspondence and spent increasing time with her two other daughters, flying to visit them and their families. Daughter Betty wrote in 1980: "*She is a remarkable lady . . . so cheerful, so positive in her outlook on life. All of these qualities have been hers all of her life and are serving her well at age 87.*"

Elizabeth's body was to outlive her personality. When her mental decline had entered its irrevocable course, her's two younger daughters, Katharine and Jean and their husbands took responsibility for her and relieved Betty, now in her sixties, of the multifold daily tasks of caring for Mama. After twelve years with Betty in Louisville, Nan moved - more accurately - was moved - to

Nan Elizabeth Huey Taylor, baby Betty

Winston-Salem, to live in a nursing home near daughter Jean and her husband, Henry Taylor.

In the deepening darkness, Nan lived on for ten years. But she entered the twilight with dignity and little expression of fear or resentment. Grandson, Cecil Virgil Cook III has written, "When she saw the end coming to her logic she told me not to come see her in the nursing home that way . . ." But of course, Jean and her family did come and see Elizabeth *that way*. Mama's habitation in shadow was another kind of gift to her family. "One catches patterns of life as one sees life lived out," Betty has written. "I have observed two generations before me caring for the older family members, not only parents but aunts and uncles. One gets the message: *this is the way we live in our family*." The pattern of care that Mama had given her parents was repeated for her by Betty, Katharine and Jean.

Elizabeth was beloved by those she loved. She knew this and responded with words and deeds of her own. On January 1, 1974, in a letter to her three daughters, Mama wrote,

"Fifty-eight years ago today, about this time of day was our wedding day. That was the beginning of it all. A good and happy day that certainly was enriched by you three girls." A few months later, she wrote, *"How very thankful I am that you three girls came through as you did and have become what you are."*

SOURCES:

For genealogical data: Betty Taylor Cook's unpublished genealogical book. For many of the details of Nan Elizabeth life, including all quotations: **Nan Elizabeth Huey Taylor: "The Heirloom Seed"** Editors: David Cook, Reade Taylor and Nancy Vonk (1993).

"A NEVER ENDING PARTY"

Noted composer and music critic, Virgil Thomson (1896-1989), and his two sisters, Ruby Richardson and Hazel Louise, were third cousins of **Nan Elizabeth Huey** by way of their Gaines ancestors. Virgil was born in Kansas City, Missouri on Nov 25, 1896, son of Quincy Adams Thomson (1862-1943) and Clara May Gaines (1865-1957). Clara's parents were Mary Eliza Graves (1836-1879) and Benjamin Gaines (1832-1932), a son of **James Gaines** (1798-1868) and **Virginia Watts Gaines** (1803-1883). Benjamin was a brother of **Amanda Gaines** (1821-1895), the wife of **Joseph Addison Huey** (1819-1896), Nan Elizabeth's grandparents. (See below, pages 53 and 89.) Virgil Thomson, who was awarded a Pulitzer Prize for composition, wrote his autobiography (**Virgil Thomson**, 1966), generally considered the best by an American composer. In it Virgil has invoked family recollections, but with few details. From pages 5 and 9:

I do not know when it all got started in Virginia, this business of their being always Baptists, though family records show persecutions for it in the eighteenth century. And certainly there had long been Baptists in Wales, where many came from. It may be that the Welch ones (and my mother's people seem all to have borne Welch names) were Baptists when they landed...

Benjamin Watts Gaines, born in 1832, had lived in a wide Boone County [KY] house full of children and visitors. The Civil War, less passionately viewed, I gather, in Northern Kentucky than in central Missouri, had passed him by. Along with his brothers, he had offered himself to the Confederate troops; but he was refused for lacking two fingers. . . . As with so many Kentuckians, life at his house was a never ending party.

"JACK WAS NEVER MISSED"

John Oliver Taylor, Jr

Father of Betty Taylor Cook (1918-2000)

John Oliver Taylor Jr was born on Jan 20, 1891 and died May 25, 1960. Although much of his life was lived elsewhere, both events occurred in Northern Kentucky. John Taylor Jr was the first son and second child of six, and was named for his father **John Oliver Taylor Sr** (1862-1922). His mother was the formidable **Mary Baldwin Moore Taylor** (1863-1936). Family lore accurately records that John Jr and his five siblings were kept out of the public schools, "the common schools" so called. Allegedly, this was because the schools were "not good enough" for Minnie's children. Allegedly, the Taylor children were taught at home. This informal hit-or-miss schooling served the children ill. Some of them remarked to various relations, how disabling the absence of a diploma was; they could not prove their educational attainments. John's younger sister, Nancy stated this to me. The children did grow up in a house full of books; their letters reveal a high degree of articulate ease with the written word.

Those who knew John Taylor Jr, remembered a man who adored his wife and treasured his daughters. John was also a great admirer and defender of President Franklin Roosevelt and all his works. John Jr was known to debate politics to the point of discord, taking on (when few others would) his younger brother, the loud and deep voiced Marmaduke ("Booch"). John brought the larger world of national and international events into the perspectives of his three young daughters. From John, they learned to debate and defend their views with tenacity. John sustained a life-long protective devotion to his own mother, whom he may have viewed as a victim of the appalling circumstance of her marriage to John's father.

John Oliver Taylor Jr

John possessed a dispirited and pessimistic temperament. His daughter Betty recalled that he always had a bad word to say about an employer. Of anyone placed in charge to hold him accountable, John's critique was relentless and bitter. Daughter Betty was especially impressed with the low qualities of one particular supervisor, whom her father vigorously condemned and scorned. Years later, she attended the man's funeral just to see if anyone came and if so, were the man's abusive traits publicly condemned. As Betty suspected, many people attended and the alleged mistreatment of his work force by the defunct received no mention among the grieving.

John's strident disdain for his managers seems to have been his particular expression of a family characteristic. John, like his mother and father, was possessed of a personality colored in somber tones.

As Betty wrote, contrasting her parents, "Mother was always sunny and optimistic, while Boba tended to be moody and if faced with a choice looked on the down side of every event." But is the child best positioned to assess the emotional state of the parent? (Some of us hope not – or at least hope that the children wait a decent interval before publishing their assessments to the world.) Perhaps John's personality pushed to the fore a quality of directness, which could be mistaken by a child for harshness. I can testify to a wrong conclusion drawn by a grandchild about John. He was fond of calling grandsons, "Bub." This always seemed harsh to me – until 2007, when I discovered that John's father referred to himself as "Bub" in an 1886 letter he wrote to his sister Jean. For John, *Bub* was a treasured family endearment.

Is there reason to assign blame for the scuffling career stratagems to which the Taylor boys were reduced? Daughter Betty thought so as did her aunt, John's sister, Nancy. The problem, they concluded, was parental: John Taylor Sr was absent, leaving Mary Moore Taylor to raise their six children. Mary must have felt abandoned by her husband for the sake of his traveling job, a job which produced very little income. She responded to this betrayal by emotionally carpet bombing the home front; she combined notions of success with a peculiar strategy that kept her children away from any program of education that could match her airy plans for them.

"JUST IN TIME FOR THE DISHES, OR RATHER, THE DISH"

As young men, newly wedded, John and his brother Mayo worked as farm supervisors in Alabama. They were employed by moneyed individuals situated at the top of a predatory share cropper system which, at the end of the day, rewarded no one. The Taylor boys had been raised to speak their minds. From "Sunnybrook" Farm, Wheeler, Alabama, John wrote home to their mother that he grew impatient with Mayo's employers, Miss Birdie and Miss Annie Wheeler, to the point of demanding to know, if Mayo was so lacking in the requisite skills, why did they not just fire him?

Both John and Mayo were unsuited for farm supervision responsibilities in Alabama in the '20s. John once wrote that share croppers, "colored and white," were meeting to protest their rental arrangements. Mayo was dispatched to attend and represent the interests of the owners. At the meeting, John says, Mayo "on his own hook" told the renters their complaints were justified, to the consternation of the employers "Miss Birdie" and "Miss Annie" Wheeler. Mayo himself wrote to his mother that the ladies were waiting for "the shade" of the patriarch, General Joseph Wheeler of Civil War fame, to arise and put everything right – without the need to spend a cent.

The "god-forsaken" (Mayo's words) share cropper system and its mostly barter economy kept everyone cash poor, tied to a stubborn piece of unyielding soil. The fundamental problem for Mayo and John Taylor was the deliberate "reconstruction" of the ante-bellum plantation system, which the Alabama establishment imposed in the 1880s and '90s as a reaction to potential local Black political and economic gains after the Civil War. White

Southerners of the Deep South (Alabama, Georgia, South Carolina, Florida, Mississippi and Louisiana) established local political dominance and legalized a "lien" system of leases, which gave land owners first claim to the crops raised on land rented to share croppers. With landowner liens on the harvest, the risk of farming was placed almost entirely on renters, which deprived share croppers of credit or cash with which to buy seed, or tools.

The letters of both brothers reveal that rural Alabama in the 1920s had not yet entered the twentieth century. Travel was by horseback or wagon; simple one- and two-room homes were lit by gas lamps. The brothers maintained both a longing to return to Kentucky and a sardonic humor about their poverty. In one of his countless letters to their mother, Mayo wrote: "It's past eight and I am just in time for the dishes, or rather, the dish."

Neither brother could make a success of the farming venture. Both eventually left, John first. Mayo returned to Erlanger, KY and John moved to Montgomery, AL, and then Louisville, where he could install his family while following his father's career as traveling salesman. Given the necessity of going out into the world of work with no true education or demonstrable credentials, John was unable, through parental fealty, to fault his mother or father for this circumstance.

John aimed his work-day frustrations at a more acceptable target, the boss. In conversation with her sons, John's daughter Betty went further. She concluded that in the semi-tragic life of his mother and the catastrophe that was his father, John Taylor Jr's outer-directed rancor was a symptom of untreated depression, born within him in childhood. No one can ever know for sure. John was aware of his gloomy nature. He wrote to his sister Jean, that in contrast to himself, "You have a philosophy that makes life give you something every day." The unstated corollary was that John expected very little from life.

Within his family, John's affect may have been dour but his actions were gentle. He was attentive to his grandchildren as he had been towards his children. He was

John Oliver Taylor Jr with banjo & baby Betty

a patient teacher, taking satisfaction in telling you what he knew to be true. Having lived on the road in hotel rooms and at the YMCA, "Boba" took time to demonstrate how best to fold a pair of pants so they would look presentable when removed from a suitcase: always fold the pant leg above the knees. Having helped his wife in the operation of a bookstore, Boba would demonstrate across the bookshop counter or on the dining room table, how to "break in" a hardback book so as to protect the spine: with the book on a flat surface, open it wide then, every 40 pages or so, slide your hand up and down the inside of the spine. Boba always had a nickel for a grandson. And he enjoyed a good laugh. A smoker whose health was utterly ruined by middle age from severe emphysema, Boba's laugh is remembered by grandchildren as a wide mouthed, soundless grin.

John Taylor Jr may have suffered career disadvantages from a lack of formal education, but he certainly married well. On January 1, 1916, he wed **Nan Elizabeth Huey** (1893-1993), an exceedingly attractive young woman from Union, KY. Nan Elizabeth, for two years, had attended Stephens College in Columbia, Missouri. Not long after she returned from Missouri, Nan Elizabeth and John met at a party in Erlanger. They discovered they had grown up a mere seven miles apart, but had never before met. They also discovered they were immediately taken with each other. John, in horse and buggy, began to call on Nan at her parents' home.

John and Nan were remembered by their children as very much in love and quite contented in each other's presence. John enjoyed cooking roasts and lentil soup for his wife and three daughters, who perceived his long absences from home as a heavy burden upon both of their parents. As they faced the trials imposed upon them by scant income and then the Great Depression of the '30s, the sense of Robert Frost, iconic poet of their generation, resonated with this couple: "*I counted our strength – Two and a child.*" With Katharine and little Jean added to daughter Betty, there would be the strength of five.

John never indicated the least disappointment that

he had fathered three daughters but no sons. In January 1948, as daughter Betty awaited the birth of her fourth child (David), John sent an affectionate letter to her. "Betty Girl," he wrote, in recall of Betty's own birth in 1918, "we were expecting either Jack or Betty and Jack was never missed."

"YOU CAN WORK IT UP INTO A MORE ACCEPTABLE FORM"

Although his brother Mayo Taylor was the avid family historian of that generation, John seems to have had more than a passing interest in genealogy. In March 1945, he wrote to daughter Betty, *"I worked up the enclosed from some facts cousin Mary Lawrence gave up, knowing you would be interested and it really is something to have even one line of our family for three hundred years. And to look at Billy and Dick and say Boys, this is in your little bodies, something that all these that have gone on pass on to you. Maybe with this you can work it up into a more acceptable form. Don't you like to think your great-great-grandfather journeyed into Boone County to find your great-great grandmother. Then comes your father going back to same county to find Muhie* [his wife, Nan Elizabeth]. *And further back Daniel Mayo and Mary Putnam started out in New England, getting together in Northern KY or southern Ohio. And still further back, Mayos and Putnams coming from England. Your past, with all of it going into what you and your boys are today."*

Nan, a practicing Baptist, may have been concerned before their marriage, about John's lack of religious interest. At best, he was a nominal Methodist. John's grandparents **Charlotte Gamewell** and **Charles Taylor** had been the first missionaries commissioned by the Methodist Church, South. They had gone to China in 1849. Returning to South Carolina after five years, they had given forty-five years to Charles' career as a Methodist educator and pastor. Charles and Charlotte's devotion was not carried forward by their son John Sr and his wife Mary ("Minnie") Baldwin Moore Taylor. Nor by John Jr.

As young children, John Jr and his five siblings were baptized but only at the instigation of their oldest sister Jean, who arranged this when their mother was out of town. Minnie was remembered by daughter Nancy to have remarked, "I had a happy home until Jean and Mayo got religion." Her son John Jr was excluded from Minnie's slight, which suggests that John Oliver Jr, despite his surreptitious sprinkling, had, like his parents, only a trifling interest in sectarian concerns. When it came down to cases, after his marriage to a practicing Baptist, John attended the Baptist church with Nan Elizabeth and was proud of his three daughters' leadership in church activities. But that was it.

At their wedding in 1916, John's sister Nancy played, *Believe me if all those Endearing young charms*, the bride's chosen song, which was her favorite, Nan Elizabeth said, sixty-years later. The ancient English melody, with words added by Thomas Moore, about 1827, expressed sentiments well suited to the marriage that followed.

Believe me if all those
Endearing young charms
Which I gaze on so fondly today
Were to change by tomorrow
And fleet in my arms,
Like fairy gifts fading away

Thou would'st still be adored
As this moment thou art
Let thy loveliness fade as it will
And around the dear ruin
Each wish of my heart
Would entwine itself
Verdantly still.

It is not while beauty
And youth are thine own
And thy cheeks
Unprofaned by a tear
That the fervor and faith
Of a soul can be known
To which time will but
Make thee more dear

The heart that has truly loved
Never forgets
But as truly loves
On to the close
As the sunflower turns
On her god when he sets
The same look which
She'd turned when he rose.

John and Nan Elizabeth Taylor are buried in Highland Cemetery, 2167 Dixie Hwy., Covington, KY near the graves of both their parents, James A. and Sara Crouch Huey and Mary Moore and John Oliver Taylor Sr (and at least one unnamed infant of theirs). Mary Moore's parents, Benjamin and 'Rilla Mayo Moore are also buried at Highland.

John Oliver Taylor Jr

SOURCES

For genealogical data: Betty Taylor Cook's unpublished genealogical chart book.

For the details of John Taylor Jr's life, and personality including Betty Taylor Cook's quotation: **Nan Elizabeth Huey Taylor "The Heirloom Seed"** Editors: David Cook, Reade Taylor and Nancy Vonk (1993, page 16).

Other quotations are taken from the letters and reflections of Nancy Collier Taylor Johnson, John's sister and from Mayo Taylor, his brother, whose letters have been preserved by cousins Anne M. Gibbs (granddaughter of John's sister, Jean, and Paul Carter) and Mary Taylor Ecton (daughter of Mary Alice Stevenson and Mayo Taylor), whose generosity in sharing is acknowledged with gratitude.

I counted our strength – Two and a child: Robert Frost: *Storm Fear*, **Robert Frost's Poems** (Pocket Books, 1955, page 245)

For the history of political, economic and social developments in the American South after the Civil War, see the excellent **Reconstruction, America's Unfinished Revolution** by Eric Foner (New York: Harper Collins, 1988, 2005).

> "*Porgy and Bess*, a white man's view of life among Blacks, has circled the globe. Its power and charm put it not far below Bizet's *Carmen*, which is after all a Frenchman's view of Spain." Virgil Thomson (see above, page 40) (**Virgil Thomson: A Reader** by Richard Kostelanetz, Routledge 2002, page 182)

"BEST TO TRY TO BRITEN THE CORNER WHERE WE ARE"

James Addison Huey
Sara Crouch

Nan Elizabeth Huey Taylor (1893-1993)
Betty Huey Taylor Cook (1918-2000)

Sara Huey Crouch (1861-1956) was born Aug 19, 1861 near Ghent in Gallatin County KY and died in her home in Union, KY on March 20, 1956. She had been named for a favorite aunt: Sara Huey.

Sara Crouch married **James Addison Huey** (1862-1961) on June 29, 1881. Over the next twenty years, James and Sara had three children, Joseph Addison (1884-1963), **Nan Elizabeth Huey** (1893-1993) and James Gaines (1901-1935). Sara's religious nature was an early and constant feature of her long life. In 1875, at age 14, Sara was baptized into the Oakland Baptist Church in Warsaw, KY and promptly became a Sunday School teacher there.

In 1886, Sara and husband James were charter members of the Union (KY) Baptist Church and attended there for sixty years. Sara was active in various Baptist women's organizations and was a teacher of the Women's Bible Class, giving it up only late in life as a result of failing eyesight.

James and Sara have passed down two very tiny, thick hymnals. One of them is *The Christian Hymnbook*, "selected by A. Campbell and others" (Cincinnati, Ohio, 1868). This hymnal and its association with Alexander Campbell indicate that it emerged from a church controversy of the early and middle decades of the nineteenth century. The dispute in question was a divisive debate among Baptists in Ohio, Kentucky, Indiana and Illinois, which had to do with Alexander Campbell (1788-

Sara Huey Crouch

1866), a charismatic preacher, who held strong opinions about the need for unity among evangelical Protestants. Campbell's convictions included hostility toward human slavery. But he also held strong views about the mode of musical instruction within the churches. Campbell insisted that non-believers should not be permitted to sing hymns. Nor did he think hymnals should include musical notations, but only the words, as notation could distract from the object of worship. Campbell's efforts led not to the merging of denominations (is anyone surprised?) but to the creation of a couple more, the Church of Christ and the Disciples of Christ. The hymnbook in question, passed down through the Huey-Taylor-Cook family, was authorized by Campbell in 1864, to be published after his death in 1866 by the American Christian Missionary Society. The family's 1868 edition eschewed the objectionable musical notation, though an edition published two years later is said to have added them. The hymnal's gold leaf pages are not much marked, suggesting this hymnal was rarely used. James and Sara Crouch Huey did not become Campbellites; they would not have warmed to Campbell's rigid rules about congregational hymn-singing.

The second hymn book left by James and Sara Huey is a much worn copy of **The Baptist Hymnal**, 682 numbered pages, divided into two parts, "hymns" and "songs." A child (or several children) drew lines up and down and across every blank page. The name "James" appears in a child's hand. The book is missing its front matter and any publication details. However, a final unnumbered page advises that the book is the work of "Mr Mason, the author of Mason's Harp, whose celebrity as a composer and teacher of music is everywhere acknowledged."

Lowell Mason (1792-1872) was a New Englander, a music teacher, composer and arranger of hymns, who contributed much to the music education of children in the public schools. Mason also campaigned to transform hymn singing in the Protestant churches of America. Mason found great fault with the "singing school" approach to hymn-teaching, a highly popular method of choral and congregational instruction which had developed in the eighteenth century in New England and spread into the South and West in the nineteenth. The "singing school" stressed the teaching of hymnody by the printing of songbooks, with musical notes appearing in a system of shapes - thus the shape-note system. The memorization of the shape of the notes permitted the singer to follow the melody, which would be given its own name, and thus applied to different words. The learning of hymns in this manner was of a highly social character, as church members would gather weekly for practice.

Mason's main complaint was high-brow: shape-note systems were taught by unqualified itinerant instructors, ignorant of European hymnody. Mason's energy, skill as a teacher and knack at self-publicity resulted in the displacement of shape-note singing by Mason's own "round note" method. This system drew inspiration from European sources, but, it must be admitted, favored more tuneful, easily remembered melodies. Mason's substitution of a *round note* format did not completely wipe out *shape note* instruction.

Mason and his followers, notably William Bradbury (1816-1868), succeeded in relegating shape note singing in the 19th century to primarily small, rural congregations and to an ever smaller fraction of choral instructors and singers, who remained loyal to the shape note tradition. Shape note singing is still popular today, embraced by its practitioners and by musicologists as both a respected form of American church music and a mode which preserves uniquely American hymnody. Shape note singing draws upon musical phrases, melodies and theological formulations dating from the colonial period.

Lowell Mason wrote more than a thousand hymns, many of which are still sung today. These include *Joy to the World, My Faith Looks Up to Thee,* and *Nearer, My God, to Thee.* The Hueys' well-worn **Baptist Hymnal** was one of Mason's later hymnbooks. Think of **James** and

Sara Huey, standing together a hundred years ago in the Union Baptist Church, doors and windows open to the Kentucky spring, turning to No. 3 of the "Songs," noting the tune is "Italian Hymn" and singing Mason's *Come, Thou Almighty King*.

Early on, James Huey found his life's spot. It was the hamlet of Union in Boone County KY, to where his parents had moved from their farm on Rice Pike, near Big Bone, when James was seven or eight. Sent away to Georgetown College in Frankfort, KY, he returned home after a few weeks and, with one short exception, never again lived away from Union. James had inherited vast properties, which he maintained as farmlands and pasture. With the aid of his sons, James farmed some 500 acres and also owned an "upper" farm. He and Sara lived and raised their family in what had been his parents' home.

In the 1920's, after their children were grown and had homes of their own, James and Sara sold some farmland and moved into Erlanger. They soon regretted this decision. They missed their farm home and so moved back to Union, able, apparently, to reacquire the very home they had sold not long before.

In later life, James adopted the practice of selling his lands for needed cash. This activity was compounded because, in addition to farming, "Boss" (as he was called by everyone in Union) served on local bank boards in Erlanger, Richwood and Union. James' procedure was to sell off lands, to be subdivided and developed by others into parcels for resale. His land sales increased during the Great Depression, when James had to deal with personal liabilities that resulted from the failures of banks on whose boards he sat. Then in 1935, Gaines Huey, Sara and James' youngest child and second son, died after being kicked in the stomach by a colt. This calamity combined with advancing age, meant James was not able to farm as before. The sell-off of farmlands seems to have accelerated.

Sara and James Huey maintained an affectionate and welcoming household for their three children and their families. Daughter **Nan Elizabeth Huey Taylor** (1893-

James Addison Huey

1993) certainly remembered it that way and always looked forward to opportunities to take her own children "up home." In July 1918, John and Nan's daughter Betty was born in nearby Cincinnati. (Nan's week long hospital stay cost $31.21, including a $1.11 laundry bill and .10 for medicine.) In 1920, Nan, husband **John Oliver Taylor** (1891-1960) and baby daughter Betty (age one and a half) were enrolled in the Boone County census, as residents of the Huey household, along with **Nancy Williams Crouch** (1843-1923), Sara's 76 year old widowed mother, who was called "Nanny Crouch" or "Maw."

James and Sara Huey arranged for their children to be taught at home. They set up a school room compete with school desks, book and various supplies and employed "Cousin Flora" to teach their children and other children in the neighborhood. This arrangement worked well enough to prepare their children for high school in Covington.

Nan and John Taylor's daughters, Betty, Katharine and Jean recalled happy summer sojourns with the Hueys. The little girls acquired status among their school mates in Louisville, when they announced they would be spending the summer in the country.

Everyone loved to visit "Mama and Daddy Huey." Betty Taylor recalled how her grandfather, Daddy Huey, would slip out of the house, to appear a moment later as a ghost at a window, howling and draped in a sheet. The appearance of "dumb Ellen" was a tradition that extended to several generations. In a letter to daughter Elizabeth, in September 1910, after she had gone to Columbia, Missouri to attend Stephens College, James wrote, "We have just had supper and my promise is out to Gaines to cut some melons for him and while he and his chums are eating I am to appear as Dum Ellen so I must close."

Playfulness was typical of both Sara and James. They could entertain and be entertained at an advanced age, by a pop-up toaster, whose spring was so strong the toast would be sent flying. Their home in Union had an

Sara Huey Crouch

upstairs bedroom, which required a step down to enter (and of course, a step UP to leave). Great grandchildren were warned not to forget about "the step down room." The writer recalls falling into and then tripping upon exiting "the step down room." There was a spinning wheel in the living room and rocking chairs on the front porch of the Huey's white farmhouse home. Daddy Huey, born during the Civil War, was known to lament how federal soldiers stole the family's silver and chickens, while he, no more than two or three years old, marched behind them.

James and Sara celebrated seventy-five years of marriage. They were, in the words of Wordsworth: *a double tree with two collateral stems sprung from one root*. Both Sara and James lived well into their tenth decade, cared for by doting children and grandchildren.

In the 30's, James was told he had colon cancer. He submitted to surgery, and afterwards, was informed that the surgeon had discovered cancer but intended to close the incision and tell James there was nothing to be done. But James' family doctor told the surgeon he had promised the patient, whatever dangerous growths were discovered, would be taken out. The surgeon then did remove what he could of the cancer. James lived on for 30 years.

Boss was remembered for his generosity to neighbors in need. Before he quit farming, he would preside at annual hog killings. On these occasions, *Boss* would insist that a dressed hog be delivered to a family in the neighborhood, who were going through a rough time.

Sara Huey died on March 10, 1956, five years before James. On the first anniversary of Mama Huey's death, a solicitous granddaughter wrote Daddy Huey a note of condolence. James wrote back on March 20, 1957,

Dear Betty,
Your letter this A.M. So nice of you to remember and write. Yes it is a blue day but best to try to briten the corner where we are. Thank you for your remembrance of what March 10 meant to me.
Love, Dady

NANCY WILLIAMS AND JOHN CROUCH

Sara Huey Crouch Huey (1861-1956) was the daughter of **Nancy Williams** (1843-1923) and **John Crouch** (1835-1903). Nancy was born on June 15, 1843 and died Jan 23, 1923. John Crouch was born Feb. 17, 1835 and died Oct 7, 1903. John and Nancy were married in September, 1860, in Glencoe, KY.

The five children of Nancy Williams and John Crouch are as follows: Henry, **Sara** ("Sally"), Myrix Josiah (a physician, named for his mother's father), Jenetta (approximately named for her grandmother Junietta, but called "Junie"), Lula (Quizenberry), and George. The Crouch family is enrolled in an 1870 Gallatin County Census, which lists the following individuals: **John**, 35, **Nancy**, 27, Henry, 10, **Sally**, 8, Myrix J. 5, and Jenetta age 3. Mary, age 47, is listed as well. The family is also registered in 1880 and in the 1900 federal census.

The 1900 census confirms John's age and records that he was born in Kentucky, and married to "Nannie," a name given to her granddaughter, **Nan Elizabeth Huey** (1893-1993), by Nancy's daughter, Sara. John Crouch was remembered by daughter, Sara, as very strict and "a little snobbish." Sara's husband, James Huey, confirmed to his granddaughter Betty Cook, that John Crouch "liked the blue beards."

John and Nancy's son, Dr. Myrix Crouch, took an active interest in local history. In 1894, he delivered a paper before the Grant County Medical Association, entitled "Big Bone Springs." The event was reported in the *Boone County Recorder* Dec 26, 1894 (page 2).

After her husband, John, died on Oct. 7, 1903, Nanny Williams Crouch lived with her daughter, Sara and son-in-law James Huey, in Union, KY. "Maw" was recalled by grandchildren as an old lady who loved to garden. On Sunday afternoons she would collect slips and cuttings from the neighbors and transplant them to her own patch.

John Crouch

Maw would attend to the family's sewing and mending chores. For this labor, she would recruit other relatives, who were visiting her at the Huey family home.

In 1914, the venturesome "Maw" Crouch made a cross-country automobile trip, with two other elderly female friends, keeping a diary along the way. The journal is over full of weather-related comments (Oct 26 1914: "Jack Frost in all of his glory"). There are notes on church attendance but there are occasional, descriptive remarks.

>
> *Duro wood the name of the auto we drove . . .*
>
> April the 8th went to Long Beach and the first time in my life I beheld the great Pacific Ocean. We also went to Ocean Park. It was a sight to watch the people bathe and see them ride the waves of the mighty deep . . .
>
> April the 15th, we went to the Caneston Ostrich Farm. The life of the Ostrich is 65 years. They lay 15 eggs, set 42 days. Male sits on the eggs 16 hours out of the 24. The oldest they had was 20 years old. Their names were George & Martha Washington; they also had Col. and Mrs Roosevelt and Major and Mrs McKinley. Major McKinley killed his first and second wife because they did not want to set. They then chose a wife for him and she makes him stand around and take notice.

Nanny Crouch's diary covers more than her remarkable cross-country trip. She kept other journals, sometimes writing in the margins of an old calendar, which she up-dated by marking the current year at the top of the page. On Jan 14, 1915, Nanny Crouch wrote, "My poor child left us one year ago today." This reference is to her son Henry, who died on Jan. 14, 1914. Nanny had also buried a daughter, Jenetta, on Jan. 28, 1911. John and Nanny Crouch are themselves buried in the New Warsaw Cemetery, Highway 42, Warsaw, Gallatin County Kentucky.

WELSHMEN IN THE KENTUCKY WILDERNESS

Nancy Williams Crouch was a daughter of **Myrix Josiah Williams** (1811-1897) and **Junietta Gouge** (Feb 25, 1815-June 17, 1846). Junietta and Myrix were married in Grant County KY on Nov 8, 1831. They were the parents of four children, Louisiana (June 8, 1834-August 4, 1934, named for an aunt); Sarah (?-?); **Nancy** and John, who died in 1846 at age 19. Louisiana married Henry Clay Castleman in 1850. Sarah married Washington Huey and was the mother of four: Lee; Oscar M., a pastor of Crescent Hill Baptist Church in Louisville, KY and friend of **Cecil V. Cook Sr** (1871-1948); Annie (Gaines); and Samuel. Nancy, as stated, became the wife of **John Crouch** (1835-1903) and the mother of **Sara Crouch Huey** (1861-1956). Two other children were born to Myrix and Junietta, who died quite young; they were Mary Jane (1838-1842) and Joannah (1845-1845), who lived but five months.

Junietta Gouge's older sister, Louisiana, had married Kavanaugh Williams in Grant County on Feb 20, 1830. It would appear, then, that Junietta married her sister's brother-in-law when she married **Myrix Williams** in 1831. Myrix' name is at times misstated in census records as "Max" or even "Miax." The name seems to be of Welch origin, a permutation of Miricks or Myrick or even today, Merrick. Myrix' grandfather's middle name was "Miricks" changed two generations later to *Myrix* by an indifferent speller (as were many) or a conscientious clerk with a good ear and a creative pen.

MYRIX JOSIAH WILLIAMS: TALL, PROPER, SEVERE

Myrix Josiah Williams was born near Richmond, KY on July 14, 1811, a son of **John Williams** (c. 1764/7-1816?) and **Elizabeth Collins** (?-?), both from Virginia but believed to have met in Madison Co KY, where they married. They named Myrix for his grandfather **William Miricks Williams** and his great-grandfather, **Josiah**

Stone (see below).

Betsy Collins Williams was the daughter of **Nancy Anne Garland** (?-?) and **John Collins** (?-?). Both the Williams and Collins families had settled in Madison County VA (later, KY) after moving into KY from VA. The Williams were located on Tates Creek, while the Collins family lived on Muddy Creek. Both families attended Viney Fork Baptist Church. In about 1830, John and Betsy Williams relocated their family from Richmond, KY to Napoleon in Gallatin County KY. This was the year before Myrix and Junietta got married in Grant County.

John Williams' parents were Welshman **William Miricks Williams** (abt 1735-1814, Madison County KY) and **Elizabeth Stone** (April 14, 1749, Stafford County Virginia-b/f 1787?). In addition to son John, William and Elizabeth Stone Williams were the parents of two other children, William Jr (c. 1764/7-?) and Mary (1770-?). Elizabeth and William were married in Prince William County VA in 1764. Elizabeth was a daughter of immigrant **Josiah/Josias Stone** (abt 1725-1790) and **Mary Coleman** (abt 1720-1789). Josiah Stone was born in England and married Mary Coleman on June 17, 1747 in Stafford CO Virginia. In 1778, Josiah Stone bought land and a slave from William Miricks/Mirix Williams. Josiah Stone died in Stafford County VA in 1790; Mary, his wife died the year before.

It is believed William's first wife, Elizabeth, died before 1787. In that year, a census and tax assessment was conducted in Madison County Virginia (later, Campbell CO KY). William Miricks Williams was enrolled together with one son below the age of 21. William M. Williams' property is listed as 4 horses/mules, 10 cattle and one adolescent slave. William M. Williams' second wife was Ann(a) Milam (?-by 1810). According to the Madison County KY census of 1810, Wm M. Williams is the owner of three slaves. No free white female is enrolled in his household. Since no wife is listed in the 1810 census, it is reasonable to conclude that William's second wife, Ann(a) Milam had died before the 1810 Census was conducted.

In 1830-31, Myrix built a home for Junietta in Dry Ridge, Grant County KY. They lived there until Junietta's death in 1846. Myrix Williams was the owner of a number of slaves; it is reasonable to conclude that in fact, Myrix and Junietta' s home (indeed each of Myrix's subsequent homes) was build by his slaves. Myrix moved to Glencoe after Junietta died, where he saw to the construction of a two-story brick home overlooking the community. Myrix served as Glencoe Magistrate for 40 years.

Myrix' granddaughter, Sara Crouch and her husband James Huey, told their granddaughter Betty Cook that Myrix, tall, proper and severe, required everyone to come to breakfast properly dressed. He read the Louisville *Courier Journal* every day and looked up in his dictionary any words he did not know. Rain or snow, he saw to his riding horse every morning. Myrix was remembered as generous and hospitable but "ruled with an iron hand," Sara said. (For a photo of Myrix, see page 394, below.)

Junietta Gouge Williams died a month before her 31st birthday. She is buried on a gentle slope in the cemetery at Ten Mile Baptist Church, Tapering Point Road, in Napoleon, Gallatin County KY. In June 2006, her double great granddaughter, Jean Valette Taylor, and a small entourage of other relatives, visited Junietta's grave. Young Junietta died of an unremembered cause. The culprit could have been the harsh gauntlet of childbirth, far more deadly in those days, to mothers than to their babes.

Space was left for Myrix in the Ten Mile Baptist Church Cemetery. But soon enough Myrix married Martha Turley (Dec 22 1821-Nov 14 1871). Myrix and Martha were the parents of five children: Taylor, Billie, Jimmie, Betty and Frank (Joseph Franklin). In 1874, Myrix, widowed once again, married Minerva Donaldson and with her became the father of Maggie Williams (Mrs. J.E. Wolford), who lived in Louisville. Myrix was buried in a family cemetery in Glencoe. Although Myrix had been an active Baptist, the funeral took place in his home and the graveside ceremony was conducted by the Masons. Myrix had been Grand Master of the Kentucky Masons in 1865-

66. He also served in the KY legislature in that year. His headstone could still be read in 2006.

The sudden death of young Junietta and the prompt second marriage of her husband, is a reminder of duties owed to the living. Myrix quickly got a mother for his young children, including daughter Nancy, then three years old. Junietta, in her dying, may have made Myrix promise to re-marry. We cannot know. But we do know that little Nan Williams, with hardly a memory of her mother, grew up to be an articulate, extraverted and literate woman, a venturesome widow and an honored matriarch in the home of her daughter, Sara Crouch Huey, in Union, KY. Sara named her only daughter after Nan. We must not, then, forget to salute Martha Turley, the second bride of Myrix Williams, who raised little Nancy and her young siblings plus five children of her own, with Myrix. Martha Turley Williams died (of exhaustion?) before her children could honor her in old age.

JAMES AND ELLEN GOUGE: LATE HUGUENOTS, EARLY BAPTISTS

Junietta Gouge, Nan's mother and Myrix Williams' wife, was one of nine children born to **James M. Gouge** (1777-1858/60) and **Ellen (Ella) Jane ("Nellie") Jewett /Juett** (1789-1849) of Grant County, KY. James and Nellie were married in 1807. In addition to Junietta, their children included Louisiana, James M., Marietta, William Taylor, Thomas Jefferson, Lafayette P., John Quincy, and Henry Clay Gouge. Of these children, perhaps the most locally prominent was T.J. ("Uncle Jeff") Gouge, a farmer and sometime hotelier in Williamstown and the father of seventeen children.

James Gouge was from Virginia and lived in Bourbon County KY before settling permanently in Grant County. It has been said that James moved to Kentucky as early as 1798, with his widowed mother. James is listed in the Grant County Census of 1820. In 1824, James Gouge bought a lot in Williamstown, Grant County. He is presumed to have built a home on this lot. It has also been recorded that by 1814, James Gouge was operating a tavern near the hamlet later to be named Mason. However, the tavern owner appears to be a James Gough, not James Gouge. Confusion linking Gough and Gouge has lingered for centuries; James Gough has been mistakenly said to be buried in the small Gouge family cemetery, a half mile north of the spot where the Gough tavern was located on Route 25.

Ellen Jane Jewett and James Gouge are buried in a now-isolated Gouge Family cemetery in Mason along Route 25. Their graves are on a rise of ground, in a thicket between the highway and the tracks of the Southern Railroad, a quarter mile south of the Lawrenceville Road in Grant County. In June 2006, their two gravestones were located by a covey of their relatives, who found the markers completely hidden in underbrush and for that, surprisingly well preserved. A third stone marker is that of Joseph Juett, Oct 26, 1792-Nov 12, 1849, a brother (I believe) of Ellen Jewett Gouge.

James and Nellie Gouge were active Baptists. James was listed as a member of the Fork Lick Old Baptist Church. The formal name of this church was "the Particular Baptist Church at Fork Lick." Prior to the founding of this church, the Fork Lick members had been associated with what they themselves called the "Baptis Church at Dry Ridge." James and Nellie Gouge and the few others who organized the Fork Lick Old Baptist Church had been released to do so by the Dry Ridge Church, probably for reasons of distance. In 1826 James and two other Fork Lick members convened a commission to consider the orthodoxy and beliefs of the Dry Ridge Church, as it reconstituted itself. The committee from the Fork Lick church gave approval and the Dry Ridge Church, the oldest church in what became Grant County, was reorganized.

Now is as good a time as any to try to distinguish "Particular" Baptists from "General" Baptists. As all congregations and church hierarchies define themselves as the 'true' church, real distinctions are found to lie elsewhere than in self-descriptions. In essence, the Particular and General Baptists are distinguished by a difference of opinion concerning election by God versus the decision of the individual to obtain salvation, by faith in Jesus. Particular Baptists in 19th Century Kentucky believed that God designates who is among the Elect and who is not - who is "saved" and who is not. As God's "foreordaining" of salvation occurs beyond time and apart from any human initiative, there is little reason, by implication, to evangelize in the world. On the other hand, "General" Baptists were of the opinion that the personal choice of the individual whether to accept Jesus as the savior of humanity is all important. For General Baptists, then, evangelical work was necessary since every human being should be extended an invitation to join God's elect: humans cannot know who may or may not be among the 'elect' of God.

The distinction has worn away, but in the early decades on the nineteenth century in the Kentucky bluegrass, Baptist churches took most seriously the question whether one's entry into salvation was entirely based upon God's predetermined will (Calvinism) or upon an invitation offered by the evangelical elect (Arminianism). Tiny churches scattered across the hills and in the crossroads of rural villages would split up over the question.

As the nineteenth century progressed, the Particular Baptists' strict adherence to the Reformist (John Calvin's) rigid doctrine of election became much modified in practice. An example of the melding of evangelical fervor with Calvinism and its severe doctrine of election is **Abraham Cook**, (1774-1854). (See **All of the Above, II**.) A well known Baptist preacher of Shelby County KY, Abraham's double great grandson **Cecil V Cook Jr** (1913-1970) would marry **Betty Taylor** (1918-2000) in 1941. Betty was the great granddaughter X 3 of Ellen and James Gouge. Abraham Cook was described in the 1880s by a near-contemporary as a Calvinist BUT also evangelical. J.

H. Spencer, publishing his **History of Kentucky Baptists, From 1769 to 1883**, was careful to write in 1886 (vol 1, page 435), "In doctrine Mr. Cook was Calvinistic, and was very firm and decided in his principles, contending for them with earnest boldness; but he regarded it his duty to warn sinners to repent and believe the gospel."

Most Kentucky Baptists of the second half of the nineteenth century were heirs of rural Particular Baptist congregations, such as the Gouge family helped to found in Grant County KY. But they would follow such as Abraham Cook, in sacrificing the virtue of consistency for the greater virtue of practical compromise and thus would come to maintain both election and evangelism as correct doctrine and proper practice. (This was a hundred years before the Southern Baptist Convention, in the latter half of the twentieth century, placing idiots in charge of the asylum, would abandon both integrity and compromise and show the door to any who declined to adopt the half-baked and bigoted creeds of radio pulpiteers and televangelists.)

The eventual melding of Anabaptist evangelical practice and Calvinist doctrine was unthinkable among the sectaries of Europe in the 1500 and 1600s. It was hard enough to bring off in Kentucky, even on the sparsely populated frontier of the 1820s and '30s. Separation was often preferred to conciliation. No sooner would a small congregation of say, 25 families, organize into a gathering of Baptists than the strongly opinioned members would find themselves wrapped around the axle. Were they all "general" or "particular" in their notions of God's election? If they found themselves in harmony, they would proclaim themselves Particular or General in their beliefs. If they fell out over election, the already tiny church would split.

And so, in 1826, to settle this question within a fledgling congregation, it was necessary for James Gouge and two or three others to be formed into a commission of inquiry by the Fork Lick church. The commissioners were under a mandate to investigate the beliefs of those who wished to reconstitute the Dry Ridge Church, which had been the parent church of the Fork Lick congregation. According to church documents, the newly reorganized congregation won the commissioners' approval and the tiny congregation was encouraged in its reconstruction under its new name, the Williamstown Church of Christ, Particular Baptist.

In Kentucky, in the early nineteenth century, both Particular and General Baptists looked back with nostalgic fervor to Baptist beginnings in Virginia Colony the century before. Both groups claimed to be the spiritual descendents of those persecuted pioneer preachers, who stoutly resisted state church (Episcopal) pressure to desist from preaching and teaching the freedom of the individual conscience to worship God outside of the legally sanctioned, tax-supported colonial church. Many of these "new lights," also called "professors," migrated into Kentucky, where they gathered one or two Sundays a month to worship in their own manner. Their "soul freedom" was linked with the successfully fought Revolution and with the notions of freedom of religion as the deist Thomas Jefferson had articulated these ideas. In Kentucky, Baptists such as William Hickman (1747-1830/34) who could remember the Revolution referred to themselves politically as "Whigs of the Country," which meant something akin to but not wholly identical with Jeffersonian agrarian democracy. (Hickman's memoir is appended to the companion to this volume.) The embrace of Jefferson by Virginia/Kentucky Baptists lasted little more than a decade after the Revolution. By the 1790's Baptists in Virginia were denouncing Jefferson as an infidel.

JEWETT = DE JOUET ?

Ellen Jane (Nellie) Jewett Gouge's parents were **William Jewett/Juett/Jouett** (abt 1766-abt 1821) and **Anna Falkoner (Faulconer)** (1769-1834). In 1779/80 William and Anna are thought to have moved from Virginia to Bourbon (now Harrison) County Kentucky, where Nellie was born.

The Jewett family of Virginia seems to have been Huguenots (French Calvinists) whose surname in France may have been *De Jouet*. After 1685, many Huguenots immigrated to America, fleeing political and religious persecution in France. These troubles were precipitated during the Protestant Reformation of the previous century. In France bitter and bloody sectarian fighting was only temporarily and intermittently settled by the 1588 Edict of Nantes, which divided French cities and regions into Protestant and Catholic enclaves. The edict offered a measure of security to both camps, but was revoked by Protestant King Henry of Navarre, who converted to the Catholic faith in order to be made the French King.

The 1685 revocation of the Edict of Nantes provoked renewed slaughter. This new and decisive turn downward in their fortunes caused many thousands of Protestants – Huguenots - to leave France, immigrating in vast numbers to the nearby German Palatines ("Paltz"), and to Amsterdam, London, and, after a generation or more, to America. Many Baptists, looking with pride to their Huguenot origins, draw inspiration from the tragic history of the Huguenots - victims and not conquerors in their worldly struggles against malign forces. Ironically, John Calvin, who gave the Huguenots their theology, was as critical of the re-baptizing Anabaptist sects as ever he was of 'Popery.'

William Jewett's parents were **John Jewett** (?-?) and **Mourning Harris** (?-?). John's parents were **Mathew Jouett** (?-abt 1734) and **Susannah Moore** (?-?). John Jewett's grandson (and therefore cousin of Nellie Jewett/Juett Gouge) was Matthew Harris Jouett (1788-1827), a well known portrait painter of Lexington, KY. William Jewett's brother and the father of the painter, was Captain Jack Jewett (1754-1822), who, after the Revolutionary War, settled in Woodford County KY on Craig's Creek Pike. In 1781 Captain Jack raced from Cookoo Tavern in Louisa County VA to Charlottesville to warn Virginia Governor Thomas Jefferson and the colonial legislature of the approach of British soldiers. The governor and the legislature got away just in the nick.

FALCONER & CRAIG ANCESTORS: BRYANS' STATION, BOURBON WHISKEY & THE TRAVELING CHURCH

As stated, the mother of Ellen Jewett Gouge was **Anna Falkoner** (1769-1834), daughter of **(Re)Joyce Craig** (1732-1812) and **John Faulconer** (prob 1722-179_). John and his brothers (cousins?) Nicholas and Johnston have been identified as soldiers in the American Revolution from Spotsylvania County VA. John has been identified as a son of **Sybilla/Sebalah** _____ (?-?) and **Nicholas Faulconer** (abt 1660-b/f 1743), son of **David Faulconer** (abt 1625-1692/3) and **Judith** _____ (?-?). David was a son of indentured servant **Thomas Faulconer** (abt 1594-?), who was in VA by 1622. Twenty years later, Thomas was recorded as Anglican minister in Isle of Wight County, now Smithfield.

John Faulconer and Joyce Craig moved with their family from Virginia (probably Essex County) into the Bluegrass region of central Kentucky in 1779, taking the famous Wilderness Road. In 1844, their daughter-in-law, Francis Nelson Faulconer, then quite aged, was interviewed and provided many details of the family's early days in KY. "March 10, 1780, there was an army coming and we all had to scatter." This is in reference to combined British and Indian attacks on the American settlements ("stations") in Kentucky during the American Revolution.

Joyce Craig was the child of **Mary Hawkins** (1716-1804) and **Taliaferro (Toliver) Craig** (1704-1799) of Spotsylvania County, VA. Mary "Polly" Hawkins was born in King William County VA and died in Craig's Settlement, Clear Creek KY on January 6, 1804. She was buried in a cemetery since destroyed, at Great Crossings Baptist Church in Scott County, KY, under the inscription: "Mother of Many Faithful." A charcoal portrait of Polly Hawkins is said to hang at the DAR headquarters, Duncan's Tavern, Paris, KY. Notably, Mary Hawkins was the daughter of **Mary Long** (?-?) and **John Hawkins** (?-

?), whose brother was William Hawkins, lineal ancestor of Betty's husband, **Cecil V Cook Jr** (1913-1970), by way of William's son, Reuben (1747-1812), and grandson, "Black Head Billy" Hawkins (1781-1845), father of Katherine Hawkins Farmer (1814-1851), mother of Sue Farmer Cook (1838-1890), Cecil's grandmother. (Please see **All of the Above II**, pages 97, 123 for details.)

Mary Hawkins and Taliaferro Craig were married in Spotsylvania County VA in about 1730. Their children are: (1) John (2) **Rejoice,** aka, **Joyce** (3) Lewis (4) Taliaferro (Toliver) Jr (5) Elijah (6) Jane (7) Joseph (8) Sarah ("Sally") (9) Benjamin (10) Jeremiah and (11) Elizabeth (Betty). Several of these children are noted in the larger history of their times. Lewis Craig (1737-1828), Baptist preacher, brought a group of Baptist settlers into Kentucky from Spotsylvania County, Virginia in 1781. The caravan has entered Kentucky State history as "the traveling church." Lewis' (and Joyce's) parents, Polly and Toliver, were in this group. It is believed that Joyce Craig and her husband John Faulconer were already in Kentucky by 1781; John sold his remaining Spotsylvania County VA lands in February, 1780. The Traveling Church settled on Gilbert's Creek in Lincoln (now, Garrard) County. As a group the congregation relocated to the South Elkhorn in Fayette County.

Joyce Craig Falkner's brother John Craig (abt 1730-1815), oldest son of Toliver and Mary Hawkins Craig, was in charge at Bryans' Station (Fort) during the British and Indian siege in August, 1782. The defenders successfully "forted up" the stockade and repelled the attackers, who withdrew after three days. The eighty or so Kentuckians who relieved Bryans' Station then made a fatal decision. Hot to get into some action against an enemy they believed to be in flight, the Kentuckians pursued the British and their Canadian and Indian allies and were defeated with great loss of life. The Battle of Blue Licks took place on the Licking River near present day Mount Olivet, Robertson County KY. All of these events occurred the year *after* Cornwallis had surrendered to Washington at Yorktown,

VA in 1781. (Huey ancestors, Samuel and Jane Mason Huey were at Bryan's Station a few years later - page 80.)

Another of Joyce Craig Falkner's brothers was the Reverend Elijah Craig (1738-1828/29), the founder (1787) of an academy which became Georgetown College in Georgetown, Kentucky. Elijah, an entrepreneur and the founder of several businesses, was said to have invented Bourbon, that is, whiskey created by aging corn in charred oak barrels. That is the essential step but it is doubtful if Elijah first took it. Many farmers distilled their own whiskey in his day including Elijah and other Baptist ministers. (See Abraham Cook in the companion volume to this book.) Elijah Craig was not credited with inventing Bourbon Whiskey until late in the nineteenth century, when it might have seemed droll to claim that a prominent Baptist preacher had a hand in creating Kentucky's signature liquor.

The father of Elijah, John and Joyce Craig was the above mentioned **Taliaferro (Toliver) Craig** (1704-1799), whose mother was **Jane Craig** (?-?). Jane gave birth to Toliver aboard ship bound for America from her home in Scotland. Jane, it has been said, was married to a John Craig (?-?) who died shortly before the voyage. Pregnant, but with her two brothers making the journey with her, Jane came anyway. She died shortly after arriving and Taliaferro Craig was raised by his uncles. Members of the Craig family have recorded that Taliaferro was the son not of John Craig but of ship's captain, _____ **Taliaferro.** Hence, the name Jane Craig gave to her son. Jane Craig's great grandson, Tolliver Craig, began a memoir of his life and family with these words, "My grandfather was the illegitimate son of Jane Craig who was from Scotland and he married Mary Hawkins by whom he had Twelve Children."

Sara Crouch Huey - Sally

The first Toliver Craig's paternity of Joyce Craig Faulconer has been proven beyond any doubt. He gave a slave to his daughter *"Joyce Falkner"* in a deed of gift dated April 19, 1791: *"a negro girl Gemima otherwise called Mima. I give her to the above Joyce together with said Mima's increase forever and the only use of the said Joyce, to will and dispose of as to her seemeth fit."* This giving of one human being to another prompted litigation peculiar to ante-bellum jurisprudence. At issue was not the moral catastrophe of legally sanctioned ownership of one human being by another. No. The complaint turned on the gift *to* a female, that is, whether a gift to a daughter remains in her estate when a *male heir* of the donor seeks to reclaim the property. The gift of an enslaved person to a free person was merely a fact incidental to the case. This litigation focused on a tree while the entire forest was ablaze.

THE CROUCH FAMILY

As stated, **Nancy Williams** (1843-1923), Myrix and Junietta's daughter, married **John Crouch** (1835-1903). John was the son of **Elijah Crouch** (May 14 1790- Feb 16 1849). An Elijah Crouch received a land grant near Warsaw, KY in 1797 and a second parcel in 1810. The first grant may have been given to Elijah's uncle and his namesake, for Elijah, father of John Crouch, was but seven years old in 1797. Assuming the second conveyance of land in 1810 was to the **Elijah** born in 1790, a further surmise would be that this young free holding farmer felt sufficiently emboldened as a property owner to marry **Sallye (Sallie) Ladye (Lady)** (April 12, 1790 -March 1863), which he did on Nov 11, 1813.

It is left to future research to determine if a fascinating person is represented by the fascinating name, Sallye Ladye. This moniker has resonated down the family as 'sara,' 'sarah' and 'sally.' The 1860 census records Sallye Ladye Crouch as "Sally" Crouch, head of household, living with a Mary Crouch, 40 and Sally's son, **John Crouch**, 27.

Elizabeth Taylor Rubio, third great granddaughter of Elijah and Sallye Crouch has confirmed that this couple was buried on the farm of their son, John Crouch. Elizabeth Rubio has disclosed several additional details about the earlier generations of the Crouch family, i.e., that Elijah and Sallie Crouch were the parents of six children: Elkanah, Margaret (Mary?), Noah, Henry Elijah, **John** and James.

The parents of Elijah Crouch were, Elizabeth Rubio records, **Jesse Crouch** (April 25, 1760-abt Dec 22 1841) and **Mary Sarah Nance** (May 30 1770-Jan 1 1842). Both Jessie and Mary died in Washington County, Tennessee, and are buried at the Old Falls Branch Baptist Church (aka Hopper Graveyard). Including Elijah, their second child, the fourteen children of Jesse and Mary Crouch were William, Sarah, John, Joseph, Martha, Susan, Ruben, James, Mary Ann, Isaac, the twins Jesse Hiter and Jonathon Mulky and Allen.

The parents of Jesse Crouch were **John Crouch** (1727/30-1811/15) and **Sarah Barbee (Barbary?)** (1730-1782). John and Sarah were born in Virginia (both probably in King George County, where John was known to have been born). Their marriage began in Virginia in 1748. The seven children of John and Sarah Crouch were: Joseph, Anna, Martha, John, Elijah, **Jesse** and James. In 1781, John and Sarah moved their family from Virginia to Claybourne County, TN and may subsequently have moved to Washington County NC as Sarah is known to have been buried at Buffalo Ridge Baptist Church Cemetery in Washington County, NC, now, Tennessee. (See Sources, below, for directions.) After Sarah's death in 1782, John Crouch married Elizabeth Cloud. It is not known if they had children together.

The parents of the first John Crouch (b. 1727) were **Anne Reeds** (?-?) and **Joseph Crouch** (?-1741/42). Joseph Crouch is known to have died intestate in King George County Virginia on March 5, 1741/1742. Anne and Joseph were the parents of three sons: **John**, Joseph (1731-?) and James (1741-?). Joseph may have been the son of **John Crouch** (Crowche?) (?-?) and _____? No Crouch family connection has been made to prominent 17th century English writers, Nathaniel, scholar of the topography of Palestine and John, poet, or with John's brother, Captain Gilbert Crouch.

Although Sara Crouch Huey (wife of James Addison Huey) was a devoted Baptist, there were many active Methodists in the Crouch family. They served as members and leaders in the Warsaw, KY Methodist Episcopal Church from its organization in 1844. In 1845, the presiding elder of the church was the Reverend Benjamin T. Crouch. The national Methodist Church split in 1844 over slavery. The Warsaw church allied itself the following year with the Southern branch, renaming itself the Warsaw Methodist Episcopal Church, South. For twelve years after its founding, the congregation had no building and met in various members' homes. In 1857, the church rented the building of the Missionary Baptist Church for one Sunday each month. This arrangement lasted until 1873, when the Methodists bought the building of the Christian Church, and have been using this building ever since.

THE HUEYS - A LIKELY HUGUENOT LINE

James Addison Huey (1862-1961), Sara Crouch's husband, was the son of **Joseph Addison Huey** (1819-1896) and **Amanda Watts Gaines** (1821-1895). Joseph and Amanda were married on October 28, 1841. They were the parents of four daughters, before son James was born: Mary Malvina (July 2, 1843 – June 26 1845), Paulina G. (Jan 28 1845 – 1877) Virginia Ann (March 20, 1847 – Feb. 1852) and an unnamed girl baby, born April 12, 1860)

Joseph Addison Huey was born in Boone County KY on Nov 16, 1819 and died in Union, Boone County KY on Feb 1, 1896. Joseph was the son of **Samuel Huey** (Sept 19, 1771-Jan 17, 1831) and **Jane Mason** (Dec 20, 1778-Feb 2, 1859), whose father was said to have been killed by Indians when Jane was four years old. Samuel and Jane were married March 1, 1797. They made their first home near Bardstown, KY and later were at Bryan's Station, that famous early settlement near Frankfort, KY, associated with the Bryan Brothers, Daniel Boone and the Craig ancestors of **Betty Huey Taylor Cook**. (See page 74.)

Additional research among Mason ancestors may find Jane's father's name among those Kentuckians killed in the ill-advised Battle of Blue Licks (1782). This was one of the last major Battles of the Revolution, when impatient Kentuckians were tricked into attacking a concealed and much larger combined force of British Regulars, Loyalists settlers, and Ohio Indians. (See above, page 75.)

Jane and Samuel Huey settled finally at Big Bone Lick, KY, the site of discovery of mastodon bones, that so fascinated President Thomas Jefferson, inspiring him to send across the continent the party of exploration led by Meriwether Lewis and William Clark. Samuel Huey is enrolled in both the 1810 and 1820 federal census of Boone County KY. Many Masons and Hueys, including the widow Jane Huey, were enrolled as founders, on May 25, 1843, of the "Baptist Church of Christ at Big Bone."

Samuel and Jane were the parents of 12 children (page 88), including, as stated, **Joseph Addison Huey**, father of **James Addison Huey**. With their young daughters, Samuel and Jane Huey are buried in Big Bone Cemetery, off Route 536 (Hathaway Road) in Boone County KY.

Sam Huey is recalled in family lore as an acquaintance of Daniel Boone. Betty Cook wrote that Samuel and Jane "lived a rough, hardy pioneer life." Both died from violent accidents. Samuel, in 1831, "was killed by the felling of a tree by his own hand." Jane Huey died in 1859, after a hard fall from a horse, when she was 81. Sam died while he and his brother William were cutting down a tree on their several-thousand acre land grant along Big Bone Church Road (near present-day Big Bone Lick State Park). A hand-hewn pork scalding and salting box is said to have been made from the tree which killed Sam Huey. In 1975, the box was given to the Boone County Parks and Recreation Department by Mrs. A. Stanley Kasper, a niece

James Addison Huey - "Boss"

(second great niece) of Samuel Huey. The scalding box, no doubt much weathered and the worse for wear, by 2006, had disappeared.

Samuel Huey was born in Pennsylvania, where his family had lived for three generations. He was the oldest son of **Robert Huey** (1757-1842) and **Agnes/Nancy Elliot** (?-?). Samuel was named for his paternal grandfather. (see below.)

In 1782, when Samuel was eleven years old, Robert and Agnes (or Nancy) moved from Lancaster County, PA to Waterbury, Virginia and from there to Boone County Kentucky. Although Samuel Huey settled in Big Bone Lick, KY, his parents may not have; both Robert and Agnes (Nancy?) Huey are buried in Dayton, Ohio.

Most probably, Robert and Agnes (Nancy) moved in their old age (if not sooner) to Dayton to live with a daughter, Margaret Huey Fulkarth (1775-1865), who had married John Christopher Fulkarth. Margaret is also buried in Montgomery County (Dayton) Ohio, near her parents.

Robert Huey, named for his father's father, was the son of **Samuel Huey** (?-?) and _____ **Russell** (a widow), both of Churchtown (Churchton), PA. Samuel was the son of **Robert Huey** (est. 1700-1770) and **Esther** _____ (?-1770), also of Churchtown. In addition to this first American Samuel Huey, the other children of Esther and Robert Huey were James, Henry, Elizabeth and Mary, all of whom were born in Churchtown (Lancaster County), PA. Prior to the appearance of the first Robert in Churchtown, the Huey ascendancy is murky. We cannot as yet tell from where they immigrated or what language they spoke when then did. (Some passenger lists have a Johan Wilhelm Huey reaching PA on the (*Snow?*) *Molly* in 1741.)

The old country Hueys, like the Jewett ancestors, are remembered (in our branch of the Huey family) as descended from Huguenots, part of some half million French Protestants hounded out of France at the end of the 17th century. The forced exodus followed the revocation, in 1685, of the 1588 Edict of Nantes by Louis XIV.

While in France, Huguenot rowdies conducted considerable violence as well. Some of the hottest of the Huguenot hot heads insisted that statues be destroyed from atop Catholic churches and cathedrals; they climbed up into belfries and on to roofs to do this work themselves. These excesses surely must have contributed to popular rejection of the Huguenots' otherwise well-taken criticism of medieval Catholic corruption in France. The Edict of Nantes was a Reformation era gesture towards civil harmony, which mandated reduced harassment of the Huguenots, who were so called, apparently, as partisans of a Zurich politician, Hugues Besançon (c. 1491–1532?). Under the Edict a theoretical freedom for diverse religious observances would be permitted throughout France - except where it wasn't permitted: Paris, Rheims, Toulouse, Lyons, and Dijon.

The Edict was rescinded (page 73, above) by the ironic Protestant, Henry of Navarre. Henry converted to Catholicism in order to become King of France. On that occasion, Henry supposedly muttered to himself, apparently within earshot of a contemporary blogger, "Paris is well worth a mass."

Just as Spain emptied itself of its Moslems and Jews in the fifteenth century, France, in the seventeenth, caught, killed and chased away its Protestants. These self-inflicted wounds to both Spain and France caused the loss of vital human energy and talent, and required centuries to mend, even partially. The role of Hueys in the religious troubles of the sixteenth and seventeenth centuries is not clear. The origin of the name itself is lost in the fog of medieval migrations.

We believe, then, that these Hueys wended their way from France to England, stopping there for a generation or two, long enough to learn English. From England, Hueys (one or more) crossed the Atlantic. Our Huey ancestors settled in Churchtown, PA for three generations, before moving into Kentucky. There they fetched up at Big Bone Lick, and then in Union, while some were found across the Ohio River, settled at Dayton, Ohio.

Where does the proper name *Huey* come from? Etymological studies are uncertain but suggest that Huey is a variation of *Hughie* which is an endearment for *Hugh*. Suppose you were the court jester to Hugh Capet, 10th century King of France. During an entertainment, you might have gotten away with calling him *King Huey*.

So far so good, but Huey-from-Hughie-from-Hugh presupposes the English and French languages and *Huey Studies* point to Germanic as well as Gaelic origins. *Huey* has been connected to the old German word, *hug* which is given the meanings *heart, mind,* or *spirit*. This may or may not be either helpful or accurate, since *heart* and *mind* and *spirit*, taken as human attributes in a figurative sense, do not represent the same organs or concepts.

The Gaelic terms, carried into English as *Huey*, appear to have merely phonetic associations. Some believe Huey is derived from AODH, a popular ancient and Irish name *(Áed), fire* which has been associated with UISDEAN, the Scottish Gaelic EYSTEINN, which is itself a derivation from the fusion of Old Norse elements, *ey (island)* and *stein* (stone). EOGHAN, Old Celtic, may mean *born from the yew tree* or may be a Gaelic form of *Eugene*. Eugene is Greek, *(Eugenios)*, meaning *well born*, a conflation of *ev (good* or *well)* and *genes born*.

But wait. John L. Huey, in 1908 (see Sources, below) writes, "It appears that the Hueys originally came from the French Huguenots, who spelled the name *Huet* (the *t* being silent)." This information is credited to a Family Bible in the possession (in 1908) of Frank W. Hughey, of Pittsburgh, PA. If correct, then the etymological tracings of *Huey* and the linkage of the proper name to a Swiss politician, named Hugues Besançon (see above) are merely chimeral speculations. It is *Huet* in France, which was changed in England and English America, to *Huey, Hughey, Hewitt,* and *Huyett*. Perhaps. Prior to departures from France, stimulated by assaults provoked by the 1685 revocation of the Edict of Nantes, the Huets may have been concentrated in the province of Anjou, as suggested by baptismal and other records.

SOURCES:

Huey, Crouch and Williams genealogy and letters: Betty Huey Taylor Cook's collected data and her unpublished book. Betty's records included selected pages from **Genealogy of the Huey Family**, by John L. Huey (100 pages, 1908). For *Huet*, see page 14. Etymology of *Huey*: "Behind the Name" at behindthename.com.

Huey information has also been obtained in conversation with J.M. Huey, M.D., grandson of James and Sara Huey, whose memory of events extends across 9 decades.

Helpful Williams data, including the names of the children of William Miricks and Elizabeth Stone Williams, their residency in Virginia, and details of the life of Josiah Stone and also the Williams connections to Viney Fork Baptist Church, has been researched and posted on the web by Williams family historian Sally Williams Black.

A useful Stone family website, with Williams connections, has been placed on the web by: The Stone DNA Surname Project at familytreedna.com.

Biographical details concerning William Faulconer: **The Faulkner History**, by Peggy Grace Faulkner Sersain, (1973), on the web at eccchistory.org/HawleyFaulkner.

Williams genealogical details are found in a document of Betty Cook's, which was prepared by Major (U.S.M.C.) Lee N. Uts, entitled "History of the Williams Family" (1941).

For Lowell Mason and the Singing Schools, conversations with music historian Harry Eskew; also, see on the web, "Understanding the Music, An essay by John Newsome" at lcweb2.loc.gov/cocoon/ihas/html/ohio/ohio-newsom.html

Information concerning James and Nellie Gouge in Grant

County: **History of Grant County Kentucky**, Grant County Historical Society (1992), John B. Conrad, editor.

Jewett/Juet family information (which may have been a source for Betty Taylor Cook): **Huguenot Emigration to Virginia and to the Settlement at Manakin-Town**, by Robert Alonzo Brock (1886, 1962). For the Huguenots in France: **A History of the Christian Church**, by Williston Walker (1959, pages 388-89.).

For the gift of a slave girl: Jo Thiessen, Ed., "*Slave Entries in Wills, Deeds, etc.,*" on the web: *slave doc* at mindspring.com and at other websites.

Samuel Huey and the Pork Scalding Box, made from the tree that killed him: ***Cincinnati Inquirer***, December 15, 1975, generously provided by Jean Valette Taylor, granddaughter of Sara Crouch and James Addison Huey.

Additional Crouch genealogy details have been generously provided by Elizabeth Taylor Rubio, great-granddaughter of Sara Crouch and James Addison Huey.

Taliaferro Craig biographical information may be found in **Descendants of Thomas Bryant Parker and Thomas Ross**, Ella Parker Ogden (1965), on the web at:nhn.ou.edu./parker/genealogy. Different (better?) information, citing sources, may be found at: Ancestors of Nancy Carol ARNOLD - farmerfamily.org

William Myrix Williams' ancestry and descendents, through John and Myrix and his second wife, Martha Turley: Maryland Genealogical Society, Maryland members Ancestry, may be found on the web, www.mdgensoc.org/genealogyfortng

Nineteenth Century Kentucky census data: Baltimore County Public Library, at bcplonline.org

For John Calvin's theology, **Calvin**, by Francois Wendel (New York: Harper & Row, 1950).

The Gouge family cemetery was surveyed in 1981; see **Grant County Cemeteries**, compiled by Virgil Chandler, Sr (Grant County Historical Society, 1988).

Directions to the Buffalo Ridge Baptist Church cemetery where **Sarah Barbee Crouch** (1730-1782) was buried: In East Tennessee, take Exit 42 off I-181 going east toward Gray. Go to the 1st traffic light and turn right on Old Gray Station Rd. Go 7/10 of a mile, then right onto Hales Chapel Rd. Go 1.6 miles (7/10 mile past Hales Chapel Christian Church on left), take a right onto Holly Lane. Then immediately turn right on Freeman Lane. Buffalo Ridge Cemetery is on the right on top of hill just before Freeman Lane dead ends. From: the restorationmovement.com

a double tree with two collateral stems sprung from one root: William Wordsworth's poem, "Written After the Death of Charles Lamb" and quoted in **The Devil Kissed Her, The Story of Mary Lamb** by Kathy Watson (New York: Jeremy P. Tarcher/Penguin, 2004, page 236).

The 12 children (& spouses) of Jane and Samuel Huey:

William – Florence Whitaker, Mary Bradford, 4 children
Robert – Matilda Brady, 12 children
John – Matilda Rice, 12 children
Harriet – Squire Grant Scott, 6 children
Thomas Addison - Elvira Garnett, 7 children
Mary Pauline – John Scott
Agnes – George Scott
James – Mary Corn, 2 children
Joseph - Amanda Gaines, 5 children
Oscar Woodford – Elizabeth Gaines (sister of Amanda)
George Washington – Sarah Williams, 4 children
Samuel – Harriet Scolds, 7 children (5 died in infancy)

"CAN YOU FEEL OR FIND A HEART TO PRAY FOR ME?"

Joseph Addison Huey
Amanda Watts Gaines

Amanda's parents:
Virginia Watts
James Gaines

James Addison Huey (1862-1961)
Nan Elizabeth Huey (1893-1993)
Betty Huey Taylor Cook (1918-2000)

Joseph Addison Huey (1819-1896) and **Amanda Watts Gaines** (1821-1895) were the parents of **James Addison Huey** (1861-1961), father of **Nan Elizabeth Huey Taylor** (1893-1993) and grandfather of **Betty Huey Taylor Cook** (1918-2000). Joseph A. Huey was too old to see service in the Civil War (1861-65) and his son James (1862-1961) was much too young, but Joseph, Amanda and their family certainly suffered from the war, which ruined the economy of Kentucky. They were also subjected to the indignities and dangers of occupation, as Kentucky was kept loyal to the federal government by way of a heavy handed military regime. This was so in spite of the fact that more Kentuckians fought in Union Blue than in Rebel Gray.

Some occupying federal troops tended to see all White Kentuckians as disloyal. The property of such people was available for the taking. Many a northern soldier wrote home to brag about his unit having captured and eaten a "sesesh" hog or cow. Joseph and Amanda's family sustained these kinds of losses. On more than one occasion, federal troops came through their farm, taking whatever they pleased. They entered the Huey home and made off with silver, jewelry and other valuables. Their son, James, three at the end of the war, told of marching

Amanda Watts Gaines Huey

behind the soldiers as they chased the family's chickens. Loyalties were divided up and down the state and also in Union. After the war, Amanda one Sunday saw a family heirloom broach on the dress of a neighbor.

At 6th and Main Streets in Covington (Kenton County), Kentucky, there is a sober historical marker (Number 1863):

Slave Escape

> *On a snowy night in January 1856, seventeen slaves fled, at foot of Main Street, across frozen Ohio River. Margaret Garner was in this group. When arrested in Ohio, she killed little daughter rather than see her returned to slavery. This much publicized slave capture became focus of national attention because it involved the issues of federal and state authority. [Reverse] Controversial Judgment - Decision regarding Margaret Garner fueled fires of abolition. Fugitive Slave Law supporters wanted her returned to master. Garner wished to remain in Ohio, even at risk of death for her crime. She was returned to Ky., with master's agreement to extradite her to Ohio. But soon afterward Garner was sent south and never heard from again. Presented by City of Covington.*

The marker neglects to identify Margaret Garner's owner. Nor does it give the name of the "little daughter" killed by her own mother. The owner of Margaret Garner was Archibald Gaines, who bought her from his brother, John. The three-year-old murdered girl was Mary Garner. Archibald Gaines' lawyer admitted in court that Mary was his client's daughter. (See note on page 111.)

There had always been slave escapes and escape attempts in the Colonies and in the young United States, but there had not always been newspapers to report these events. By the middle of the nineteenth century, technology had improved. Every major city and many towns and hamlets had newspapers, with the larger towns boasting of a half-dozen or more, contending with one another for readers (and therefore, advertisers) among an increasingly literate population. When slaves escaped into Ohio from Kentucky, the newspapers in Cincinnati and beyond published hair-raising headlines followed by the hysterical details. Such was the case on January 29, 1856, when the *Cincinnati Inquirer* ran the headline:

> Stampede of Slaves
> A TALE OF HORROR!
> An Arrest by the U.S. Marshal.
> A DEPUTY U.S. MARSHAL SHOT.
> A Negro Child's Throat Cut from Ear to Ear
> by its Father or Mother, and others wanted:
> CORONER's INQUEST
> Writ of Habeas Corpus Taken Out.
> GREAT EXCITEMENT!

Kentucky slaves attempting a race to freedom in Ohio were common in the eighteen fifties. An increasing proportion of White citizens in both states turned their disgust at the horrors of slavery into active support for those slaves who managed to cross the Ohio River. By word of mouth, slaves in Kentucky had heard that any who escaped might expect to be hidden away in the cellars and barns of Quakers and other anti-slavery activists, who would spirit the fortunate escapees into Michigan and on to Canada and freedom. This was the Ohio version of the "underground railroad."

Many winter-time escapes were attempted, when ice on the Ohio River made for a treacherous but not impossible vault from one frozen slab to another. The hunt of course would not end at the river's edge. Kentucky slave owners and their neighbors gave chase. From their point of view, valuable property ought to be returned to them.

The Kentucky slave owner benefited from the protections of federal law, enforceable even in Ohio, KY, and beyond. The Fugitive Slave Act required an officer of the Federal Court to enforce the return of any captured escapee. Court procedures required an expedited hearing at which the slave herself was not permitted to testify, except by special permission. In many instances the only issue before the court was the question whether the human being standing in irons before the judge or commissioner had in fact been the property of the complainant, who had recaptured her and was seeking her return.

By the mid-eighteen fifties, opinion had hardened in Ohio and Kentucky and these convictions were headed in opposite directions. There was no lack of respected and well known Ohio politicians, community leaders and lawyers willing to speak up for slaves just escaped from over the river in Kentucky. Even in Cincinnati, where pro-slavery sentiment was vocal and popular, a handful of prominent attorneys would represent an escapee *pro bono*. Such counsel would look for arguments that might justify a release, delay a return to Kentucky or move the matter into state court, which could be friendlier to the idea of emancipation and not necessarily bound to enforce federal law. But all this was an uphill legal battle.

The slaveholder could rely upon a surprisingly aggressive enforcement mechanism lodged in the courthouse itself. Friendly commissioners could order federal marshals to act in place of the local sheriff. Even more controversial was the deputizing of citizens who would join in the hunt and expect to be paid a stipend for their services. These temporary deputies created a spectacle in and around Cincinnati in the 1850s. More than once, a handful and sometimes up to a dozen or more rowdy young White men on horseback appeared at full gallop on the streets and highways around Cincinnati. These were men from the river towns of northern Kentucky and they were on a mission. Transformed by an oath from "nigger hunters" into armed federal employees, they were empowered to surround or even break into a home in

Cincinnati and wrestle to the ground and hog tie a screaming and resisting Black man, woman or child. When Kentucky slaves escaped, the chase into Ohio was on!

Amanda Gaines (Dec 13, 1821-June 3, 1895) was one of ten children born to **James Gaines** (1798-1868/72) and **Virginia Watts** (1802-1882). Virginia's parents were **Susan Davis** (?-?) and **Johnson Watts** (1762-1813) of Orange County, VA and then of Boone County, KY. Virginia and James Gaines were members of Bullittsburg Baptist Church and are buried there in Lot 55 of the Old Section of the Church Cemetery, 2616 Bullittsburg Church Road, Petersburg, KY. Members of the Gaines, Watts, Dicken, Graves, Huey and other related families were among the founders and active early members of nearby Sand Run Baptist Church (organized in 1819), Hebron, Boone County KY and also of the Bullittsburg Church. In the wilderness fervor that led to the founding of these churches, James' father, **George Gaines,** was moved to seek baptism by preacher John Taylor, imploring Taylor, "Can you feel or find a heart to pray for me?" Preacher John could, and did.

James Gaines, father of ten, was one of eight children born to **George Gaines** (1764-1845) and **Susan** or **Susanna Graves** (1764-1845). George and Susanna were married December 18, 1788. From an ancient Bible record, created apparently by his granddaughter Amanda, we learn that George Gaines was born on Dec 20, 1764 and died March 17, 1845. George and Susan Gaines were members of the Bullitsburg Church.

After 1819, George was listed as the owner of a slave, Asa, a preaching member of the church. In 1839, Asa and his wife Rachel were dismissed by letter from the membership of the church, which suggests they were either sold or freed. It seems likely Asa and Rachel were freed to move into Indiana, where slavery was forbidden; their dismissal from the Bullittsburg Church was sponsored by a "Bro E. Ferris." This was probably Elder Ezra Ferris, the pastor in Lawrenceburg, Dearborn County Indiana.

James Gaines

Susanna Graves, named for her father's mother, was the daughter of the long lived couple **John Graves** (1737-1825) and **Ann Rice** (1741-1826). Ann was the daughter of **William Rice** (?-?) and **Sarah Helm**, (?-?) of Culpeper County VA. John Graves was from Culpeper also, where his ancestors had lived for several generations, after departing Virginia's foundation community, Jamestown. In 1797, John and Anne Graves moved to Boone County Kentucky, where they lived for a quarter century and were buried. Knowing that John and Ann Graves' daughter Susanna and her husband, George Gaines also settled in Boone County, it is likely the younger couple moved from VA with her parents. They probably traveled overland to the upper Ohio River, then downriver by boat. (For such boat trips, see pages 232 and 285-86.)

JAMES GAINES' GRAVES, COTTON AND STONE ANCESTORS

James Gaines, through his mother, Susanna (Susan) and her father, John Graves, is a descendent of **Katherine** _____ (?) and **Thomas Graves** (?-by 1637), a founder of Jamestown, Virginia Colony. The lineage, we believe, is as follows. Susanna was the daughter of **John Graves** the Third (1737-1825). It seems likely that this is John Graves, a founding member of Bullitsburg Baptist Church in Boone County and the owner (before **George Gaines**) of Asa, a slave and church member, who was encouraged by the church "to appoint evening meetings about that his brethren may have a chance of hearing him & get their minds better informed concerning his Gift."

John Graves the Third was the son of **John Graves Jr** (1706-1747) and **Susanna Dicken** (1714-1784). John Graves Jr was the son of **John Graves Sr** (1677-?) and **Rebecca** _____ (?-?). John Sr was the son of **Thomas Graves** the Third (1639-?) and **Mary** _____ (?-?). Thomas Graves the Third was the son of **Thomas Graves Jr** (1609-1677) and _____. All of these Graves generations were inhabitants of Virginia Colony, in and around the earliest settlements.

The parents of Thomas Jr were **Katherine** _____ (?-?) and **Thomas Graves** (?-by 1637), who arrived at Jamestown in 1608. In 1617, after 10 years in Jamestown, a settlement was made by some Virginia Colony adventurers on the eastern shore of the Chesapeake Bay. The community was called Smythe's (later Southampton) Hundred. Apparently, after a return to England (where Thomas Jr may have been born), Thomas Graves, in 1619, was placed in charge of Smythe's Hundred. In that same year he was a member of the Virginia House of Burgesses, when it convened as the first legislative assembly in Virginia Colony. He served in that body (off and on) until 1632.

THE VIRGINIA HOUSE OF BURGESSES: FIRST REPRESENTATIVE ASSEMBLY IN AMERICA

As a member of the earliest Assembly ("House") of Burgesses, **Thomas Graves** was elected to a body which was created under the idealistic but disastrous governance of Sir Edwin Sandys, who was made treasurer of the Virginia Company in 1619 by the London investors. With a reputation for bold action in Parliament against James I, Sandys was authorized to devise a plan, which called for an end to all taxes in Virginia Colony. Sandys also attempted the integration of the Indians into the settlers' communities, in the manner in which Cortez had "integrated" indigenous peoples into the hacienda system of New Spain, a century earlier. In 1622, objecting to their enslavement, the Indians rebelled, killing some 347 settlers and coming close to wiping out the entire English colony. In 1624, Charles I revoked the charter of the Virginia Company and tried to rule Virginia colony through committees of the Privy Council. The King acted after it was discovered that the Virginia Company was bankrupt and that many (most?) of the newly arrived colonists Sandys recruited had died of disease – more even than had lost their lives in Indian attacks.

In 1625, Charles I (successor to King James) explicitly declined to authorize the continued existence of the Burgesses. However, the assembly continued to meet for 150 years. It did not disappear until it morphed at the time of the American Revolution (1776-83), into the state legislature. In the 1600s, the Burgesses continued to meet partly because effective Royal control was in the hands of the royal-appointed governor and his Council after 1624 and partly because (especially during the 1620s) everyone in power (the King, the governor and his close assistants and appointees, and the big planters) was making real money from inflated tobacco prices in Europe. Just as the Burgesses ignored Charles' order for their dissolution, Charles I, grateful for the heavy flow into his treasury from Virginia, ignored the refusal of the Burgesses to dissolve. A gush of money can lift all boats over dangerous shoals.

The 1620s tobacco "boom" ended in the 1630s. But by then a Royal demand for the dissolution of the House of Burgesses would have been resisted not only by the planters but by the governor. The crown-appointed governor needed tranquil relations with the owners of the large tobacco plantations, even if the Royal treasury was seeing reduced income from tobacco. The main fact that kept the Burgesses in place was the wide Atlantic Ocean, separating Virginia and London.

Among the first acts of the first Assembly (under Sandys) were prohibitions against excess in fancy clothes and strong drink. Most likely, **Thomas Graves** would have supported these measures. He stands out as a person of religious convictions, a trait more widespread in New England than in Virginia, where pretentions to aristocracy operate against egalitarian expectations, even in Heaven.

Thomas Graves was acquainted with another of Betty Cook's ancestors, **William Stone** (1603-1660), first Protestant to be appointed proprietary governor of Maryland. (Please see page 363.) In 1635, Thomas Graves and William Stone were both members of the first Vestry of Hungars Episcopal Church, Eastville, Northampton County VA. Thomas Graves was buried in the ancient Hungars

Church cemetery on Virginia's Eastern Shore.

William Stone and Verlinda Stone are lineal ancestors of Betty Taylor Cook through their daughter, **Mary** (?-1683/86), wife of **Robert Doyne** (?-1689) and then by the Dawson line of Prince George's and Montgomery County Maryland and the subsequent PA and KY Moore, Scott, and Taylor lines. (See other sketches in this volume, including Verlinda and William Stone's.)

It has been stated that William Stone married Verlinda *Graves,* Thomas Graves' daughter. However William Stone's wife may have been Verlinda *Cotton* (?-c. 1675), sister of William Cotton (abt 1600-1640), first rector of the Hungars Church. In his Aug 20, 1640 will, William Cotton acknowledges his "brethren in lawe Capt. William Stone." This suggests William Stone's wife was William Cotton's sister, Verlinda. But William Cotton's will also mentions "my well beloved wife Ann Cotton." Ann was another of Thomas Graves' daughters. This could also explain why Cotton refers to William Stone as his brother-in-law, if Stone was married not to Cotton's sister but to Cotton's wife's sister. A supplementary theory (lacking evidence) is that William Stone married the two Verlindas, successively. Betty Taylor Cook is yet a descendent of Katherine and Thomas Graves back through her Huey-Gaines line even if Verlinda Stone was a Cotton and not a Graves (and then also, Betty's ancestor back through her Moore-Dawson line).

Ann Cotton, wife of William Cotton, is possibly (though not likely to be) the writer of an engaging history of Bacon's Rebellion (1676). By that time, Ann, widow of the unfortunate William Cotton, had re-married twice. Her second husband was the Rev. Nathaniel Eaton, first president of Harvard College. Eaton wound up in Virginia Colony after his dismissal from Harvard, for gross mismanagement. After marrying Ann, he sold off some of her lands and absconded to England. Ann's third husband, in 1657, was the Rev. Francis Doughty. With two husbands after William Cotton, Ann is unlikely to have signed herself thirty-six years after his death, "An Cotton"- the name of the writer of the history of Bacon's Rebellion. (For additional information about Bacon's Rebellion, and the historian An(n) Cotton, please see page 367 and **All of the Above II,** page 287.)

FIRST SLAVES RECORDED IN VIRGINIA COLONY: CHATTEL IN WILLIAM COTTON'S WILL

William Cotton, Episcopal rector (whose sister may have been Taylor ancestor **Verlinda Stone**) has been recorded as the owner of slaves brought early into Virginia. Arriving in the colony by 1632, Cotton was given 250 acres for having transported five persons into the colony: Eleanor Hill, Richard Hill, Edward Eason, and Domingo and Sambo (Saconyo?), both *Negroes*. Early Virginians and English colonists in general took an ambiguous view of the legal status of the Africans in their midst. Some of these laborers were called "servants" and were subject to an indenture for a term of years rather than to lifetime servitude. Imported into Virginia and Maryland in increasingly larger numbers and against their will, the status of Africans was clarified in colonial custom and then in law (pages 369-70) well before the end of the seventeenth century: they were slaves. These laborers became increasingly preferred to servants from England.

Except for convicts, English servants had to be enticed to come to America; they could not be worked as hard or treated as harshly as field hands; they could work off their indenture or might simply disappear before their time of service was over. As the first settlers began to die, their African workers were deemed chattel in the early wills, subject to transfer to heirs. Thus in 1640, did William Cotton convey his slaves. In the presumed absence of heirs (there may have been one born shortly after William Cotton's death - daughter Verlinda), William Cotton's slaves were to pass to his widowed mother, **Joane Cotton** (?-?) immigrant, from Cheshire, England – our ancestor - if in fact she was the mother of Verlinda Stone.

GAINES, PENDLETON and TAYLOR FAMILY TIES

George Gaines (1764-1845), husband of Susanna Graves and father of **James Gaines** (1798-1868/72), is believed to have been the first of his family to settle in Boone County, KY followed shortly by two of George's brothers, William and Churchill and a first cousin, Abner, who was one of the earliest residents of the community of Walton, KY. The town was said to have been named for the carpenter who built Abner Gaines his log house.

George Gaines was the son of **Martha George** (?-?) and **Henry Gaines** (1731-1810), Henry was the son of **William Henry Gaines** (?-1796) and **Isabella Pendleton** (1712-1790). William Henry was the son of **Richard Gaines** (1666-1755) and **Dorothy Rawlings** (1664-1750). Richard's parents were the first **James Gaines** (1620-1692) and **Mary Pendleton** (?-?). The first James' parents were Welsh immigrant **Thomas Gaines** (1584-?) and _____. In Wales and early Virginia, the surname may have been *Games, Gane, or Gaine*.

Archibald Gaines and his siblings, the children of Abner and Elizabeth Gaines, were great grandchildren, X 3, of **James Gaines** and **Mary Pendleton Gaines**, and therefore first cousins (four times removed, I think) of **Amanda Watts Gaines Huey** 1821-1895), great grandmother of **Elizabeth Huey Taylor – Betty Cook** (1918-2000).

Abner Gaines married Elizabeth Mathews, and with her had eleven children: Elizabeth, Archibald, James M., John P., Abner W., Benjamin P., William, August, Richard, Mary and Mildred. The most renown of Abner and Elizabeth Gaines' children, was John P Gaines (1795-1857), who was a United States Senator, Whig Congressman, prisoner of war in Mexico and (after former Whig Congressman Abraham Lincoln declined the appointment) Governor of the Oregon Territory (1850-53). It may be of interest that a great grandson of Abner Gaines was Lindsey Burke, killed in the Congo Free State, at the end of the 19th century - in the service of King Leopold of Belgium.

As noted, George Gaines' grandmother (wife of William Henry Gaines) was **Isabella Pendleton** (1712-1790). Isabella was an older sister of the justly famous Edmund Pendleton (1721-1803).

EDMUND PENDLETON (1721-1803)

In even a brief history of **Isabella Pendleton Gaines'** family, the career and accomplishments of her singularly talented brother are worth a mention. Thomas Jefferson said of Edmund Pendleton "taken all in all, he was the ablest man in debate that I ever met with." Jefferson's opinion would not have been idly offered. Edmund Pendleton took a leading role in Virginia prior to, during and subsequent to the American Revolution. A member of the Virginia House of Burgesses, Pendleton was chosen a member of the Virginia committee of correspondence in 1773. He was a member and then President of the colonial convention and was sent by that body to the first Continental Congress. With George Washington, Peyton Randolph, Patrick Henry, Benjamin Harrison, and Richard Henry Lee, he went to Philadelphia in 1774. As president of the Virginia convention, he was at the head of the government of the colony from 1775 till the creation of the Virginia constitution the following year. In May, 1776, Pendleton presided again over the convention. He drew up the resolutions of rebellion, using words that were afterward incorporated almost verbatim into the Declaration of Independence, *"that the delegation be instructed to propose to declare the United Colonies free and independent states, absolved from all allegiance or dependence upon the crown or parliament of Great Britain."*

Edmund Pendleton was a leader of the "cavaliers," as the old planter class became known in eighteenth century Virginia. He was an opponent of the populist Patrick Henry. The Baptists in their histories have preserved a friendlier place for Patrick Henry than for Edmund Pendleton. **Betty Huey Taylor Cook** (1918-

2000), multiple great niece of Edmund Pendleton, but also wife of a Baptist minister, the Rev. **Cecil V Cook, Jr** (1913-1970), and herself a loyal Baptist, made the following notation part of her research. *"The Baptists found an able advocate in Patrick Henry, 'being always a friend of liberty. He only needed to be informed of their oppression.' A letter from Judge Spencer Roan to William Wert, Henry's biographer, states that Mr. Edmund Pendleton on the bench of Caroline Court justified the imprisonment of several Baptist Preachers who were defended by Mr. Henry, on the heinous charge of worshipping God according to the dictates of their own consciences."* **The Baptists of Virginia**, Ryland (page 76).

After independence from England, Pendleton was appointed, with Chancellor George Wythe and Thomas Jefferson, to revise the colonial laws. In March, 1777, despite a crippling fall from his horse, he was re-elected speaker of the House of Burgesses, and after the organization of the chancery court, he was unanimously chosen its president. In 1779, on the establishment of the court of appeals, he became president of that body, holding office until his death. In 1788, he presided over the Virginia State convention that ratified the constitution of the United States.

JAMES TAYLOR (1609/15-1698) AND
SOME OF HIS PROGENY

Isabella Pendleton Gaines and her eminent brother Edmund were the children of **Henry Pendleton** (1683-1721) and **Mary Bishop Taylor** (1688-1770). Mary and Henry Pendleton's other children were James (1703-1761), Philip (?-1778), Nathaniel (1715-1794) and John (1719-1799). Mary Taylor, Henry Pendleton's wife, is said to have been a daughter, by **Mary Gregory** (1665-1747), (second) wife of English immigrant to **James Taylor** (1635-1698), son of immigrants **Elizabeth** _____ (?-?) and **John Taylor** (1607-1651).

> Taylor Family genealogist Elizabeth Marshall Taylor Rubio has demonstrated that she and her siblings, are descended from ancient Taylors not only through their maternal Taylor, Huey, Gaines and Pendleton ancestors but also through their father, Henry Anderson Taylor Sr and his paternal (Taylor) line: Cary Buxton (1895-1964), Thomas George (1860-1935) Henry Alley (1825-1898) Lewis Jr (1784-1870), Lewis Sr (1751-1820), Edmund (1723-1808), and John (1696-1780), son of **James Taylor** (1635-1698) and **Mary Gregory** (1665-1747). Elizabeth Taylor Rubio and her brothers, David Reade, Henry Anderson Jr, and John Buxton Taylor are thus related to Taylor patriarch **John Taylor** (1607-1651), James father, through both Henry Taylor, their father, as well as their mother, Jean Vallette Taylor (Taylor), sister of **Betty Taylor Cook**.

The parents of **Mary Gregory Taylor** were immigrant **John Gregory** (1623-1676) and **Elizabeth Bishop** (?-?), lineal ancestors of James Madison (1750/51-1836), fourth President of the United States. Madison was also a descendent of the above mentioned immigrant, James Taylor. Madison's grandmother was Francis Taylor Madison (1700-1761), granddaughter of this James Taylor, ancestor not only of President Madison but also President Zachary Taylor (1784-1850). Zachary's father, Richard Taylor (1744-1827), moved his family from Orange County VA to near Louisville, KY in 1785. A daughter of Zachary and Margaret Smith Taylor (?-?) was Sarah Knox Taylor (1813-35), wife of Jefferson Davis (1808-1889), President of the Southern Confederacy during the Civil War.

As stated, Mary Bishop Taylor was married to Henry Pendleton. Henry's father was **Philip Pendleton** (1654-?) of Norwich, England, who probably came to Virginia Colony in 1676, where he married **Isabella Hunt (Harp/Hart)** in 1682. Philip was the son of **Elizabeth Douglass** (?-?) and **Henry Pendleton Jr** (1614-1682).

Henry was the son of **Susan Carmen/Camden** (?-?) and **Henry Pendleton** (1583-1635), who apparently were married in England in 1605. Henry was the son of **Elizabeth Pettengale** (?-1625) and **George Pendleton** (1558-1603). They were married at St. Peter's Norwich, England. George was buried at St Stephens Church, Norwich (1603).

The Huey (page 80) and Gaines families were united in the persons of **Joseph Addison Huey** (1819-1896) and **Amanda Watts Gaines** (1821-1895), who were married on October 28, 1841. They moved to Union, Kentucky in about 1869, from Big Bone Lick, KY. Even though they had moved to nearby Union, Joseph and Amanda were buried back in the Big Bone Cemetery, off Route 536 (Hathaway Road) in Boone County, KY. The graves of Joseph's parents, **Samuel Huey** (1771-1821) and **Jane Mason Huey** (1778-1859) are there as well.

THE ORDEAL OF MARGARET AND MARY GARNER

The cousins, **Amanda Gaines Huey** and Archibald Gaines, shared a time and place peculiar in import and drama. It was they who inherited the catastrophic consequences of the decision of their grandparents' and parents' generations, that human slavery must be sanctioned and preserved in Kentucky. It was their generation, reaching maturity in the antebellum south, who, with their children, experienced Civil War, and were required to take the post-war reins of responsibility, in a defeated and largely devastated land. But it was their parents and grandparents who, in their time, settled on their progeny a vigorous and uncompromising defense of human slavery.

Abner Gaines, a first cousin of **George Gaines** (1764-1845) and Archibald's father, was an energetic and opportunistic entrepreneur. In 1813, he bought a tavern and inn, and built an impressive residence on the property. He was a justice in Boone County from 1805 to 1817, and was then appointed sheriff. In 1818, he became the owner of the first stagecoach line between Cincinnati and Lexington, carrying passengers on a trip that took thirty-four hours. In his 1839 will, Abner, noting that he had previously given $2,000 to each of his children, left his "plantation" to his youngest and yet unmarried daughter, Mildred, with the usual proviso that his wife have the lifetime use and enjoyment of this property. The donation to Mildred included "all my negroes, stock of Horses, cattle, sheep, hogs &c. farming utensils &c. &c." To Abner's wife, Elizabeth, went the "Black woman called Aggie."

The will signified the passing to his children not only of a donor's property but also his values. Thus, by Abner to his children, so also by **James Gaines** to his, and **Johnson Watts** to his, slaveholders each and all, passed along slaves and the appreciation of slavery to their heirs. Their children, innocent at their births, inherited the demons that had been released into the slavery-endorsing world of their ancestors and their fathers and mothers, demons that were as potent and destructive in the daytime of commerce as in the night time of other all-too-human pursuits. (See NOTE, page 111.)

By 1850, Kentucky's pioneer generation had passed and their children were in charge. In that year, John P. Gaines sold a farm and slaves to his brother Archibald. Included among the property was Margaret Garner, a young woman who, by then, was the mother of three mulatto children. By way of an admission made on his behalf by his lawyer (see page 111), we know that Archibald Gaines was the father of Margaret Garner's children, including the murdered Mary. (At her trial in Cincinnati, when asked how she had received the injury that left a scar from her forehead to her cheekbone, she replied simply, "White man struck me.")

The sale of brother John's slaves to him may have begun Archibald's troubles. After that, he often found himself rushing over the Ohio River into federal court in Cincinnati, to secure a warrant for the return of escaped slaves. In January, 1856, Archibald was at it again, to fetch back Margaret Garner, her children, husband and others.

This time, seventeen escaped slaves had run away, crossing the iced up river on foot at Covington. On the Ohio side, they split into two groups, so as to draw less attention. Nine slaves slipped into Cincinnati and found daytime hiding places in the northern part of the city, from whence they were taken to Canada. But the second group asked directions to the home of an elderly former slave, to which they were directed. Their location was reported to pursuers from Kentucky and the house was soon surrounded. Those within barred the doors and windows and also fired weapons at any who tried to enter. At least one "deputy" was wounded by gunfire when he tried to come in through a window. With the barricaded house surrounded and no hope of escape, Margaret grabbed a butcher knife and cut deeply into her daughter's throat. While little Mary bled to death on the floor, Margaret and the rest were soon overpowered and taken to prison.

The State of Ohio wanted to try Margaret Garner for murder. Archibald Gaines wanted his property returned to him. After many maneuvers and motions during a sensational two-week trial, the federal anti-fugitive slave law prevailed. The court ordered Margaret Garner to be taken back across the Ohio River, to Archibald Gaines' farm.

The escape and capture of Margaret Garner, her children, and her husband, was a national uproar. An enslaved mother had killed her own child before seeing her returned to slavery. This was an event with little precedent in the national psyche. Any occurrence falling outside the expected patterns of behavior can deliver a shock. The murder of enslaved, little Mary certainly did. The shock has resonated, off and on, ever since.

Toni Morrison's Pulitzer Prize-winning novel **Beloved** is premised upon Margaret and Mary's anguished lives. A play, *Margaret Garner* has recently hit the boards. Efforts have been made to preserve the homestead area of Maplewood, the ancestral Gaines plantation where Margaret Garner was born in 1834. The gently sloping farm, as beautiful today as its ante-bellum tableau must have been, is 18 miles south of Cincinnati, a few miles west of Richwood, KY, on U.S. Route 25.

Despite her desperate act, Margaret and her remaining children were doomed. Returned to Kentucky by court order, she was promptly shipped south to a Gaines plantation in Arkansas. On the journey, the boat in which they were confined was hit by another boat and sank in the Mississippi River. Although Margaret was saved, her infant son was drowned, a death which is said to have caused her to rejoice. Margaret Garner is believed to have died of typhoid fever shortly before the start of the Civil War.

A GIFT TO A DAUGHTER-IN-LAW

After the war, people in Kentucky picked up their lives. In the Huey households in Union, KY, the start-up included a gift to a daughter-in-law, in 1886. Amanda Gaines inscribed a book of poetry to son James's wife - "to Sallie C. Huey from her mother Huey." Doubtless Amanda was mighty pleased to have Sarah for a daughter. Amanda had given birth to three daughters, all of whom had died young. (Page 80.) The gift book was **The Union of American Poetry and Art**, edited by John James Piatt (Cincinnati: Dibble, 1882). This enormous volume of poetry and woodcuts contained, among its many themes and conceits, poetry on the subjects of slavery and freedom. Paul Hamilton Hayne's *The Hanging of Black Cudjo* is printed here (page 465). Its narrative is built around the refusal of a slave to accept his freedom after the Revolutionary War. The loyal Cudjo submits to torture from the Tories, including a botched lynching. The stalwart, suffering Cudjo refuses to reveal the hiding place of his "Mass Tom." After he saved *Mass Tom* and is offered his freedom, Cudjo declares his preference to remain as overseer on the plantation of his birth. Why? *"I got all ting tat I want, wid not one tax to pay. Now go long, Massa! Wha' you wish fur dribe ole Cuj away?"*

What good is freedom?

Not much, to *ole Cuj* because:

> *I nebber see free nigger yet*
> *but what he lie and steal,*
> *lie to 'e boss, 'e wife, 'e chile*
> *in cabbin an de fiel."*

Printed in a treasured family book, a gift to a young woman from her mother-in-law, the poem might be dismissed - 120 years after the gift was made - as very dated and unimportant posturing. But we note the vile sentiments. From a literary point of view, the poet is adopting a counterfeit persona. He is flying under false colors, aiming for a bit of humor at the expense of the formerly enslaved but now freed subjects of his day. The problem is not that the poem has little or no literary merit. The problem, the tragedy of the verse, is that it does have value, shining a light on its own time, as the poet used his skill, such as it was, to demean and ridicule those most wounded by a commonly shared, bitter history.

This is *Nigger Verse*, poetry of abuse. It is obsessive and fanciful, fixated on denying the humanity of freed slaves, who are tricked up with a contrived dialect and fraudulent notions of noble suffering on behalf of a representative, White slave owner. A non-existent world is conjured out of class defeat and resentment and displayed to the reader in imitation of supposed African-American submissiveness and sonorities. Irwin Russell offers similar sensibilities in the same volume (page 515). Russell serves up spurious insights by making a former slave lament the dire circumstances of "Mahsr John" after the Civil War.

> *Well, times is changed! De war it come an'*
> *sot de niggers free,*
> *An now ol' Mahsr John ain't hardly wuf as*
> *much as me;*
> *He had to pay his debts, an' so his lan' is*
> *mostly gone—*
> *An' I declar' I's sorry for poor ol' Mahsr*
> *John.*

And we're sorry, as well. Sorry to acknowledge this poetry on the bookshelf, which says more about the brutish perspectives of the versifiers then it ever did about their fanciful subjects. We are sorry not to be able to know what the much venerated **Sarah Crouch Huey** made of these poisonous sentiments, coming to her in the guise of gentle verse, as a token of familial love, from her equally well remembered mother-in-law, **Amanda Gaines Huey**.

SOURCES:

Gaines Family genealogy: Betty Huey Taylor Cook's unpublished genealogy book; material has also been generously provided by family genealogist John C. Gaines. Valuable research has been conducted and shared by Elizabeth Taylor Rubio, great, great granddaughter of Amanda Gaines Huey. A Gaines genealogy is posted as *Gaines Family History,* members.tripod.com, which is part of *the Pendleton Family* at geocities.com

For the early history of colonial Virginia: **American Slavery, American Freedom**, by Edmund S. Morgan (New York: Norton, 1975, 2005), winner of the Parkman Prize.

Many Doyne, Stone, Cotton, and other documents (such as William Cotton's 1640 will) were generously provided to the writer in 2006 by Anne Moffett Gibbs, descendent, who typed and preserved a lengthy 1924 report, with exhibits, by well known genealogical researcher Hester Dorsey Richardson. Ms. Richardson certified under oath that she had examined and copied documents "gleaned from the original records in Maryland."

Evidence for Gaines settling in Boone County: *Supplement to the Boone County Recorder, Illustrated Historical Edition*, R. E. Berkshire, Publisher, Burlington, Kentucky, Thursday, September 4, 1930.

For additional Watts, Gaines and especially Graves genealogical information: the extensive, well researched and maintained material at the Graves Family Foundation website: gravesfa.org. See especially the file (often revised) "CAPTAIN THOMAS GRAVES, 1608 Settler of Jamestown, Virginia, and His Descendants (ca. 1580-2006)."Additional Graves information, including mention of the location of the gravestone of Thomas Graves: tsgraves.com

Histories of the Baptist Churches in Boone County KY: microfilm at the Boone County public library in Union, KY, reproduced on the web at various family history and Baptist history websites, such as "Baptist History Homepage."

On the career of Edmund Pendleton: famousamewricans.net/edmundpendleton

For collateral Taylor generations from Immigrant John Taylor, see Janet Green's postings, esp. geocities.com/janet_ariciu/Taylor.

can you feel or find a heart to pray for me? – George Gaines, quoted in John Taylor's **A History of Ten Baptist Churches** (Nelson County KY, 1827, page 134)

NOTE: Was Archibald Gaines the father of Margaret Garner's children? The *New York Times* covered the trial and on Feb 16, 1856, published a report of the testimony of Doctor Elijah Smith Clarkson, who swore that he knew Margaret ("Peggy") Garner and her children to be the slaves of Archibald Gaines. In response to the question put to him on cross examination, "Is he [Archibald Gaines] the father of those children?" Archibald's lawyer interjected, "We admit that." See above, pages 105-08.

In the evening of another day, and thru the leaved branches of the big oak right out there in the pasture I can see the moon as it slowly advances along its watch. . . . It really helps one in the moments of doubt and perplexity, just to behold life in all its constancy; simple of manner yet sublime of action, unassuming of wealth yet rich in sweetness and beauty.

I give my belief in the divinity into which human nature could grow thru the inherent tendency on the part of all things living to grow toward the light.

Mayo Moore Taylor
(1893-1982)

Letters to his mother, Mary Baldwin Moore Taylor: Sept 29, 1923, & undated

"... SORRY ENOUGH WAS THE STAY"

John Oliver Taylor Sr
Mary Baldwin Moore

John Oliver Taylor Jr (1891-1960)
Betty Taylor Cook (1918-2000)

On May 10, 1922, Edward W. Hawkins, an attorney in Newport, KY, wrote to the just-widowed **Mary Baldwin Moore Taylor** (1863-1936) that her husband **John Oliver Taylor** (1862-1922) "never knowingly harmed or hurt a single living creature." Unintended hurts can be freighted with special sorrows inside the family.

John was born in Spartanburg, South Carolina during the Civil War, where his father, former Methodist missionary **Charles Taylor** (1819-1897) was President of Spartanburg Female College. Infant John Oliver was named for his two prominent grandfathers. **John Gamewell** (1756-1827), an English seaman, plying Atlantic and Caribbean waters, gave up the life of surf and swell to become a pioneering Methodist evangelist in South Carolina. John Gamewell was the father of John Oliver's mother, **Charlotte Gamewell Taylor** (1828-1910). **Oliver Swaine Taylor** (1784-1885), John's paternal grandfather, was a much-traveled educator, medical doctor and Presbyterian evangelist, whose long and active retirement (1850-1885) in Auburn, New York, added an affirming *gravitas* to a life already full of accomplishment.

In 1867, Charles and Charlotte Taylor moved to Kentucky. There Charles accepted the presidency of Kentucky Wesleyan College. John and his siblings grew up in Northern Kentucky, as their father pastored several Methodist Churches, each of them allied to the Methodist Episcopal Church, South. This was that branch of American Methodism that had been captured by slave-holding sentiments before the Civil War and dominated by these same opinions for decades after.

Mary Baldwin Moore

In the 1880 census for Covington, KY, John Oliver, age 17, is enrolled as a resident in his parents' home, employed as a grocery store clerk. This census details the rest of the household as follows: Charles Taylor, 60, wife Charlotte Taylor 52, daughter Mattie, 24 a music teacher, and Charlotte B, age 15. There is also a servant, Lizzie Wilson, age 20.

Although his father Charles and paternal grandfather Oliver were both college graduates (NYU, with honors, and Dartmouth, respectively), John Oliver never attended college. John's working life was remembered by his children and grandchildren exactly as he was listed in subsequent census records, a "traveling salesman."

John Oliver met **Mary ("Minnie") Baldwin Moore** (1863-1936) at his father's church, when they were sixteen or so. Minnie told her children John was the best looking man she had ever seen in her life. Even so, they did not marry until some ten years passed, on March 29, 1887. At their marriage, Mary B. Moore and John Oliver Taylor Sr, shared a common set of ancestors: the immigrants **Sarah _____** (abt 1600-1672) and **Isaac Morrill** (abt 1587-1661), a Roxbury, MA blacksmith. (See pages 186 and 324, and *Morrill* in the Index.)

For reasons no longer known, John Taylor and Minnie Moore were married in the home of Robert T. Snowden in Oldham County, KY. The wedding was recorded as performed by J.J. Johnston, not by the groom's clergyman father. Perhaps the Rev. Doctor Taylor participated and even presided, while deferring to another minister to sign his son's marriage certificate.

John Oliver Taylor was remembered with unfriendly ambivalence by his daughter Nancy, who described him as a sometime doting but routinely insolvent father. Can Aunt Nancy be relied upon as a source of intelligence? Her writings may conceal as much as they reveal. "Whenever he was capable of making a dime he would give me a quarter, sometimes," wrote Nancy Collier Taylor Johnson. Every line Nancy wrote demonstrates an

John Oliver Taylor Sr

arresting method of recounting what she pretends she does not want to say. She is our main source and authority concerning her father.

Grandchildren and great grandchildren preserved a distant and un-emotive affection for John Oliver. They recall him as a drinker. Some say, flat out, that John Taylor was an alcoholic. Family lore has preserved the memories of his children, going out in the night to look for their father to bring him home.

On September 12, 1963, his birth date, but forty-one years after John's death, daughter Nancy penned a spectral meditation. *"Today, I would say to him, 'You were not a very satisfactory father' and he would say, 'I never wanted to be anybody's father.' Maybe I misunderstood you but you acted as though you could not care less what happened to us . . . and to mother. Mother so often said the first ten years of your marriage was her heaven, then your weakness over-came you and you seemed so beaten and alone from then on."* What his daughter Nancy perceived and remembered as John's rejection of her could just as likely be the socially destructive symptoms of an addictive disease - still poorly understood.

Is it fair to point at John Oliver Taylor, Sr as nothing more than an inadequate father and an alcoholic? What good can this characterization serve? Perhaps a blighted life from an age long past may cast an admonitory shadow upon us. Perhaps some cautionary aspect might be detected by the observant descendent who may then be watchful of oneself. Perhaps, too, there was a more capacious circumstance to John Taylor, a larger history that, if understood, may bring a degree of comprehension to a life not fully lived.

John Oliver Taylor's British ancestors were mostly English in origin, that is, they were not Scot, Celtic or Irish. His ancestors were then, from cultural and literary influences, given to a sober rumination of the fates. Such existential discordance might be expressed in the individual as a disconsolate searching. If John Oliver inherited the sardonic gene, he passed it along. His son,

John Jr (1891-1960) seems to have suffered in this way and so did **Betty Taylor Cook** (1918-2000), his granddaughter. In conversation with her adult sons and with others, Betty acknowledged her habit of brooding about life and its trials. Betty recognized a predisposition to despondency within her and fought it with uncommon candor and fortitude. In her spoken reflections about her ancestors and their morose aspect, Betty traced it back through the Moore and Taylor lines, as has Anne M. Gibbs, a great-granddaughter of John Taylor Sr, who has shared her thoughts in conversations with the present writer.

As Betty and Anne surmised, the Taylors of Northern Kentucky seem to have been melancholic to a high degree. Today, we call it depression. In any day, a symptom can be alcoholism, which seems to have been a lifelong hazard for John Oliver Taylor Sr. If the Irish drink to forget, the Brits drink to remember - in case their morbid nursery rhymes, passed down from one unsuspecting generation to another, are not enough. *And if I die before I wake* comes from the plague years, tricked up as a gentle bedtime prayer, by people who have forgotten the terror but yet find themselves enveloped in sadness.

Alcoholic depressives in the family attic ought to be instructive to us, the progeny of these dispirited strugglers. Read the message in the bottle. Then search out, with guiltless clarity, for medicinal and clinical relief. The children of darkness may yet join the children of light. Don't wait until your depressed existence has run its course and your reputation within your family is, with justice, fixed, and you are spoken about at the end, as having never deliberately hurt anyone. If John Oliver Taylor could tell us something, he might tell us that.

The English depressed? If you don't believe me, you can look it up in their literature. There you will find a fondness for themes and metaphors associated with despondency. Their poetry and theatre are full of it to a startling degree. Peter Ackroyd (see Sources, below) believes the motif of melancholy is unique in its Englishness. Elegiac tendencies and the contemplation of mortality have "always been there," Ackroyd writes, from the Britons and the Saxons on through to Philip Larkin and Ted Hughes. The vivid Celtic legend of Arthur, *rex quondam, rex futurus* – once and future king – is the model. Arthur is invoked in Welsh poetry in the tenth century as, even then, a figure of the remote past. He is the reticent commander in battles that are fought audaciously but then lost: "*courage must be the firmer as our strength grows less*" – is one of the most forlorn lines in all literature.

Arthur is the inspiration of the melancholic, backward-facing literature and the very self-identification of these island peoples, constantly invaded, constantly overwhelmed, ceaselessly brooding over a lost past. Even the occupying Normans, losing Normandy itself within two centuries, encouraged an identity with their new homeland, England, and a reverence for its shadowy past. Albion is the mysterious land to which Arthur was taken to be buried. Albion is England. Just as the Normans endorsed the old legends, the Tudors endorsed genealogy, as a way of linking themselves to the old ways. This impetus for recall has not weakened, as the reader of this volume can attest.

Malory, Milton, Spencer, Shakespeare, Donne, Gray, Keats, Tennyson, and countless lesser literati can all be found tracking the ancient and well worn paths through the forests of the Druids and the little people who are in hiding. Among the witnesses is found one **John Moore** and his **Map of Man's Mortalitie** (1617). John Moore gave his book a very full title: "*A mappe of mans mortalitie. Clearly manifesting the originall of death with the nature, fruits, and effects thereof, both to the vuregenerate, and elect children of God. Diuided into three bookes; and published for the futherance of the wise in practice, the humbling of the strong in conceit, and for the comfort and confirmation of weake Christians, against the combat of death, that they may wisely and seasonably be prepared against the same. Whereunto are annexed two consolatory sermons, for the afflicted*

Benjamin Moore

Christians, in their greatest conflicts. By John Moore, minister of the word of God, at Shearsbie in Leicestershire." The book may yet be in the stacks at the Union Theological Seminary in New York City.

To cite a seventeenth century *map of mortalitie* by a certain John Moore is to bring us round to his possible descendent, our **Mary Baldwin Moore Taylor** (1863-1936). For it is not only our Taylors but also our Moores who struck and held a lingering note of despondency. Minnie spoke to her children of her father, **Benjamin Moore** (1837-1894) as a whiskey drinker, who read bedtime Shakespeare to her. The union of dispiriting Moore and Taylor strains in Minnie and John may have become a perfect storm of melancholia – for their kids.

Although Minnie Moore aimed to have her sons become "professional men" (as daughter Nancy Collier recalled), she seems to have bequeathed to several of her children and grandchildren a high quotient of her own very peculiar anguish. Her youngest child went unnamed for two and possibly four years. "Booch" (for beautiful baby boy, or some such), was finally given a name, but only when Aunt Jenny, frequent visitor, occasional boarder, intervened, as recalled by Minnie's daughter, Nancy Collier Johnson: "*She said, 'Minnie, that child should have a name!' Booch was about four by then, and had never been called anything but BOY! And mother said, 'Well, how about Ishmael?" And he was that for a few weeks, and Aunt Jenny said, 'Why not name him after Pa?' . . . who was Marmaduke Moore . . . so Marmaduke Littleton it's been . . . and I often think Booch had three strikes against him before he ever came up to bat.*" Booch signed himself, in letters to his mother, as "Boy." On the day of his tryout with the *New York Football Giants* in 1925, he surely announced himself to the coaches as "Duke," not Marmaduke or Booch. His visit to New York got Booch a wife but not a position on the football team. On July 2, 1927, Thelma Sybil Goldsmith and Marmaduke Lyttleton Taylor were married in Yonkers, NY. Booch's sister Nancy wrote that Casper, a hired man in Minnie's house, once inquired "where mother got those no-good names. From a book?" Yeah, Casper. From the Casper book.

With a husband absent even when he was present, Minnie Taylor presided over a ménage she filled with paying boarders, kinfolk, and two adolescent, orphaned sisters, Nettie and Mary. Minnie took them all in. Her parents **Mary Aurelia Mayo** (1839-1901) and **Benjamin Moore** (1837-1894) lived with Minnie, in their final years, as did Aunt Nanny Collier, from Cynthiana, KY, who (the story goes) came for the wedding of Minnie and John's daughter, Jean, to Paul Carter and stayed for forty years. There were maids who came and went, proving that lots of Erlanger families were in worse straits than the hard-pressed John Taylor household. These boarders, orphans, helpers and aunts were in compliment to six children: Jean Valette (Nov 21 1888-July 18, 1965); **John Oliver, Jr** (Jan 23, 1891-May 25, 1960); Mayo Moore (Jan 16 1893-May 7, 1980); Dwight Parsons (Nov 2, 1894-May 20, 1962); Nancy Collier (Dec 15, 1896-Dec 5, 1986); Marmaduke Lyttleton (May 17, 1904-Jan 14, 1982). The primary boarder was "Deakie," so called (in ridicule?) as he had at some time been an Episcopal deacon.

"Deakie" was Daniel Ruffner; he became so accustomed to living in the home of the much-decamped John Taylor, that when the family moved, Deakie moved with them. On birthdays and at Christmas, Deakie was known to give the children valuable gifts, such as sterling silverware (Georgian pattern), with date and initials engraved, sometimes adding his own name. Deakie's room was usually the finest, the one with a fireplace and not just a grate. Christmas largess was spread on his bed for the children to come and get. When the circus came to town, the children went; Deakie footed all costs.

John and Minnie's children were descended on both sides from notable educators, especially Taylors and Dwights. From this heritage Minnie somehow drew the conclusion that she should refuse her children even a rudimentary public school education. Accordingly, she kept her children at home and saw to their education only

Mary Baldwin Moore Taylor

fitfully, either with the occasional tutor or by her own efforts. In this way, Granny Taylor guaranteed that hers and John's children entered the twentieth century without even a high school diploma.

Absent credentials, the children were reduced to physical labor, low wages, schemes and dreams. The writer heard Nancy Collier speak of her own and her siblings' life-long humiliation and sketchy employment prospects, a result, Aunt Nancy said, of having no way to certify their schooling and education. A mild irony may be seen in Minnie's sometime presidency of the Erlanger PTA, presiding at parents' meetings at the school she refused to let her own children attend.

The home schooling project might have worked better but for a fire, which destroyed the family home. With an inheritance from life insurance left to Minnie by her unmarried brother Hunt Mayo Moore (1873-1906) who briefly lived with her, Minnie decided to build a brand new house. While the new home, "the beaches," was being built by her soon-to-be son-in-law, Paul Carter, the family moved into two rough buildings in a lumberyard. As trash was burned in the kitchen stove in one of these structures, the upper floor caught fire and the entire dwelling was consumed by the flames.

Writing some seventy years later, in a style reflective of James Joyce or of her make-do education (or both), daughter Nancy created a narrative (reproduced verbatim) about the calamity. *"In the process of moving from the two temporary buildings we had shared while our beautiful home was being built, the stove was being filled with unwanted and hopefully gone up in smoke . . . soon blaze was coming from the roof and what had not been removed, which was mother's life time of books . . . BOOKS! . . . and many other cherished items . . . only at this hour do I feel the real loss . . . I stood there with the rest of the family . . . especially mother . . . bitter hard for her."* In the pictures that have survived, one may see in Mary Moore Taylor a dread of what the next week, day or hour might bring to her.

We may speculate - as we have - about the causes of the dolorous melancholy that afflicted the personalities and the marriage of Mary Moore and John Oliver Taylor. But a strict honesty requires the admission that we just do not know what was the matter. Some of their children may have escaped completely the numbing grip of depression. Daughter Jean (1888-1965), the oldest, was remembered by granddaughter Anne Moffett Gibbs and niece Betty Taylor Cook as a joyful and engaged lady. Her surviving letters show an affectionate face to her often anxious siblings.

Son Mayo (1893-1980) was effervescently popular in Erlanger, KY, where he lived most of his life and was feted in his old age as a localized version of Will Rogers. Mayo's brother, Dwight Parsons Taylor, served the community as mayor. But there is no question each of the boys hustled to make a simply living and there is little question about the despondency of their siblings, John Oliver Jr, Nancy and the alcoholic Marmaduke Littleton ("Booch").

Somber questions persist about their parents. Were John and Minnie a bad match? Should Minnie have reconsidered her marriage to John, when her mother **Mary Aurelia Mayo Moore** (1839-1901), asked Minnie if truly she wanted to marry a drinker like her father, **Benjamin Moore** (1837-1894)?

Perhaps John and Minnie would have been inclined to brooding whether together or alone. Perhaps they were exquisitely vulnerable to their straitened surroundings. John and Minnie lived out their lives in the only section of the United States that - up to their own time - had suffered defeat in war. Minnie and John, two War infants, grew to maturity in the immediate aftermath of The Lost Cause, among people who refused to recognize their defeat and who insisted on restoring their domination of African Americans. In social, political and psychological terms, the Northern Kentucky environment of their adulthood was a toxic continuation of the war itself.

Mary Aurelia Mayo Moore

The 1861-65 conflict has forever become embellished in HISTORY as the "civil" war. But there is little that is "civil" about a civil war. In Kentucky the bloody conflict was a bitter, clannish affair, with moral overtones and moralistic undertones. The struggle undermined the economic and social structures of Kentucky, even as it failed to replace with anything better, the regional and racial mythologies that had sustained the households of Minnie's and John's parents and grandparents. These mythologies actually increased in political strength, resentment and verbosity during Reconstruction, the years of John and Minnie's maturity. Kentucky's reactionary embrace of Jim Crow legislation was in full throat by 1900, and never actually let up for fifty more years. That ought to have been enough to depress everybody.

John and Minnie's time and place made them part of a generation of backward glancing, White Southerners, many of whom were embittered and adrift. Perhaps Minnie and John absorbed into their persons defeatism from their surroundings. Perhaps they reworked a community ethos of collective misfortune into private convictions about the unfairness of it all.

Did they feel compelled to live unwelcome lives in economic, physical and psychological discomfort not of their making? Were they archetypal victims, assigning cosmic guilt to the "*sun, moon and stars for the surfeit of their own behavior*"- as the besotted Benjamin Moore might have read in *King Lear* to little Minnie Moore in her bed? We don't know. If with John and Minnie Taylor we observe personal tragedies of Shakespearean scope, we should recall the most important scene in any play. It is the curtain call, when the vilest and deadest character is up again, out front, smiling, seeking applause. In Erlanger, KY in the 1880's and 90's and beyond, occasions for bowing to an appreciative and paying audience were limited.

Some of John's sibs got out of town. They and their children could be found, before the close of the nineteenth century, in Alabama, Texas, Oklahoma. John never left, unless you want to count the frequent rambles of a traveling salesman. Was John's defeatism *cum* alcoholism the cause of his absenting himself from his wife and children? Is it as simple as this? Probably not. Did Minnie, missing John, take up a larger pattern of revenge, and assail her children's futures? We don't know.

JOHN TAYLOR SPEAKS FOR HIMSELF

Before our harsh judgment upon John is put before the world, John ought to be given a chance to speak. The written statements that we have are spread across his life and appear (to this reader) to share common themes. John Taylor could articulate great love for his family, especially his children. John did not like to be put upon or ordered about by anyone. John had no patience for hypocrisy. Each of these traits resonates through John's family, before and after him. Each is positive in a private context. John's resistance to taking directions and his nose for pretense probably complicated his relationship with his father and limited his prospects for a satisfying career, especially a career as a travelling salesman, which would have required him to smile at the pretensions of prospective customers, and marshal the fortitude to keep on smiling even after the hope of a sale had vanished. John's objections to being put upon are on display at age 12, in 1874, when he wrote, in a bold hand, a statement he entitled "Gardening."

> *Gardening is not very pleasant sport for me and I don't think any other little boy likes it. There is one reason why I do not like for summer to come because I have to go right home and go into the garden and pull up weeds and many other things. Some evenings when I come home from school Pa tells me to come on and have some fun with him in the garden. But I don't stay in the garden all the evening. As soon as he goes away I stop and go to playing. One day I told Pa that I did not like to plant anything that I did not like to eat. I told him there would be some use in some watermelons or musk*

melons. There is one thing which he plants which I like that is sweet potatoes. That is the only thing I like to plant.

On March 29, 1886, John, 24, wrote to his sister Mattie ("Dear Mat"). The event inspiring this letter was the appointment of their father to the Taylor Street Methodist Church in Newport, KY. John and Minnie Moore married in March, 1887, and lived their first married year with his parents in this parsonage. His father is "the doctor."

Dear Mat,

I speak for the little room between the church and the house, and then when the sexton is sick you know I can run in, light up, sweep out & I can't imagine anything more delightful. I can hear the doctor saying already Forward March and in we go through the tunnel up from behind the pulpit on to the front before the eyes of the inquisitive multitude and again, 'Ma, I don't think that you are well enough to go in today. You can draw your chair close up to the door in John's room and get the full benefit of the singing, sermon, etc.'

And me, I'll be there all the time. Won't have to get up even. Oh! How nice. And when our rushes of company come, why we can use the seats in the church at night. Tell Lee that she can have first choice, dress circle or balcony. The pulpit we reserve for sister Stock. She gets that when she comes to stay a week to get over the trip.

You said something about the meetings I believe, how is it? Monday night an experience meeting to tell how much each one enjoyed the experiences of the day before. Tuesday night. A kind of social gathering to discuss the future welfare of the church and how we can best reach the outsiders, in fact a general talk among ourselves about our neighbors. Wednesday night. Regular prayer *meeting. Thursday night. A kind of musical entertainment. All are invited. Calculated to bring those who never attend and to hold outsiders after we reach them. Friday night we meet to scheme for money. Strawberry or oyster suppers (depends on the weather) whichever is ripe. Might be other societies (to which I won't belong) lectures, concerts, etc. Saturday night we want you particularly to remember as we wish the whole Sunday School to go over the lesson for the morrow. Sunday night services at the regular hour except in summer or winter when it will be changed about thirty minutes.*

Now the other nights in the week you can do just as you please.

Good by.   'Bub'

Some thirty years later but on a date unknown, John tore off a piece of a ledger sheet and wrote to one of his sons, perhaps placing the note in a "grip" (suitcase).

You know that I have never been given to wild demonstrations either in words or in action, and when I say my boy I'm not only going to miss you for a day but miss you until you come back. It means as much as many countless pages. May God watch over and keep you and give you all success in your new work and send you back to us safe when your work is finished. This is now and will be the prayer of

Father

John wrote a birthday greeting to John Jr around 1919-20. His son was away from wife and baby daughter, Betty.

Dearest John Boy,
Once again, Father Time calls upon you. O Gracious isn't he some speedy chap. I'm sorry for you that your family couldn't be with you for the day. . . .
Good night, I love you.

"MARRIAGE ISN'T ALWAYS THE LONG SWEET SONG IT PROMISES TO BE"

John seems to have loved well those nearest to him but gave in to a sense of helplessness about himself. Minnie is a more interesting figure and for that, harder to understand. The harsh denial of a standard education for her children may have seemed to Minnie a fitting response to their lost Moore-Mayo and Taylor-Dwight heritage of academic excellence, prestige and accomplishment. Minnie's bitter approach to mothering might have been a spiteful answer to her sober and respectable in-laws, **Charlotte Jane Gamewell** (1828-1910) and **Charles Taylor** (1819-1897), who presented to her their irresolute, alcoholic son for a husband. Trapped in a profound and life-long disappointment, did Minnie try to will herself back to her grandfather Pappy Duke's stately Covington home with its imagined ease, and its servants?

Minnie may have decided, or acted on a conviction without any decision, that her circumstance required her to look only inward for solace. Did her outward severity conceal an inner sorrow? Perhaps her daily stratagems of bluster and belly laughs were aimed at reducing her attachments and so shield her from additional hurts. Her grandchildren seemed to have picked up on polarizing extremes within Granny, who displayed to them either affection or harshness.

Minnie's household, as recalled by some of its denizens, was full of raucous laughter but little joy. She took pride in her accomplishments as a reader, but there is slight trace of the effects of this pursuit in her letters. For Christmas, 1893, husband John gave Minnie a volume of Robert Burns' poems but the book's only turned-back pages are at the drinker's ballad, *John Barleycorn* and *Man was Made to Mourn (a Dirge)*.

Mary and John Taylor

Minnie or John probably never got hold of the poetry of that reclusive refugee of their parents' generation, Emily Dickinson (1830-1886). But if so, did Emily get hold of Minnie or John? Lacking Emily's lyricism, but sharing with Emily an austere candor not at home on this earth, Minnie might have found comfort in Emily, the Solitary. Both women suspected that the high arc of their interior meandering might be all the heaven there is. John, too, would have savored Emily, the Unbelieving Believer, who insisted to "Daddy Above" that a blissful mansion must await the rat, if it awaits anyone at all. John, a preacher's kid not lacking a sardonic wit, would have liked that.

In the 1930's, the final decade of her life, Granny Taylor initiated a round of genealogical data collection from cousins and beyond. This work was continued by her son Mayo, daughter Nancy, granddaughter Betty Taylor Cook, and great granddaughters, Anne Moffett Gibbs and Elizabeth Taylor Rubio. Mayo's efforts were memorable. Decades before photocopying, Mayo Taylor made a collection of family Bibles, from which he cut out the birth, marriage and death records. He saved them separately, and thereby permanently disconnected the genealogical trove from the books in which the information had been recorded. This is a plus-minus gambit. The information is no doubt easier to preserve and pass around but a question mark is branded like a tattoo upon the provenance of genealogical information, cut away from its repository. Isn't a question mark a good way to end a short narrative of the lives of Mary Baldwin Moore and John Oliver Taylor?

The last word should come from Minnie, seldom at a loss for one. Shortly before her son **John Jr** married **Nan Elizabeth Huey** on New Years Day, 1916 (see above pp. 31, 47), Minnie wrote to the bride-to-be. Her letter is a meditation on opportunities lost. With typical ferocity and frankness, Minnie exposes her disappointment in the course of her own marriage to the "little girl" she mistakenly took Nan Elizabeth to be.

Minnie Moore

Love disappointed is still love. Aside from the shadowy aspersion cast by Deakie the boarder, there is no hint in family lore that Mary Moore Taylor stopped loving her John. Minnie left instructions that hers and John's ashes be mingled together in the Moore plot at Evergreen Cemetery in Erlanger. If *love-him-always* is the advice Elizabeth got from Minnie's letter, this may have been enough. For Nan Elizabeth and John Taylor Jr created a wonderfully loving marriage. Whatever the message delivered by Minnie or received by Nan, the letter proved a keeper. Granny Taylor's stark counsel to a future daughter-in-law was guarded away by Elizabeth and has been preserved for three generations, and more.

Minnie Moore Taylor was a woman with a broken heart. She needs your prayers and so does her John. Embraced by a Providence that knows them better than we know ourselves, they may be praying for us.

Lisabeth honey

I want to tell you why our plan for a day together and a time for heart to heart communication gang a gley. The Aunt, Miss Collier, is of the household and has been very near always in her interest in the children and to have left her out would have hurt her so it couldn't be done even tho I was denied the opportunity I had looked for. She by the way in her quiet way accepted you wholly and as we all do feel John has reason to rejoice in the gain of that priceless beyond rubies. Let me hasten tho to entreat you to carry the likeness no farther. That paragon of virtue who rose while it was yet dark to give portions clothed her husband in scarlet and then let him loaf around the gates with the elders had in my mind lost a few. Don't do it. The place for that gentleman as I see it was home being handy and pleasant.

Now for what you asked in your letter. I think if you are decided in mind that you are ready to cast in your lot with John for weal or woe with all it may ask of forbearance and sacrifice in order that you may begin the common structure of your lives marry him and go back with him. Understand, little girl, this is not advising you against your own or the judgment of your family. I could not do that. I can only answer you as I see it and remembering always I do not know what you ask of life nor the standard to which you hope to build. I'm acting from self knowledge and what I've learned of the normal woman and that is she comes to the time when life calls her (she thinks it does anyhow) to go with the one man that her destiny may be fulfilled and all she can do is to go. Not wanting to rob you or any woman of her right to dream I feel forced to say while marriage isn't always the long sweet song that it promises to be it sure is a means of growth and that is really what we are here for. I suppose if you don't you always feel you've missed something and if you do you know you haven't, not a thing and that ought to help some. As I tried to tell you yesterday I think marrying John now may call for the exercise of some traits you have heretofore not needed but if you love him more than other things there will be compensation also I think it will be wise for you to have quite a voice in the standards of your living and insist on being a full partner in all that concerns you both. I know his great fear at present is that you may find the new conditions hard and he not able to prevent. That you know is something only you can work out. You see I confronted just this problem and because "nobody did that way" I stayed at home and sorry enough was the stay. I've learned since that It isn't precedent that counts but what contributes most to the working out of the best we can do for our happiness and development. From where I've journeyed you need not fear being a burden. John need not fear for you to live your own life but you should both be ready to accept this great adventure as your life work as well as its joy and in that you will find all the happiness you seek. I hope I've not been prosey. I will be glad to know of any plans you may care to tell me and maybe we can have another chance to "make acquaintance". Did you get cold before reaching home?

Yours in great friendliness
Minnie Moore Taylor

SOURCES:

For Taylor and Moore genealogical data: Betty Taylor Cook's unpublished genealogy book. For all Nancy Johnson quotations and for data concerning the appraisal of John Oliver Taylor and Benjamin Moore by children and grandchildren: letters and documents written by Nancy Collier Taylor Johnson (1896-1986), daughter of John Oliver and Mary Baldwin Moore Taylor, many preserved by Betty Taylor Cook, many others gathered and generously shared by John and Mary's great granddaughter Anne M. Gibbs.

Courage must be the firmer – The Battle of Maldon (991 AD), mss Otho A.xii. For currents of depression in English literature: **Albion, the Origins of the English Imagination**, Peter Ackroyd London: Chatto and Windus (2002)

The appraisals made of Mary and John Taylor by Betty Taylor Cook and Anne M. Gibbs: in conversations with the writer.

The gift-giving of Daniel Ruffner to John and Minnie's children: from the letters and reflections of one of the children, Nancy Collier Taylor; also, conversations with Anne M. Gibbs. Deakie's sterling silverware gifts are in Anne's possession.

Minnie's letter to Nan Elizabeth: from Jean Valette Taylor, Nan Elizabeth's daughter, with copies also to be found in the files of Betty Taylor Cook, in the possession of the writer.

The three great inventions that have exerted a stronger influence than any other in the civilization of mankind - the art of Printing, Gunpowder, and the Mariner's Compass - all claimed by Europe, and as comparatively of modern date, besides many other useful arts - were known and in universal use by the Chinese, while nearly all Europe was as yet a wilderness of savage barbarians.

The albatross, a magnificent bird, generally white, wheels about the vessel in its pathway of airy circles, on such delicately poised wing - so still while moving - that you can look into its large, mild, beautiful eye, as it sweeps swiftly past.

Oh! Ye shadowy phantoms of earthy grandeur and glory, and is this all ye have to give the most devoted worshipper that ever bowed at your shrine?

Charles Taylor
Five Years in China *(1860)*
pages 211, 390, and
403 (on St. Helena, at Napoleon's tomb)

"WHAT IS YOUR HEART MADE OF?"

Charles Taylor
Charlotte Jane Gamewell

John Oliver Taylor (1862-1922)
John Oliver Taylor Jr (1891-1960)
Betty Taylor Cook (1918-2000)

Charles Taylor (1819-1897) was born in Boston, MA on Sept 15, 1819 and died in Courtland, Alabama on Feb 5, 1897. Charles was reared by his parents, **Catherine Gould Parsons** (1791-1865) and the exceedingly long living **Oliver Swaine Taylor** (1784-1885). In a biographical sketch of his father, Charles indicated that he grew up in homes Catherine and Oliver established in Boston and Hadley, MA and then in Homer and Auburn, NY. But Oliver may have been more traveled than this. Charles also wrote that his father was employed as a teacher in several western and southern states.

Charles probably attended one or another academy administered by his scholarly and well educated father. Consonant with his heritage, Charles demonstrated superb intellectual aptitudes, particularly in the study of languages. He graduated from the University of New York with highest honors in 1840, working as a store clerk in New York City to pay his bills and assisting Professor Samuel Morse in his experiments with the telegraph. After college Charles immediately became a teacher of ancient languages. A few years later, Charles, like his father, became a doctor, obtaining a medical degree in 1848 in Philadelphia, a center of medical education made famous by Benjamin Rush (1745-1813). Betty Taylor Cook has recorded that Charles was "converted in a Methodist Church" while attending college in New York City where he met a "Dr. Wightman who urged him to come South." This Dr. W. M. Wightman (1808-1882) was later Methodist

Charles Taylor

Bishop Wightman. After graduation, Charles moved immediately to South Carolina.

In 1844 Charles was admitted to the South Carolina Conference of the Methodist Church and appointed "a junior preacher." His presiding elder was William Capers, Jr (1790-1855), subsequently a Bishop in the Methodist Episcopal Church, South.

> A note about Bishop William Capers Jr and some of his descendents is not out of place in this sketch. William was the son of Mary Wragg (?-?) and William Capers, Sr (Oct 15, 1766-?). William and Mary were married on Nov 11, 1792 and were the parents not only of William Capers Jr but also of the Rev. Samuel Wragg Capers (Mar 5, 1797-June 22, 1855), the father of Richard Thornton Capers (Feb 1, 1834-Dec 19 1915). Richard and his wife, Mary Hurd (Mar 4, 1841-Nov 25 1919) were the parents of Helen Capers (1889-1975), who married Paul Lathrop Miller (1885-1962) of Bridgeport, CT. Paul and Helen Miller were the parents of two daughters, Marjory and Barbara and a son, Paul L. Miller, Jr (Feb 4, 1923-), who married Sara Katharine Taylor (Jan 5, 1922-Aug 16, 2004). Paul and Katharine had four children: John Taylor, Douglas Thornton, Nancy Lathrop, and Katharine Leigh. Sara Katharine was a daughter of **Nan Elizabeth Huey Taylor** (1893-1993) and **John Oliver Taylor Jr** (1891-1960), a grandson of **Charles** and **Charlotte Taylor**. Sara Katharine was a sister of **Betty Taylor Cook**.

In his new surroundings, Charles Taylor's intellectual gifts were noted, encouraged and rewarded. In South Carolina, he quickly became a language teacher in the Methodist Seminary at Cokesbury, specializing in Greek and Latin. His medical studies in Philadelphia were sponsored by the Methodists, who sent Charles as a doctor to Shanghai in 1849, the first Southern Methodist Missionary to China.

In 1844, the same year Charles was ordained a

Methodist preacher, he volunteered to go as a missionary to China. Because the distance was so great and the possibility of sickness likely, "it was thought best to have another missionary to go along. Nearly two years elapsed before one was found." But one was found. As **Betty Taylor Cook** put it (apparently quoting Mary Moore Taylor, Charles and Charlotte's daughter-in-law, who referred to Charles as "grandfather"): "Benjamin Jenkins, a printer, became so moved when he read an editorial in the Southern Christian Advocate while setting type that he volunteered to go with Grandfather." Charles spent the intervening two years studying medicine in Philadelphia where he received an MD degree.

On his return from China in 1854, Charles accepted a professorship at Spartanburg Female College. He was made president of that institution in 1857. (The college survived the Civil War but closed in 1871.) After the Civil War, Charles Taylor became president of a college soon known as Kentucky Wesleyan University, in Millersburg, KY. He subsequently pastored Methodist Churches in northern Kentucky. At some point in his career, Charles is said to have served as Presiding Elder of the Wadesborough District (North Carolina) of the Methodist Church, South. Like his father Oliver S. Taylor, Charles actively promoted the Sunday School movement throughout his life.

Charles' career as an educator, especially in Kentucky, is well documented. In 1866, as noted, he was elected President of Kentucky Wesleyan College and held that post for four years, before returning to pastoral work. The college was then located in Millersburg, KY. Its Methodist patrons had called Charles Taylor to the Presidency because of his credentials as a missionary, writer, educator and administrator. The Methodist Board of Directors was determined to open the school promptly in 1866, despite the devastation and bitter divisions of the just-concluded Civil War. An energetic and well known Methodist leader and former missionary, who was academically gifted and already a school president, would have been an attractive figure to the Board, especially as Charles had personal ties to the North, where much needed funds might be raised. Charles and Charlotte moved to Millersburg, probably in the summer of 1866.

Classes began the first Monday of September, 1866. The academic year was divided into three sessions, with tuition for the first session set at $16.00 and $12.00 for the two following sessions. Freshmen were to study Virgil and Homer in Greek and add to that Herodotus in English, geometry, surveying and navigation. Sophomores were to take up ancient, medieval and modern history, physics (electricity and magnetism) and Latin prose composition. Juniors continued with Latin and Greek classics and added chemistry (organic and inorganic), differential and integral calculus, physics and mechanics. Seniors were to study astronomy, geology, logic, political science and moral philosophy. Students planning to enter the pastoral ministry could substitute Hebrew and Biblical literature for some of these requirements. Science students would take civil engineering, anatomy and physiology in place of some of the ancient language courses.

Although the first Wesleyan catalogue was virtually free of rules, by 1869, these had been added. Surprisingly, the early rules focused on faculty conduct rather than that of the students. It would appear that Charles Taylor was in a power struggle with members of the faculty. Included in the 1869 rules were requirements that all faculty attend daily morning prayers and take turns conducting worship, as directed by the school's president, who also required faculty members' attendance at weekly faculty meetings. The president assumed authority to assign rooms "to faculty, students and literary societies, at his discretion." The faculty were to report student misconduct to the president, and "a student excused by the president shall be excused by every member of the faculty."

President Taylor was able to report in 1869 that the school's enrollment had increased from 90 in 1866 to 144 students. During the brief intervening years, he had not only reined in the apparently too-independent faculty but had added a dormitory and presided over the school's first commencement, in 1868, when a transfer student, Benjamin Best graduated with a Bachelor of Science degree.

Charles Taylor's great personal interest, as he reported annually, was that "pious students" be sent into the service of Methodism. He highlighted the creation by his students of Sunday Schools in nearby churches, where they "held meetings for prayer and exhortation." By 1870, Charles resigned from the presidency of Kentucky Wesleyan and devoted himself to pastoral duties in Maysville and Newport, Kentucky until his retirement. At that point, he and Charlotte Jane moved from Kentucky to Alabama.

Charles Taylor was a linguist and prolific writer. While in China for the Methodists, he published in Mandarin a *Harmony of the Gospels* and several other texts. In 1860, he became the author of a memoir of his China years, which he entitled **Five Years in China**; he subsequently published **Baptism in a Nutshell** for the Methodists.

Charles and Charlotte's influence within and without the family is well known. An interesting note appeared in a Methodist journal, *The Southwestern Advocate* on April 27, 1937. The subject was "Our First Missionaries," which featured Charles and Charlotte Taylor, with information provided by one of their children. The editor wrote, "Last Monday, Mr. H.P. Taylor of Dallas was an appreciated visitor at the Advocate office. He is a son of Dr. Charles Taylor, and was born in Shanghai China. On account of his mother's poor health his parents did not remain in China many years but returned to this country. Mr. Taylor is a retired railroad man, having worked for the Cotton Belt for 41 years. He is now 87 and a devoted Christian and member of Trinity Heights Methodist Church."

For years, Charles Taylor was held up by Methodism as a model missionary. His and Charlotte's stimulus upon family members to serve the Methodist

Church has extended down among their descendents. Their grandson Mayo Taylor was a faithful and active Methodist laymen all of his life. Great-granddaughter, Charlotte Taylor, a daughter of Mayo and his wife, Mary Alice Stevenson, was a church worker in Congo for ten years, serving there as secretary to Bishop Newell Booth. Another great-granddaughter, Sara Katharine Miller (1922-2004), daughter of **Nan Elizabeth Huey Taylor** (1893-1993) and **John Oliver Taylor Jr** (1891-1960), was a life-long active Methodist layperson in New Jersey.

THE GAMEWELLS OF SOUTH CAROLINA

On December 27, 1846, two years after moving to South Carolina, Charles married **Charlotte Jane Gamewell** (1828-1910). She was 18, he 28. Charlotte was of a prominent Methodist family. Her father was **John Gamewell** (1756-1827), who had immigrated to America from England with his brother William when both were young. John became a mariner and made voyages from Philadelphia to Nassau. According to Betty Taylor Cook, John "gave up the seafaring life to preach. He was converted and licensed to preach by Bishop Asbury." Betty has also written that John Gamewell "was one of the pioneer preachers in the South Carolina Conference." In 1800, John Gamewell was enrolled as a Methodist Episcopal preacher in South Carolina. In 1801, he was recorded as pastor of the Rainbow Methodist Church, Snow Hill, Green County North Carolina. John Gamewell preached and pastored churches in the Carolinas until his death in 1827. The "bishop" who converted him was the famous, spectacularly energetic circuit-riding founder of Methodism in the American South, Englishman Francis Asbury (1745-1816).

John Gamewell's first wife was Anne Welch. They were married Dec 2, 1793. Anne died four years later, leaving one son, James (born Nov 29, 1796) and twin girls, four-month old, Lucy and Sarah. John Gamewell then married **Delilah Booth** (?-?) on Dec. 12 1812. Deliah's parents were **Thomas Booth** (?-?) and **Martha Woodbury** (?-?). John and Delilah had six children. The oldest was Whatcoat Asbury (1814-1869), namesake of two prominent Methodist Episcopal leaders. One was Bishop Richard Whatcoat (?-1806), who was registered as a Methodist preacher in South Carolina as early as 1769. The man who gave little Whatcoat his middle name was the above mentioned tireless church organizer, Francis Asbury. John and Delilah's other children were Tom, Wilson, Martha Ann, John Nelson, Francis, and the baby, **Charlotte Jane**. Charlotte was born on May 28, 1828 and died in Courtland, AL in 1910. Charlotte never knew her father, who died just months before her birth.

There are many Booth lines in the United States but tracing Delilah's lineage has proven fruitless (so far). A reasonable guess would be that Delilah Booth's father (and mother?) were English, by way of Nassau in the Bahamas or perhaps Barbados or some other Caribbean locale, a region frequented by the first John Gamewell and his brother. These island ports proved to be interim destinations for many venturesome English, themselves island people. A high percentage of early South Carolina settlers were English, arriving from the Caribbean, as they followed the trade in slaves and other commerce between these destinations.

THE "FIRE ALARM TELEGRAPH"

Mention of the Methodist Gamewell family of South Carolina requires a pause at the careers of Charlotte's brothers, John Jr and Whatcoat Asbury Gamewell. John Gamewell Jr (1822-1896), an entrepreneur and inventor, moved his family to New Jersey just before the Civil War. John is remembered for his invention of a fire alarm used by fire departments across the United States and Canada. In 1855 John was a postmaster and telegraph operator in South Carolina and attended a lecture at the Smithsonian Institution, Washington DC, on the *Fire Alarm Telegraph.*

Delilah Booth Gamewell

John was so impressed that he found backers in New York, bought the patent and the licensing rights for southern and western states and went into business. The "Electromagnetic Fire Alarm Telegraph for Cities," was an adaptation of Samuel Morse's telegraph by a Boston doctor, William Channing and an inventor, Moses Farmer. It was a device designed to permit an individual, by winding a crank in a call box, to report a fire to the municipal fire department. The electromagnetic fire alarm was a vast improvement over the existing, centuries-old "system" that amounted to running out in the street and shouting "Fire!" until a church sexton heard the appeal, ran up into the belfry and rang the bells – at which time, a horse drawn fire wagon might be dispatched – to the church. By 1859, John Gamewell had secured the entire rights to the Fire Alarm Telegraph and began to interest cities throughout the country.

The Civil War intervened. In 1865, owing to John Gamewell's Southern sympathies, the federal government confiscated his patents and offered them for sale to the public, blocking Gamewell from bidding on them. But the astute entrepreneur obtained the assistance of an employee, John F. Kennard of Boston, who purchased the Fire Alarm Telegraph patents and returned them to Gamewell. Kennard had been prepared to bid up to $20,000 for the patents but secured them for $80.00. The two men went into business as Kennard and Company in Newton Upper Falls, Massachusetts. Meanwhile, Gamewell had moved from South Carolina to Hackensack, NJ.

In 1879, John Gamewell Jr became the sole proprietor of the Gamewell Fire Alarm Telegraph Company. By 1886, the Gamewell fire alarm system was installed in 250 cities in the US and Canada and became the standard fire alarm system until the advent of wireless communications in the 1970s. Today, Gamewell alarm boxes are collector's items, available for sale from municipalities and on the internet. On July 24, 1896, John Gamewell died at his home in Hackensack, where there is a street named for him.

John's son, Francis, attended Dickinson College in Carlisle, PA and went to China as a Methodist Missionary as his aunt and uncle, Charlotte Gamewell and Charles Taylor had done a half-century before. Frances returned to the US and obtained a PhD in physics from Columbia University and then went back to China. In 1907, Francis' wife, Mary Porter Gamewell, published a record of her unhappy career as a Christian missionary at the end of the 19th century and the opening decade of the 20th. She and Francis were in China during the "Boxer" Rebellion against the occupation of China by European powers. (Because they practiced martial arts, foreigners called the insurgents "Boxers." The rebels called themselves, "The Fists of Righteous Harmony.")

"SLAVES OF THE NORTH"

John and Charlotte's older brother, Whatcoat Asbury Gamewell (1814-1869) was, like his father, a prominent Methodist Episcopal clergyman. Whatcoat was remembered as tall, with a deep voice and a commanding pulpit presence. A picture of Whatcoat suggests a strong resemblance to his baby sister (Charlotte: page 160): a broad forehead, high cheekbones, thin lips and a placid but penetrating expression. During the Civil War, Whatcoat, a strident secessionist, was pastor of the Washington Street Methodist Church (Washington and Marion Streets) Columbia, SC. In his pocket diary, Whatcoat wrote in 1866, of the difficulty of attending to his pastoral duties in defeated and devastated South Carolina, while farming at the same time to take care of his family. In a note from July 4, of that year, Whatcoat writes, "This is independance day: but alas what independance for us whites of the South! We are more the Slaves of the North than our fathers were to the crown of Great Brittain."

In 1835, Whatcoat made a record of his visit to a synagogue in Charleston, SC. His observations are an arresting description of Jewish worship in that time and place:

I have frequently passed this place of worship while they were at service but through some cause or other had never entered, though I have determined to do so at some time before I left this place. A friend and myself were passing on one of their feast days and concluded to walk in and witness their proceedings so far as we could. It was quite a commodious house with a galery; in the centre of the lower floor was something like an alter which was used as a pulpit or desk. The males occupied the seats in the lower floor and the females the galery so that it would seem they were in some measure excluded from the immediate service. The males had each a scarf about his shoulders and retained their hats on their heads. One of the number who was not in any respects distinguished from the others ascended the desk and commenced reading when all rose to their feet; at intervals the whole assembly would respond or rather join the reader. After having read and sung for some time, the reader took up something resembling a small bunch of green branches bound closely together, and shook them in a variety of ways during which he seemed to be quite animated, though himself and audience throughout preserved a considerable degree of solemnity. They had proceeded probably half an hour when one of the company opened a closet in one end of the house and took out something which when shaken would make a tinkling sound which I took to be a cymbal, and ascended the alter followed by several others where they continued to read and sing with apparent fervency after which the instrument was replaced and the officiating person addressed several individuals as though he was interrogating or Chatechising them which closed the services the whole of which was performed in hebrew.

Charlotte Jane Gamewell Taylor bore Charles nine children, only five of whom reached adulthood. The little ones who died have been recorded as: J. William Taylor, born Sept 18, 1849 in Shanghai (Kiangsu) who died at five weeks on Oct 24, 1849; Frank Taylor, born July 31, 1857

(Spartanburg, SC) and died Dec 10, 1860 (Columbia, Richland County SC); Catherine Taylor, born Feb 14, 1860 (Columbia SC) and died May 14, 1865 (Cheraw, Chesterfield, SC); Edward Paul Taylor, born Nov 29, 1867 (Millersburg, Bourbon County Kentucky), died June 30, 1870.

The children who lived were Charles G, born in 1848, Henry Parsons, born Sept 30, 1851 (Shanghai); Martha ("Mattie") Wilson, born April 19, 1855 (Camden SC); **John Oliver** (1862-1922), born Sept. 12, 1862 (Cheraw, Chesterfield County SC), who was named for his two grandfathers; and Charlotte ("Lottie") Booth (1865-1926), born May 12, 1865.

Even for the nineteenth century, the deaths of an infant and three toddlers between three and five years of age would have been losses of exceptional devastation. In 1849, the composed young Charles recorded in his journal the death of baby William and conveyed the note to his China book (page 178) ten years later. "On the 24th of October, our own dear little babe, aged five weeks and one day, was transferred from the dark land of China to the bright paradise of God."

The death of baby William engendered a grief so great that Charles tried to adopt a Chinese baby to replace their own lost infant. The project failed as the foundling he spotted was not the motherless waif he had imagined. Charles wrote about it in his China book. Encountering a naked toddler crying in a Shanghai street, Charles inquired and could not find any parents or other family nearby. He assumed the child was abandoned. Arranging for someone to look after the baby, he raced home to ask Charlotte if she wanted this little girl. Charlotte did. Charles ran back to where he had left the child, only to discover that the child was not there. He was told the distraught mother had arrived looking for her baby, who had been stolen not far away but soon abandoned after thieves made off with the child's clothes. Charles did not describe to his readers what

Charles Taylor

he felt as he walked home to Charlotte to give her this news.

In her genealogical records **Betty Taylor Cook** has transcribed a narrative of the Taylor's missionary saga, remembered as having been written by her grandmother, that is, by Charles and Charlotte's daughter-in-law **Mary Baldwin Moore Taylor**. Necessary factual corrections to this narrative appear in brackets.

On April 4, 1848, the two couples set sail on the ship Cleone for China. Mrs. Jenkins was so feeble by the time they reached Hong Kong that the Jenkins left the ship there. The Taylors sailed on to Shanghai. They were met there by missionaries of the Southern Baptist Board ([including] Matthew T. Yeats). The Baptists had rented a home for them. The following October, they moved into a home they had built. A little girl [boy: William] was born this year. She [he] lived only five weeks. After three years Grandmother's health was shattered. She wouldn't consent to leave because she did not want to take Grandfather from his work. An opportunity came for her to return with some Americans. She returned [February, 1852] with two babies [one baby, Henry Parsons Taylor (Sept 30 1851-?) and a toddler, Charles G, born in 1848] and a native nurse. The following year the Jenkins returned, Mrs. Jenkins dying on the voyage home. Grandmother's health failed to improve and Grandfather had to return five years to the day after he arrived.

Family genealogical narratives (such as the one you have in your hands) create a double difficulty. They should be neither too readily dismissed, nor relied upon uncritically. Such narratives are often written with a spirit of sentimental uplift, which does not hint at any degree of interior conflict. But because they lived in prominence through the most traumatic period of the nation's history, and were allied to the losing side, a descendent may wonder what might have weighed upon Charlotte and Charles. We permit ourselves to imagine.

Doubt about Charles Taylor's intellectual brilliance is ruled out on many grounds. There is the prominence of his public positions, first in South Carolina and then in Kentucky, twice selected to preside over locally significant educational institutions. There is also the record of his academic achievements in New York and Philadelphia. In 1869, New York University, his *alma mater,* awarded him an honorary doctorate. There is his book, **Five Years in China** (1860), which demonstrates a seeming effortless ability to create astute and well-crafted observations. A paragraph (page 123) serves to demonstrate the skills as well as the evangelical motives he brought to his missionary work in Shanghai:

There now lives in the next house to the one we occupy, a little boy who has been blind from his infancy, in consequence of a severe attack of the small pox. His mother is dead, and her body is the one contained in the coffin above described as being but one step from our door. He is a very sprightly, active and affectionate little fellow but has a gloomy prospect before him for life, as his friends are all very poor. It makes one feel sad to meet a blind person in a Christian land, whose mind and heart may yet discern the truths, and feel the power of the blessed Gospel, and who can, with an eye of faith, look forward with sweet anticipation to a bright world, where the glorified body shall enjoy perfect vision. But it is sadder still to see one twice blind--the inner man sealed up in moral, as the outer is in physical, darkness.

To these literary gifts, Charles added a remarkable ability with languages. As noted, by the time he had graduated from college, Charles had mastered Latin and Greek so as to qualify for high academic honors and then to teach these languages to seminary students. In Shanghai he learned Mandarin well enough to travel around the city and countryside by himself and to write several works, (as noted above) including a "harmony" of the Gospels. The writing projects suggest a surprising proficiency in both spoken and written Mandarin.

Charles, and surely also Charlotte Jane, brought a sacrificial, energetic thrust to their missionary endeavors. We know that Charles' approach to evangelical work was not for the timid or the withdrawn. There is also a naiveté in Charles' activities in China, which at times lead him to simplistic conclusions and an absence of caution.

THE TAIPING REBELLION (1850-64)

After Charlotte had returned to South Carolina, Charles encountered, in Shanghai, some people involved in the Taiping Rebellion (1850-64), the largest uprising in modern Chinese history. The rebels were lead by *Hong Xiuquan* (1814-64), whom Charles named, *Hung-siu-tsiuen*. Hong wished to eliminate from China: the smoking of opium, slavery, foot binding, and idol worship. These reforms were popular with masses of Chinese, but Hong, apparently as a result of some exposure to Protestant missionary teachings, led his followers to denounce Confucius. Some of the rebels also announced that Hong was the younger brother of Jesus Christ. Rejection of Confucius combined with the hostility of the Han upper classes and the support of British and French forces on behalf of the weak Qing dynasty ended the rebellion. It is estimated some thirty million Chinese lost their lives. (Only in ignorance of events in China, may the just-past 20th century be described as the bloodiest one hundred years in all history.)

During the rebellion, Charles visited rebel camps in and around Shanghai and in theory, supported their cause. He did so despite the chaos and bloodshed because of Hong's earlier exposure to Christian teachings and the Bible. "The hand of the Lord certainly is in these commotions," Charles wrote in his journal (page 380 of his China memoirs). He had a giant banner made, proclaiming the worship of "the One True God" and saw that it was posted prominently in Shanghai after the city had fallen to the rebels. "If we can get the doctrine of but one true God before the people, as set forth in this proclamation, our object is in part obtained," he wrote.

During the rebellion, Charles' breakfast was interrupted one day when his "servants" rushed in to shout that six men were robbing a boat on the stream near Charles' house. "I hastened through my study," Charles wrote, "where I seized an unloaded pistol and rushing out reached the gate at the same moment with the robbers. I pointed the pistol at them and ordered them to stop. Four of them escaped, but the two hindmost obeyed. One of them raised his sword to strike me, but I held the pistol to his breast and demanded his weapon, and did the same to the other. They finally, after much parleying, gave them up with much reluctance." After this, Charles secured from the United States acting consul, a two-member Marine guard for his residence. A few days later, Charles with the two Marines, stood down a crowd he estimated at 2,000, who had "issued from the north gate" of Shanghai and were marching to raid a nearby village. Charles and the Marines refused them passage. The mob took another route and razed and burned the targeted village before returning to Shanghai.

In his final published piece, written in January 1897, a month before his death, Charles describes his activities in and around Shanghai a half-century before. Speaking of himself in the third person, Charles writes:

After acquiring enough of the spoken dialect to make himself readily understood, the missionary would take daily walks into the city, conversing with the natives in their shops and stores, discoursing to crowds in their places of public resort, and distributing tracts to such as could read.

The most noted place of public gatherings was the large open space in front of the "Ching Wong Miam" - the 'City Guardian's temple.' Here would assemble jugglers, gamblers, cricket fighters, tooth pullers, displaying nearly a peck of teeth which they claim to have extracted, quack doctors and mountebanks of all imaginable varieties.

The missionary would take his stand on the topmost steps of the temple, its wide portals open behind him, and with the huge idols in full view and pointing to them would descant on the folly of worshiping such objects, the work of their own hands. The at that time novel sight of a foreigner, and hearing him speak their own language, soon drew the crowds from all the other centers of attraction, leaving them deserted and venting their wrath in abusing him, who had so unceremoniously drawn their customers and listeners to himself.

[. . .] He also established a day school by renting a room and employing a native teacher, requiring him to use our Christian books as soon as the pupils had learned to read. He also visited the families in the neighborhood, inviting them to send their children, free of charge, with the understanding that they were to be taught Christian doctrines while learning their own language. [. . .] Occasional excursions by boat to the surrounding cities and towns constituted an interesting feature of his work. He would on such occasions take along a supply of medicines as well as books and tracts, and administer to such as could come to him at his boat. [. . .] Besides his dwelling, he built a chapel on the same lot, and into this he moved his Sunday School, so as to emphasize its sacredness and give it greater prominence.

FROM THE MEDINA OF ANTI-SLAVERY TO THE MECCA OF SLAVERY

The length of years given to Charles and Charlotte incorporated events momentous and mundane. Education, marriage, the choice of a career, care of a family – these quotidian, personal choices may assume a heroic aura in a specific context. Charlotte and Charles made their choices and lived with them. As we look back from 150 years and more, we observe that they both demonstrated a lifelong fidelity to the important commitments made when young. But we feel uneasy. We confess a curiosity about Charles' motives behind his choices. The passage of the decades, stretching now into centuries, does not aid our understanding of him. In his career decisions, Charles allied himself with a section of the country - and a state in that section - which was boisterous and extreme in leading the region's defense of slave labor.

South Carolina's most prominent and popular leaders, including the famous politician, John C. Calhoun, insisted that race slavery was an essential component of South Carolina's way of life. As such sentiments were gaining in stridency in South Carolina, Charles united for life with the slave-holding South.

After graduation from college in 1840, Charles Taylor never again lived in his old home states of Massachusetts or New York. Except for his two years of medical studies in Philadelphia, 1844-46, followed by five years in China, he is never found residing anywhere outside of the southern United States. Did Charles, at the end, come to see his alliance with the South as a misalliance? Had he severed himself from the values he had learned from his parents? Had he made a grave error? Did Charles, or Charlotte, living out their lives in a defeated region, come to feel mocked or derided by the large events of their time?

Charles' writings do not betray the slightest awareness of irony. He and Charlotte chose to travel a world away from South Carolina, to seek converts of another race on behalf of an American denomination, which explicitly endorsed and practiced race slavery. There is more than irony here. There is grave moral failing, in tandem with an impossible contradiction. Did they see this? Did they feel it? If not before the Civil War, then surely after? Charles if not also Charlotte (mute, in our records), must have had private regrets. Mustn't they?

Their missionary career was aborted by Charlotte's poor health, but in the decades before and throughout the Civil War, Charles' career moved from strength to strength. Their prominence as early missionaries was followed by his eminence as president of two institutions of higher learning. These posts were succeeded by pastorates and administrative roles in the Methodist Episcopal Church, South. But the absence of any specific family reminiscence suggests that it all may have culminated in a dispirited winding down into old age. By the 1890s, the elderly Charles and Charlotte Taylor decided to leave Kentucky for Courtland, Alabama, to live with their daughter Charlotte ("Lottie") (1865-1926) and her husband, locally prominent Jack Shackelford (1858-1937), who were wealthier than the Kentucky Taylors. Charlotte and Charles Taylor are buried in the Courtland Cemetery, at the end of Vanburen St., Courtland, Lawrence County Alabama.

Charles certainly was not a passive bystander in ante-bellum South Carolina. This was true in church matters if not also in other public affairs. The year Charles was formally accepted into the Methodist Church and licensed by it to preach, was the same year, 1844, that the Methodist Church, South split away from the rest of American Methodism. The southern faction insisted that slavery must be maintained.

In 1860, Charles dedicated his China memoirs jointly to his father and to James Osgood Andrew (1794-1871). Andrew was Bishop of the Methodist Episcopal Church in South Carolina, whose refusal to give up his slaves in 1844 lead to the north-south split. It was at the 1844 (Louisville) and 1845 (Richmond) meetings that the southern Methodists decided both to affirm slavery, organize themselves into a separate denomination and settle upon sponsorship of a mission to China. Charles was certainly in the midst of these discussions as he promptly and prominently volunteered to found the China mission. Upon his return from China, after five years in Shanghai, he was embraced by South Carolina Methodists and passed the Civil War years in Spartanburg as a college president.

Charlotte Jane Gamewell

What was Charles Taylor's public role during the Civil War? Research is needed here. The "just war" rationale as well as "total war" strategies (inherent in civil conflict) were openly discussed by Southern clergy and politicians during the conflict. Did Charles, from a Methodist pulpit, allow himself any criticism of the premises and purposes of his own side? or the other side? Did he publicly endorse the Southern Cause? As a college president in South Carolina, with the wellbeing of an institution as his main professional concern, did he fall silent before the possibly overwhelming and insistent power of wartime Southern patriotism? Did he write to his father and mother in Auburn, NY about any of this?

What of Charles' role in Kentucky after the war? What part did Charles play among Kentucky Methodists, who were divided after 1865, more bitterly than they had been during the war? Did he argue for or against an end to military occupation? Did he become a vigorous proponent of the "Lost Cause?" Did he revere the battle flags of the South and encourage the growth of the Ku Klux Klan? Or was his a voice of church unity and reconciliation? Looking further back to his early adulthood, other questions arise.

What motivated Charles in his choices? Might it all be comprehended in his attraction to the luminous Charlotte Jane Gamewell, who gave herself to him at age 18? Charlotte was so statuesque that a daughter-in-law, Mary Baldwin Moore Taylor, later confessed to her daughter, Nancy, a reluctance to go to church to be seen with Charlotte. The dilemma was made doubly trying, Mary added, because "grandfather was the preacher." Charlotte proved capable of traveling with Charles to China, suffering the privations of Civil War, birthing nine children and burying four of them. For half a century, Charlotte made a home for Charles amidst household moves every few years. Charlotte may have been the prize and then the consolation for Charles in his life choices. But in simple fact, his inner motives remain undocumented to us and possibly never stated to anyone.

Perhaps we ought to conclude that Charles was

about what he says he was about; he wanted to be an agent in the service of God for the salvation of humanity. After two years in China, Charles, 32, full of energy and hoping to motivate his sponsors on the other side of the globe, wrote back to them:

Still we are far enough from being discouraged. We have blotted that word from our vocabulary. Ours is the task, nay privilege, to try and break up the fallow ground, and cast a few seed; but the harvest is not yet, though we may, and shall expect to see some little fruit, to gather a sheaf or two before we die. The hearts of this great one third of the human race, steeped in the soul-debasing influence of idolatry and abominable superstitions, for thousands of years, will not be induced to renounce them in a day, except by a miracle. The gradual emancipation scheme is the one on which we must work here, but we implore you, brethren, by the love of Jesus, by the love of souls, by the hope of heaven, not to be so distressingly gradual. A half million Christians abounding in means, send two men as their share to help convert three hundred and sixty millions of idolaters!

Charles sounds like a young man moved to action by the fervor of the so-called *Second Great Awakening* (approximately 1800-1840). This resurgence among evangelical Christians swept the country (the first *Great Awakening* having occurred in the 1740s).

Do we mock Charles by pointing to the unreflective paradox of his appeal? In writing to his slavery-embracing sponsors, Charles speaks of "gradual emancipation" – not of the slaves back in South Carolina but of the Chinese people, whose ancient ways he was intent upon upending. Charles' rhetoric describing his energetic efforts to lift up "the Chinese" can assume the aura of a Bible parable (his memoir, page 373-4):

I came upon a family consisting of a man, his wife and two little children, who had been wrecked and lost their boat. *The poor man, bursting into tears, told me one of their children was drowned. He had saved nothing but an oar, one or two planks, and some other articles of little value. They were living under a shelter formed by a few mats, placed against a high bamboo fence. I gave him some cash for his wife and children and requested him to follow me, without telling him for what purpose. Leading the way for about a mile and a half, I brought him to our boat and, pointing to it, asked him if he would like to have it. His face fairly shown as he replied in the affirmative. I told him it was his. The poor fellow dropped upon his knees, his eyes filled with tears and he bowed his head to the ground. Immediately, I lifted him up and told him he must kneel to the true God and offer his thinks, but not to me. . . . The kindly hand of time may heal even that ["the wound of their hearts, bleeding for their drowned little boy"] but the religion of Jesus would do it much more sweetly and surely. Oh that they had its blessed consolations.*

Charles' zeal for Jesus as Savior of the Chinese is in high contrast to his dismissive description of the unnamed Black cook on the American ship *Torrent*, which carried Charles home from China in 1854 (his memoir, page 387-8). His common language is matched to his ugly opinions:

Our cook was a curiosity of fossilized filth. He was about the dirtiest, greasiest most slovenly old negro you ever saw. I espied him one day standing at the windward door of the galley, carding his ebony fleece with a right good will and accompanying each pull of the card with a display of his entire stock of ivory. It was therefore no matter of surprise to find the mess, called a stew (that was on the table for dinner that day), embellished with curls.

Charles, your great-granddaughter Betty Taylor Cook would have said, "That comment is unworthy of you."

Charles' repellent commentary, directed at a Whites-only audience, adopts a literary affect far cruder than his description of the noble-but-soul-threatened Chinese. Notwithstanding his natural gifts, superior education and high-minded vocation, Charles, himself, was made brutish by the enslavement he took to be the natural fate of the brutish African. Reconciled in mind to the rightness of slavery in his adopted South Carolina, could Charles have been forever ignorant through his long life, of the effect his terrible acquiesce to human degradation had on his judgment, his conscience, and even on his writing style? (The contrast is stark, if the two just-quoted passages are read aloud, back to back.)

Charles' glimpse of the ship's cook was important enough to him for inclusion six years later into his published missionary saga. This galley-cook vignette, then, must be factored into our attempt to understand Charles Taylor's true sense of personal mission and his place in the world. Can we avoid the conclusion that our Charles, despite his many qualities, was nothing different from a routine American racist, holding views about Black people, typical of much of 19th Century White America? His ideas of slavery and his ideas of Africans were interchangeable. One set of notions supported the other. Such is the insidious workings of race enslavement on the slave-holding class. The *Torrent* took Charles from China to New York in 1854 but he was not home until he reached antebellum South Carolina.

A DESCENDENT OF GOULDS, PARSONS, GRAVES, MATHERS & DWIGHTS

Charles' biography does not begin with himself. No one's does. There is family, with its time-worn modes of embrace and rejection, routine and wonder, ennui and drama. The contours of Charles Taylor's life began to be formed in the home of his parents. Something of this early influence can be detected even now, despite 175 years of silence and lost information. For generations Charles' family had been New Englanders, often of reforming and patriotic accomplishment. His father was the centenarian

Oliver Swayne Taylor (1784-1885), who, like Charles, was a physician, educator and evangelist - caught up also in the fervor of the Awakening of the 1800's.

Oliver S. Taylor followed his several careers mostly in New England and New York State, where Charles was raised. But here the paths of father and son separate dramatically. Or so it seems from our vantage. Oliver lived the final 35 years of his long life in Auburn, NY, the hometown of William H. Seward, the best known anti-slavery politician of the decades before the Civil War. Auburn, New York, and William Seward were to the anti-slavery cause what Columbia, South Carolina, and John C. Calhoun were to the advocates of slavery. In the 1850's Auburn became the home and headquarters of Harriet Tubman and her "underground railroad." Seward helped Tubman acquire the property in Auburn that she used for her activities. It is no exaggeration then to say that after college in New York City, Charles Taylor moved from the Mecca of hostility to slavery to the Medina of slavery's embrace.

Through his mother, Charles was related to generations of venerable New Englanders, including prominent members of the Parsons and Dwight families. His mother was **Catherine Gould Parsons** (1791-1865), whose father, **Nathan Parsons Jr** (1752-1823) served with Washington throughout the Revolutionary War. Nathan died in Bangor, Maine, possibly on land he was granted for military service. Nathan's father **Nathan Parsons Sr** (?-?) was a sergeant in the French and Indian War (1754-1763). His parents were the Rev. **David Parsons** (1679-1743) and **Sarah Stebbens** (1686-1758). Sarah was the daughter of **Abigail Munn** (1650-1691/92) and **Thomas Stebbens Jr** (1648-1695), both of Springfield, MA. Sarah was orphaned of both parents by age nine. Abigail Munn Stebbens, dying at forty-one, was named for her mother **Abigail** (1629-1691/92) whose second husband, **Benjamin Munn** (1619-1675), born in England, was Abigail Munn Stebbens' father.

After Abigail's death in 1691-92, who raised her

165

little daughter Sarah, she, who grew up to marry David Parsons and become the mother of Nathan Parsons Sr. The credit for Sarah's productive life should probably go to Mary Day Ely Stebbens (1641-1725), who married widower Thomas Stebbens in 1694, the year before he died. Mary Day was already widowed herself, having married Samuel Ely (1639-1691) and become the mother of seven children. At the death of Thomas, her second husband, Mary Stebbens would have had responsibilities for the youngest two or three of deceased Thomas and Abigail's seven children. Three hundred years after, Mary Day Stebbens is recognized and appreciated for her widowed, maternal embrace of some ten children, including little Sarah.

Thomas Stebbens Jr was the son of immigrant couple **Hannah Wright** (1620-1660) and **Thomas Stebbens** (1620-1683). Thomas Sr, born in Essex, England, was the child of **Ro(w)land Stebbens** (1592-1671) and **Sarah Whiting** (1591-1649). Roland and Sarah immigrated to America, as did their son Thomas and his wife Hannah, all living in Springfield, MA, where Sarah Whiting died. After her death, Roland lived in Northampton, MA, dying there in 1671.

The Rev. David Parsons, husband of Sarah Stebbens, father of Nathan Parsons and great grandfather of Catherine Gould Parsons Taylor, died in Worcester, MA. David was apparently the first Parsons in a line of Congregational ministers that reached well into the nineteenth century. David's parents were **Elizabeth Strong** (1647-1736) and attorney **Joseph Parsons** (1647-1729). Joseph and Elizabeth were buried in the Bridge St. Cemetery, Northampton, MA.

Catherine Gould Parsons' paternal grandmother was **Amy (Brewster?) Gould** (1725/8-1798), wife of **Nathan Parsons Sr**. Amy's parents were **Mary Cruttenden** (1690-1776) and **Thomas Gould** (1689-1746) of Gilford, CT. Thomas' parents were **Elizabeth Robinson** (?-1745) and **Benjamin Gould** (?-1718). Elizabeth's parents were **Mary ____** (?-1668) and **Thomas Robinson** (?-1689) of Gilford as well.

Catherine Taylor's paternal great grandmother, Mary Cruttenden was the child of **Susanna Gregson** (16345-1712) and **Abraham Cruttenden Jr** (1635-1694), who was the son of immigrants **Abraham Cruttenden** (abt 1610-1682/83) and **Mary Hinkson** (1612-1664). The first (American) Abraham Cruttenden was born in Cranbrook, Kent, England. Mary and Abraham were married in England in 1630. They settled in Gilford, Connecticut, a state where Crittendens are located still.

Catherine Parsons Taylor's mother, **Susanna Graves** (1769-1859), was the daughter of **Joseph Graves** (1735-1796) and **Eunice Dwight** (abt 1742-1807) of Belchertown, MA. Joseph was the child of **Jonathan Graves Jr** (?-1787) and **Margaret Strong** (1710/11-68/69). Jonathan was the son of **Jonathan Graves Sr** (1665-1736/7) and **Sarah Parsons** (?-?) of Hatfield, Hampshire, MA. Jonathan Sr was the son of immigrant **Isaac Graves** (abt 1620-1677) and **Mary Church** (1630-1691), whose half-brother, Benjamin Church (1640-1717/18) was the once-famous militia Captain, Indian fighter and savior of New England during King Philip's War (1675-76). (Page 188.) Isaac, son of immigrant **Thomas Graves** (?-1662) and **Sarah** _____, was born in England, married Mary Church in Massachusetts and is believed to have been one of the many colonists (some 600) killed by Indians during the war. Mary Church, was the daughter of Englishwoman **Ann Marsh** (1611-1683/4) and **Richard Church** (1609/10-1667), who was born in London and immigrated to Hatfield, Hampshire, MA. In this line then, Catherine Parsons Taylor, Charles Taylor's mother, was a seventh generation American; the number of the generation to Betty Taylor Cook is eleven.

Catherine's maternal great-grandparents (parents of Eunice Dwight) were Capt. **Nathaniel Dwight** (1712-1784) and **Hannah Lyman** (1709-1794). Staying in the Dwight line, Catherine's double great-grandparents were **Mehitable Partridge** (1675-1756) and Justice **Nathaniel Dwight** (1666-1711). Mehitable was the daughter of **Mehitable Crowe** (1652-1730) and **Samuel**

Partridge (1645-1740) of Hatfield, Hampshire, MA. Mehitable Crowe was one of eleven children of **Samuel Crowe** (1610-1685) and **Elizabeth Godwin** (?-?) of Hartford, CT. Samuel Partridge was one of eight children of **Mary Smith** (1624?-1680) and immigrant **William Partridge** (1622-1688), born at Berwick upon Tweed, England. William lived in Hartford, CT, where his wife Mary died, and then in Hadley, Hampshire, MA, where he died.

Nathaniel Dwight's father was **Timothy Dwight** (?-?), the great-grandfather of the famous militant evangelical, who bore his name. This second Timothy Dwight (1752-1817) was a grandson of Jonathan Edwards and president of Yale University from 1795 until his death. The father of the first Timothy Dwight was **John Dwight** (?-?) who came to America in 1634, bringing Timothy with him and settling his family in Dedham, MA.

Hannah Lyman, mother of Eunice Dwight, was the second wife of Nathaniel Dwight. His first wife was a Mary Lyman (?-?). Hannah was one of eleven children of **Benjamin Lyman** (1674-1723) and **Thankful Pomeroy** (1679-1773), whose families were both of Northampton, Hampshire, MA, where Benjamin and Thankful raised their own large family. Thankful was the daughter of **Medad Pomeroy** (1638-1716) and **Experience Woodward** (1643-1686). Medad's parents were **Eltweed Pomeroy** (1585-1672) and **Margery Rockett** (1605-1655), who were married in Crewkerne, Somerset, England in 1629.

Experience was the daughter of **Henry Woodward** (1606/7-1685) and **Elizabeth Mather (1618-1690)** from Winwick, Lanshire, England. In addition to Experience, Henry and Elizabeth named two other children, Freedom and Thankful. Henry Woodward is believed to have been a doctor, arriving in America on the *James* in 1635 and, with Elizabeth, moving to Northampton in 1659, where they helped to found the first Congregational church.

Charlotte Jane Gamewell Taylor

Henry was said to have died in a grist-mill accident. The accident may have been a lightening strike at the mill. Elizabeth Mather has been identified as the daughter of Margaret (Margarite) Abram(s) (1618-1690) and Thomas Mather (1575-1633). If true, she would be related to the famous Mathers, notably Increase and Cotton. This association is more aspirational than actual.

Prior to the Civil War, in the era of Charles Taylor's youth, the Dwights, staying in New England, devoted considerable political and literary energy to active resistance to human slavery in America. But "facts are stubborn things." The Dwight family had not always been abolitionists. Indeed, generally in eighteenth century America, the attitude toward slavery was more accepting and the laws were tolerant of the system of lifetime servitude for Africans. Not until the early decades of the nineteenth century did opinions harden on all sides. And so we are not surprised to discover that the anti-slavery work of the Dwights in the decades before the Civil War had an earlier counterpoint in the activities of the famously devout Timothy Dwight, President of Yale University. In 1788, Timothy Dwight purchased a woman, Naomi. President Dwight of Yale expected the slave Naomi to labor in his service, until she had compensated him for her purchase price, and at such time, he would free her.

With his acquisition of the slave Naomi, Timothy Dwight was matching his personal practice with established public principles. Her provisional bondage to him was treated as conditional, with the conditions entirely under his control. This was perfectly legal and in keeping with the policies of Connecticut, which had legislated gradual emancipation in 1784. Dwight held to his views. As late as 1814, Dwight asserted that slavery was only "a question of local interest." Its abolition, the devout university president insisted, ought not to be pursued at the risk of "dissolution" of the Union.

At this time, when the opponents and defenders of human slavery were beginning to coalesce into bitter, warring camps, Dwight drew a distinction between slavery as practiced in the West Indies by European governments and slavery in Connecticut. In a poem, Timothy Dwight complimented himself on his gentility as a slave owner and proclaimed enslavement to be a benefit to the slave:

"... kindly fed, and clad, and treated, he
Slides on thro' life, with more than common glee ..."

Timothy neglected to contrast the "glee," that ought to have been felt by slaves, with their actual longing for freedom, which led them to rebel, more often than our routine histories of the period like to admit. Nor do we easily acknowledge the Scriptural warrant invoked by the enslaved rebels, the sermonic texts touted by Dwight and all other evangelicals of the period. Consider the participants in Gabriel's Plot, who were slaves executed in Virginia in 1800. Their plan to take over Richmond was brought to light and they were placed in the dock. At their show trial, the rebel slaves offered a Biblical rationale. These condemned, American, freedom fighters invoked an escape narrative, which must have been preached by Timothy Dwight on many occasions. If Moses led the Israelites to freedom, should not we, too, be free?

Charles Taylor might have found an affirming resonance in the evangelical career of his collateral ancestor, Timothy Dwight. But Charles' contemporary Dwight relatives - northerners and patriots - did not feel bound to follow the self-interested gradualism concerning matters of race, which had been the perspective of their family's patriarch. Could Charles have missed the Dwight's current support of the back-to-Africa colonization movement? In the decade before the Civil War, could he have been unaware of the Dwights' fervor on behalf of the anti-slavery "free soilers" in Kansas? During the War, several members of the Dwight and Parsons families served with high rank in the national army, seeing action and receiving wounds at Antietam, Port Hudson and elsewhere.

The Dwights' vigorous Civil War-era opposition to Southern slavery is in vivid contrast to the life Charles chose for himself. Perhaps in the privacy of his own thoughts, with the lovely Charlotte at his side, and with the well being of Spartanburg Female College his personal responsibility, Charles may have tapped into distinctions rooted in the eighteenth century customs of his prominent, well regarded Dwight cousin. Did he long to live in an earlier, seemingly less complicated age and place, when the slave Naomi was imagined to be held to service for her own benefit and then, perhaps, in a kindly expression of the open heart of her owner, beneficially freed? With public acclaim heaped upon her patrician benefactor?

CHARLES TAYLOR REMAINS TO US A CIPHER

The move south put youthful Charles in a prominent position. Linked by birth to New England, he became, by calling, marriage and career, linked to the South. Charles spent his youth and college years in the home of his parents, an evangelical but socially distinguished couple, established in a prosperous and relatively cosmopolitan northern state; he passed the remainder of his life in that part of the nation which militantly embraced race slavery. Educated in New York City and Philadelphia, he would ever after – on his return from a missionizing crusade in China - reside in small Southern towns. In this setting, Charles' visible public positions required at least a tacit endorsement of an ethos of harsh consensus. The consensus required of Charles, for the first twenty of his Southern years, that he endorse race slavery; for his remaining thirty years, his context required that he maintain a posture of defeated victimhood.

The transition from slave ownership to victimhood entailed a catastrophic military struggle, which ended in the humiliating refutation of the Old South's self-idealization as a happy, God-blessed, pastoral realm. The enforced transition, spanning the years 1861-65, found Charles, in his full maturity, a civilian partisan in a failed war of rebellion undertaken by his adopted region, against the nation his ancestors had helped to found and to protect. What did he make of himself in all this?

Did Charles Taylor become an emblem of regret or even condemnation by some of his distinguished New England relatives? (Dwight and other family letters and documents have not yet been examined on this point.) Did Charles hear and feel the sting of family laments made over him? Did he suffer regrets of his own? In the exuberance of youth, had Charles Taylor misinterpreted the whispers of a zealous, evangelical spirit, which, he thought, bid him turn toward the enslaved South? Was his inner, guiding light truly the lofty Benevolence he imagined? Was Jesus truly manifest in the South Carolina of John C. Calhoun? Or in the modest home Charlotte made for Charles in Shanghai? Or in benighted and defeated post-bellum Kentucky? Did Massachusetts-born Charles Taylor see himself in these unlikely locales, sacrificially but happily dedicated to the heart-warming Methodist Episcopal Evangel, celebrated in the hymns of Charles Wesley and the preaching of John Wesley? Or had he gotten it all wrong? Did Charles ever wish he had stayed with the science of Samuel Morse, to which he was exposed in college in New York City?

John Wesley - the guide star of Methodism - had harsh words for such as Charles Taylor, and by inference, also for our silent and long-suffering Charlotte, loyally and heroically by his side. Charlotte Taylor, who left children buried across the globe, near all the homes she ever had, Charlotte would have cringed under the zealous, pious, self-righteous, mocking denunciation, directed at her by John Wesley. One wonders. Did Charlotte or Charles ever read these words? In 1774, addressing himself to the colonies from England, Wesley wrote,

> *You have carried the survivors [of kidnapping in Africa] into the vilest slavery, never to end but with life; such slavery as is not found among the Turks at Algiers, no, nor among the Heathens in America.*

May I speak plainly to you? [. . .] Is there a God? You know there is. Is he a just God? Then there must be a state of retribution; a state wherein the just God will reward every man according to his works. Then what reward will he render to you? O think betimes! before you drop into eternity! [. . . .]

"Are you a man? Then you should have an human heart. But have you indeed? **What is your heart made of?** *Is there no such principle as compassion there? Do you never feel another's pain? Have you no sympathy, no sense of human woe, no pity for the miserable? When you saw the flowing eyes, the heaving breasts, or the bleeding sides and tortured limbs of your fellow-creatures, was you a stone, or a brute? Did you look upon them with the eyes of a tiger? When you squeezed the agonizing creatures down in the ship, or when you threw their poor mangled remains into the sea, had you no relenting? Did not one tear drop from your eye, one sigh escape from your breast? Do you feel no relenting now? If you do not, you must go on, till the measure of your iniquities is full. Then will the great God deal with you as you have dealt with them, and require all their blood at your hands.*

In this 1774 appeal, John Wesley penned a preemptive gloss upon the life of Charles Taylor. The founder of Methodism, that movement to which Charles and Charlotte gave themselves so fully, announced condemnation upon all who allowed themselves to be carried astray by a misguided sanctity - missionizing the world with slaves in tow.

Charlotte's father, the (apparently) conscience stricken **John Gamewell** (1756-1827), seems to have heard Wesley and heeded the appeal. He rejected the vocation of a seaman-slaver and turned to the pulpit. Yet there is no record that John, any more than Charles, his son-in-law, ever denounced the life-long, brutal bondage of the slaves he might have brought from Barbados to South Carolina.

What did Charles Taylor make of John Wesley? What did Charles make of himself? Did he come to see himself as Wesley surely would have - subjected to a severe, eternal destiny, in which his quest for the doing of good deeds could lead only to cosmic punishment? What of Charlotte? Her views are unknown on this and every other point. To Charles and Charlotte Taylor, was Wesley a prophet or a hectoring, petulant scold? Did they see themselves crucified for their South in order to redeem it - somehow?

Charles Taylor's most important book remained unwritten, a book in which we might truly encounter him. The unknowable essences of Charlotte and Charles find a resonance in a phrase from Walt Whitman (1819-1892), the greatest poet of theirs and of any American generation: *"the real me stands yet untouch'd, untold, altogether unreached."*

SOURCES:

For Charlotte and Charles Taylor's and Taylor genealogical data generally, Betty Taylor Cook's unpublished genealogy book and her copy of a family narrative written by Charles Taylor in about 1884.

Data about Kentucky Wesleyan University: **1866-1870: In Pursuit of the Dream: A History of Kentucky Wesleyan College**, by Lee A. Dew & Richard A. Weiss (pages 27-40), generously shared by Anne M. Gibbs, second great granddaughter of Charles and Charlotte Taylor.

Parsons and Gould genealogy: Betty Taylor Cook's genealogical research and *"Elder John Strong Comes to New England,"* see geocities.com/sfaapage/elizabeth.html.

Taiping Rebellion in China: *"Armed Conflict CHINA, 1800-1999,"* at onwar.com/aced/nation/cat/china - See also: **Chinese Roundabout** by Jonathan Spence (Norton, 1992) esp. page 152

Charles Taylor's 1897 description of his work in China: *"Beginning of the Southern Methodist Missions in China,"* **Gospel in All Lands** (1897), and all quotations from Charles and Charlotte's granddaughter Nancy Taylor Johnson: material collected and shared by Anne M. Gibbs, second great granddaughter of Charles and Charlotte Taylor (1819-1897).

Details of the career of John Gamewell Jr and his fire alarm system:firehallmusieum.org. The book by Mary Gamewell (Francis Gamewell's wife) about their career as missionaries in China: **Mary Porter Gamewell and her story of the siege in Peking** (New York: Eaton & Mains; Cincinnati: Jennings & Graham, 1907.)

Whatcoat Asbury Gamewell's pocket diary, other papers and sermons are in the manuscripts collection, "Papers of the DeSaussure, Gamewell, Lang, and Parrish Families," South Caroliniana Library at the University of South Carolina, Columbia, SC. - www.sc.edu/library/socar/uscs/1993/desa93.html

The genealogy from William Capers, Sr to Paul L. Miller, Jr: a genealogical chart created from family records by Helen Capers Miller (1889-1975), generously shared by her son, Paul L. Miller, Jr, widowed husband of Sara Katharine Taylor Miller, great-granddaughter of Charles and Charlotte Taylor, and sister of Betty Taylor Cook.

facts are stubborn things – John Adams addressing the Boston Massacre jury; see page 332, below.

Timothy Dwight's purchase of the slave Naomi: "Yale, Slavery and Abolition," visit yaleslavery.org/WhoYaleHonors/dwight2.html.

For excerpts from Timothy Dwight's poem, *Green Hill:* on the web at yaleslavery.org/WhoYaleHonors/dwight3.

the real me stands yet untouch'd – From **Leaves of Grass**, Walt Whitman, *Sea-Drift*: "As I Ebb'd With the Ocean of Life" (New York: Airmont, 1965, pages 186-87).

John Wesley on slavery: *Thoughts Upon Slavery*, John Wesley (1774) (emphasis added): on the web at http://gbgm-umc.org/umw/wesley/thoughtsuponslavery

---

During the American Revolution, Connecticut lawyer Samuel H. Parsons, second cousin of **Nathan Parsons Jr** (p. 165), contributed to the shaping of the central federalist idea of shared powers. See **The Ideological Origins of the American Revolution**, Bernard Bailyn (1967, 1992, pages 356 n. 37, 360 n 40). The notion of shared powers was a commonplace in the American colonies, arising from the rules of government of New England town meetings, such as the first set of such rules - drafted for Dorchester, MA, by a four-member committee, which included **John Maverick** (page 210). The town meetings proved no threat to colonial legislatures. These experiences helped Americans to answer in their federal system the ancient English fear of dual sovereignty: if the king is sovereign, then Parliament cannot be, and vice versa. Samuel Parsons was also a stockholder in the Ohio Company, led by Rufus and **Israel Putnam, Jr.** (See page 283 f.)

Could I but give voice to the sweetness that these thots bring, to the joy they lend to daily living, to the clarity and purity with which they present life's most helpful visions, I would feel the attempt would be worth the reading. But as that can only be expressed in the realm of feelings, I hope that somehow, between the lines you will find the melody I am trying to sing and understand.

As I sit me down it looks so easy to decipher the code in which the Ruler of All wrote his instructions, but paradoxically, to the world of things, the rising sun fails to bring clarity.

Mayo Moore Taylor
(1893-1982)

Letters to his mother, Mary Baldwin Moore Taylor: undated from 1920s

"LEFT OFF WITH BETTER APPETITE THAN HE BEGAN . . ."

Catherine Gould Parsons
Oliver Swayne Taylor

Charles Taylor (1819-1897)
John Oliver Taylor (1862-1922)
John Oliver Taylor, Jr (1891-1960)
Betty Taylor Cook (1918-2000)

Oliver Swayne Taylor (1784-1885) was born near New Ipswich, New Hampshire, December 17, 1784 and died in Auburn, New York, April 19, 1885. Oliver and **Catharine (Catherine) Gould Parsons** (1791-1865) were married Nov 16, 1816, probably in Enfield MA, where her parents lived. Oliver was the son of **Bridget Walton** (1746-1851) and **Thaddeus Taylor** (1744-?). Thaddeus was born in Dunstable MA, one of eleven or perhaps twelve children. He was a farmer, who established a home in the southwest corner of New Ipswich. Oliver attended Dartmouth College, graduating in 1809.

Oliver Taylor's émigré ancestors appear to have been part of a wave of seventeenth century immigrants from the south of England. In contrast to the earlier Pilgrims and Puritans, these later arrivals were of the laboring class of the late medieval age, with slight education and even slighter prospects in England. Oliver and Catherine's son, **Charles Taylor** (1819-1897), has recorded that their Taylor forbearers settled in Lynn, Mass in 1642. Charles also wrote that many Taylor ancestors are buried in Concord, MA.

The first arriving English Taylor of Oliver's line was **William Taylor** (1625-1696), whose wife was **Mary Merriam** (1630-1699). William is said to have arrived from England on the ship *True Love* in 1635, on the same voyage which brought over a John Mayo (1598-1676). This Mayo should not be confused (but has been) with family ancestor John Mayo (1630-1688). (See page 334 and

Truelove in the Index.) Mary and William's son was **Abraham Taylor** (1656-1729), who married **Mary Whittaker** (1660-1681/2). Their son **Abraham Jr** (1681-?) was born just before Mary died.

Abraham Jr was the husband of **Sarah Pellet** (1685-1710), whose parents were **Mary Dane** (?-?) and **Thomas Pellet** (?-?). Sarah Pellet and the second Abraham Taylor were the parents of "Deacon" **Samuel Taylor** (Oct 1, 1708-Oct 28, 1792), who, with his wife, **Susanna** or **Sarah Perham** (1712-1798), were the first of this line to move from Concord to Dunstable, MA. They were the parents of eleven (or twelve) children, including **Thaddeus Taylor** (1744-?). They were Oliver Swayne Taylor's paternal grandparents.

Oliver Swayne Taylor's mother was, as stated, **Bridget Walton** (May 23, 1746-Jan 22, 1851) of Reading, MA. Bridget and Thaddeus Taylor married in 1767. Bridget's parents were **John Walton** (12 Feb 1709-14 Apr 1785) of Marblehead, MA, and **Mary Swayne** (Williams) (?-1781). Mary's last name has been recorded as either Williams or Swayne. The confusion is cleared up by observing that Mary was a widow when she married John Walton about 1738; her last name was "Williams" because her deceased first husband was John Williams, whom she married in 1734. Mary Walton's maiden name was Swayne, variously spelled as "Swain" or "Swaine," which became Oliver's middle name, spelled by him, *Swayne*.

THE EARLY WALTONS

Many of Oliver Taylor's ancestors - not Taylors, *per se* - were among the more influential of the earliest New Englanders. Some were people of imposing fervor, holding locally important positions among those who defined themselves as "godly." They shared a powerful impulse to place under zealous authority an English church badly in need of continued reform (as they thought). They also brought a severe critique to political, economic, and social affairs and personal relations as well. The impulse to purify through control is what made them Puritans – a designation they may never have used of themselves.

Through his mother, Bridget Walton and Bridget's father John Walton, Oliver Swayne Taylor is descended from prominent early Puritans and Pilgrims. John Walton, Bridget's father was the son of the first **John Walton** (1684-1774) also from Marblehead. His wife was **Mary** _____ (?-?). The first John Walton was the son of **Sara Maverick** (1640-1714) and **Samuel Walton** (1639-1717), an early settler of Reading, MA. Samuel's parents were **Elizabeth L. Cooke** (?-abt 1682) and "the Reverend" **William Walton** (1605-1668). Elizabeth's parents were **William Cooke** (?-?) and **Martha White** (?-?).

William Walton, great grandfather X 3 of Oliver Swayne Taylor, was born in Devonshire, England. He attended Emmanuel College, Cambridge (degrees in 1621 and 1625) and may have become a separatist minister soon after he left the university. A nineteenth century source (James Savage) states that William Walton was "no doubt ordained" and served at Seaton in Devon. But our source does not specifically state that Walton served as clergy there.

If William Walton was ordained when a young man, he was undoubtedly influenced in his theology by Calvinist professors at Cambridge who had dominated the chairs of religion there for the previous forty or fifty years. By the 1620s, non-conformists increasingly were being pressed to conform. As a consequence, the influence of these professors was in decline as was the larger network of English clergy, who looked for inspiration to continental Protestantism and had used their influence to place like-minded young clergy in secure and promising clerical positions.

In 1625 William Walton graduated from Cambridge with his second degree (M.A.?). This was the midpoint of a decade which marked the beginning of William Laud's ascendancy through the Episcopal ranks of the Church of England, culminating in his appointment as Archbishop in

1633. The year, 1625, also marked the coronation of Charles I, King of England, and the beginning of a reign of political and religious controversy, which would end with Charles' beheading in 1649.

Also in 1625, the poet John Milton (1608-1674) entered Cambridge University, with the priesthood in mind. But Milton declined ordination because of his hostility to Episcopal authority; he preferred priestly control exercised at the parish level. While at Cambridge, young Milton learned to hate the centralizing initiatives of William Laud and the new King. Milton later learned to hate the Presbyterians as well. He turned away from everyone except that severe and enthusiastic executioner, Oliver Cromwell (1599-1658), who employed Milton to translate official communications, into Latin. Milton hovers over the hysterical violence of his epoch, the most learned yet quarrelsome, magisterial yet despairing English poet.

It would be good to know more about William Walton's participation in the divisive affairs, which swirled around all churchly circles in England in the decade of his years at Cambridge. All this is lost in history. By 1635, William is found in America, which suggests (but does not prove) that his sympathies were with the non-conformists. This faction looked beyond England for a better life and livelihood while obsessively worrying themselves and everyone else about the need to please God. The Puritan has been called "a natural Republican, for there is none on earth that he can own as master." We have inherited the republican principle but without, any longer in civil matters, the weight of the God corollary. Just as well.

William and Elizabeth Walton had nine children. This large family seems to have immigrated to America with other Puritans in what many have termed the "Great Migration" (approximately 1620 – 1634). This movement of several thousand included some propertied families as well as at least a handful of generally well educated male heads of households. William and Elizabeth Walton were among these promising early settlers. Their journey away forever from home and family was stimulated (we infer) both by official pressures directed against dissenting religious opinion and by the separatists' own hopes of better economic prospects and freer religious observance in New England.

The English non-conformists were people who expected to influence events. They carried this expectation over the ocean to America. They were offended, before they left England, at the constraining initiatives directed against them by church and crown. The official assaults were sometimes lethal and at all times pinched the conscience and the pocketbook of a Puritan. William and Elizabeth Walton's community in the New World was an assertive, stubborn, future-directed people.

If William Walton was ordained in England, he seems to have pursued other activities in Hingham, Lynn, Manchester and Marblehead, MA, where he was living when he died in 1668. James Savage, our nineteenth century source (everyone's source) who says he checked the documents, stated that Walton received a ministerial allowance in Marblehead. Savage speculates that Walton may have been employed as a teacher during winter months. Savage found William Walton the proprietor of an establishment in Manchester called Jeffery's Cove. These surmises indicate that William and Elizabeth arrived in America without great wealth. (What kinds of activities did the Puritans permit to take place in the Cove?)

Papers filed in probate court in Marblehead, which undertook to settle his intestate property, refer to William as "Mr" Walton and make no references that might infer clerical activities. (But "Mr" was a generally applicable term.) His widow, Elizabeth, was permitted to administer her husband's affairs and was instructed by the court to keep the estate together during her life and to pay William's debts. After her death, Elizabeth Walton's children returned to court in 1683 to affirm they had reached agreement among themselves as to the disposition of their parents' possessions. Son **Samuel Walton** was given a cow and leased another from his siblings, to be paid for from his part of the residue of the estate.

MAVERICK AND SWAIN ANCESTORS

Sara(h) Maverick (1640-1714), daughter-in-law of William and Elizabeth Walton, was the wife of their son, **Samuel**. Sara's parents were **Elias Maverick** (abt. 1604-1680) and **Anna Harris** (abt 1613-1697), of Reading, MA. Anna Harris' parents were **Elizabeth Williams** (abt 1587-1669) and **Thomas Harris** (1590-1634) of Chelsea. Like her husband Elias, Anna Harris Maverick was a member of the Congregational Church at Charlestown, Suffolk County MA. Anna's father Thomas Harris operated a ferry between present day Chelsea and Charlestown. It is believed this was the first ferry established in America. After Thomas' death, his widow Elizabeth married William Stitson.

Elias Maverick, Anna Harris' husband, arrived in America with his parents on the ship *Mary & John* in 1630. In 1632, Elias was living in Charlestown, Suffolk County MA and seems to have lived there for the remainder of his life. In 1634 he was granted land in what is now Revere, MA (sometimes called Pullen Point or Rumney Marsh). By 1635, Elias had married Anna Harris. Their daughter, **Sara**, was the 4th of eleven children. Sara is mentioned in her father Elias' will as "Sara Walton." Elias' parents were **Mary Gye** (app 1580-aft 1666) and the Rev. **John Maverick** (1578-1635/6), English immigrants who were among the earliest settlers of Dorchester, MA. (Please see the sketch devoted to this couple, page 201.)

We return now to Oliver Swayne Taylor's maternal grandparents, John Walton (1709-1785) and Mary Swayne (Williams) (?-1781). Mary's parents were **Thomas Swayne** (1705-1759) and **Hannah** _____ (?-?). Thomas was a physician in Reading, MA. In addition to Mary, the many children of Thomas and Hannah included Oliver Swayne (1740-1773), a physician, like his father and his nephew, our Oliver. It is now clear that our Oliver Swayne Taylor was named for his mother's brother, Oliver, who died at 33, nine years before Oliver Swayne Taylor was born.

Thomas Swayne's parents were **Benjamin Swayne** (Swaine) (1669-1741) and **Margaret Pierpont** (1672-1713) of Reading. Margaret's parents were English immigrant **Robert Pierpont** (1639-1694) and **Sara Lynde**, 1639-1724. Benjamin's parents were **Mary Smith** (1648-aft 1714) and **Jeremy/ Jeremiah Swayne** (1643-1710). They were married in Reading, MA in 1664 when Mary was fifteen. Mary's parents were **Catherine Morrill** (1635-1662) and **John Smith** (1621-1706). John Smith was a member of the militia, with the rank of Lieutenant in the 1660s and Captain in the 1690s. His wife Catherine died in 1662 at the age of 27. She was buried in the cemetery in North Chelsea (Revere), Suffolk County MA. John was buried there 44 years later.

One wonders if young Mary Smith, in 1664, willingly made herself into a wife to Jeremy Swayne at age 16. Her mother Catherine had died two years earlier. A year later (1663) her father had re-married. Did John Smith simply want his adolescent daughter out of his house? John's second wife was Mary Bill (abt 1645-1693/4). The young bride was only three years older than Mary, her stepdaughter. This circumstance suggests but certainly does not prove that the mother-orphaned Mary Smith was not entirely welcome any longer in the home of her father. In Puritan America there was a strong preference for young people to marry; suspicions and sanctions were directed against the unmarried. Jeremy Swayne, 21, would have gotten himself married with an eye on colonial laws. These laws imposed higher taxes on unmarried young men and opened the door to the prosecution of those young men who lived alone.

John Smith was the son of **Francis Smith** (?-1649/50) and _____. Francis, early immigrant, was in Watertown, MA by 1628. In 1647, he was living in Reading, MA. John Smith had a son named for his own father. This son was "Deacon" Francis Smith, who married Ruth Maverick, a daughter of Elias Maverick and Anna Harris.

As mentioned, another of Elias and Anna's daughters, **Sara**, was the wife of **Samuel Walton**.

> A NOTE REGARDING THE COMMON ANCESTRY OF MARY BALDWIN MOORE TAYLOR AND JOHN OLIVER TAYLOR SR, HUSBAND AND WIFE:
>
> Catherine, wife of John Smith, was the daughter of **Sarah Clement** (abt 1600-1672) and **Isaac Morrill** (abt 1587/8-1662). James Savage, tenacious genealogist, stated (1862) "it is very vexatious to be unable to tell more" about Isaac. We do know a bit more. Catherine Morrill had a sister, **Hannah** (1636-1717), who became the wife of **Daniel Brewer** (?-?). Daniel and Hannah were the parents of **Hannah Brewer** (1665-1721), wife of **John Bowen** (1662-1718) and thereby the mother of **Abigail Bowen** (1700-1775), wife of **Caleb Kendrick** (1694-1771) and mother of **Esther Kendrick** (1725-1775), wife of **Joseph Mayo** (1720-1776), whose son, **Daniel Mayo** (1762-1838) was the great-grandfather of **Mary Baldwin Moore** (1863-1937). Therefore, at their 1887 marriage, Mary B. Moore, descendent of Hannah Morrill Smith, and **John Oliver Taylor S**r (1861-1922), descendent of Catherine Morrill Brewer, shared a common set of ancestors: **Sarah Clement** (abt 1600-1672) and **Isaac Morrill** (1587/8-1661), the parents of Hannah and Catherine. (For additional details, see Page 324 and Morrill in the Index.)

SARAH AND ISAAC MORRILL

The descendents of Sarah and Isaac Morrill benefit from the work of family genealogists and local historians of centuries past. (See Sources, below.) Isaac and his wife are said to have come to America on the *Lion*, arriving on Sept 16, 1632, and settling in Roxbury, MA on Dorchester Road, between Warren and Washington Streets. His lands were later called the Auchmuty estate (fourteen acres). Isaac also owned a tract called the "fox holes" (26 acres). A colonial "freeman" (voting privileges) in 1633, by 1638, Isaac was a member of the artillery company of the militia. Isaac, like his brother Abraham, was a blacksmith. His forges survived usefully well into the eighteenth century, and were employed by descendents who followed his trade.

It comes as no surprise that a blacksmith would maintain a significant supply of weapons in his home. "Arms were a common possession. Those of Isaac Morrill of Roxbury, hung up in his parlor were a musket, a fowling-piece, three swords, a pike, a half-pike, a corselet and two belts of bandoleers." (For more information, see Colonial Militia Company, in the Index) In 1669, Isaac was a constable and a literate, wealthy man. In his lifetime, his property was enumerated for tax purposes: "two houses, two forges, one barn with out housing and two orchards and a swamp."

Sara and Isaac's Morrill's three sons died without issue, but their daughters all married and produced numerous Smith, Brewer and Davis progeny. No doubt, these descendents number in the multiple thousands, today. Isaac Morrill died on Dec 21, 1662; Sarah Morrill died on Nov 6, 1672. They were buried in an ancient cemetery, the "Old First Burial Ground," Roxbury (annexed to Boston in 1868), at the corner of Eustis and Washington streets. Many decades ago, a refurbished marker was installed by descendent (of Abraham Morrill), Annie Morrill Smith.

KING PHILIP'S WAR (1675-77) AND THE TAYLOR LINE

Jeremy/Jeremiah Swayne (1643-1710) was a physician, selectman, justice of the peace and military officer. He has been recorded in the histories of King Philip's War (1675-77) as having served from the town of Reading. ("King Philip" was the English name given by the settlers to the Wampanoag leader, Metacomb.) Jeremy Swayne is listed as a Lieutenant under Capt. Samuel Appleton and as having been wounded in the destruction of the Narraganset Fort in December, 1675. In this same battle, others of Betty Taylor Cook's ancestors were engaged. One was Captain **William Hathorn II** (1606/07-1681), son of the first American representatives of the Hathorn-Putnam-Mayo-Moore-Taylor line. His parents, **Sara** (?-?) and the first **William Hathorn** (?-?), had come to Plymouth Colony in 1630. In the war with the Wampanoag, the second William Hathorn, great, great grandfather of the iconic Nathaniel Hawthorne (1804-1864), was given command of the hundred-member force from Salem, after the death of their highly regarded commander, William Gardiner, who was shot in the head after entering the Narragansett fortress. In his memoir, Benjamin Church, one of the "brisk blades" present during the battle, said that Captain Gardiner was shot from the direction of the attacking colonists. Church reported to the commander, Governor Winslow, that "the best and forwardest of his army [. . .] were shot in their backs and killed by them that lay behind."

Other ancient relatives were mobilized, wounded and killed in this war. A Samuel Taylor of Ipswich was killed at Narragansett. **Isaac Johnson** (1610-1675) of Roxbury and **Henry Bowen** (1633-1723), both of them ancestors of the Mayo line, fought the Narragansett; Henry (probable son of Welch Immigrant **Griffith** and **Margaret Bowen**) assumed command of his company after Isaac Johnson was killed. (Details elsewhere; see page 323 and also 300). The defeat of the aboriginal peoples of Massachusetts, Connecticut and Rhode Island meant the extermination of the Wampanoag and the near annihilation of the Narragansett people.

After hostilities had ended in overwhelming victory for the English settlements, Jeremiah Swayne joined with other soldiers to petition the General Court of the Colony that they be given lands as promised by the governor. In December 1675, the governor had announced to the soldiers assembled on Dedham Plain, if they "played the man, took the fort, and drove the enemy out of the Narragansett country, which is their great seat, they should have a gratuity of land, besides their wages."

Jeremiah Swayne and the other soldiers "valiantly performed the service, and the war long past, the soldiers were not forgetful of their claim, nor the colony unmindful of its obligations." Unfortunately, the land offered was too remote to be of much value for a generation or more.

The following description of the organization of a colonial militia company, the "train band" (*trained* band?), was provided by Ellis (1847) and reproduced by Gameila Morrill Grant (see Sources):

"All males between sixteen and sixty were required to be provided with arms and ammunition. The arms of private soldiers were pikes, muskets, and swords. The muskets had matchlocks or firelocks, and to each one there was a pair of bandoleers or pouches for powder and bullets, and a stick called a 'rest' for use in taking aim. The pikes were ten feet in length, besides the spear at the end. For defensive armor, corselets were worn, and coats quilted with cotton. The train-band had not less than sixty-four nor more than two hundred men and twice as many musketeers as pikemen, the latter being of superior stature. Its officers were a captain, lieutenant, ensign, and four sergeants. The commissioned officers carried swords, partisans, or leading staves, and sometimes pistols. The sergeants bore halberds. The flag of the colony bore the red cross of St. George in one corner, upon a white field, the pine-tree, the favorite emblem of New England, being in one corner of the four spaces formed by the cross. Company trainings were ordered at first every Saturday, then every month, then eight times a year. 'The training to begin at one of the clock of the afternoon.' The drum was their only music."

OLIVER SWAYNE TAYLOR

Oliver Swayne Taylor (1784-1885), the principal subject of this sketch, great-great grandson of **Jeremiah Swayne** and great-great grandfather of **Betty Taylor**

Cook, was the eighth of nine children, four sons and five daughters. Charles, Oliver's son, recorded that all of Oliver's sisters married and many of Oliver's siblings were long-lived, though none as long as Oliver. Charles, demonstrating a lingering family interest in the abstraction of dates and time lines, wrote that two of Oliver's sisters died between 50 and 60 years of age, another at 63, one at 82, and one at 94. The oldest brother died at 96, the second at 92 and the third at 82. Oliver Taylor lived to be 100. Charles left us this much, but neglected to match particular names with the carefully kept chronologies.

Long life, in Oliver's case at least, was credited to daily disciplines of diet and exercise. Walking was a favorite activity, which Oliver adopted early and practiced three or four times a day throughout his life. His son Charles has written arrestingly of his Dad. *"With an appetite that was always keen, he did not indulge it to the extent of its demand, but left off in the midst of his meals with better appetite than he began."* Now, go back and read this statement, aloud. If you can write about your father in a rhyming manner, does that mean you love him more?

Oliver is remembered in the family as a literal teetotaler, who drank but one cup of weak tea or coffee, never drank cold water and as son Charles, curiously wrote, "not once a year felt any thirst."

> Dec 31 Conversation -
> Charles: Father, were you thirsty this past year?
> Oliver: Not Once.

Oliver and all of his brothers were said to have avoided tobacco in any form. This is all fine but for longevity, genetics probably counts, too. One should not overlook the span accumulated by Oliver's mother, **Bridget Walton**, which descendent **Betty Taylor Cook** (1918-2000) recorded at 105 years, 1746-1851. No one has left us a word about Bridget Walton Taylor and her habits of life.

Oliver's early education was at the public school in the New Ipswich district (NH), which was open to him only six weeks each winter and perhaps a few more in the summer. The scant opportunity for formal study was owing to the inability of the poor population to subscribe the school for longer periods. Despite these limitations, Oliver was encouraged, evidently at home, to think of higher education. On his mother's Walton-Swayne side, he was descended from physicians, including his uncle and namesake Oliver Swayne, his grandfather Thomas and his double great grandfather Jeremy/Jeremiah Swayne.

As an adolescent, Oliver boarded at and attended the Academy of New Ipswich and there determined to go to college. During the year following his graduation from the academy Oliver prepared for his college examination by teaching school for five months, doing farm work and studying Latin. The family has passed down a record of his youthful accomplishments during that year. In a few brief months, young Oliver is said to have mastered Latin grammar well enough to read through a lessons book in five days; he also read nine books of Virgil's *Aeneid*, other Latin classics and the Four Gospels (presumably in the Latin Vulgate).

Oliver Swayne Taylor entered Dartmouth College in 1805. His class of forty included Levi Woodbury, who had been Oliver's roommate at the Academy and was so at Dartmouth. Woodbury became a U.S. Senator, New Hampshire Governor, Secretary of the Navy and then Treasury in President Jackson's and Van Buren's cabinet and a justice of the Supreme Court of the United States (1845-51), appointed by President Polk. Although Dartmouth had only four faculty members, Oliver was exposed there to the wider world. Daniel Webster (Dartmouth class of 1800) spoke to the Phi Beta Kappa Society, of which Oliver was a member. While at Dartmouth, Oliver taught three winters in the district school he had attended and in his senior year was principal of the New Ipswich Academy, where he had only recently been a student himself. He graduated from Dartmouth in

1809. After college, Oliver taught for three years at the New Ipswich Academy.

Oliver also attended medical school at Dartmouth, graduating in 1813. The then tiny Dartmouth Medical School (founded in 1797) was only the fourth medical school established in North America, having been started by Nathan Smith (1762-1829). Smith subsequently moved on to teach medicine at Yale, a newer medical school founded under Yale President Timothy Dwight; Dwight was a distant relative of Oliver's wife, Catherine, through her mother's family. (Details may be found in the sketch devoted to Charles Taylor and Charlotte Gamewell, esp. pages 168-172.) There were no more than three or four lecturers, when Oliver studied medicine at Dartmouth. The medical students were expected to supplement their academic program by way of apprenticeships.

A calling into religious service came early to Oliver Swayne Taylor and shaped the remainder or his long life. His son, Charles, recorded that in 1812, while in medical school, Oliver made a public profession of his Christian faith, uniting with the Presbyterians. This personal commitment came during a period of religious revival and missionary fervor in America, remembered by historians as the "Second Great Awakening." Oliver Taylor's subsequent activities and associations show that he was an active participant in this movement.

Until 1817, Oliver practiced medicine in Dover, NH and in Belchertown and Hadley, MA. It is likely that Oliver met **Catherine Gould Parsons** (1791-1865) during his medical practice in Massachusetts. They married on Nov 16, 1816, and had five children: Catherine Gould Taylor (1817-1890); Elizabeth M. (abt 1816-1851), who married Delos M. Keeler (1815-1868); **Charles Taylor** (1819-1897); Henry Martyn Taylor (c 1825-?) and Edward Payson (Parsons?) Taylor (?-?). In Hadley, Oliver curtailed his medical career and devoted himself thereafter to the education of children and, in retirement, to prisoners.

In 1817, Oliver and Catherine moved to Boston. There, for five years, Oliver worked with Jeremiah Evarts at the American Board of Commissions for Foreign Missions (A.B.C.F.M.). He prepared articles for Evarts' religious publication, *The Panoplist Or the Christian's Armory*, renamed *The Panoplist and Missionary Herald*. Oliver was invited by Dr. Samuel Spring, one of the founders of the A.B.C.F.M., to go as a missionary doctor to Ceylon (Sri Lanka). Oliver agreed to go and was appointed as a missionary, but the funding fell through. While in Boston, Oliver became the director of one of the first Sunday Schools established in America, founded by the father of the inventor, Samuel B. Morse. While living in Boston, Oliver and Catherine Taylor became the parents of Betty Taylor Cook's great-grandfather, Charles Taylor (1819-1897).

Beginning in 1822 Oliver Taylor resumed teaching full time in Boston and Hadley, MA and virtually gave up the practice of medicine. (In later census records from Auburn NY, Oliver lists himself as a retired clergyman.) In 1826 he took charge of an academy at Homer, New York and in 1830 moved to Auburn, NY. Remembering that Oliver's mother's maiden name was Walton, we may speculate that re-settlement in Auburn may have been encouraged by the fact that a John Walton had received a grant of Revolutionary War Bounty Land in Cayuga County, NY. Between 1830 and 1850, son Charles Taylor reports, Oliver taught and supervised schools in Plattsburg and Henrietta, NY and also in Indiana, Michigan, Ohio, and South Carolina. These locations seem surprisingly extensive and unconnected. Perhaps an inquisitive descendent can track down the details.

Oliver was licensed to preach June 17, 1840 at Weedsport, in the Presbytery of Monroe, NY. He was fifty-six. Oliver preached frequently for the next ten years, in churches near the schools where he was teaching. In 1850, Oliver retired from public teaching and returned with Catherine to Auburn, where they remained the rest of their lives. Catherine was enrolled in the 1860 census but not the 1870. The Fort Hill Cemetery records indicate she died in 1865.

Retirement for Oliver Taylor was an opportunity to more fully engage in religious enterprises and to continue his teaching, both of private pupils and in the churches. Oliver usually taught Bible classes in one and sometimes two Presbyterian churches. In addition, for seventeen years, up to the age of 90, he conducted a Bible class in the state prison at Auburn. The classes were held at about 7:30 on Sunday mornings. On Sunday afternoons Oliver Taylor attended meetings at the "Home of the Friendless" in Auburn. (How would you like to live in a place called *Home of the Friendless*? It could have been worse. In Louisville, KY there used to be a residential facility called "Home for the Incurables.")

Auburn, NY was the site of a number of significant events in Oliver and Catherine Taylor's lifetime. In July 1831, Alexis de Tocqueville and his friend Gustave de Beaumont, visited the prison at Auburn. Toqueville's book, **Democracy in America** (1834), is required reading for historians of America. But it is not generally recalled today that the primary purpose of his visit to the US, was to examine prison systems. The likelihood of a meeting between Taylor and Tocqueville is reduced because Oliver is not known to have had a connection with the prison until about 1858. Furthermore, Beaumont and Tocqueville recorded the names of those persons with whom they met in Auburn and the surrounding area. They list warden Gershom Powers, prison chaplain B.C. Smith, and an unidentified clerk; there is no mention of interviews with teachers at the prison.

Auburn, NY was notable for the vigorous anti-slavery environment that existed there prior to the Civil War. Auburn was the hometown of William Seward, who as governor of New York State, and then as United States Senator, was probably the most prominent and articulate anti-slavery politician in the country before 1860. Prior to Lincoln's election to the Presidency in that year, Seward campaigned hard for the Republican nomination, which Lincoln received. Seward lost the nomination because of the widely held opinion among Republicans, that Seward's anti-slavery views were too vigorously pressed and divisive. Republican convention delegates, even if personally sympathetic to Seward and perhaps holding views similar to his, concluded that Seward had little chance of winning the electoral votes of the slave-holding border states, Kentucky and Maryland.

A further, telling indication of the anti-slavery environment in Auburn was the welcome the community extended to anti-slavery proponent Harriet Tubman (1820-1913). She selected Auburn as her headquarters during her efforts to organize Quakers and other activists into the informal (and illegal) "Underground Railroad." This was a network of homes and farms which spirited escaped slaves from the South to Canada. William Seward, as governor of New York, helped Tubman secure property in Auburn for her headquarters. When Tubman got married in Auburn in 1859, her wedding was a grand and well publicized event.

After his stint as a teacher in South Carolina, and elsewhere, Oliver and Catherine Taylor returned to Auburn in 1850. They lived there during the intense decade prior to the Civil War, and for the rest of their lives. They may have moved to Auburn in order to live with one of their children. For whatever reason and we wish we knew what it was, Oliver and Catherine opted to live in one of the most vigorously anti-slavery communities in the United States. This environment stands in dramatic contrast to the circumstances of their son Charles, who, like his father, was a medical doctor and Christian minister, but who spent his long career in the South.

There are many similarities in the careers of Oliver Taylor and his son Charles. Both were well educated scholars with degrees from highly regarded private universities; both trained as medical doctors; both elected not to practice medicine but rather to devote themselves to church work and to education; both maintained a specific and active interest in fostering the burgeoning nineteenth century Sunday School Movement within the Protestant Churches. Both father and son were possessed of a religious temperament that rose to the level of a calling.

Oliver Taylor must have understood Charles' turn of mind and therefore his son's decision to choose church-related educational work as a career. Oliver, late in life, did the same thing. In 1840, at age 56, Oliver secured a license to preach and on Dec. 8, 1848, was ordained a Presbyterian evangelist. This was near in time to his son's decision (1844) to pursue an explicitly church-related career. Oliver and Catherine Taylor also knew South Carolina, where, son Charles has recorded, Oliver worked both as teacher and preacher.

But for Charles, a turn toward the church entailed a public affiliation with a branch of the Methodist Episcopal Church, which boldly endorsed human slavery. In 1844, the White Methodists of the South separated themselves from the national Methodist Church. Debates, arguments and threats of schism had taken place at regional and national Methodist gatherings for at least twenty years prior to the 1840's, but the precipitating event for the split was the refusal of the Methodist Bishop of South Carolina, James Andrew, to free slaves he had inherited.

After Charles Taylor concluded his missionary activities (sponsored by the Methodist Episcopal Church, South) and returned from China to South Carolina, he wrote a book about his experiences in China. The book, **Five Years in China** (1860) was dedicated jointly to his father, Oliver Swayne Taylor and to Bishop James Osgood Andrew. (See above, pages 144 & 154.) At this distance in time and without having discovered any records on the point, one can only speculate about what Catherine and Oliver Taylor thought of their son's decisions. One wishes for letters or other documents, which might reveal what passed between Catherine and Oliver in New York and Charles and Charlotte in South Carolina.

In 1884, the Rev. Dr. Oliver Swayne Taylor's hundredth birthday was publicly celebrated in Auburn. Speeches were delivered; accolades were bestowed; Oliver was made a member of the local historical society. It is likely Dr. Charles Taylor, 65 years old, who wrote his father's biography for the occasion, was in attendance.

On April 21, 1885, Oliver Swayne Taylor was buried at Fort Hill Cemetery, 19 Fort Street, Auburn, New York (Glen Haven Section, Lot 3, grave 12), next to the grave of William Seward and not far from Harriet Tubman's. Catherine preceded Oliver in death by 20 years, and is also buried at Fort Hill Cemetery.

SOURCES:

In addition to Betty Cook's notes, the source for some biographical details about Oliver Swayne Taylor was found on line at: Virtual American Biographies, //famousamericans.netsamericans.net. See also websites with content concerning cemeteries in Concord, MA.

Catherine Parsons and Oliver Swayne Taylor's genealogy information, generally: the unpublished book (including notes) of Betty Taylor Cook. Among Betty's notes is a three-page biography of Oliver Taylor, in the language of his son Charles, written during Oliver's lifetime, probably for the public celebration in Auburn, NY when Oliver reached 100 years of age.

For additional Swaine genealogy data: Pierpont Genealogies - ccat.sas.upnn.edu/rs/rak/gen/pier/piergen

Swayne (Swain), Smith and other New England genealogies may be examined at: Steve Condarcure's New England Genealogy Index - www.genealogyofnewengland.com/sjc.

For William Walton: **A Genealogical Dictionary of The First Settlers of New England, Before 1692 (1860-62) *4 Volumes*,** By James Savage (see Vol 4). This document may be purchased (CD) or try: usgennet.org/usa/topic/newengland/savage/bk4/intro.

For additional information about John Maverick and the founding of Dorchester, MA: research of Clovis LaFleur, on the web at: Aaron Starke Family Chronicles; see also Descendants of the Founders of Ancient Windsor, Inc." at colonialwarsct.org/1633.

For details cited concerning Nonconformity in England in the seventeenth century: **Archbishop Laud**, by Hugh Trevor-Roper (London: Phoenix Press, 1988).

the war long past, the soldiers were not forgetful of their claim, nor the colony unmindful of its obligations - For Jeremiah (Jeremy) Swayne's service in King Philip's war: See Mass. Colonial Records, vol. V. p. 487; and on the web at worldroots.com; see also SOLDIERS IN KING PHILIP's WAR, Chapter 28, Part I (from James Savage, **A Genealogical Dictionary of the First Settlers of New England before 1692**), cited above.

"the best and forwardest of his army [. . .] were shot in their back:" Excerpts from Benjamin Church's memoir appear in **King Philip's War**, by Eric B. Schultz and Michael J. Tougias (Woodstock, VT: Countryman Press, 1999, page 326).

For the records of John Walton's Cayuga County NY bounty land: rootsweb.com/~nycayuga/land/mtractuz.

Revolutionary War Bounty Land in "The Military Tract Of Central NY" (For The Area Within Cayuga County, New York) - from the book: **The Balloting Book and Other Documents Relating to Military Bounty Lands, In The State Of New York** (Albany: Packard & Van Benthuysen – 1825) (Available from the Cayuga County Clerk's Office, Records Management Division, 160 Genesee St, Auburn, NY 13021).

Helpful Smith Genealogical materials may be examined at: LIEUTENANT & CAPTAIN JOHN SMITH, (1621-1706) - alumni.media.mit.edu/~kristin/family/Smith/JohnSmith.

For Morrill details: **The Morrill Name in America,** Gameila Morrill Grant (1923, 1969: San Jose, CA), which provided a description of a colonial militia company, taken from **The History of Roxbury town**, Charles M. Ellis (Noston: Samuel G Drake, 1847).

Portions of Gameila Grant's book may be found on the web: familytreemaker.genealogy.com. Tocqueville's visit to the prison at Auburn: a chronology produced by George Wilson Pearson at Yale University in 1931, and available at the Cayuga County (NY) Historian's Office, Auburn, NY.

with better appetite than he began - from Charles Taylor's biography of his father, Oliver, prepared for the community celebration of Oliver's one hundredth birthday in Auburn, NY, 1884.

For Charles Taylor's dedication of his book, plus citations from it: **Five years in China With Some Account of the Great Rebellion and a Description of St Helena**, *by Charles Taylor, M.D. Corresponding Secretary of the Sunday-School Society of the Methodist Episcopal Church, South (Nashville: McFerrin, New York: Derby & Jackson, 1860).*

Information about the burial of Oliver and Catherine Taylor: helpfully provided, in writing, by Elaine Hutson, Fort Hill Cemetery Association.

The Puritan *a natural Republican* - **Religion and the Rise of Capitalism**, R.H. Tawney, (1922, 1966, page 201)

What we owe the future - Wendell Berry, *At A Country Funeral,* **Selected Poems** (Berkeley, CA: Counterpoint, 1999, page 92, Copyright by Wendell Berry, Reprinted by permission of Counterpoint). See page 200, below.

*What we owe the future is
not a new start,
for we can only begin with
what has happened.
We owe the future the past,
the long knowledge that is
the potency of time to come.*

Wendell Berry

At A Country Funeral
Selected Poems

"FAITHFUL IN FURTHERING THE WORK OF THE LORD IN THE CHURCHES & CIVIL STATE"

John Maverick
Mary Gye . . .
Charlemagne (747-813/14) . . .
Charles Martel (689-741)

Elias Maverick (app. 1604-1680)
Sara Maverick (1640-1714)
John Walton (?-?)
John Walton (1709-1785)
Bridget Walton Taylor (1746-1851)
Oliver Swayne Taylor (1784-1885)
Charles Taylor (1819-1897)
John Oliver Taylor (1862-1922)
John Oliver Taylor, Jr (1891-1960)
Betty Taylor Cook (1918-2000)

The Rev. **John Maverick** (1578-1635/6) and his wife **Mary Gye** (c. 1580-aft 1666) and children were among the earliest settlers of Dorchester, MA. John was born in Awliscombe, Devonshire, England. The date of his baptism in Awliscombe was Dec 28 1578. John Maverick's parents were the Rev. **Peter ("Bull") Maverick** (c. 1550-c. 1616) and **Dorothy Tucke** (?-?). Peter Maverick was reported to have died a violent death. No details have been uncovered. The well-educated John Maverick received a B.A. (1599) and an M.A. (1603) from Exeter College, Oxford. John Maverick was ordained a priest in 1597 at Exeter, Devonshire. His friends would come to think of him as an 'evangelical,' his enemies a 'nonconformist.' A separator from the Church of England he surely was.

John finished at Oxford while its theological curriculum was under the control of stout Calvinists. Oxford's Church of England critics thought of the university as "a colony of Geneva" for good reason. The appeal of Geneva was practical as well as theological.

In the dawning of a new century, numbers of restive English folk continued to look to continental Reformist enclaves and their open embrace of capitalism. Self-governing Geneva invited the merchant class throughout Europe to make its own laws in its own interests. Standing fiercely against Rome, Geneva would exercise a powerful appeal to English merchants, who were themselves energetic island dwellers and enthusiastic sponsors of ocean-going, globe-crossing voyages of discovery-cum-piracy. Hearty English Protestants welcomed every rationale to validate their competition with the Catholic monarchies of the Continent. In the words of their leader in Massachusetts, John Winthrop, Mary and John Maverick set out to build their own "City on a Hill," not to be hid under any bushel. And not intended to lose, but rather to make money for their sponsors.

A minority of this English minority in the *New* World would be, in the new 17th century, of a temper that fully embraced Calvin's notions of comprehensive church control of civil affairs. These "puritans" would carry their convictions to extremes that would be rejected by many of their own descendents. The salvation theology of the first American generation of Puritans was always tempered by the business plans of their sponsors, and then by the land acquisition stratagems of their heirs. The heirs of Puritanism would increasingly focus their minds on acquiring title to portions of the literal earth, reserving the Sabbath for their reflections on the deferred rewards of heaven and its more problematic real estate. But the settlers, arriving with Winthrop in 1630, in addition to their own mission, were on one for God - to purify the civil government of its devilish ills. The stridency of such impulses, in the following two generations, would lead zealous reformers into religious warfare in England and increased immigration abroad. Any sense the aboriginal occupants of *New* England (so called) could make of all the confusion was whatever they might discern, while trading their lands for tools or peering into the business end of a blunderbuss.

The instinct to purify would plague dissenting and "free church" sectaries down the centuries. Even into our own day, believers periodically denounce and separate from one another over theological nuances or the minutiae of private behavior. In the days of John and Mary Maverick, the list of taboos was long and harshly enforced. Official scrutiny and its attendant condemnations extended to matters of attire and the personal convictions of otherwise passive colonial subjects. The Church Militant of every age and stripe finds more resonance in the Old Testament imposition of sanction and punishment than in the New Testament appeals to consider the lilies or turn the other cheek.

On Oct. 28, 1600 John Maverick married **Mary Gye** (app 1580-aft 1666). Mary Gye's documented genealogy is so vast as to extend some eleven generations back from her into thick medieval mists. Even though these fogs have never lifted and are not likely ever to lift, tenacious researchers of this line have tracked Mary Gye's ancestry to **Charlemagne** (747-813/14) and even to his Belgian grandfather, **Charles Martel (*the Hammer*)** (689-741), and on to Charlemagne's great grandfather, **Pippin the Middle** (aka **Pippin the Fat**) (635/40-714) and to Pippin's girlfriend, **Alpaida (Elfide, Chalpaida)**. Charles Martel, ruler of the Franks, is credited with leading the forces, which stopped Moorish advances into France from Spain at the once-famous Battle of Tours in 732. But a modern lineage which connects to *the Hammer* is genealogical fairy dust that ought to be blown away.

A line of descendents that covers 30 generations is an imposition upon Mary Gye's blameless progeny. They are made to closely read medieval royal sagas to answer the simplest query: tell me about your family. Let us leave Charlemagne alone with his pretensions to the creation of a new Holy Roman Empire. Let us think only of Mary Gye and only where we find her: an adolescent girl and the young wife of an evangelical priest, then mother of a large family in the Tudor-Stuart England of Shakespeare, then middle aged immigrant, and finally New World widow.

Mary Guy divided her long life almost equally between Devonshire, England and Dorchester, Massachusetts.

"MR. MAVERICK WAS DESIROUS TO HAVE A BREED OF NEGROES"

Mary and John Maverick were the parents of seven children, at least two of whom deserve notice. Son Samuel Maverick (app 1602-1669/76) was the first of this family to come to New England, arriving in 1623 at age 21. He is considered one of the earliest settlers of Boston. Samuel's written reports back to his family and others stimulated many to decide to join him in the unspoiled (so called) New World. Young Samuel seems to have crossed the wide ocean with thoughts other than the building upon earth of God's Kingdom. No doubt, many settlers came with mixed and perhaps contradictory motives, hoping to serve God and make profits as well. This paradox may have burdened only a minority among the earliest New Englanders, who survived the voyage, and the early, starving years, and through all this remained true religious dissenters. We know that, unlike his parents, who followed him to Massachusetts, Samuel Maverick was no dissenter. Bad luck for Sam, because the Puritans were the ones in charge; they represented the financial backers in London. They were organized. They ran the local government. They left most of the written records. History's spin is controlled by the well placed and the literate.

In 1630, when the famous Winthrop-led flotilla arrived full of the judging and judgmental, Samuel Maverick was already a colonist and a freeman. As such, he was grandfathered in, that is, he was made a voting stockholder in the holding company which managed the colony. Soon, company affairs were no longer directed from London but from Massachusetts itself. The early buying out of the original investors established a precedent favoring local control over local affairs. This arrangement blossomed 140 years later into political independence for Massachusetts and all the other English colonies.

Samuel's seniority seems to have made him exempt from the soon-established voting limitations based upon congregational church membership. Inclined more toward Anglicanism, Samuel joined a freemen's faction hostile to Winthrop's rigorous and reformist governance of Massachusetts. Samuel allied with those who complained about the civil privileges accorded newcomers merely because of their congregational church membership.

Samuel, a true *Maverick*, piped his own tune in Puritan-dominated Massachusetts. He was said to have given shelter to accused adulterers seeking to escape punishment at the hands of the authorities. He caused scandal among his neighbors for attempting to force his African slaves to procreate, viewing such offspring as an enlargement of his wealth. The record of a visitor to his home: "*Mr. Maverick* was desirous to have a breed of Negroes and therefore seeing [that his "Negro woman"] would not yield to persuasions to company with a Negro young man he had in his house; he commanded him will'd she nill'd she to go to bed to her which was no sooner done but she kickt him out again, this she took in high disdain beyond her slavery."

There seems to be no record suggesting the Puritan establishment, which justified race enslavement of Indians and Africans on "just war" theories, ever prosecuted or otherwise pursued Sam Maverick for trying to force his slaves to copulate. Sam could get into trouble for refusing to go to church but not for abetting the rape of an African woman. So in New England, as in the southern Colonies of Maryland and Virginia, legislation followed custom. In the South it would require the humiliation of Civil War and in New England, a decline in the cash value of human chattel for the heirs of Puritanism to accord civil status to such as the Maverick slaves of the seventeenth century.

John and Mary Maverick's second son (Samuel's younger brother), was **Elias Maverick**, (1604-1680) husband of **Anna Harris** (1613-1697). Elias and Anna were the parents of **Sara Maverick** (1640-1714), the wife of **Samuel Walton** (1639-1718). Through this line of descent, **Betty Taylor Cook** (1918-2000) is reached. (Additional details of Elias Maverick and Anna Harris are found in the sketch devoted to Oliver Swayne Taylor.)

After serving as rector for fourteen years (1615-1629) in the West Country, at Beaworthy in Devonshire, John Maverick resigned in order to sail to New England. John Maverick's religious principles allied him with many other militant idealists who wanted to cleanse the Church of England. By the close of the 1620's they had come to doubt the "reforms" begun in the time of Henry VIII a century before. Dissenters who became Separatists did so when they concluded that no cleansing would continue and England would not in fact become a godlier nation. Accordingly, as with John Winthrop and other reform-minded entrepreneurs and their families, a momentous decision was made. Encouraged by enthusiastic reports sent them by their son Samuel, Mary and John Maverick decided to embark with their family for America and there create an evangelical nation in the wilderness, truly under the sovereignty of God alone. So they believed.

The English nonconformists were influential in England more for their growing numbers and their fortitude than for any unique or outstanding theological creativity. The Separatists denounced Established Church stipulations of only approved sermonizers and they objected to prescribed prayers. They resisted the collecting of multiple dioceses under the control of a single bishop and complained of the non-residency of these bishops. But in all this there were conformist critics as well. Some of the purifiers went further, being of a general anti-clerical bent. They objected to the consecration of churches on the grounds that individual conscience sanctifies any place where conscience is truly exercised. Some denied the divine origin of the Church of England. Many viewed Episcopal structure itself as "Romish" and the devil's handiwork. Some were anarchists, rejecting all governments in all spheres of life. It was said of John Lilburne, who passed like a meteor through and beyond the reformist ranks, "if there were none living but himself

John would be against Lilburne and Lilburne against John."

We do not know with certainty where **John** and **Mary Maverick** placed themselves on the continuum of Protestant Dissent. Nor is it clear how much of the turmoil might have been caused in the first instance, by the poverty of the English churches, which lost much property during the Tudor confiscations of the previous century. For the hope of revenue, many priests permitted secular activities such as cock fighting and gambling to be conducted on church property. Was such a priest corrupt or simply poor? Was he venal or looking for ways to add to the cash flow of the parish? The dissenters' notion that God may be worshipped in any place is at least a second cousin to the idea that any place may be utilized for any convenient purpose. Thus, poultry may roost in the belfry and hogs may be lodged in the chancel. To an impoverished, married cleric, the father of children, who is denounced for such efforts and harassed into bishops' court, a *new world* can be inviting.

Puritans carried a combination of religious and secular notions into New England. There they mixed the rigors of doctrine with an insistent quest to improve their economic prospects. Their settlements were established with both God and their backers' profits in mind. Is this mixture of self-defined orthodoxy and avarice not part of the Puritan heritage in America? Is it only a coincidence that today's evangelists, like carnival barkers, proclaim to large and approving audiences that Jesus wants you to become rich? Where else in the world is this sort of rank quackery passed off as gospel preaching?

The Nonconformists' cause in England was greatly aided by its antagonists, with pride of place belonging to Archbishop William Laud (1573-1645), who was vindictive, cruel and ineffective. During his tenure as Bishop in London and finally at Canterbury, Bishop Laud looked increasingly to the unpopular Charles I (1600-1649) for the enforcement of church dictums. What brought Laud down was his failure to notice that churchly powers are more latent and apparent than certain and substantive. Reliance by religious authority upon the prosecutorial powers of the state is a failure of faith, an implicit confession that gentle persuasion must be backed up by force, or the dove that is carrying your message will be shot out of the sky.

Laud's attempts at coercion simply multiplied the opposition - a lesson constantly taught and constantly unlearned. The number of Quakers increased in Massachusetts as the shrinking Puritan Establishment criminalized their practice. In the next century Baptists multiplied in Virginia as the self-subtracting Anglicans looked to local magistrates to enforce Episcopal privilege. It did not work. Zealotry eats official disapproval for lunch.

Laud set himself against Parliament at a time when Parliament would assert itself against the King. The inflexible and unimaginative Laud staked all on Charles I. As a result, the two-way ecclesiastical denunciations of the 1620's became root-and-branch political warfare through the 1630's and bloody military battles in the decade following. In 1641 Laud was put in the Tower of London and, in the midst of three consecutive civil wars (1642-45, 48-49, 49-51), was beheaded in 1645. Charles I lost his head four years later.

Prior to his 1630 departure for America, John Maverick had been a West Country rector for fourteen years. For twenty years John Cotton preached in the east, in Lincolnshire, before leaving for New England. These long pastoral tenures in different parts of England seem to have been largely untroubled. This relative tranquility suggests that in the decades prior to 1630, evangelical clerics had won enough adherents among the people and the hierarchy to offer an imperfect but tolerable protection to all but the most strident preachers.

Severe religious persecution in medieval England had been sporadic and local. However, after Henry VIII (1491-1547) shattered the official Catholic consensus, efficient persecution was centralized in church and crown, receiving a guiding prosecutorial impetus from the heights of the royal and the clerical establishments. The spies whom Elizabeth I (1533-1603) dispatched, found state enemies everywhere, but Protestant dissenters were not hounded wholesale. Unless you were Catholic, you had to denounce the Queen herself before you would lose your nose or your ears. Elizabeth's nephew and successor, the Scot, James I (1566-1625, ruled England: 1603-1625) tried to stifle the more extreme preachers. He attempted to enforce conformity, in the interests of the national church and of his own crown, which he saw as all of one piece. But James' rule was dominated by international relations. His disputes with Parliament meant James lacked the finances to go after dissenting clerics or their supporters. Archbishop Laud tried to change all of this after the coronation of Charles I in 1625.

Archbishop Laud, in one of his numerous inconsistencies, was hostile to immigration to America. The West Country population, though perhaps pressed, was not actually persecuted by Laud and his agents, who wanted people to submit but also to stay put. The best evidence for the *de facto* local protection of nonconformity is that immigration to New England was encouraged and even organized, as we have noted, by the Dorchester Vicar John White, who obtained a royal charter for the Company of the Massachusetts Bay. After 1629, White's company sponsored the renewed colonization of New England.

The 1630 ocean-crossing Separatists looked back from Massachusetts with fondness upon their forsaken homes. Lingering affection for lost ties is seen in the naming of their new communities. The early residents did not forget to name their greatest town for that Lincolnshire "nursery of inconformity," Boston. Just to the south, Dorchester, MA was so named to honor the West County Vicar of Dorchester, the Reverend John White, primary patron of the settlers' voyage.

Before their 1630 departure for America, the 140 reformer-immigrants gathered at Plymouth, chose **John Maverick** as one of the teachers of the Puritan church there. He was then selected one of two ministers to come to New England aboard the ship *Mary & John*. The Maverick family sailed from Plymouth in March 1630. Their ship was not formally associated with the seventeen ships in the convoy lead by John Winthrop. But the *Mary & John*, sailed with those ships and with the same destination, Massachusetts Bay Colony. They arrive safely.

In 1632, the Reverend John Maverick was one of a committee of four, convened in Charlestown, to decide whether Governor Winthrop was at fault in a complaint made by the deputy governor, Thomas Dudley. Winthrop was accused of malfeasance for failing to move his residence to a new town ("Newtown") from Boston, after he had agreed to do so. Deputy Governor Dudley, apparently given to sudden anger, "began to be in a passion" over a number of other complaints he raised to the committee against Winthrop. When the two officials rose angrily towards each other, Maverick and the other committee members intervened to keep the governor and the deputy from coming to blows. The committee found some fault with Winthrop but not so much as Dudley would have wished.

In 1633, John Maverick was chosen one of four men, two ruling ministers and two deacons, who established the rules of government for the town of Dorchester, MA. With twelve men of Dorchester chosen in 1633 as selectmen, Dorchester's was the first organized New England town government. The old town encompassed areas, which were eventually renamed as the population increased: Milton, Canton, Stoughton, Sharon, and that part of Boston called Dorchester Heights, which was fortified by a later and collateral ancestor of **Betty Taylor Cook**. This was engineer Rufus Putnam, acting upon the orders of General Washington on March 4, 1776.

When he died in 1635-6 at about 60 years of age, John Maverick was eulogized by Governor Winthrop and others. Maverick was described as a man "of very humble spirit, and faithful in furthering the work of the Lord here, both in the churches and civil state." That last phrase indicates the gentle John Maverick was of a Puritan and not merely a Pilgrim temperament. His urge to purify may account entirely for his willingness to move with wife and family to America in the first place. Already an elderly cleric by 1630, he left behind all security for the new venture, promoting morality through both churchly discipline and State action.

The speculation of genealogists has arrived at the idea that all American Mavericks descend from Mary Gye and John Maverick. This would include the prominent nineteenth and twentieth century Texas *Mavericks*, who gave their surname as the very definition of going-your-own-way. Samuel Augustus Maverick, a Texas rancher and signer of the Texas Declaration of Independence in 1836, is said to have been lax about branding his cattle. Since everyone else's cattle was branded, his unidentified cattle could be easily distinguished. "Maverick" cattle belonged to the *Maverick* who refused to go along with the branding.

John and Mary Gye Maverick's gravesites are unknown. The location of the earliest Dorchester cemetery and meeting house is unrecorded.

SOURCES:

For additional information about John Maverick and the founding of Dorchester, MS: research of Clovis LaFleur, on web at: Aaron Starke Family Chronicles; see also "Descendants of the Founders of Ancient Windsor, Inc." URL http//www.colonialwarsct.org/1633.htm

For details concerning John Maverick, Elias Maverick and the Maverick lineage generally: "Genealogy of Kristin C. Hall" and related webpages; /alumni.media.mit.edu/~kristin/fambly/Maverick/JohnMaverick.

Samuel Maverick's efforts to breed his slaves: John Josselyn, *An Account of Two Voyages to New England* (1675), quoted in **White Over Black**, Winthrop D. Jordan (1968, Norton: 1977, page 71) For old Dorchester and its founding: *Dorchester Atheneum*, which is found on the web: dorchesterathenium.org

For the descendency from Charles Martel and Charlemagne see "Mary Gye's Importance" and related webpages by Kristin C. Hall: alumni.media.mit.edu/~kristin/family/CoolLines/MaryGyeLines.

Details cited concerning Nonconformity in England in the seventeenth century: **Archbishop Laud**, by Hugh Trevor-Roper (London: Phoenix Press, 1988) and **Religion and the Rise of Capitalism**, by R. H. Tawney (Penguin Books, 1966). For Samuel Maverick's activities in Massachusetts: **John Winthrop: America's Forgotten Founding Father**, by Francis J. Bremer (Oxford University Press, 2003). For the sixteenth century Tudor background: the excellent **Henry VIII, The Mask of Royalty**, by Lacey Baldwin Smith (Chicago: Academy, 1982).

What motivated the Pilgrims? David H. Fischer looked at the prevalence of church membership and concluded (1989) that the "spiritual purposes of the colony were fully shared by most men and women in Massachusetts." (**Albion's Seed**, page 40). Fischer seems not to take into account that colonial voting privileges were contingent upon membership in the Congregational Church. Nor does Fischer note that the London financial backers of Plymouth objected to Puritan leaders' enforcement of conformity on a resisting population. The investors in the 1620 *Mayflower* expedition (probably including Cook ancestor **John Beauchamp**) wrote to the leaders at Plymouth Colony, complaining they were "*contentious, cruel and hard hearted, among your neighbors and towards such as in all points, both civil and religious, jump not with you.*" (**All of the Above II**, page 87.) An insistence by Puritan leaders upon religious submission was in tension with the backers' hopes for profits. But everyone agreed on the objective of getting land away from the Indians, for the settlers and their children.

"I WANT TO TELL YOU A GREAT DEAL BUT HAVE NO ROOM"

Marmaduke Moore
Jane Hedges Baldwin

Benjamin Moore (1837-1894)
Mary Baldwin Moore (1863-1936)
John Oliver Taylor Jr (1891-1960)
Betty Taylor Cook (1918-2000)

Jane Hedges Baldwin (1809-1893) grew up in Springfield, Clark County Ohio; **Marmaduke Moore** (1808-1883) near Cynthiana, Harrison County KY. With Baldwin, Moore and Harrison relatives in Clark and Harrison Counties, Duke Moore and Jane Baldwin would have had plenty of family occasions to get acquainted. They were half first-cousins. A portrait by an unknown and probably itinerant (p. 214) artist suggests that little Jane liked kittens, and grew up in a household commodious and affluent enough to accommodate large portraiture.

Jane Hedges Baldwin (1809-1893) was the daughter of **Sarah Scott** (1791-1817?) and **Jonah Baldwin** (1777-1864). Jane's maternal grandmother was also the maternal grandmother of Marmaduke, her husband. This was the one and only **Valette Lyttleton** (1759-1842) whose first husband was **Nicholas Dawson** (1745-1789). That they shared the same grandmother proved no impediment to the marriage of Duke and Jane.

Marmaduke's parents were **William Moore** (1780-1859) and **Elinore/Elinor/Ellen Valette/Violet Dawson** (1781-1834). Elinor's mother was the above mentioned **Valette Lyttleton** (1759-1842). Marmaduke was born into a family tenacious in naming infants for venerable ancestors; he was probably named after his maternal great-grandmother, **Catherine Marmaduke** (?-?). Catherine was the wife of **Lawrence Harrison** (1710-1772) and the mother of **Mary Harrison** (1761-1835), wife of **Thomas Moore** (1745-1823). But there

Jane Hedges Baldwin

were other *Marmadukes* who might have been recalled in the naming of Marmaduke Moore. Descendent Nancy Collier Johnson (1896-1986) wrote in her source notes in 1965 "Copied from notes of R.M. Collier, Cynthiana Kentucky 1965 [. . .] Eleanor Dawson – Descendent of Marmaduke Tilden and Marmaduke Medford [. . .] The Medfords – ancestors through both Moore and Littleton line." Nancy said that Robert Menifee Collier, grandson of William and Elinore and a nephew of Marmaduke, wrote a history of the Moore family in 1898. (Where is this document?)

Marmaduke's first name was shortened in daily usage, to "Duke." He sometimes referred to himself as *M D Moore*. In subsequent family generations he has become *Pappy Duke*.

Duke and Jane were married in Springfield, OH, in 1834 (page 339). From surviving letters, we know that Jane and Duke Moore were close to their Ohio kin. In the 1840's or early '50's Jane wrote to "Mrs Anne E. Baldwin, Springfield, Ohio," with a salutation to "my dear aunt and cousin" (p. 354). Jane pleads for news, begs for a summertime visit, talks of how much she misses everyone in Springfield and sends her love to all but especially "to grandmother and grandfather Baldwin," Jonah and his second wife, Amelia were Anna's grandparents (page 232). There is no mention of her maternal grandmother, Valette Lyttleton Dawson Scott, who died in 1842 (page 337). Jane mentions her oldest daughter Ellen (b: 1834) who "is going to school and is progressing fine, she says." This comment suggests that Ellen might be an adolescent. In a corner of this letter, a different and teasing hand has written, "I want to tell you a great deal but have no room. M. D. Moore."

In a second letter, undated as to the year but written on May the 14th, Jane addresses her sister ("my dear Nancy") taking up much of two pages to explain why her sister ought to write to her. Jane is pleased that her nephews Joseph and James remembered her. Joseph's verbal skills surprised her but little Joseph "astonished me more walking to papa's." Once again her husband

Marmaduke has added a note, running up the side of the page and concluding, "I love all. Your Brother, M.D. Moore"

For a year, they lived at Stony Point, Harrison County KY, where MD's father William Moore had built a log house. From Stony Point, Jane and Duke moved (according to family tradition) to "the Lindsey Farm." Duke was county sheriff. Leaving Kentucky and the farm, in the 1840s they are found in Bellefontaine, Ohio and then in Covington, KY by about 1850. In Covington Duke opened a lumberyard. Great granddaughter Nancy Collier Taylor Johnson has written that the yard burned and was not rebuilt, an event believed to have severely injured the fortunes of the family.

In 1860, the census taker, in a good faith but failed attempt at first name accuracy, listed Marmaduke Moore as "Marma Moore." In this census Duke is given the profession, "master tobacconist." He was at that time a tobacco wholesaler.

With the move to Covington, KY, Marmaduke Moore installed his family in a stately three-story home at Second Street and Garrard. Nancy Moore Johnson records that her great grandparents' home often received out of town guests, with a Moore carriage regularly meeting the train. In the twentieth century, the Moore home, with its iron fence, grillwork front and recessed porches, found its way onto guided tours of Covington, typical of what the newspaper called "the dignity and charm of years gone by." The *gone by* years witnessed slaves in the Moore home. The 1850 Slave Index for Covington lists M D Moore as the owner of two unnamed female slaves, ages 25 and 8, probably mother and daughter.

Duke and Jane Baldwin Moore took family responsibilities seriously, providing home and shelter to orphaned and needy nephews and nieces. Duke's sister Katherine (1815-1851) had married Robert Collier, who like his wife, died young, leaving four small children, James, Nancy, Dick and Elanor.

Marmaduke Moore

I hear a low faint voice that says
"Pa and Ma are dead"
It comes from the poor orphan child
that must be clothed and fed

No doubt, Jane was especially touched by the plight of bereft children. Sarah, her own mother, had died when Jane was not yet ten years old. The Collier children grew up in the Moore's Garrard Street home. They called their uncle, "Pappy Duke," a name used by all of the children in the household, and taken up by grandchildren.

Death frequently cast its disconsolate shadow over the Moore household. Six of the ten children of Duke and Jane Moore died at an early age. Their children were (1) Ellen (Oct 3, 1834-?), who married William Winston and had four children, Lina, William, Marmaduke and Joe; (2) Joseph B. (Jan 24, 1836-Sept 10, 1836); (3) **Benjamin** (March 24, 1837-June 19, 1894), who married **Mary Aurelia Mayo** (1839-1901); (4) Caroline (Dec 3, 1838-Nov 13, 1901); (5) Mary S. (Oct 9, 1840-March 1841); (6) Marmaduke Jr (Aug 20, 1843-Aug 29, 1846); (7) William (Feb 13, 1846-Jan 4, 1847); (8) Jane Baldwin (Aug 9, 1848-?); (9) Martha McDowell (Sept 6, 1851-April 1, 1852); and (10) Sarah Scott (1853-1857). It is as if wee Joseph, Mary, Marmaduke Jr, William, Martha and Sarah peered suspiciously into this world and quickly withdrew:

We do not want your bread, they cried,
Nor do we want your wine
For yonder stands our Savior Lord
In Him we all design.

The causes of the deaths of these infants are no longer known, if ever they were. But the general unhealthiness of that time and place should be noted. Typhoid fever and cholera were prevalent, and were greatly aided by generally poor sanitation. Malaria, spread widely by mosquitoes, was so common that "the shakes" were considered normal. Milk fever, resulting from the consumption by cows of a poisonous weed, was a lethal threat, especially to young children. The standard diet relied heavily on potatoes, fried fat and salt pork. Fruits and vegetables were honored seasonally but not otherwise. Duke and Jane were doubtless comforted in their home by the four orphaned Collier children, surrogates for their own lost six.

How did the Moore household met the Civil War? Little is recalled. In the summer of 1864 Marmaduke Moore was arrested on the authority of the federal military occupation. He is believed to have spent some considerable portion of the rest of the war in a prison for disloyal civilians. Duke could have been held in Louisville, at a federal prison then located on Broadway between Tenth and Eleventh streets. He might have been transferred to Ohio.

Family tradition maintains that Duke's arrest and detention for manifest rebel sympathies was all a mistake. Duke Moore had many personal ties to the free state of Ohio, where he was born and where he had found and married his wife. Until recently there were no known records, which indicated slave ownership by Duke Moore. This absence of data prompted his grandchildren to pass down the thought that Duke was an innocent civilian, a victim of the bloody civil conflict in Kentucky that divided families, cut down passive and active sympathizers of all stripes and ruined the economy for everyone. But the now uncovered fact (reported above) is that the socially prominent Marmaduke Moores were slave owners. This information alone does not explain the military arrest of the elderly, non-combatant Duke Moore. But it is suggestive of a greater investment in the old ways of the South than had been earlier believed.

Union General Jeremiah Boyle, a native of Kentucky, and his successor, General Stephen Gano Burbridge, were responsible in 1863-5 for maintaining order in Kentucky, as Military Commanders of the Commonwealth. To meet this objective, the military command adopted the self-defeating policy of arresting prominent citizens who were known to hold or express vigorous Southern sympathies. The goal was to intimidate that part of the population (perhaps no more than half of the citizenry) to stop their visible support of violent acts of harassment (small arms fire, lynching) that took the lives of federal employees such as mail carriers, slaves working for the military occupation and soldiers on solitary patrol. But the arrests often were carried out without any clear evidence of active and violent resistance to the army or to the state government the army maintained in place.

There is no question that Generals Boyle and Burbridge were facing a widespread and lethal insurgency in Kentucky. Throughout the war, dozens of federal soldiers and 'northern' sympathizers were bushwhacked and killed. But efforts to counter the guerrilla war by the implementation of a program of preemptive arrests of prominent citizens and the retaliatory executions of prisoners surely backfired. Hostility merely increased across the white, civilian south-sympathizing population. After the war ended, Jeremiah Boyle could not return to his native Kentucky and found his exile in Brooklyn, NY. That he was merely following the orders of General Sherman did nothing to repair his reputation in his home state. The bitterness lingered. Kentucky joined the South after the war in fostering repressive, segregationist legislation.

Duke Moore may have been a passive observer of the somber events of the war. He may simply have been caught in Boyle's too-widely cast homeland security net. Justifiable or no, Pappy Duke's incarceration was doubtless a great personal aggravation, probably a humiliation, possibly a threat to his life and certainly an economic catastrophe for this middle-aged man and his family.

The public expression in Kentucky of unpopular opinion was no more welcome before or after the Civil War than during it. Jane and Duke Moore's Covington hometown was a place where the assertion of detested views often was met with vilification, mob violence, night-

Jane Hedges Baldwin Moore

time gunfire and general lawlessness. The outbreak of a shooting war in 1861 only heightened a disorder the war did not create. A cherished southern tradition is to move quickly away from the opinion expressed and focus on the alleged cultural betrayal and low personal qualities of the one whose views are beyond the pale. In the 1850s, this reaction could be sprung like a hair-trigger when the subject was race-and-slavery, race-and-sexuality, race and anything at all. During the 1860s' shooting war, the pendulum swung against white supremacist opinion; afterwards, it swung back the other way, hard.

As before the war, when local law enforcement and the public prosecutor looked indifferently upon vigilante action, so during the war, an army of occupation, confronting a bloody insurgency, adopted a blanket arrest approach, bypassing local courts. After the formal ending of hostilities, the region descended even further into terror, with the emergence of semi-secret armed groups, who proclaimed an illusory vision of the "old South" and imposed a return to White rule by way of whippings, shootings and lynchings of freed slaves and others. All this occurred even though twice as many Kentuckians served in the federal army as had served in Rebel ranks. Duke and Jane Moore's views on these events are no longer known.

Duke Moore lived until August 8, 1883, dying of a "stone in the bladder and exhaustion." Jane Baldwin Moore died at age 83 in 1892. Jane suffered from cataracts as did her father, **Jonah Baldwin** (1777-1864/5) and her grandmother, **Vallette Lyttleton Dawson Scott** (1759-1842). Jane and Duke Moore were buried in the old Linden Grove Cemetery, on Holman Street, in Covington, KY. A visit to the cemetery in June 2006 by their great, great granddaughter Jean Valette Taylor and other relatives, found broken headstones but no sign of Duke and Jane.

Moore, an Irish name, also has an English origin. An etymological inquiry is resolved unsatisfactorily. Surmises are based on frequency of usage. The name is among the twentieth most common in Ireland, they say. Old Irish *Moore* is traced to *O'Mordha* (great), from the

Gaelic. *Moore* may also be Welsh, for big (*mawr*) man. But *Moore* is also ranked by the name-rankers as among the fortieth most common names in England. The English Moore (also *More*) derives from the Anglo-Saxon *mor* (marsh), first applied, in 1086, as the name of a dweller in or near a marsh (*moor*) or (perhaps) of a resident of the town of Moore in Cheshire. This early More might have been Saxon rather than Norman. Then there is the use of *Moor* in France or Spain (*moro*) for someone of dark complexion. Don't know any Moore than that.

The etymology of *Marmaduke* seems a bit more straightforward. The experts tell us the name is derived from Old Irish, *Mael Maedoc*, which means "a disciple of Saint Maedoc," an Irish saint of the 6th century, not to be confused, certainly, with St. Madoc of Wales or with St. Modoc of the 3rd or 4th centuries.

SOURCES:

Moore, Baldwin, Scott genealogy: Betty Taylor Cook's unpublished genealogy book. Robert Menifee Collier's 1898 history of the Moore family was probably a main source.

Details of life in Covington and listing of Duke and Jane Moore's children: Anne Carter Moffett Gibbs, who credits Mayo Moore Taylor (1893-1980), Duke and Jane Moore's great grandson. In 1979, Anne created a document from Mayo's notes and records, and shared it with me.

We do not want your bread, they cried: from "The Three Little Babes," or "The Wife of Usher's Well," #79 in Francis James Child's **English and Scottish Popular Ballads** (1882-1898); also transcribed from Appalachian singing, 1924-54, by Patrick W. Gainer, **Folk Songs from the West Virginia Hills** (Seneca Books: Grantsville, W V 1975).

Cause of death of Marmaduke Moore: investigated and reported by descendent, Elizabeth Taylor Rubio, triple great granddaughter of Jane Hedges and Marmaduke Moore.

I hear a low faint voice that says "Pa and Ma are dead" - Lyrics from A.P. Carter, *"Poor Orphan Child"*

For the etymology of the Moore name: The Etymology of Last Names at EnglishWiz.com; see also AUTOBIOGRAPHY OF FLORENCE (MOORE) WILBER: freepages.genealogy.rootsweb.com/~lynn5/page3.

Note to 'Rilla Mayo Moore, on the death of her husband, Benjamin Moore (pp. 120-122, 125, 218)

June 22, 1894

My dear sister Rilla,

There is but little consolation in this your hour of grief and sorrow, but it is in your power and not mine, to ask Him who holds all our lives in the hollow of his hand, to give you health and strength to bear the grief that is weighing you down at this time. I often wish that I was made of the same stuff that my sisters are, to be able to call on a higher power for aid and comfort, as I know they do and is often a great help to them in hours of great trials and troubles, as it is with you at this time . . . Give my love to Minnie and Mayo [his brother] and others of the family. Hoping to hear the particulars of poor Ben's sickness, etc, soon.

Your affectionate brother,

Dudley [Daniel Dudley Mayo, see page 277]
Denver, Colorado

"A REMARKABLE MEMORY OF CIRCUMSTANCES AND DATES"

Jonah Baldwin
Sarah Scott

Jane Hedges Baldwin Moore (1809-1893)
Benjamin Moore (1837-1894)
Mary Baldwin Moore (1863-1936)
John Oliver Taylor Jr (1891-1960)
Betty Taylor Cook (1918-2000)

In 1804, **Jonah Baldwin** (1777-1864/5) made his way to Clark County in central Ohio, on the Western frontier. Born during the War for Independence, Jonah would live to see the Civil War. Although 83 when the war began, he took an active interest in it.

Jonah probably journeyed to Ohio from his parents' home in Berkeley County, in present day West Virginia. Jonah was one of seven children of **William Baldwin** (abt 1716-1785) and **Jane Hedges** (1752-aft 1785). It is believed all of these children were born after William Baldwin moved from Pennsylvania to Virginia. Since Hedges family members were in the panhandle in the 1770s (then, Augusta County VA), it is probable Jane Hedges was living with her parents before meeting the much older widower, William Baldwin.

William Baldwin was a tanner. Jonah learned the trade of saddlery, no doubt from his father, but Jonah never worked at this trade in Ohio. In Clark County, Jonah became a farmer and rancher, first near New Moorefield, buying and selling cattle and driving them himself to markets east of Springfield, and perhaps to the river town of Cincinnati. Jonah was also a surveyor, a likely indication of the high quality of his (Episcopal?) schooling. He was employed off and on in laying out roads in Ohio and Indiana.

Young Jonah attended private school in Winchester, Virginia. His early education formed in Jonah

Jonah Baldwin

the habit of reading, a habit he followed and recommended throughout his life. To speak of Jonah's regular practice of reading, invites us to remember that Jonah lived and died before electricity would have enabled him to illuminate his home. Jonah read by fire, candle or perhaps lamp light. He developed eye trouble; perhaps faint indoor lighting was the culprit.

Jonah Baldwin built the first two-story house in Springfield. This residence also served as a tavern. Although a tavern owner, Jonah was recalled as temperate and even hostile to alcohol. From his tavern-owning days to his death, Jonah's views on alcohol might have changed. In 1871, six years after Jonah's death, local historian John Ludlow of Springfield, Ohio, spoke of Jonah Baldwin as strict, honest, conscientious and possessing considerable "natural ability" including "a remarkable memory of circumstances and dates." Jonah's early schooling in Virginia may have been sponsored by the Episcopal Church. He was a member of the first Episcopal vestry in Springfield; that first church was located on the southwest corner of High and Limestone Streets.

Jonah travelled widely as a surveyor. In 1824, he was commissioned by the federal government to survey a post road from the unincorporated town of Chicago to Detroit. The survey was published in 1825, as *The Plat of the United States Road from Detroit to Chicago, as surveyed and marked by James McClosky, Jonah Baldwin, and Laureat Durocher, C'om.s, copied by John Farmer,* (1825).

An 1876 history of Porter County, Indiana (relying on early reports) records, "*The road surveyed between Detroit and Fort Dearborn was merely a verification of the old Indian trail across the Southern Lake region. Landmarks were established, a few bridges, strongly built of unhewn timbers, were thrown across some streams, a few hillsides were graded, and little else was done or needed. The trail was established upon ground naturally firm and solid. It avoided quagmires and other obstacles, and as the only vehicle to pass over it was the mail* wagon--a sort of buckboard, guiltless of springs, drawn by Indian ponies--which came one week and returned the next, no deep wheel ruts marked the still unbroken sod."

The surveyed road was soon constructed. The earliest users of the new road were soldiers, who carried the mail in knapsacks. In 1832, soldiers and civilians, including Abraham Lincoln, participated in the so-called "Black Hawk War," and marched over the route. A year later, stage coaches were carrying passengers and baggage three times a week. Jonah Baldwin's surveying activity was recalled in the family, as the following letter indicates.

A Bit of History

I have been reading of the great growth of Chicago and I thought I would tell what I remember.

My father Jonah Baldwin was appointed to survey a road from Chicago to Detroit when there was not a building at Chicago except Ft. McKensie [Fort Dearborn]. General McKensie was there at the time with soldiers. It was the year eighteen twenty four.

I know it was the same year that General Lafayette last visited the United States. My sister, a young girl at the time, was visiting a friend in Pennsylvania. They gave a reception to the General. She was introduced. He shook hands with her and made some remark. I have forgotten what it was. She always thought it an honor. My sister was Mrs. Duke Moore of Covington, Ky. Has been dead three years.

My father always predicted a great future for Chicago - said it would be one of the great cities of the west.

If you think this is worth publishing, I would be glad.

Yours respectfully,

Mrs. N.E. Perrin
(in her 83rd year of age, 1896)

This letter was written by Jonah's daughter, Nancy Baldwin (Mrs Joseph) Perrin (1813-?), Harrison County, KY. By then, Chicago had a population of some 500,000, a startling rise from the 3,000 or so, who lived in Chicago when Jonah Baldwin conducted the survey of the Chicago-Detroit road seventy-two years before.

SARAH SCOTT BALDWIN

Jonah's wife, **Sarah Scott** (1791-1817) fourteen in 1805, moved in that year with her parents, **Solomon Scott** (?-?) and his (second) wife **Valette (Violet) Lyttleton (Dawson)** (1759-1842), to Springfield. Jonah and Sarah married, presumably in her parents' home in Pleasant Township and presumably by 1809, when their daughter **Jane Hedges Baldwin** (1809-1893) was born. Local historian John Ludlow stated in 1871 that the marriage took place in 1809. Graham's 1881 **History of Clark County**, with a section devoted to Pleasant Township written by James Arborgast, states the marriage occurred around 1805-07.

Sarah was raised in the Anglican faith by Valette, her mother, who likely would have insisted on an Episcopalian wedding for her daughter and would have taken whatever steps necessary to accomplish this, as she did when her daughter **Eleanor Dawson** married **William Moore**. (Page 253.) Jonah, himself also an Episcopalian, likely would have made arrangements for a priest to be on hand just as his father-in-law had done for Eleanor in the backwoods of Kentucky in 1804.

At her marriage, Sarah would have been sixteen or so, Jonah a surprising thirty or thirty-one. Why did Jonah Baldwin not marry sooner? He is known to have arrived in Springfield a single man in 1804. Arriving single invites the thought that Jonah had married earlier in Virginia but then was widowed.

After her marriage to Jonah, Sarah Baldwin, in her brief life, probably never lived away from Springfield except in nearby New Moorefield. If she had lived, Sarah might have visited Philadelphia in 1824, with her daughter, **Jane Hedges** (named for her father's mother) when young Jane met the Marquis de Lafayette. The old general was making his grand finale tour of the country he had helped to found a half-century before. But Sarah Scott Baldwin was dead by 1824. Jonah had remarried in 1823 (see below). There is a slight piece of material evidence that Sarah had died in 1817. For close to 200 years, the family has cherished an ancient, framed, cloth "sampler," of a headstone which contains the embroidered words, "In memory of S. Baldwin 1817." This is a bit of sewing done (we assume) by a daughter, to keep close the memory of her mother, dead when Jane was no more than eight or nine years old.

As with so many frontier women, Sarah Scott Baldwin is a cipher to us. She is known to her descendents only through marriage and childbirth. She and Jonah had three children, **Jane Hedges** (1809-1893), Nancy, and Joseph. Sarah remains all the more behind a shade drawn by history because she died at 26, before her children could remember her and her descendents might venerate her.

Nothing of Sarah's dying has been passed down to us. Perhaps she died in childbirth. Perhaps she died at the mercy of some infection or illness, routinely defeated today by treatments then unknown. In the failing light of her own life, did Sarah call Jonah to her and make him promise he would find a good woman to raise her babies? Such desperate pleas must have been common in frontier Ohio. Far too many young mothers closed their eyes on little ones only just aware that *mama is a'bed*. Far too many little girls and boys on the frontier lost the memory of a mother who would laugh at their antics, smooth their tangled curls and wipe away their tears.

As mentioned, Sarah learned her observances from her mother **Vallette Lyttleton Dawson Scott** (1759-1842). Valette insisted a priest be present when her daughter Elenor married Kentuckian William Moore in 1804. Solomon Scott, Vallette's second husband and step-father of the bride, traveled 30 miles to find a priest and bring him back to preside at the Blue Lick, KY nuptials.

Valette and Solomon Scott, Sarah and Jonah Baldwin surely were counted among the "wandering lambs" of the Episcopal Church, so described by the first Bishop of Ohio, Philander Chase (1775-1852). These words are found in Bishop Chase's appeals, in a mostly failed attempt to raise funds and priests for Ohio from the eastern states. Did Sarah Scott Baldwin, dying in a tiny village in the Ohio wilderness, meet her death without the ministrations of an Episcopal priest? Seventeen long years would pass from Sarah's death in 1817 before there would be an Episcopal church in Springfield.

For our **Sarah Scott Baldwin**, we make the sign of the Cross, which she learned from her mother. This sign was her seal both of solace in this life and assurance of a future one. This sign Sarah shared too briefly with Jonah two hundred years ago. May this forever young mother, our ancestor, pray for us now and in the hour of our death.

After Sarah died, Jonah remarried. His new wife was Amelia Needham (?-?), a daughter of Dr. William A. Needham, who came from Vermont to Springfield, Ohio in 1814, and practiced medicine there until his death in 1832. Jonah and Amelia married in 1823. A record of early Springfield settlers states that Jonah Baldwin's wife (unnamed) was the first person confirmed in the first Episcopal Church in Springfield. This first church was the Parish of All Souls, organized on December 7, 1834, and renamed Christ Church, at Christmas, 1841. These dates indicate that Jonah's wife who was the first person confirmed in Springfield would have been Amelia.

In 1827, Amelia and Jonah moved to King's Creek in Champaign County where Jonah conducted a large stock operation. In 1835, Jonah and Amelia returned to Springfield and in 1839, to Pleasant Township.

Jonah and Amelia were the parents of five children, Sarah, Mary, Minerva, Bettie and Henry, with Jonah the father of a total of eight. Note the first of Amelia's babies: Sarah Baldwin; did Amelia permit Jonah to name their first child for his first wife? Their only son and youngest child, Henry Baldwin, married Maria Dawson. A daughter of Henry and Maria was Anna Baldwin (?-?), family historian of the Dawson, Lyttleton and Baldwin lines.

EARLY SPRINGFIELD

Over the first two decades of the nineteenth century, Clark County Ohio became dotted with villages. Settlers pushed overland following the buffalo trails and Indian traces across the Alleghenies and continuing on into Ohio Territory. Perhaps more commonly, they floated down the Ohio River, to Losantville (renamed, thankfully, Cincinnati) and then overland, northeast, eighty miles to Springfield village. In imagination, one may sense something of the excitement of new possibilities these families must have felt, as they floated down the widest and longest river they had seen in their lives, taking in on both riversides, vast meadows and vaster forests, all, to them, untouched and open. Their parents had won a Revolution. They would win the wilderness.

Jonah's niece, Eli, married James Dunn in 1801 in Washington County, MD. In about 1810, they moved to Warren County Ohio. Their grandson, Frank, has left this written reminiscence: *"Grandfather came down the Ohio River from Wheeling, (now West) Virginia, to Cincinnati on a flatboat ... They came in the autumn ... The river was low and there were six weeks making the trip. The boat would stick on the sand bars."*

The process of the settlement of Springfield had begun in the spring of 1795 when two members of a survey party, David Lowry and Jonathan Donnel, became excited at the quality of the land in this region northeast of Fort Washington, built in 1789 on the Ohio River, to protect 'Losantville.' On returning to Ft. Washington, they partnered with Patten Shorts, who had already purchased and entered the land they were interested in and who needed surveying services to determine the boundaries of his property. Lowry and Donnell moved fast. By autumn, 1795, they were established on their lands.

Other sojourners in early Clark County included father and son, **Thomas Moore** (1745-1823) (p. 251) and **William Moore** (1780-1859) (p. 257). Their interest in central Ohio may have been stirred by Thomas' military service under Anthony Wayne or George Rogers Clark. Although the Moores were in the Springfield area frequently enough to have figured in its earliest history (conference with Tecumseh, p. 237, below), to refer to either of them as a "settler" of Clark County is probably inaccurate. In 1799, a William Moore joined Samuel Kenton and three others – all from Kentucky – who established New Moorefield Township in Clark County. This Moore may be William, son of Thomas, although he would have been only nineteen years old in 1799.

Many Moores settled in Clark County Ohio but by the early 1800's Thomas and William and their families were established south of the Ohio River, in Harrison County Kentucky. This was the site of a large concession of land made to Thomas Moore. The Kentucky land probably had been a grant to Thomas by virtue of his service to VA Governor Dunmore, in a boundary dispute with Pennsylvania (page 262). Family ties to Kentucky were strong with the Moores. Harrison County was named for Thomas Moore's brother-in-law, Benjamin Harrison (1750-1808), brother of Thomas Moore's wife (and William's mother), **Mary Harrison** (1761-1835).

Extended family relations continued to draw the Moores back to Ohio from Kentucky. Doubtless William brought son, Marmaduke, from Harrison County, KY to Clarke County OH. The travel was frequent enough for Marmaduke to have met his half-first cousin, **Jane Baldwin**, whom he married in Clark County. William and Elenor Moore of Harrison County KY and Jonah Baldwin of Springfield lived to see the Jan 1834 wedding of their children, **Marmaduke Moore** (1808-1883) and **Jane Hedges Baldwin** (1809-1893). For Elenor Moore, this wedding would be one of the final family celebrations of her life, for 1834 was also the year of her death. It is not known if she was well enough to attend.

Jonah Baldwin, suffering with cataracts

An early Clark County history records as few as fourteen families in Springfield when **Jonah Baldwin** arrived in 1804. By 1810, a small number of English-speaking settlements had been established. Clark County, incorporated in 1818, was named for General George Rogers Clark, who opened the region for settlement. In Aug 1780, Clark came upriver from Louisville, with 1,000 men and destroyed the nearby Shawnee town of Piqua (pages 239, 256). Who could have foreseen how completely would be the transformation of the old Shawnee territory?

A hand written note in Clark County archives preserved the information that in 1820 the population of the hamlet of Springfield had increased to 510. These few early arrivals continued the far-sighted planning of the surveyors Lowry and Donnell. In 1818, the year of the county's incorporation, leading citizens of Springfield offered to subscribe $2,215 for the construction of the county Courthouse.

The subscribers knew a courthouse would mean attentions from the legislature, a higher community profile, regular government employment. With a courthouse Springfield would become the residence of a judge or two as well as home to lawyers and clerks. Perhaps of most importance, a courthouse would mean quotidian traffic to and from Springfield for anyone in Clark County who needed to register land, apply for a marriage license, or conduct any other routine legal business. This would, in turn, mean banking and land title services would be needed. As a consequence, surveyors and other businesses would be drawn to the town. Springfield got the courthouse, with Jonah Baldwin subscribing $100. In that same year Jonah Baldwin was elected one of three of the original trustees of Springfield Township. In 1823, Jonah was elected a grand juror.

Even before he helped subscribe and build the courthouse in 1818, Jonah Baldwin was seen as a founding community leader of the hamlet of Springfield. On January 11, 1812, he was elected Justice of the Peace, thereafter conducting official business from his tavern.

In 1834, a number of male citizens of Clark County, Ohio petitioned the federal government to re-charter the National Bank, which President Andrew Jackson had closed. The signatures of *Solomon Scott* and *Joseph Baldwin* appear on the petition. This Joseph is probably Jonah's son, whose wife Eliza Bacon was a daughter of John Bacon, president of the First National Bank of Springfield. The 1820 federal census places Joseph Baldwin in Clark County. Solomon Scott, also a petition signer, could be Solomon Scott, father of Sarah Scott Baldwin, although he would probably have reached at least eighty years of age by 1834. The petition was an endorsement of the Henry Clay-lead Whig Party's opposition to President Andrew Jackson's revocation of the charter of the Bank of the United States. Alarmed that the closure of the central bank would cut off their access to credit and cheapen their money, the petitioners stated that *"the wealth of our county consists almost entirely in its agricultural productions"* and is *"the source of the little wealth we possess . . . We pray, therefore, that the public moneys of the United States be restored to the safe keeping of the Bank of the United States; and that Congress do extend the resent [sic] charter of the Bank of the United States . . . ."* This appeal from Clark County Ohio fell on the deaf ears of President Jackson, who refused to renew the bank's charter or restore federal money to it.

ENGLISH SETTLERS vs. THE SHAWNEE

The founding Clark County surveyors, David Lowry and Jonathan Donnell, had good reason to move fast into the region they wanted for farmland. On their first visit, the land was occupied, if intermittently, by the Shawnee. The two surveyors no doubt suspected and hoped that a wave of humanity was headed into Ohio from Pennsylvania, Virginia and other eastern points. Soon enough, the great wave did, indeed, hit Clark County and with such force the land itself was forever changed.

In 1807, although a newcomer to the community (but who wasn't?), **Jonah Baldwin** was designated a Commissioner to represent the community in a council with Tecumseh. A record of this council states, *"One of the Commissioners in the council with Tecumseh held in the village in 1801 [1807] was Jonah Baldwin, who was selected because of his sound judgment and excellent character."* In addition to Jonah Baldwin, another of the Commissioners was the previously mentioned Maj. **Thomas Moore**. (See page 257.)

The Commission had been convened to determine the circumstances of the murder of one of the White settlers:

"The council assembled in Sugar Grove. that then stood on or near Main Street, opposite the Foos tavern. Two bands of Indians attended the council, one from the north in charge of McPherson; the other, consisting of sixty or seventy braves, came from the neighborhood of Fort Wayne under the charge of Tecumseh. Roundhead. Blackfish and other chiefs were also present. There was no friendly feeling between these two parties; and each was willing that the blame of the outrages should be fixed upon the other. The party under McPherson, in compliance with the request of the Commissioners, left their weapons a few miles from Springfield. But Tecumseh and his party refused to attend the council unless permitted to retain their arms. The reason Tecumseh gave was that his tomahawk contained his pipe and he might have occasion to smoke. After the conference was opened, the Commissioners, fearing some violence still, made another effort to have Tecumseh lay aside his weapon. This he positively refused to do. At this moment, Dr. Richard Hunt, a tall, slim young man recently from Pennsylvania, and a boarder at Foos' tavern, thinking to reconcile matters with Tecumseh, cautiously approached and handed the chief an old long-stemmed earthen pipe intimating that if he would give up his tomahawk, he might smoke the aforesaid pipe. Tecumseh took the pipe

between his thumb and finger, held it up, looked at it for a moment, then at the owner, who was gradually receding from the point of danger, and with an indignant sneer immediately threw it over his head into the bushes. The Commissioners then yielded the point and proceeded to business.

"After a full and patient inquiry into the facts of the case, it appeared that the murder of Myers was the act of a single Indian, and not chargeable to either band of the Indians. Several speeches were made by the chiefs, the most prominent of which were those by Tecumseh. He gave a satisfactory explanation of the action of himself and the Prophet in calling around them a band of Indians; disavowed all hostile intentions toward the United States, and denied that either he or those under his control had committed any depredations upon the whites. His manner of speaking was animated, fluent and rapid, and, when understood, very forcible.

"The council then terminated. During its session, the two tribes of Indians became reconciled to each other, and peace and quiet was gradually restored to the settlement. The Indians remained in Springfield for three days, amusing themselves in various feats of activity and strength such as jumping, running and wrestling, in which Tecumseh generally excelled. At this time, Tecumseh was in the thirty-eighth year of his age, five feet ten inches high, with erect body, well developed and of remarkable muscular strength. His weight was about one hundred and seventy pounds. There was something noble and commanding in all his actions. Tecumseh was a Shawnese; the native. Pronunciation of the name was Tecumtha, signifying 'The Shooting Star.' He was brave, generous and humane in all his actions."

This charitable assessment of Tecumseh might not have been shared by many English-speaking settlers on the Ohio and Indiana frontier. For years after the gathering in Springfield, Tecumseh led Shawnee and other tribes in opposition to the loss of hunting grounds and the destruction of Indian towns. Of the two, the future of Ohio and of the continent belonged not to Tecumseh and the "Originals" but to Jonah Baldwin and his kin and neighbors.

But Tecumseh did his best. In 1780, at age 12, he was present at the Shawnee defeat at Piqua in central Ohio. He spent the rest of his life attempting to rally Shawnee and other tribes against the encroachments of European settlers. His brother Tenskwatawa (better known as "the Prophet") developed a theology, which emphasized a monotheistic Creator. The Prophet preached repentance to the aboriginal peoples, who might then prove worthy recipients of a divine restoration of their ancestral lands.

Tecumseh tirelessly visited eastern tribes from Georgia to Michigan, urging unity and a refusal to sign away lands. Many tribal chiefs, however, were in debt to traders for weapons and other items. They were willing to have their debts written off in exchange for signing a paper, which purported merely to grant access to lands they might themselves continue to occupy. The traders then used these deed documents to win favor from state governments, eager to have any writing, which might justify an extension of state sovereignty over the western regions their citizens were anxious to exploit. Similarly, after defeat in war, a chief, said to be acting in the name of one or more tribes, would be pressed to sign a treaty opening lands to settlement. Such was the Treaty of Greenville in 1795 between certain defeated and terminally weakened tribal groups, who could be said by their conquerors to be a defeated "nation." General Anthony Wayne signed for the United States and announced the agreement as a treaty.

Greenville generally opened Ohio for settlement but Tecumseh refused to acknowledge the Treaty and denounced it. Shawnee and other tribal resistance to the settlement of Ohio continued intermittently for fifteen more years. A definite end to Indian opposition was finally reached with General William Henry Harrison's victory at Tippecanoe, Indiana Territory, in 1811.

Tecumseh was an ally of the British during the War

of 1812 (the "second War with England"). He was killed in the Battle of the Thames, Ontario, Canada in 1813. This battle marked the complete defeat of the Shawnee in North America, who, with other Indians, fought desperately while British soldiers surrendered wholesale without fighting at all. Notably, **Anthony Crockett**, (1756-1838) an ancestor of **Cecil Virgil Cook Jr** (1913-1970), husband of family historian, **Betty Taylor Cook** (1918-2000), fought in the Battle of the Thames. Afterwards, Crockett returned to Frankfort, KY, an honored, victorious veteran and resumed his duties as Sergeant of Arms in the state legislature.

A TOWN IN A HURRY TO CREATE ITSELF

The 1852 Springfield City Directory serves as a convenient benchmark for Springfield compared to its early years. By 1852, the population of Springfield was 5,567. In that year, the city directory reported several taverns, a railroad and railroad station, a cotton mill, oil mill, flour mill, machine shop, print shop, two newspapers, and two banks, as well as the courthouse. Wittenberg College was chartered by the Ohio legislature in the winter of 1844-45 and was located just outside of town.

The entire community was in a hurry, nineteenth century style. Everyone wanted to *better* themselves and make an improved community for their children. Everyone had decided the way to do this was to found something or join something. By 1852, there was in Springfield, a lending library, and a high school, where French was taught. These institutions may have seemed rough by later standards but not if compared to the earliest schools, which were nostalgically described in 1881:

Clad in the home-spun of the times, and generally barefooted, the children at short and irregular intervals attended the schools in the cabin schoolhouses, which were built by a few persons, each donating a certain amount of labor, and a stated number of logs. The houses were beyond question ill adapted for the purpose for which they were designed. Instead of glass for the windows, pieces of oiled paper were used.

Rude benches served as seats; and to add to the too numerous discomforts, the cold in winter - as this was before the introduction of stoves - was by no means agreeable.

Great severity was used in the school government, and it was no uncommon thing for young men even to receive the most severe corporal punishment.

That no transgressor might lose his reward, the instruments of correction, gathered with care from the adjacent thicket, were constantly kept in full view; and with these the schoolboy was urged forward along "the flowery path of knowledge."

There may have been many schoolmasters then, but there certainly were few teachers, for the methods of that day, if they did not utterly repress, at least must have checked the loftiest aspirations that belong to youth.

Text-books were few and imperfect. The beginner learned the alphabet from a thin piece of wood, upon which the letters were printed. The first lessons in reading were learned from the Testament.

The schools were maintained by subscription, the tuition being about $2 per scholar for a "quarter," consisting of sixty-five days.

A number of circumstances conspired to render the education of the young very defective. First, the tuition for even a small family could ill be spared from the scanty savings accumulated by the most rigid economy; and secondly, that the assistance of each member of the family was demanded; lands were to be cleared, rails made, and fences built, crops planted, cultivated and harvested.

Books and papers were exceedingly scarce; the American Preceptor, the English Reader and the Testament, were generally the literary treasures of the family.

In Springfield by 1852, there was also a female seminary, as well as the Greenway Boarding School for Boys. The town could boast of at least eight churches and two newspapers. A temperance paper, *The Moss Covered Bucket*, had been started in 1847 but discontinued after six issues. There were two literary societies, the "Excelsior" and the "Philosopohian" in addition to the Springfield Lyceum, which offered regular lectures in the winter months. By 1852 there existed a Springfield Branch of the Ohio State Medical Society. A bewildering number of secret and semi-secret societies and social clubs met regularly. These included the Odd Fellows, Masons, the Mad River Encampment, the Temple of Honor, the Social Degree, and the Ancient Order of Perdons.

Jonah Baldwin tried the secret society of the Masons but apparently dropped out. In 1809, he and Samuel Simonton attended an organizational meeting of Masons in Urbana. This lodge alternated its meetings between Urbana, Dayton and Springfield, but the difficulty of travel prompted the Springfield and Urbana Masons to seek their own charter and lodge, which was granted in 1810. After 1815, the members from Springfield applied for a charter under the name Morning Star Lodge, No. 27. The charter was granted in 1818, but there is no record of any meetings or of any participation by Jonah Baldwin after the earlier dates.

The City Directory enumerated, located and published the hours of operation of the organizations in this fledgling Ohio community, where founding something or joining something seems to have been a civic and social obligation. Not being a joiner, Tecumseh had no chance.

Over the next hundred years, any vital memory of the earlier hunter-gatherers of the Ohio Territory was as effectively erased as were the peoples themselves. Gone into eternity with them were clan memories of the harmonies and the dissonances of a world they had occupied for ten thousand years. Soon enough, no one was left who could recall with pride the victory of the Miami Indians in October 1791. This event occurred on the banks of the Wabash River, when Little Turtle, their greatest military leader and his warriors – already victors in 1790 over an American army – engaged in hand-to-hand combat with American militia and regular soldiers. The Miami were fighting in defiance of what, to them, was incomprehensible: *ownership* of the land and its rivers such as the Wabash, where the clans and the buffalo, deer, fox and turkey had come down from the hills to drink for uncountable centuries. The desperate battle Little Turtle conducted on the banks of the Wabash sent the English-speaking survivors into a chaotic retreat. The victory was probably as sweet to the aboriginal conquerors as it was short lived. By the twentieth century, Hoagy Carmichael and Sidney Arodin could write with jaunty innocence about the "lazy hazy" river of blessed but selective memory.

> *Up a lazy river by the old mill stream*
> *That lazy, hazy river where we both can dream*
> *Linger in the shade of an old oak tree*
> *Throw away your troubles, dream a dream*
> *with me*
>
> *Up a lazy river where the robin's song*
> *Wakes up in the mornin', as we roll along*
> *Blue skies up above . . . everyone's in love*
> *Up a lazy river, how happy we will be, now*
> *Up a lazy river with me*

HEDGES AND BALDWIN ANCESTORS

Jonah Baldwin's parents were **William Baldwin** (abt 1716-1785) and **Jane Hedges** (1752-aft 1785). William Baldwin was born in Chester County PA and died Sept 7, 1785 in Berkeley County, West Virginia (then part of Virginia). William was married twice and fathered a total of 14 children. His first wife was Mary _____ (1723-abt 1771), who bore William seven children. After her death, he married **Jane Hedges** in 1773. They also had seven children, including **Jonah** (1777-1864). When they married, William Baldwin was 57 and Jane Hedges, 21.

In 1750-51, William and Mary Baldwin moved from Chester to near Winchester, VA. Brother Frances Baldwin moved also, a relocation which coincides with the opening of land offices in western PA and VA, to accommodate thousands of colonists and immigrants, moving west from Chester, Lancaster, Bedford and York Counties, PA. William was a son of **Thomas Baldwin** and **Mary Beal**, married on March 20, 1714, at St. Paul's Episcopal Church in Chester. Thomas' parents were **Frances Baldwin** (?-1712) and **Cicely Coebourne**, of Chester, PA. Francis and brothers, Thomas and John, were from Oxford shire, England, sons of **Mary** _____ and **William Baldwin**.

Jane Hedges, second wife of William Baldwin, was a daughter of **Agnes Powelson** (abt 1720-aft 1804). Her father was **Jonah Hedges** (?-?). Jonah Hedges' mother was **Catherine Stalcop** (1688-1749) of Newcastle City, DE, granddaughter of Swedish immigrant **John Stalcop** (aka **Andersson**) (?-?), who reached America (New Sweden) in Nov, 1641, on the ship *Charitas*. John's wife was **Christina Jonsson/Carlsdotter**, from Finland.

Jonah's father was English immigrant **Joseph Hedges** (?-1732), who died in Monocacy, Maryland. Joseph's father was **Charles Gent Hedges** (?-1730) who died in England not long before Joseph's own death in America. Charles Gent Hedges was the son of **Sir Charles Hedges** (1649-1712/14), who graduated from Doctors College Oxford in 1675.

The Hedges of England are a well remembered clan whose presence on that island began with the Norman Conquest in 1066. As with much medieval genealogy, we are dependent upon the common occurrence of surnames, the common use of first names and the coincidences of location as the sum of our knowledge. This is the Hedges case, to a tee. The Hedges of Cornwall were known as de Lacy (de Laci) in the early records. For centuries, they were either *de Lacy* or *de Lacy alias Hedges*. Beginning in the 1600's it is all Hedges and no more de Lacy.

Before the Conquest, back in Normandy, the brothers Walter and Ilbert de Lacy held eight estates. Normandy itself had been acquired in a bold act of piracy by Rollo the Viking in 911. Piratical habits die hard, if at all.

Who could have been surprised when William, nicknamed "the Conqueror," and the wealthy but greedy Norman lords with him turned to England and Ireland for enlargements upon their property? Rollo the Viking was their ancestor and role model.

Hugh de Lacy went to England with William and was given Dublin Castle (and dungeon). If you think you cannot read this snippet from the Song of Dermot (1172), try it out loud:

> Li riche rei ad dunc baille
> Dyvelin er garde la cite
> E la chastel e le dongun
> A Hugh de Laci le Barun

And we're off! Roger de Lacy (1179-1211) was Constable of Chester. John de Lacy (?-1249), Earl of Lincoln, was one of twenty-five Barons, who forced the Magna Carta upon King John at Runnymede in 1215. John's cousin, Roger de Vere, Earl of Oxford, was also at Runnymede. Henry de Lacy (?-1312) was made Earl of Lincoln in 1272. Notable and loyal Catholics, the de Lacy/Hedges family saw their holdings in Ireland much reduced when Oliver Cromwell confiscated the entire country in 1549. But in the Restoration, the Lacy/Hedges were restored. Charles II knighted two of the clan and the family could thereafter be found either in their seat in Youghal, County Cork or at Burton Burks or Wiltshire, or in London. They were also in possession of Wallingford Castle, Clapcot, and Berkshire.

John Lacy alias Hedges (?-1594), Berkshire, had one daughter (who did not count as a holder of any property) and three sons. Their names and property: William (1571-1645): Kingsdowne, Wiltshire; Richard (1583-1640): Stratton, St Margaret; and **Henry** (?-?): Burton, Burkshire. John's son, William of Wiltshire, had (who cares how many) daughters and five sons. Their names and their properties are: John Lacy alias Hedges (24 Feb 1597-?): Kingsdowne; Thomas Lacy alias Hedges

(1601-?): Wiltshire in 1626); Robert Lacy alias Hedges (1604-1670): Yougal, Cork; William Lacy alias Hedges (1615-1645): Cheney Wilts; and Tobit Lacy alias Hedges (1618-1645). Tobit Lacy alias Hedges, as you might have noticed, had no holdings; there were too few properties for too many sons. Thank goodness for the New World and Catholic Lord Baltimore's proprietorship of a piece of it. But poor Tobit died too young to make his plans.

John's son Robert Hedges (of Cork) had daughters and two remembered sons: Sir William Hedges (1632-1701) was Sheriff of London. Robert Hedges (1637-1687), seated at Burrows, Queens, in Ireland, had several daughters and three sons: Robert Hedges (1658-1689), William Hedges (1671-?) and Richard Hedges (1668-?), seated at Macroom Castle, Cork. John Hedges (1688-1737), son of Sir William, was a Member of Parliament.

Henry Lacy alias Hedges (?-?), Berkshire, son of **John Lacy alias Hedges** (?-1594), had one son and heir, **Henry Hedges** (?-?) of Wanborough, Wiltshire, who was the father of two sons, Henry Hedges (1651-1689) and Sir **Charles Hedges** (1649-1712). Sir Charles was Secretary of State to Queen Anne (1665-1714; Queen: 1702-1714). This was back in the day when the Secretary of State was a secretary. A note has been preserved. Queen Anne to Sir Charles: "send me some good pens, for those I have are soe bad I can hardly make them writt." Difficulty with the pens may have been the tipping point for Sir Charles' grandson, **Joseph Hedges** (?-1732), who came, as we have seen, to America in about 1713/14, stopping in Monocacy, western Maryland, as a good Catholic might do.

In the 1880's, beginning in Bourbon County, KY, English lawyers rummaged around in search of Hedges heirs. We do not know if they located the elderly **Jane Hedges Baldwin Moore** (page 214, 221) in her home in Covington or **Benjamin Moore** (p. 120), her only surviving son. No satisfactory candidate was found. As a result, this sketch has been prepared on a computer in Cockeysville, Maryland rather than with one of Queen Ann's good pens, at a desk in Berkshire, Wanborough,

Wiltshire, Burrows, or Macroon Castle, Cork.

> COOKS' TOUR THRU THE TAYLOR GENEALOGY
>
> The eldest son of **Joseph Hedges** was Solomon Hedges (c. 1710-1797), husband of Rebecca Van Meter (c. 1711-1770). Her parents were Margaret Mollenaur (1687-aft Aug 13, 1745) and John Van Meter (1683-1745). John Van Meter (Van Meteren) was born in New York and moved first to New Jersey, then to Maryland and finally to the upper Shenandoah Valley of Virginia. John's first wife was Sara Bodine (1687-1709). Sara and John were the parents of Maria (Mary) Van Meter (1709-aft 1752). Mary and her husband Robert Jones (c. 1696-aft 1796) moved from New Jersey to Maryland and then on to the upper Shenandoah Valley with Mary's parents. (See **All of the Above II**, page 249 f.)
>
> Mary and Robert Jones were the parents of John Jones (c. 1733-c. 1793) and (perhaps) Margaret (c. 1734-1797), the wife of William Cook Jr (abt 1730-abt 1790). Wm and Margaret Cook were the parents of Abraham Cook (1774-1854). John Jones and Mary Rentfro (?-?) were the parents of Sarah Jones (1777-1857), Abraham's wife. Abraham Cook and Sarah Jones, possible first cousins, when they married, were the great-great grandparents of **Cecil V. Cook, Jr** (1913-2000), the husband of **Elizabeth ("Betty") Huey Taylor Cook** (1918-2000), a great granddaughter x 3 of **Jonah Baldwin**, whose mother, **Jane Hedges Baldwin**, was a granddaughter of **Joseph Hedges** (see above, page 244).
>
> How are Cecil Cook Jr and Betty Taylor Cook related by way of the marriages of Hedges, Jones, Cooks, Rentfros and Van Meters in the seventeenth and eighteenth centuries? I can't figure it out.

SOURCES:

For Baldwin and Moore genealogy: Betty Taylor Cook's unpublished genealogy book, plus materials given her by Anne Moffett Gibbs, a lineal descendent of Jonah Baldwin and Sarah Scott Baldwin. The Hedges genealogy is taken from a one-page document titled "Hedges" and sent to Mary Baldwin Moore Taylor by Cass K. Shelby, Hollidaysburg, PA in August, 1932. Additional Hedges data may be found in **The History of Bourbon, Scott, Harrison and Nicholas Counties, Kentucky** by William Perrin (Chicago: O. L. Baskin & Co., 1882, p 471).

Cousin Elizabeth Taylor Rubio has shared her Baldwin, Hedges and Stalcop research.

Jonah Baldwin: a remarkable memory - For Clark County history, including the council with Tecumseh. **History of Clark County**, John Simpson Graham (1881). The writer of this valuable work states that his own memories of Clark County go back to 1818. Also, "A Brief Sketch of Springfield" by R. C. Woodward (published in the Springfield City Directory for 1852), which cites as sources some of the still-living founding settlers of the community.

The boat would stick on the sand bars – the 1936 memoir of Frank Dunn: posted at **Descendants of John Dunn**

Information concerning Jonah Baldwin and Amelia Needham has been passed down by granddaughter, Anna B. Baldwin, who was also a great granddaughter of Vallette (Anna called her "Violette") Lyttleton.

Details of Jonah and Sarah Scott Baldwin's life in Springfield: **A Biographical Record of Clark County Ohio** (New York: Clark Publishing, 1902); and **The Early Settlement of Springfield, Ohio (The Ludlow Papers)**, John Ludlow (lectures delivered in 1871); Clark

County Historical Society (1963). For Tecumseh and Tenskwatawa: **Facing East from Indian Country, A Native History of Early America**, Daniel K. Richter (Cambridge: Harvard University Press, 2001).

The Clark County residents' petition to Congress: rootsweb.com/ohclark/history. Historians studying the 19th century have debated recently whether President Jackson's closure of the Bank of the United States was a well aimed, if futile, cannon shot across the bow of nascent American capitalism. In some quarters capitalism was viewed with suspicion, a force which was going to sweep away Jefferson's idealized agrarian America. The debate is reductionist. Too much else was happening that single-theory histories cannot account for: resistance to the westward extension of slavery; steam power; road, railroad and telegraph construction; expansion of male suffrage; a nascent women's rights movement; the continuing settlement of the continent; the continuing arrival of waves of immigrants, many from Catholic Ireland. The Baldwins and Scotts and their neighbors, who petitioned Congress, may simply have been trying to protect their local efforts to move from a barter to a money economy, with the value of their money held secure by a national standard.

Early Episcopal Church history in Springfield, Ohio: Dec 2006 e-mail from the Rev. Charlotte Collins Reed, Pastor Christ Episcopal Church, Springfield, Ohio.

For the 1824 Chicago-Detroit road survey: "The Plat of the United States Road from Detroit to Chicago, as surveyed and marked by James McClosky, Jonah Baldwin, and Laureat Durocher, C'om.s, copied by John Farmer" (1825); for Indiana roads, see a website, which quotes from A. G. Hardesty's 1876 "History of Porter County, Indiana" (part of his Illustrated Historical Atlas of Porter County, Indiana), on the web: (/members.tripod.com/IanHistor /maps/ihr20.html).

The 1896 Perrin letter (copy) citing the 1824 survey and recalling Jane Hedges Baldwin's introduction to Gen. Lafayette is in the possession of the writer, having been found in a WW II era ration book, also preserved.

The Taylor-Moore-Baldwin-Hedges line, generally: the genealogical chart book and notes of Betty Taylor Cook. For the Cook-Jones-Van Meter line, and its connection to Joseph Hedges, see the research of William G. Scroggins, containing examinations of land transactions and posted on the web by Gary Kueber at kueber.us/. Scroggins cites the important Lyman C. Draper Manuscript Collection (431 notebooks) at the Wisconsin State Historical Society in Madison. Lyman C. Draper (1815-1891), from the mid 1830s and for the next 50 years, traveled throughout the eastern and central US, interviewing people and collecting old records, many from the 18th century.

In memory of S. Baldwin 1817 - The ancient framed sampler of a headstone which contains these embroidered words, was generously given to the writer by his cousin, and Baldwin descendent Mary Taylor Ecton in June 2006. Mary has preserved and shared countless family letters.

Lyrics to *Lazy River*, on the web at many sites; see: lyricsdownload.com

Hedges material: *"Known" Data Alternatives for Joseph of Monocacy*; and *The de Lacy Hedges*, csd.com/~rhhedgz1 /delacy, which cites a number of sources: **Irish Ancestry** Vol I, #2 (1969); **The Family of Odell**, Vol III, #1,(1970) by Brian de Breffney; **Picturesque Narrow Tower & Later Buildings**, Survey by West; **Proceedings of the Royal Irish Academy**, by T.J. Westropp – see rootsweb.com/~hedges/joseph/alternative

send me some good pens - **Queen Anne** by Edward Gregg (Routledge, 1980), cited at *Delacy-Hedges History:* ecsd.com/~rhhedgz1/delacy

"BUILDER, IN BUILDING THE LITTLE HOUSE IN EVERY WAY YOU MAY PLEASE YOURSELF"
(Robert Frost)

William Moore
Elinor [Eleanor?] Vallette [Violet/e] Dawson

Marmaduke Moore (1808-1883)
Benjamin Moore (1837-1894)
Mary Baldwin Moore Taylor (1863-1936)
John Oliver Taylor Jr (1891-1960)
Betty Taylor Cook (1918-2000)

William Moore (1780-1859) was born during the Revolutionary War and died on Dec 23, 1859. William was the son of **Mary Harrison** (1761-1835) and **Thomas Moore** (1745-1823), a Captain in that war. He was believed to have been born in either Washington County or Fayette County, PA, which is where genealogist Elizabeth Taylor Rubio, great-granddaughter x 4, has placed him.

William seems to have been the beneficiary of land grants extended to his father, who with the Harrisons, moved into Kentucky as early as 1776 and laid claim to thousands of acres. Kentucky land concessions came about as a dividend for Revolutionary War service. As narrated in ancient histories, land grants were also offered prior to the Revolution, as compensation for armed service on behalf of colonial governments, such as in the border dispute between Pennsylvania and Virginia. This appears to have been the basis for Thomas Moore's award of land in (Harrison Co) Kentucky. (For details of the Boundary Controversy, see Page 262, below, in the section of this document devoted to Thomas Moore and Mary Harrison.)

The wife of William Moore was **Elinor Vallette Dawson** (1781-1834). For at least a thousand years English peoples have practiced the custom of phonetic spelling. This habit has not served well the descendents of Elinor [Eleanor?] Vallette [Violet/e] Dawson Moore, who wish to spell her name *correctly*. Our confusion is multiplied by the probability that speakers of French had a large say in the spelling of *Valette*, surname in her mother's line. Likely as not, Elinor herself contributed to the spelling variations in her own name and was indifferent to them. However spelled, Elinor Vallette was born on Jan 12, 1781, the year that saw the victorious end of the Revolutionary War.

The circumstances of Elinor's early life placed her in proximity to well-connected families in Virginia, Maryland, Pennsylvania and finally Kentucky and Ohio. Born in Fayette County, PA (according to Elizabeth Rubio), Elinore was named for her two grandmothers, each of whom was Elenor/Eleanor. Her father was Nicholas Dawson (1745-1790), the son of **George Dawson** (1716-1783) and **Eleanor Ann Lowe** (1715-?). Elenore's mother was **Valette Lyttleton Dawson** (1759-1842), daughter of **Elenor Valette** (?-?) and **John Lyttleton** (?-?). Baby Elinore may have been presented to Martha Washington at Mt Vernon, if family traditions are in fact correct, which place Elenor's Vallette and Lyttleton grandparents and other relatives in the Mount Vernon neighborhood. (The problem is that no actual evidence of proximity to Mount Vernon has been discovered, whereas Elinor's parents are know to have been in western Pennsylvania not long after 1781, the year of her birth.) Elinore Valette Dawson Moore, daughter of Nicholas and Vallette Dawson and wife of William Moore, died in 1834, at age fifty-three, in Harrison County KY, the year her son **Marmaduke Moore** (1808-1883) married **Jane Hedges Baldwin** (1809-1893) in Springfield, Ohio. See page 213.)

It is no longer remembered how William Moore met Elenor Dawson, but their first encounter was probably in or near Harrison County, KY. Their families had ties both to Clark County Ohio, where lived Scotts, Baldwins and Moores, as well as to Harrison County, settled by Moores and Harrisons, with the Scott's living at Blue Lick Springs before moving on to Clark County, OH. The Clark County connection may have begun as early as 1799, when Samuel Kenton and four other families settled Moorfield

Township. With the Kenton party, there was a William Moore. Our William Moore, however, was only 19 in 1799, unmarried, and unlikely to have had the name of a new township settled upon him.

Elenore Dawson and William Moore were married by an Episcopal priest at Blue Lick Springs, Nicholas County KY on Feb 23, 1804. The family has preserved the memory of **Solomon Scott**, her stepfather (second husband of her mother), leading a horse 30 miles to fetch the priest. In 1804 Solomon and Vallette Scott must have been living at Blue Lick Springs, the site of their daughter's wedding. Not long after this date, the Scott's moved to Clark County Ohio, where daughter, **Sarah**, met **Jonah Baldwin** and, by 1809, married him. (Page 225.)

Newly wedded William and Elenor Moore resided for a few years in Ohio, where their first four children were born. The family then moved permanently to Harrison County, KY (named, as noted, for Elenor's uncle Benjamin Harrison). There, William build a log house and named his place "Stony Point" for the battleground in Virginia, where his father, **Thomas Moore** (1745-1823) had fought under General Gates against the British.

The nine children of William and Elenor Moore were: (1) Thomas (Jan, 1805-Nov, 1805); (2) Caroline H. (Oct 10, 1806-April 5, 1830) (3) **Marmaduke** (Oct. 16, 1808-1883); (4) Polly (April 1811-March 13, 1831); (5) Nancy (August 1803-June 1841); (6) Katherine (Oct 1815-Dec 1851); (7) Nicholas D. (March 27, 1818-?); (8) James (April 1820-?) (9) Elenor (August 1823-?).

"Stony Point," William's log house, might have been impressive to his neighbors but it would not have seemed pretentious even by frontier standards. No grandiose homes were built on the American frontier. Writing about the early settlement of Springfield Ohio, where William and Elenor had settled before moving permanently back to Kentucky, a nineteenth century Springfield historian has described the earliest homes, "*erected within a few days to last for a whole life time; how the door, made of a few split boards, often squeaked with a peculiar coarse noise as the latch-string was pulled, and the door swung open upon its rude wooden hinges. These houses were quite dry and warm in winter, and their thick logs rendered them cool during the heat of summer."*

The lack of pomp in home construction was not limited to the trans-Appalachian outskirts. Even the greatest mansions of the grandest Virginia land barons of the eighteenth century were not comparable to any one of hundreds of medieval English castles. Before the nineteenth century witnessed the arrival of the capitalist potentates of "the Gilded Age," so aptly named by Mark Twain, no one in America would have presumed to build a palace. It has taken us almost three hundred years to lose our egalitarian architecture and create a chasm separating the homes of ordinary people from the irrelevant and remote alcazars of the super rich. William and Elenor Moore probably would have been embarrassed to live in a grand mansion.

William and Elenor are buried in the "Lindsey Cemetery" in Harrison County, KY. When laid out, this cemetery was surrounded by a four-foot wall of field stones. Now the wall, the headstones and the heavy slab markers are destroyed. When visited in June 2006, the old river bottom graveyard was covered in tangles of weeds and high grass. There are some 20-30 headstones, many fallen or pushed over and broken up. Among the ruins, could still be read:

Elenor Moore,
Consort of
William Moore
Died March 11th 1834
In the 54th year of her life

No stone could be read that marked William Moore's grave, but there are other Moores at the Lindsey Cemetery. The sleepers, whose stones are still legible, include: Caroline H, who died in 1830 at age 24 and Polly, who died in 1831 at age 20 – both of them daughters of

William and Elenor Moore. Caroline and Polly apparently never married before their young lives ended and their bodies were placed in this once-cherished and secluded clearing. The early deaths of her daughters may have contributed to the death of Elenor in 1834. After she died, William lived on for twenty-five years.

The Lindsey Cemetery, which contains the Moore graves, is situated on private property in Poindexter, a few miles west of Cynthiana, taking KY 36. The marker is about one and a half miles north of KY 36 on KY 1743, "Carl Stephens Road." The cemetery is about a half mile east of the marker. The official Lindsey Cemetery Marker (Number: 1220) reads: *"Located one-half mile east, this pioneer cemetery is the burial place of settlers, among them four Revolutionary War veterans, Rangers of the Frontiers, 1778-83: Capt. **Thomas Moore**, Capt. **William Moore**, Lt. David Lindsey, John Makemson. This plot set aside about 1800 by David Lindsey, who brought his family here about 1780."*

The cemetery marker perpetuates the confusion that William Moore, husband of Elenore Valette Dawson, fought in the Revolutionary War (1776-1783). This cannot be the case for William, who was born in 1780. Perhaps our William Moore was named for an uncle, brother of his father Thomas, who did offer military service when both Moore brothers lived in western PA and also came to KY. (Perhaps Uncle William was also buried in the Lindsey Cemetery, and the marker is correct.) It was among settlers in western Pennsylvania where a local militia, "Rangers of the Frontier" was raised, from time to time in the mid to late 1700s. As were many other Kentuckians, William Moore is believed to have been a soldier in the War of 1812. If so, one would expect the marker to note this service.

SOURCES:

Moore, Harrison, Dawson, Valette, Lyttleton genealogy: Betty Taylor Cook's unpublished genealogy book.

William and Elenor Moore's marriage and family life: writings created by Anne Carter Moffett Gibbs, who credits her great uncle, Mayo Moore Taylor (1893-1980), Duke and Jane Moore's great grandson, for sharing his notes and records. For early Springfield homes: **History of Clark County**, John Simpson Graham (1881). Relevant cemetery records: *"Lindsey Cemetery"* **Kentucky Ancestors** (April, 1967, pp. 158-60) by F.P. Wood.

Builder, in building the little house - Robert Frost, *The Kitchen Chimney*, **Robert Frosts Poems** (Pocket Books 1955, p. 234)

The August, 1780 destruction of Piqua (see pages 235, 239), the Shawnee town, may have been a mistake. The order for this sortie was rescinded by General Washington after the new British commander for North America stopped paying a scalp-bounty on American settlers. But General Clark did not get the new orders in time. Cook ancestor **Anthony Crockett** (1756-1838) was part of the 1,000-man force from KY that General Clark led up-river from Louisville. (See **All of the Above II**, page 126, f.) Also on hand may have been Taylor ancestor, **Thomas Moore** (1745-1823) (below, page 257 f.) Most of the Shawnee escaped from Piqua before it was torched. A total of about 40 men were killed at Piqua, 20 on each side. Old Piqua was on the Mad River about 5 miles west of present-day Springfield. Thomas F. McGrew wrote in 1880 (**History of Clark County**) *"At the time the Indians occupied the place, the prairie was about three miles long and one mile wide. It is now fenced off into farms under the highest state of cultivation. [. . .] Behind the willow swamp was located the town of Piqua, and behind the town was a round-topped hill, rising up 100 feet from the level of the plain. From the crown of this hill the country might be overlooked for as much as five miles up and down the river. The general appearance of the locality, in its almost primitive wildness, must have been of unsurpassed loveliness."*

"THE SPRING NEAR THIS SPOT HAD THE APPEARANCE OF A LASTING ONE"

Thomas Moore
Mary Harrison

William Moore (1780-1859)
Marmaduke Moore (1808-1883)
Benjamin Moore (1837-1894)
Mary Baldwin Moore (1863-1936)
John Oliver Taylor Jr (1891-1960)
Betty Taylor Cook (1918-2000)

Thomas Moore was born at Arcadia Plantation, Kent County, Maryland Province, on March 7 1745. He died in Harrison County KY on Oct 20 1823. Some believe Thomas' father was immigrant John Moore, from Catholic Ireland. If John Moore had emigrated from Ireland in the first half of the eighteenth century, he was, most likely a Protestant, from Ulster. The timing of such an arrival in America would fit with the Treaty of Union (1706), which created a *United Kingdom* (England and Scotland). Soon after 1706, immigration to the American Colonies of Scots and Ulstermen was encouraged. But in fact, Thomas' father was not John Moore but **William** and his *grandfather* was **John Moore** (abt 1665-1728), a grandson of the first Moore immigrant. This was **Richard Moore** (?-1676), who arrived in the province long before the uniting of the two Kingdoms. Richard may have owned land in Ireland but was English, possibly Catholic, more likely, Anglican.

Thomas participated in military affairs throughout his life. During the Revolution, Thomas Moore was a lieutenant, 13th Virginia Regiment, commanded by his brother-in-law, Benjamin Harrison, and then in the 9th Virginia (the renamed VA 13th) Regiment, with a captain's rank. Captain Moore also saw service with George Rogers Clark's Illinois Regiment and, in 1793, was a Captain, 14th Regiment, KY's "Cornstalk Militia." He may have fought against the once famous Chief *Cornstalk* at Point Pleasant

(Lord Dunmore's War, 1774) as Ben Harrison commanded a company under Col. Charles Lewis (page 271). Thomas retired in 1802, a Major in 1st KY Battalion, 51st Regiment.

Thomas was the sixth child and fourth son of **Rachel Medford** (?-b/f 1779) and **William Moore** (1703-1780/81) of Kent County, MD. Thomas' older brother Augustine Moore (1743-?) married Verlinda Dawson (1755-1815). Verlinda was a daughter of **George Dawson** (1716-1783) and **Elenor Anne Lowe** (1715-?), ancestors of Betty Taylor Cook (1918-2000) through her Dawson and Baldwin lines, uniting with the Thomas Moore line by way of the marriage of **Jane Hedges Baldwin** and **Marmaduke Moore,** Thomas' grandson (page 213).

Rachel Medford Moore's grandparents are believed to have been **Fortuna Watson** (1640-1701) and **Bulmer Medford (Mitford)** (1632-1665), who arrived in Maryland in 1664 on the ship *Providence,* from Morpeth, Northumberland shire, England. Rachel's maternal grandparents were **Ann Hepbourne** (?-?) and **George Mackall** (?-?) who reached St. Mary's County MD from Dumfrieshire, Scotland aboard the ship *John of Topsham* in 1670.

Like his son, Thomas (the subject of this sketch) William Moore had been born at Arcadia Plantation, a 300 acre tract he received on the death of his father in 1728. William's parents were **John Moore** (abt 1665-1728) and **Elizabeth Doland** (1680-1718). Elizabeth was the daughter of **Amy Erickson** (?-?) and **William Dowland** (?-?), who reached Maryland from Ireland in 1667. Amy's parents were **Elizabeth ___** and **John Erickson** who immigrated to Maryland in 1658.

John Moore was probably born on Kent Island. In 1703, 1706 and 1718, he completed his purchase of Arcadia Plantation. John was vestryman and warden of St. Paul's Parish, Kent County. Arcadia remained in the Moore family until 1812, being purchased then by Isaac Caulk.

John Moore (grandfather of our subject, Thomas) was the oldest of two sons of **Thomas Moore** (?-?) and **Elizabeth Bowne** (?-?), widow of Stephen Whestone.

Thomas Moore was the eldest son of **Rebecca** _____ and immigrant **Richard Moore** (?-1676), who reached Maryland in 1652 on an unremembered ship from an unknown English port. Richard Moore's name appears in various records of both Kent County and St Mary's County between 1658 and 1676. In 1669, he recorded his mark for cattle on Kent Island. Richard Moore's plantation on the Chester River in Kent County was named "Kilworth."

As stated, the family has passed down the notion that the first immigrant Moore was from Ireland. This was the opinion of our subject, Thomas' son, **William Moore** (1780-1859). Five generations after immigrant Richard Moore, William mentioned this to his grandson, Robert Collier. Robert placed this information in his 1898 history of the family. Emmett Moore Waits, a descendent of Thomas Moore and Mary Harrison, through their son, Thomas Harrison Moore (1790-1840), conducted much original research in Maryland. In 1972, Waits stated, "The Anglo-Irish Moore of Kilworth, Moore's Park, County Cork, Ireland, was seated at Kilworth as early as the 1500's, having been first at Larden, Shropshire, England."

In 1786, **Thomas Moore** (1745-1823) and his wife **Mary Harrison** (1761-1835) were among the second party of European settlers to enter Bourbon (now Harrison) County Kentucky. They lived on a tract of 2,000 acres in what is now known as the Poindexter Section of the county. In his will, executed May 20, 1819, Thomas Moore left all his property to Mary, for her use and disposition at her death.

Thomas and Mary Harrison Moore were the parents of ten children: **William**, Lawrence, John Henry, Benjamin, Thomas Harrison, Mary, Nancy, Catherine, Elizabeth and Sally. All of these children reached adulthood.

Mary's parents were **Lawrence Harrison** (1710-1772) and **Catherine Marmaduke** (?-?), whose family name was given to her grandson **Marmaduke Moore** (1808-1883). **Betty Taylor Cook** (1918-2000), Mary's great granddaughter x 4, recorded that in her prayer book, engraved with the Harrison coat of arms, Mary Harrison made notes on the Harrison family. (Who got Mary's prayer book? The Colliers? Anna Baldwin? Where is it now?)

Mary's father Lawrence Harrison is believed to have been the son of **Andrew Harrison** (1687-1753) (descendent of immigrant **Anthony Harrison**) and **Elizabeth Battaile** (?-?), whose father was English immigrant **John Battaille** (1658-1707), under-sheriff of the Rappahannock Valley and a member of the House of Burgesses from Essex County VA. Elizabeth's mother was **Elizabeth Smith**, (1668-1770), John's second wife. Elizabeth Smith's father has been said to have been **Lawrence Smith** (?-?), owner of "Temple Farm," Gloucester County VA.

John Battaille's first wife is said to have been Catherine Taliafero (1668-90), daughter of immigrant Robert Taliaferro (1626-c.1721) and Catherine Debnam (?-?). A connection has yet to be made between this Robert Talaiferro and **Betty Taylor Cook**'s ancestors, **Taliaferro (Toliver) Craig** (1704-1799), son of **Jane Craig** (?-?) and _____ **Taliaferro**, a ship's captain who impregnated her (See pages 76.)

The *Battaile* surname had become a Harrison first name within a generation or two of the early Virginia Battailes; it then mutated further, no doubt in the script of court clerks and notaries, from *Battaile* to *Battle* Harrison. This last change seems to have so confused the family that the name fell out of use altogether. In colonial America even the owner of a name was not certain of its spelling, which was mostly a matter of indifference anyway.

From the moment he married **Mary Harrison, Thomas Moore**'s life and fate was intertwined with her family. The sketchy record we have permits inferences that Thomas was associated in a number of events with his brothers-in-law, William Harrison (?-1782) and Benjamin Harrison (?-abt. 1808). (These Harrison brothers should not be confused with the so-called *Presidential* Harrisons: Benjamin, who signed the Declaration of Independence, and his oldest son, William Henry, who was governor of the Northwest Territories, victor at the battle of Tippecanoe in 1811 and Ninth President of the United States; and then Benjamin, the grandson of William Henry, who was 23rd President of the United States.)

The William and Benjamin Harrisons, who were connected to **Thomas Moore** by his marriage to Mary their sister, are intriguing figures who left their own influence upon their peers and the lands they acquired. These Harrisons were given to aggressive and life-long land speculation. In early 1776, Benjamin Harrison and Thomas Moore were among a party of explorers and settlers that entered Kentucky and occupied lands in and around what is now Cynthiana, the county seat of Harrison County KY. (The town was named for Cynthia and Anna, daughters of an early settler; the county was named for Benjamin Harrison.)

The 1776 expedition is confirmed by a deposition Thomas Moore made "on the west bank of Stoner's Creek near James Patton's house in Clark county, on 20th November 1802 before D. Harrison and H. Chiles, J.P" (recorded in the Circuit Court of Fayette County PA) In this document, Thomas Moore swears,

Early in the spring of 1776 this deponent in company with Benjamin Harrison, John Morgan, Belles Collier and one [Robert] Keene came down the Ohio to mouth of Licking River and from thence up Licking to Hingston station and from thence we proceeded up this stream now called Stoner's Fork, being pilated by John Morgan, who had been in this country the year before, till he informed us we were about [Christopher] Gist's military survey and sometime, as this deponent thinks, in the month of April we built a cabbin covered it over and made it fit for habitation. At this spot we cleared about a half an acre or 3/4 of an acre of land and planted corn. This improvement we made for John Morgan and after making several other improvements on the right hand fork, which puts in about 300 yards above this place,

Harrison, and this deponent returned up the river, leaving Morgan and Collier at Morgan's cabbin, who were to remain there and to endeavor to prevent others from making improvements to interfere with ours, and we were to return the ensuing fall, and bring to Morgan and Collier such necessaries as they had sent for. The spring near this spot had the appearance of a lasting one was intended by Morgan as his useing spring.

Thomas Moore's 1802 deposition supported the claims of those who had arrived in and made improvements on lands in territory, which was under the authority of the governor of Virginia Colony. This region became the Commonwealth of Kentucky in 1792. Benjamin Harrison made a similar statement in the interests of the heirs of his deceased brother William and of his brother-in-law, Thomas Moore: "*I have known the 'Cave Spring' on this land since May, 1776, I was on the spot in camp with John Hinkson and John Sellers; camped there all night, 24 June, 1776; made two locations, one in name of William Harrison, for 2,000 acres; one in name of Thomas Moore and Benjamin Johnston, for 2,000 acres.*

THE VA/PA BOUNDARY CONTROVERSY
"*Done At the Command of Major William Crawford*"

Even before the Revolutionary year of 1776-83, the Harrisons, if not also Thomas Moore, were actively, violently asserting themselves with the aim of acquiring new lands. In the years leading up to the Revolution, a bitter confrontation had developed between Virginia and Pennsylvania over the ownership and control of a region of western Pennsylvania, which had been claimed by the French and which extended westward from the frontier English settlements to and west from the Ohio River. The dispute arose after the French were defeated at the end of the so-called French and Indian War (1754-1763). The Ohio Company, a corporation selling land, was established to promote settlement and trade with the Shawnee and other tribes. Many of the earliest western PA settlers were from Virginia and Maryland and held "certificates" issued to them in Virginia, which warranted to them access to Ohio lands claimed by Pennsylvania. After 1780, with the passage in PA of slave emancipation legislation, numbers of settlers in western PA, migrated into Kentucky. Before they left, they worked hard to make western PA (and, by extension, the Ohio country) part of Virginia.

Jurisdiction was not settled until after the Revolutionary War, when the two states appointed a commission that surveyed the lands. This commission simply extended westward the accepted PA-MD state line (the Mason-Dixon Line) and determined (1785) that the contested lands belonged to Pennsylvania. But for a decade or more, prior to the agreement, conflicting land sales, claims, occupations and disputed taxes and assessments caused fights, riots and arrests by local officials appointed by both PA and VA authorities.

In early 1775, Pennsylvania authorities had arrested some partisans of Virginia's claim. On Feb 7, 1775, William and Benjamin Harrison, and possibly also with their sister's husband, **Thomas Moore**, went with a rowdy company of men to Pittsburgh, entered the local jail and released the prisoners, with threats to shoot anyone who interfered. This exercise was repeated (with the arrest of PA-sponsored local judges) in the nearby hamlet of Hanna's Town (Hannastown), PA. On this occasion, Ben Harrison "was pleased to announce that it was done at the command of Major William Crawford." The popular Crawford (see Index) was a land agent for George Washington and Ben and William Harrison's father-in-law. Apparently the Pittsburgh and Hanna's Town hooligans, sponsored by Governor Dunmore of Virginia, were energized by the promise of grants of Western lands. Additional investigation might prove that the Kentucky lands Ben Harrison and Thomas Moore claimed after the 1775 foray into PA was a reward for these violent gambits.

Shortly after the Hanna's Town incident, Benjamin Harrison led surveyors into Kentucky and laid off thousands of acres of land for himself, his brother William and also for Thomas Moore, his sister's husband. Thomas' lands included a claim on 900 Ohio acres (Pickaway County), along Mill Creek, where he took legal possession in 1786; he supplemented this with a purchase of 1,000 additional Mill Creek acres, as evidenced by his will. This reach north across the Ohio River was probably the earliest connection of the Moore family into Ohio, where son William would be well known and William's son, **Marmaduke Moore** (1808-1883) would meet and marry **Jane Baldwin** (1809-1893). (See page 233, 237.)

Why would the Harrisons, with family ties to Pennsylvania, have been inclined to risk their lives to become enforcers of Virginia territorial claims against Pennsylvania in 1775? Why might Thomas Moore, with ancestral ties in Maryland for 120 years, have joined them? These events were part of the quest for more land. Thomas Moore had long since left Maryland and gone west. He was the youngest of four brothers; the oldest, John (1730-1812), had inherited Arcadia Plantation in MD, where he died, unmarried. By 1769, young Thomas had immigrated to the West Augusta District, Virginia Colony. He had first spent some time in nearby Fayette County, PA, which is probably where he had encountered the Harrisons, and specifically Mary, whom he married in Fayette County about 1778. By the middle of the 1780s Thomas and Mary Moore were living in that extension of Virginia known as Kentucky. A brief look at VA and PA land policies in the 1760's and '70's suggests why Kentucky settlers would have been prompted to side with Virginia against Pennsylvania's claims to lands along the eastern bank of the upper Ohio River.

Virginia's colonial officials were much more aggressive in sponsoring western settlements than were Pennsylvania's. Governor Dunmore of Virginia was offering outright grants of western land and was selling lands cheaper than PA was. Also, the Harrisons and Moores would have known that Pennsylvania, in October 1758, had achieved peace with some Ohio Country Indians by renouncing Pennsylvania's claims to lands west of the

Appalachian Mountains. They would have known that this agreement, the Treaty of Easton, had been made because Pennsylvania, with its Quaker and pacifist traditions, always had been slow to raise and pay for local militia to protect European settlers in the western reaches of the colony. The proprietary colony of William Penn, with its political establishment divided between Quaker pacifists, Philadelphia merchants, and impatient, land-hungry settlers, was indecisive. Pennsylvania's political paralysis on western land issues could be worked to the advantage of Virginia, or so concluded many long-established families in Virginia and Maryland, whose sons, like George Washington, were unable or unwilling to carve up and share the family's traditional lands in the established colonies and were anxious to get onto huge tracts of frontier acreage. (Dawson ancestors were recalled as "stern partisans" (of VA) in the VA-PA dust-up; see page 343.)

"WE ALL HAD TO SCATTER" - CLUE TO THE COLONIAL INSURGENTS' VICTORY

How is it that the Harrisons, the Moores and their neighbors under arms were able to defeat and even humiliate the British Army, mighty hammer of a world power? This unexpected result came about (in my opinion) because the British failed to grasp the difference between a war of opposing armies and an army of occupation, confronting an insurgency. This misperception was caused by the British mistake in placing too much faith in their pre-eminent navy. Exactly 100 years (1676) before the American Revolution (1776), a sub-committee of the Privy Council believed control of New York - "ye only fortified Harbor in all ye northern Plantacons" - would guarantee London's permanent domination of its American possessions. "The inhabitants there, by their scattered way of living and want of fortresses," could never resist British armies put ashore by an unchallenged sea power. For a century following 1676, this mistaken assumption was the foundation of Britain's colonial policy.

In an earlier sketch devoted to the Hueys, Kentucky pioneer settler Francis Nelson Faulconer (abt 1760/70-aft 1844) said (see page 74) that in March, 1780, "we all had to scatter." Flight into the woods was in reaction to an alarm that British soldiers were approaching through the Kentucky wilderness. A population scattered is not a population defeated. Failing to defeat the colonists' roving armies or to subdue the scattered rural communities or even permanently to occupy the coastal cities, the British could not and did not win the war. Failing to hold America, Britain turned toward India and crafted policies intended to assure British influence in the Middle East, so as to guarantee direct access to India. Britain maintained this short-sighted imperial focus for two hundred years. Meanwhile, America seems to have unlearned, in our day, the lessons of its own Revolution, time and again sending occupying armies into smaller but populous countries, who resist domination, just as our colonial ancestors did.

THE REVOLUTION AND THE KENTUCKY MIGRATION

As early as the 1750's, English-speaking and other European settlers were moving into the Ohio Country. The migrations were stimulated further by the 1763 Treaty of Paris, which marked the collapse of the French empire in America following France's defeat in the French & Indian (Seven Years) War. By the mid 1770's the Harrisons and Moores were part of that great migration. They would have known that the protection (such as it was) of the existing PA and VA settlements was largely the work of untrained volunteer militia, and that this haphazard pattern of neighborhood response probably would be all that the Ohio and KY settlers could count on.

The militia bands were little more than a reaction force of killer vigilantes (locally known as "Rangers") who gathered at the sight of a burned-out cabin after the occupants had been run off, kidnapped or killed. The Rangers would then chase down some Indians, or raid a village and then collect a bounty from the Pennsylvania authorities whose colonial legislature, instead of building forts, offered money for every scalp from an Indian at least ten years old. If, for the indiscriminate murder of Originals, Pennsylvania money was good, the Virginia offer of western lands was better. A hardened, Indian-killing pioneer could get both bounty and a grant of land.

After their excursion into Kentucky in 1776, both **Thomas Moore** and Benjamin Harrison (as stated) entered military service in the American Revolutionary Army. It is likely they and many other farmer-colonists viewed a stint under arms as an extension of their efforts to acquire holdings in the West. Why? They, like many frontier settlers, had an active interest in land speculation. Others, who also joined the Revolution, if not speculators, at least harbored a wistful hope for better farmland. For generations before and after the Revolution, everyone looked westward, towards the lands that ran away from them, endlessly, beneath a setting sun.

The Harrisons and the Moores and their neighbors would have known the British government stood between them and their ownership of land further west. In October 1763, Prime Minister Grenville issued from London a Royal Proclamation, intended to centralize Indian policy by declaring off limits the lands occupied by Indian tribes "who live under our protection . . . that they not be molested or disturbed." For westward facing colonists, this was an unwelcome echo of the 1758 Treaty of Easton. Worse. London wanted to impose immigration restrictions as large as the continent itself. It is entirely likely that the Moores and the Harrisons viewed British frontier policies as an unwarranted intrusion upon their personal plans. They may well have taken up arms in the Revolution for that reason alone. After five years of service, Thomas Moore, as stated, mustered out with the rank of captain. Benjamin Harrison retired in 1781 as a major.

In 1782, William Harrison was murdered after being captured at Sandusky. (Page 345). In 1783, the Treaty of Paris ended the Revolutionary War. In 1784 Benjamin Harrison sold his land in Pennsylvania, along the banks of the Youghiogheny River and moved to Bourbon County KY, and became quite active leader in civic life. Ben was a delegate from Bourbon County to the 1787 and 1788 constitutional conventions and a delegate, in 1792, when statehood for Kentucky was formalized under a new constitution. Benjamin Harrison then became a state senator. In 1798, he became a trustee of the Harrison Academy, an educational institution named for him, which operated until 1872, then becoming the Cynthiana public school. When a new Kentucky county was formed out of old Bourbon County, it was named for Benjamin Harrison.

In spite of his accomplishments in Kentucky, Ben Harrison seems to have had difficulty settling down. An old land-speculating friend from Pennsylvania, John Morgan, had been into the Louisiana Territory, in about 1789 – that part known as *Missouri*. He wanted Ben to go back with him. Missouri at the end of the 18th century was part of a vast swath of the continent, under the nominal control of Spain. A hamlet in Missouri was given the unlikely name, *Nuevo Madrid* - New Madrid. (For reasons no longer remembered, Spanish Governor Esteban Miro seems to have preferred the name, *L'Anse a la Grasse* - Greasy Bend; maybe he was trying for "grassy bend.")

The earliest New Madrid settlers, including John Morgan, and possibly Ben Harrison, sent entreaties and even a delegation down river to New Orleans. The new Missourians proposed that Spanish Governor Miro adopt policies, which would encourage English-speaking settlers to come into the Louisiana Territory. Governor Miro (gov: 1782-1791) responded with two conditions. His requirements must have seemed laughingly absurd to the energetic, practical-minded, land-taking, government-creating surveyor-farmers, who had spent lifetimes figuring out how to get onto tillable lands and who had rarely hesitated to threaten or shoot at anybody who interfered with their plans.

American settlers would be welcomed in Missouri, the Spanish Governor explained, if they all become Catholic and if they left behind in Kentucky their notions of representative government. These requirements became moot after Miro returned to Spain and Spain ceded the Louisiana territories to France in 1800. Napoleon, short of cash, sold Louisiana to the United States in 1803.

John Morgan did not remain in Missouri but returned to Pennsylvania. However, Ben Harrison, who may have been to Missouri with Morgan on his first expedition, acquired grants to land and eventually moved to Missouri about 1802. Ben Harrison died in Washington County Missouri in about 1808.

Thomas Moore did not go to Missouri with his brother-in-law. He remained in Harrison County KY but continued to be involved with the affairs of his wife's family. On March 5, 1812, in Belmont, Ohio, Thomas gave an affidavit on behalf of Battaile and Robert Harrison, sons of Benjamin Harrison, that they were Ben's true and legal heirs. Moore swore that he "had known Benjamin Harrison from the time of his marriage until his death; that Battaile Harrison, of Belmont County, Ohio and Robert Harrison, of Harrison County, Kentucky, were acknowledged by Benjamin Harrison as his legitimate children."

Thomas Moore made his will on May 20, 1819, leaving his estate to his wife, naming her to execute his wishes. Mary left lands to children, whose own children inherited in turn. Grandson **Marmaduke Moore** (1808-1883), after a stint as sheriff of Harrison County, sold his holdings and moved to Covington, KY by 1850.

The spare accounts we have about the Moores and the Harrisons are suggestive of a powerful incentive shared by hundreds, then multiple thousands of immigrants to America and also by their early descendents. The unwavering objective, extending across the generations, was to transform vast lands into property. The property motive was in high profile for descendents of colonists from the British Isles, where even the forests were off limits, as *owned* by the king. The ownership motivation brought the settlers into genocidal conflict with the aboriginal occupiers of America, whose communal ways rejected the idea of land as personal or private property.

Turning land into property seems to have been the primary motive of the settlers, even when there were other incentives, such as unfettered religious practice, or new beginnings well away from the slums of London or the rural poverty of Scotland. The harsh conditions of life may have pushed the immigrants out of Europe but the vast lands of America is what pulled them. Not long after landfall, the arriving colonials, especially those already with children in their arms and at their sides, realized what lay before them – an impossibly broad expanse of territory. For the immigrants and their descendents, for generations to come – until the end of the 19th century when the frontier was closed – life would have been full of dreams, discussions and plans with spouses, children and friends. Their subject would have been the land, how to get some of it, use it, acquire more of it, hang onto it and pass it down through the family.

Thomas Moore was buried in Harrison County, in Poindexter, west of Cynthiana. A broken headstone reads:

> *Sacred to the Memory of Thomas Moore,*
> *a Captain in the Army of*
> *the Revolution Who died*
> *October 20, 1823, in the*
> *78th year of His Life*

There is another headstone, which has a partial inscription today but which was copied some years ago:

> *Under this Stone are*
> *deposited the remains of*
> *MARY MOORE*
> *Consort of Thomas Moore:*
> *A native of Virginia,*
> *Who died 7th Febry 1836*
> *In the 75th year of her age*
> *To the memory of the fond wife*
> *kind parent good neighbor*
> *This slab is inscribed*

The Lindsey Cemetery (see pages 254-55), which contains the Moore graves, is situated on private property (the McNees farm) in Poindexter, a few miles west of Cynthiana, KY. The cemetery is about a half mile east of and directly behind a highway marker identifying the location of the cemetery. The marker is on Harrison County Route 1743, "Carl Stephens Road." You have to enter private property to get to the cemetery. Be nice.

> "The noble Shawnee Chief, *Cornstalk*, was head of the Shawnees living on the Scioto. *Cornstalk* implored Connelly [Governor Dunmore's agent] to restrain the Virginians from committing more murders. But Connelly did not want peace. He wanted war. [After the Battle of Point Pleasant] *Cornstalk* entered into a treaty of peace with Lord Dunmore, at Chillicothe, Ohio. It is said that his powerful, clarion voice could be heard distinctly over the whole camp of twelve acres. Among those present was Colonel Benjamin Wilson, who speaks thus of Cornstalk's address:
>
> *'When he rose, he was in no wise confused or daunted, but spoke in a distinct and audible voice without stammering or repetition and with peculiar emphasis. His looks while addressing Dunmore were truly grand and majestic; yet graceful and attractive. I have heard the first orators in Virginia, Patrick Henry and Richard Henry Lee, but never have I heard one whose powers of delivery surpassed those of Cornstalk on that occasion.'*
>
> "By the terms of the treaty of peace, the Shawnee were compelled to recognize the Ohio River as the eastern boundary of the Indian lands." C. Hale Sipe, **The Indian Wars of Pennsylvania** (1931, pages 492, 493, 499).

SOURCES:

The genealogy of Thomas Moore and Mary Harrison, generally: Betty Taylor Cook's unpublished genealogy book. Some of Betty's materials seem to derive from the valuable Lyman C. Draper Manuscript Collection (Madison: Wisconsin State Historical Society).

The spring near this spot had the appearance of a lasting one - The Nov 20, 1802 deposition of Thomas Moore (page 261-62, above): Complete Record Book A, pg. 339, Deposition of Thomas Moore, Fayette County, placed on the web: 2 Feb 1998, "To researchers of Hinkson" Jim Sellers, www/shawhan.com. Sellers has also published a deposition of Benjamin Harrison, taken from the Harrison County Court Order Book A, pg 356, June 8, 1804.

The establishment of Harrison County and the naming of Cynthiana: the above cited Betty Cook unpublished book; also **Pieces of the Past** by Jim Reis, Sec II, page 129, (1988).

scattered way of living and want of fortresses - **1676, The End of American Independence**, by Stephen Saunders Webb (Syracuse: 1984. 1995, page 332).

the remains of MARY MOORE – inscription published in "Lindsey Cemetery" by F.P. Wood, **Kentucky Ancestors** (April 1967, pp. 158-60).

For Moore and Harrison lines in Maryland and Virginia: "Colonial Families of Virginia: Moore of Kent County Maryland and Kentucky," by Emmett Moore Waits, *The Colonial Genealogist*, IV No 3 (Winter, 1972), with original sources cited.

Brief mention of both Benjamin and William Harrison (but not Thomas Moore) is made in: *A Biography of Col John Hinkson: Pennsylvania and Kentucky Frontiersman by Robert E. Francis, With Great Assistance from Jim Sellers*. (The Ruddell and Martins Stations Historical Associations, 2000) This document (and others) may be found on the web at: http://www.shawhan.com. The description (page 274) of the attire of the 18th century frontiersman is taken, with thanks, from this source, which adapted it from Joseph Doddridge's 1824 narrative.

For the details leading to the 1758 Treaty of Easton, PA, the text of the Royal Proclamation of 1763, and the founding of New Madrid, Missouri: **Facing East from Indian Country, A Native History of Early America**, by Daniel K. Richter (Harvard University Press, 2001).

Some valuable Harrison family details have been found in *BENJAMIN HARRISON, 1750 – 1808, A History of His Life And of Some of the Events In American History in Which He was Involved* By Jeremy F. Elliot (1978, www.shawhan.com/benharrison). Elliott states (without citing a source) that William Harrison was killed in Ohio in 1782. This is an apparent reference to Crawford's Sandusky Plains expedition against the Shawnee.

William Harrison was captured at Sandusky and killed shortly after – according to earlier histories examined by C. Hale Sipe, (**The Indian Wars of Pennsylvania** (1929, 1931, page 662): "John Stover was captured by the Shawnees and carried to one of the Shawnee towns, where he saw the burned and mutilated bodies of William Harrison (Crawford's son-in-law) and [others]."

The VA-PA Boundary Controversy is viewed differently by PA historians. Sipe (see above) states (His Supplement, page 837) that Virginia's armed partisans were "excited by rum" when they "paraded through the streets of Pittsburgh."

THE LIKELY ATTIRE OF THOMAS MOORE, 18TH CENTURY FRONTIERSMAN:

He wore a hunting shirt which hung loose and reached halfway down his thighs. The front of the shirt was open and overlapped with a pocket in the bosom where he could keep jerked meat, or perhaps a piece of bread and a rag for wiping the barrel of his rifle. The shirt might have been made of deer skin or, more likely, linsey-woolsey a material made from homespun combination of wool and flax. He wore "leggings," which covered the legs to the thighs, and were fastened to a belt by strings. The belt also held a bullet pouch, a tomahawk and a scalping knife. Attached beneath his belt in front and back and extending about a yard on both sides was piece of linen or cloth called the "breech clout." The ends of this cloth may have been embroidered, hanging down before and behind. [He] wore moccasins made of a single piece of dressed deer skin with a single seam along the top of the foot and another along the bottom of the heel as high as the ankle joint. Flaps were left on each side some distance up his legs and adjusted by thongs. When the weather turned cold, [he] would stuff the moccasins with deer hair or dried leaves to keep his feet warm. He completed his attire by wearing a coon-skin cap, with the tail dangling down behind.

Joseph Doddridge (1824)
Notes on the Settlement and Indian Wars of the Western Parts of Virginia and Pennsylvania from 1763 to 1783

"VERY ANXIOUS TO HEAR FROM YOU AND TO KNOW OF YOUR OPINION"

Henry Hunt Mayo
Louisa Winston

Mary Aurelia ("Rilla") Mayo Moore (1839-1901)
Mary Baldwin Moore Taylor (1863-1936)
John Oliver Taylor Jr (1891-1960)
Betty Taylor Cook (1918-2000)

Henry Hunt Mayo (1810-1877) was born in Newport, KY, the son of **Mary Putnam** (1773-1838) and **Daniel Mayo** (1762-1838). On his mother's side Henry Hunt Mayo was the great-great grandson of General **Israel Putnam** (1717/18-1790). Henry Hunt's father was from Massachusetts, his mother from Connecticut. His parents met in Belpre, Ohio, about 1795, shortly after this hamlet was established by a company of New England settlers led by Mary's uncle, Rufus Putnam. (See page 289.)

Daniel Mayo took an active and critical interest in the careers of his sons. Young Henry, 19 in 1829 and not then living at home, received a letter from his father. Daniel faulted Henry for having left his position with a certain Mr. Goodwin. The dutiful son wrote his father from Brookville, Bracken County, KY. to try and clarify Henry's change in employment.

Dear Father,
I was very anxious to hear from you and to know of your opinion of my leaving Mr. Goodwin. I see from your letter you have taken up a wrong idea about my quitting him. It was not because he wanted a writing of agreement between us nor because he was not pleased with my work for I do not know if ever he found fault with it or if he did he never mentioned it to me. It was because I was advised by my friends and Mr. Goodwin himself thought it would be to my advantage if we could get a good workman.

Louisa Winston

> *He was not at all displeased with me for quitting him nor never as I know of did I neglect his business. The reason he says that he could not learn me the business was that the time that I had to stay was not long enough, not because I did not pay attention to my work. I am your Affectionate Son, HHM*

Henry married **Louisa Winston** (? - ?) on Sept 1, 1831, in Boone County KY. Henry and Louisa were the parents of eleven children. Their first five daughters were: Mary Aurelia, Sarah Elizabeth, Lavenia Vance, Louisa, and Emma Bell. When the oldest child, Mary Aurelia died at age 5 in 1838, a new baby girl was given her name. Thus, **Mary Aurelia "Rilla" Mayo** (1839-1901) entered the Mayo family as a surrogate and namesake for an older sister she never knew. **"Rilla" Mayo** became the wife of **Benjamin Moore** (1837-1894) and the mother of **Mary Baldwin Moore Taylor** (-1936). Louisa Winston Mayo is the double great grandmother of **Betty Taylor Cook** (1918-2000), who has preserved much that we have about this family.

Henry and Louisa Mayo had five sons: Daniel Dudley, William Phillips, Thomas Lynch, Henry Hunt and a second Daniel. When the oldest Danny died at age three in 1838, his name was given to the next born male infant, who arrived in 1843. It is not known whether greater solace comes to grieving parents, who name a baby for a little one gone. Henry and Louisa must have thought it would help; they did it twice.

The Mayo household, near Ft Thomas, KY, was recollected down through the family as full of colorful characters, a place of gaiety and laughter. Sarah Elizabeth ("Aunt Sally") was said to be homely with a large mouth. These attributes did not interfere with her marrying Alonzo Taylor, a Confederate War veteran, who was, according to descendent and family historian, Nancy Collier Taylor Johnson (1896-1986), "quite a catch, had money." When Uncle Lonny and Aunt Sally got married and took their wedding party down the Ohio River to Louisville, people on the boat thought the bride must be "Rilla - the pretty one." Aunt Sally was remembered with great affection by her niece, Mary Moore Taylor (1863-1936), as well as by Nancy Collier, Mary's daughter. When Aunt Sally came to visit, she would rock back and forth and pound her knee and not make a sound. Mary Taylor said, "Heaven would not be Heaven if Aunt Sally was not there."

The Mayo children scattered far and wide, making homes in Denver, Wisconsin and New York. Some of this dispersal was owing to the Civil War and its aftermath, which effected this generation most directly. Many were combatants, then refugees, when prospects looked better elsewhere than in Northern Kentucky.

Before the Civil War, Henry Hunt Mayo operated a lumber yard in Newport and a mill in Covington. He used these coordinated enterprises to manufacture sashes, doors, blinds and a variety of building materials. He also conducted other business ventures. The 1834 Newport City Directory lists H. H. Mayo as a tanner and currier, on Taylor Street between Columbia & Cabot Streets. In 1840, the directory lists Henry H Mayo, as a dry goods merchant at Yorke and Taylor Streets.

Henry and Louisa's larger role in the community is not well remembered and may not have been documented. (A search of local and regional newspapers and court records has yet to be conducted.) Son Dudley, in an 1898 reminiscence given from his home in Denver, recalled that his parents saw to their children's early attendance in the Methodist church. Henry was probably a Mason; Dudley had become a Mason in Newport, KY before settling in Denver.

Both Henry and Louisa had grown up in the presence of slaves in their parents' households. Henry's parents, Daniel and Mary Mayo, had begun acquiring slaves as soon as they moved from Ohio to Newport, Kentucky in 1798. In 1820, when Henry Hunt Mayo was ten, his father owned six slaves, not counting "Harry a black man (pauper)," for whose annual maintenance the county paid Daniel Mayo $48.

Dudley Mayo reported that his father's lumberyard was destroyed by fire at the start of the Civil War. Dudley implied this was the work of the federal army. He added that even though Henry Hunt promptly rebuilt and conducted business throughout the war, he operated "at a loss" from then on. During the War Henry Hunt Mayo sent two sons to live and work on a brother's farm.

Louisa Winston was one of ten children of **John Winston** (July 28, 1756-July 28 1830). All of the Winston children were said to have reached adulthood. John Winston was from Surrey County VA but moved to North Carolina and then to Kenton County KY with his first wife, Sabella Moseby. They arrived in Kentucky with children and slaves in tow. A short stay near Lexington ended, because, as has been recorded somewhat mysteriously, John Winston became "dismayed by the canebrakes" around Lexington and moved his family to northern Kentucky.

In 1804, John Winston built a brick house between Back Lick Creek and the Licking River on Decoursey Pike. His wife Sabella died here and he married **Elizabeth Noble** (?-?). As Louisa was one of the youngest of John Winston's ten children, it is believed her mother was Elizabeth Noble and not first wife, Sabella Moseby. Elizabeth was the daughter of **Betty Claire Sedgwick** (?-?) and Dr. **Thomas Noble** (?-?), who arrived in America from Duntrieshire Scotland, in about 1732.

John Winston's father was the first **John Winston** (?-?) and his father was **Samuel Winston** (?-aft Aug 1 1758 [date of will]). Joseph Winston, a brother of the first John (and son of Sam) participated in the Battle of Kings Mountain, one of the decisive engagements of the Revolutionary War. The town of Winston, North Carolina was named in his honor. This town merged with a nearby community, Salem, to become Winston-Salem.

Samuel Winston's father is believed to have been **Anthony Winston Jr** (?-?) son of the first **Anthony Winston** (?-?). His brother, Isaac, was father of Sarah

Mary Aurelia ("Rilla") Mayo Moore

Winston, mother of famed revolutionary firebrand, Patrick Henry. Anthony Winston Jr, great uncle of Patrick Henry, was a judge in Buckingham County and member of the Virginia House of Burgesses. The first Anthony Winston is said to have been the son of **William Winston** (?-?), who is found in New Kent Co., VA about 1667. William is believed to have been one of five brothers, of Winston Hall, Yorkshire, England, a "gentlemen of fortune and family, immigrated to the colony of Virginia, in the spirit of adventure," and settling in Stocking, Hanover County, Virginia Colony. The Winstons, Nobles, Henrys and other clans of northern England brought their fierce, clannish, Presbyterian ways to America with them. They preferred marriage with other "border people" and were quick to offer military expertise and leadership in local fights. In the 1770's the fight was the American Revolution, a tussle Patrick Henry's mother, granddaughter of English highlander, **Anthony Winston**, called, "lowland troubles." (More on the *Borderers*, vol II, page 83.)

SOURCES:

For data concerning marriage and genealogy, including reminiscences by Mary Moore Taylor and Nancy Collier Taylor Johnson: Betty Taylor Cook's unpublished genealogy book; data has also been generously supplied by Anne Moffett Gibbs, including a copy of Henry Hunt Mayo's 1829 letter to his father.

For Henry Hunt Mayo's business activities: Mardos Collection; see memoriallibrary.com/CO/DenverPB.

For data concerning John Winston and his first wife Sabella Moseby and for Joseph Winston data: private communications from Glen Winston, whose material may also be found as "The Winston Family" by Glen Winston, Fourth Great-grandson of John Winston rootsweb.com/-kykenton/Winston. See also David Hackett Fischer,

Albion's Seed (Oxford, 1989, pages 605-782,) for English "border" immigration and the Winstons (page 650, note 8 & 779 for *lowland troubles* quotation.

For Data concerning William Winston and his brothers: **Kentucky: A History of the State**, Battle, Perrin, & Kniffin, 7th ed., 1887, Boone Co.

For Daniel Mayo's slave acquisitions and pauper maintenance transactions: notations in the county deed book, typed, preserved and shared by Mayo descendent Anne Moffett Gibbs.

For the listing of the children of Louisa Winston and Henry Hunt Mayo: a letter from their great-granddaughter Nancy Collier Johnson to her niece Jean Valette Taylor.

Covington Dec 25, 1901

My Dear Mrs Taylor,

On account of sickness I was unable to attend the funeral of your mother [Mary Aurelia Mayo Moore].
At such an hour words I know are vain but allow me from a full heart to offer a poor testimonial of her character and sterline worth.
I knew her well from her earliest girlhood and can remember of her nothing but good. She always carried with her a fold of sunshine. – She was a true friend, a kind and loving sister, a dutiful daughter, - a devoted wife, mother and grandmother and last she lived and died a devoted "soldier of the cross" and fills a Christian grave. – The influence of such a life as hers never dies but blossoms in the dust and lives immortal.

Your friend,

[ ] Kennedy

"ALWAYS IN MEMORY OF THE DAYS OF YORE"
John Quincy Adams to Daniel Mayo
March 1837

Daniel Mayo
Mary Putnam

Henry Hunt Mayo (1810-1877)
Mary Aurelia Mayo Moore (1839-1901)
Mary Baldwin Moore Taylor (1863-1936)
John Oliver Taylor Jr (1891-1960)
Betty Taylor Cook (1918-2000)

Daniel Mayo (1762-1838) was born in Roxbury, MA on Sept 30 1762. He was the son of **Joseph Mayo** (1720-1776) and **Esther Kendrick** (?-?), who were married on Sept 14 1745. Daniel attended Harvard College, where he was a classmate of John Quincy Adams; they were members of the class of 1787. In addition to Adams, other prominent names among the graduating class that year included Cranch, Judd, Kellogg, Lawrence, Learned, Putnam, Waldo, Whitney and Williams.

In 1791, young Daniel Mayo, fresh from Harvard, finds himself a school teacher living in a provisional, walled garrison on the Ohio River, called Farmer's Castle. His students were the children of settlers who, for two years or more, posted guards and established a semi-military discipline which governed all their activities.

By 1788, two tiny communities (Belpre & Marietta) had been established along the Ohio River. This was the work of a handful of Revolutionary War veterans and prospective frontier settlers from New England and the Mid-Atlantic States. In 1786, in Boston, these intrepid adventurers had formally organized an association with the goal of opening to farming a vast tract of western lands.

In the spring of 1788, the first of these homesteaders, arriving mostly as family groups, had established the community of Marietta on the Muskingum River near its outflow into the Ohio River. The war veterans, whose leader was former General Rufus Putnam, decided to name their town in honor of the French queen, Marie Antoinette, whose nation had given crucial navel aid during the American Revolution. Between 1788 and 1790 four different companies of New Englanders, composed of several dozen people - mostly families - arrived at Marietta and began to spread out from there.

The name of their second settlement was *Belle Prairie,* soon shortened to Belpre. **Daniel Mayo** arrived with either the first or the second party of the "Ohio Company of Associates." At least one record has Daniel Mayo arriving at Belpre "in the fall of 1788" and taking up teaching duties that winter.

The journey from Connecticut (the Putnam home state) was a trip of astonishing rigor and tragedy. Here follows an important letter written by **Israel Putnam** (1738-1812), father of **Mary Putnam** (1773-1838), the future wife of Daniel Mayo. When Israel wrote in 1795, to his brother-in-law back in Connecticut, he had already been living in Belpre and had returned to Connecticut to bring out his family, with other settlers.

To Col. Lemuel Grosvner
Postmaster at Pomfret, Conn.
Sunday morning, Belpre, October 18, 1795

Dear and Loving Brother;

I recd your favor of ye 25th ult, last Monday. Am glad to hear of your health and that of our friends and that you got so well through your reviews and ball. We passed on well from Harrisburg till we were ascending the last of the three mountains, and there Clarry [wife of his son Israel] met with a miscarriage which hindered us the day. We made a bier and carried her over to the first plantation, two miles, and there tarried eight days for her to recover and then proceeded on slowly as our cattle could bear, for their shoes were almost all off, and no possibility of getting them on. so we had to wait for their *feet to grow when worn too thin. But after all that, we arrived at headwaters [of Ohio] in two months, only abating the time we laid by for Clarry. So long I laid out to be getting to ye waters. I happened to find a boat ready built and just about large enough at the Monongahela. I bought her and put all our loading aboard, and had her afloat in 36 hours after there. I had sent to Waldo to meet us, which he did three days after we got to the Monongahela, but the next morning after he met us Israel was taken sick and unable to drive his team so that Waldo arrived just soon enough. Before we got to where we took Maum [evidently a pet name for his wife] was taken sick - both with dysentery - Matthews that drove one of our teams, left us after we passed the first mountain. So we had Waldo [the doctor] and George, with a Major White that lives up Muskingum and took passage with us, to man the boat and nurse the sick. The water was low and the passage was very slow. Mr. Cutler and I drove the cattle about 50 miles, but I had not reached there before a messenger overtook us with the information that Maum and Israel were both very dangerously sick at Elizabethtown, a little further above Pittsburgh. I returned and Butler proceeded a little further to good pasture and returned also. Maum and Israel were very low and weak but there was a clever little rise of water and all were a mind to embrace it and did - and got on slowly, for our boat had all our wagon body and its covers and loading and if the wind was ahead we floated up stream, so were obliged to come to till there was calm - Maum and Israel mending slowly.*

Mr. Butler's youngest child about 16 or 18 months old, had been sick and great part of the journey was taken with the disorder and died within a few days. When we arrived at Buffalo the water low and failing and Israel and Maum began to be able to sit up, we were resolved to wait for more favorable water and ye people's recovery. Tarried one week and set off again. Mr. Cutler's oldest daug, 7 or 8 years Old, was taken sick and died before we reached

Muskingum, which was about a month after we first took water, but sickness must be submitted to wherever it overtakes us - all along, some one, two or three of us had considerable complaint of the disorder, enough to [be] waited on if they had not been the "wellest." After all our delays, terrible sickness and deaths on board ye boat - which many times aground and all hands out in the water lifting with iron spikes, etc. we arrived at Marietta ye 18th day of September, Israel so that he could walk with a cane, and Maum a little better, Clarry and Fanny poorly. [Fanny was a little child of Clarry.]

We discharged Cutler, Israel and ye Doctor with their efforts the next day and David attended a singing meeting for Mr. Story had gone to Waterford to preach there. Monday we set off and arrived at Belpre. Tuesday bought a house. Maum and ye girls went on visit to Waldo's about three miles down ye river, George and I cleaning ye house. I believe by this time you are tired of particulars. I think the family are as well pleased with the situation and people as I expected and much better than they expected. Still they want more house room and sundry of their old cooking tools which a little time will replace. I am, or have been, as badly or worse off, for there was not a cart I could borrow and my old shaving brake they have shaved up, finally. I have meat to kill, people to say "how do ye" to and every tool to grind and helve, a shaving brake and a shelter or hovel to make for my cattle in ye winter before I could begin harvesting my corn. But now I have a barrel of good pork, some good dry venison, hams, good turkey hanging ready to roast and with plenty of good soil in ye garden, and ye family have all good health and excellent stomachs. My old shop or cabin has been a hen roost for some years and for ten shillings I bought the cabin full of hens and chickens and have plenty of eggs. Tomorrow I am going to harvesting, wind and weather permitting. Then I shall shut up a pair of hogs and bring in my fatting cow and look a little like living through ye winter. If I can obtain forage enough for my cattle.

Talmadge and Mowry are coming on and are going to reconnoitre the country. By the way Mowry is sick and can not go in person. It has been sickly up the river this season -- owing, some people think to a little standing water just by their stockades. Maum wishes you to let Mr. Barrett to have a little indigo to color some for her - wish you to mention it. As David is with you, he may send him a line. As to the debts due me I shall always be ready to receive ye money, or you may and use it. But don't distress people where it is perfectly safe; where it is otherwise, I would have the money collected, or ample security given to your full satisfaction. I expect to want money in ye spring, but don't know of wanting sooner. The family's best respects to you and yours and all friends. I received two letters from David [his son] when I arrived at Marietta. I know nothing of his views and consequently can give him no advice. You can help him to a little cash if he stands in need. If ye young mare at Captain Scarboroughs is not in foal he can break and ride her, if he chooses. Shall be happy to hear from you and him as often as anything worth offers and you may expect the same from me.

Yours etc.
I. Putnam

By 1789, the Belpre settlement consisted of a few dozen log cabins on the banks of the Ohio River. The inhabitants had purchased hundreds of acres and arranged for a survey before they ever left the East. They were now anxious to establish ownership by making improvements on the land and cultivating a crop. They began farming in the spring of that year. The Marietta and Belpre settlers were intent upon taming the territory with plow and cow. But they were cautious in this wilderness. The prudence of this well lead community was life-saving.

Ohio Country was, from the perspective of the national government, considered part of the "North West Territory." Ohio was a vast region, stretching west from the

Allegheny Mountains. The term loosely described the land west and south of Pittsburgh and included what became the states of West Virginia and Kentucky as well as Eastern Ohio.

Most of the early English-speaking settlers would not have been very well informed about the native people already resident in these potentially valuable farmlands. The existing population was made up of peoples who were called, by the English-speakers, Shawnees, Delaware and Mingoes. They were all Iroquois, and had been displaced from their homes in the east. These aboriginal settlers had populated the region beginning roughly a hundred years earlier (1600s). The country had been largely depopulated subsequently, as a result of clan warfare, epidemics and out migrations eastward by people who wanted closer trading access to the European settlements in the coastal colonies. But in the 1700s Ohio again was drawing hunter-gatherers, whose claims to the land were surely as good as the newbie European adventurers, whether French trappers or English traders. The English sometimes arrived with families in tow.

The Shawnee appear to have been among the prehistoric occupants, which would have given them an ancient claim to the Ohio Country. By 1790, the Shawnee were re-occupying what they viewed as ancestral lands, but they found themselves sharing it with other clans, who had been forced back westward by the advancing European-based migration into western Pennsylvania.

No doubt the Shawnee, Delaware and Mingoe inhabitants had varying opinions about the presence of small numbers of the English-speakers. These white settlers, unlike the French trappers, often came with wives and children and gave every intention of planning to stay. Some of the "Indian towns" welcomed trading opportunities. Others nurtured family or clan memories of having been forced once before from these very lands and then having been compelled to move back onto them by the ever-pressing Europeans. These were adamant against being forced off once again.

The clans had made friendly overtures to the leaders of the Belpre and Marietta settlements but the Indians appeared to be hostile to additional White encampments. The distinction drawn by the Indians may have been that the Belpre and Marietta settlers were not Pennsylvanians, who were seen as the main threat, having already pushed out the clans. Any such distinction was artificial; the beginning of a great European migration into the Ohio Country was under way. The stage was set for bloody conflict, which came soon enough.

FARMER'S CASTLE

In 1790 a new association was formed among more recently arrived English-speakers. This company came to be known as "Big Bottom" for the expanse of rich lands it encompassed. These associates appear to have been individuals who arrived haphazardly into the Marietta and Belpre settlements. Half of the thirty-six members of the Big Bottom partnership went immediately to establish their new settlement. They were mostly young men, impatient to begin their project. Apparently the Big Bottom settlers rejected the advice of the Belpre and Marietta pioneers, who thought eighteen homesteaders were too few to discourage attack by the people already in occupation of the lands everyone wanted. But the impatient Big Bottom settlers went into their chosen lands and built three log houses. No stockade or other defenses were erected around the block-houses.

In the winter of 1790-91 the settlement was attacked and twelve pioneers were killed. A handful of terrified survivors escaped to the other settlements, which organized an armed party and found the bodies of the victims, piled inside one of the block-houses. Floor boards had been tossed on top and the building and the corpses set afire.

The settlers at Belpre responded by gathering together and building a garrison along the Ohio River, into which all of the families moved. They called their new, walled community "Farmer's Castle" and adopted a military regimen. A commander was selected; roll was called each morning. Able bodied men were mustered, given assignments and punished with extra chores for tardiness and other lapses. A flagstaff was set up and a swivel gun ("howitz") was placed on a platform and fired frequently in the spring and summer months, echoing up and down the Ohio River.

The community soon turned to the scholarly needs of its children and established a school in one of the blockhouses. The first teacher of the older children was the young, unmarried, Harvard-educated **Daniel Mayo** (1762-1838). Daniel taught the children in Farmer's Castle during the winter months and, like the other men, spent his summers cultivating crops. Farmer's Castle seems to have been occupied until 1794. A "treaty" was signed at about that time and the threat of attack from *the originals* had largely dissipated, to reemerge again at the time of the "second war with England," that is, the War of 1812.

Before his marriage to **Mary Putnam** (1773-1838), Daniel Mayo left Belpre and moved to a downriver village, Losantville (renamed, thankfully, Cincinnati). Daniel's relocation seems to have been prompted by his appointment to the job of assistant postmaster at Cincinnati in about 1795. His connections to the Adams family might have facilitated this federal job, which was made during George Washington's presidency, when John Adams, the father of Daniel's Harvard classmate, was Vice-President.

In 1796 Daniel relinquished the postmaster appointment in Ohio but soon replaced it with a like appointment across the Ohio River in his new residence in Newport, Kentucky. Daniel held the postmaster position in Newport for the rest of his life. The 1834 City Directory for Newport lists Daniel Mayo as Postmaster with a residence at Columbia and Front Streets.

By the time Daniel moved across the river to Newport, he had begun to court young Mary Putnam, daughter of **Israel Putnam Jr**, one of the leaders of the

Marietta/Belpre settlers. Mary preserved a letter Daniel wrote to her in their courting days, from Newport, Kentucky:

> Miss Mary Putnam, Belpre Ohio
> Newport, August 14, 1796
> My dear Mary,
>
> I have written you two letters since you left Kentucky, which I hope you have received, and, agreeable to my promise, write you by this day's feast, concluding a line from me would not be disagreeable to you, and if it gives you half the pleasure in perusing that it does me in writing, I shall be amply compensated for my trouble.
> The time, dear Mary, I have is not far distant, when this way of communicating our sentiments of esteem will be useless. I anxiously wait that moment when my eyes shall once more see the objects on which my thoughts are so much employed. The [ ] are now [ ] from a 'Friend' which I hope will occupy it early in October in whose company and conversation I anticipate much happiness.
> I do not think I can content myself here in my present situation more than six weeks longer, but shall ascend the Ohio in quest of happiness. When I shall set out I shall inform you.
> Our friend Mrs. Austin appears to be very happy in her partner. She has got a very industrious and [ ] husband. She has signified a wish to accompany me this fall to Belpre on a visit to her friend, but whether she will or in what manner I shall go is uncertain. Therefore, it is as yet all talk.
> I have nothing new or interesting to communicate to you at this time. I enjoy a fine state of health and as great a flow of spirits as is feasible in the absence of <u>my friend</u>. Adieu my dear. I shall close this letter in your own words as there is no sentiment more consonant to the feelings of my breast than those you closed your last (Viz.) In a continuance of your friendship and correspondence rests the happiness of - Daniel Mayo

Daniel's sentiments found their resonance with Mary, but the wedding did not take place in Belpre until October of 1798. By then, Daniel owned nine acres in Campbell County, KY. By 1800 he was listed as postmaster of Newport, KY and the owner of 24 acres. The energetic Daniel and his bride arrived in the hamlet of Newport as landowners with a government appointment to a paying federal job. No doubt, Daniel and Mary, with their "Up East" connections and accents were accepted as prominent and important newcomers in the community.

It was soon clear Daniel and Mary had decided to invest their lives and resources in this Ohio River village, as Daniel took up a variety of official duties in his new hometown. In December 1798, he joined a half dozen other citizens as a founding trustee of Newport Academy. In February, 1799, he was appointed Justice of the Peace in Newport. In April of that year, he was appointed election superintendent. In September, Daniel was made a Commissioner to receive from the county sheriff all monies collected since the county was established. In April 1800, he was appointed "Capt. of a Patrole," with two assistants, each of whom was to commit 12 hours a month to this duty; in October he was paid 16 schillings for two wolf scalps. Also in October, 1800, Daniel was made Judge of Presidential electors, thereby assisting in the certification that year of the election of Thomas Jefferson, who defeated and replaced Daniel Mayo's family friend, John Adams, as President of the United States.

MARY PUTNAM & THE PUTNAMS, PORTERS AND HA(W)THORNS

Mary Putnam (1773-1838) was born on August 5, 1773 in Brooklyn, CT. One of eight children, Mary's mother was **Sarah Waldo** (?-?) and her father was **Israel Putnam Jr** (1738-1812), one of ten children of **Hannah Pope** (1739-1766) and **General Israel Putnam** (1717/18-1790), famous to history for purportedly shouting to his soldiers at the Battle of Bunker Hill, June 16-17,

1775. "Don't fire until you see the whites of their eyes!"

Although a tactical victory for the British, the Battle of Bunker Hill was a great boost to the morale of the raw New England militia, who inflicted 1054 killed and wounded and took only 441 losses against British regular army troops. General Gage reported to London, "Those people shew a spirit and a conduct against us they never shewed against the French."

Was Gage thinking of the colonial militia under the youthful George Washington and their embarrassing failure to oust the French from Fort Duquesne (Pittsburgh) in 1755? Perhaps, but this sorry encounter was actually a British failure to adapt their strategies to a wilderness context; Washington had acquitted himself well – and would do so again, two decades later.

General Putnam, unlike his son and namesake (father of Mary), was, we state it mildly, unlettered. Earlier biographers also have treated this topic gently. "His early instruction was not considerable" wrote Humphreys (1788), who credited Putnam with a style in spelling, which went for the sound and sense but little precision otherwise. A later observer referred to this trait as "epigrammatic laconicism," whose meaning may be: *Caint spel – don't care*. No matter. "Old Put" was fearless and direct and his soldiers loved him. In 1776, after the soldiers in his command narrowly escaped capture on Long Island, *Old Put* (who truly was elderly) was removed from command and placed in charge of recruitment.

Mary Putnam's ancestry has been traced through the Putnams to seventeenth century Salem, Massachusetts and from there to England, where an ancestor, **George Puttenham** (?-c 1590) wrote **Arte of English Poesie** (1589). Or did he? If not George then his brother Richard (?-1601) wrote this vital book. Nineteenth century scholarly opinion favored Richard as the author. He was known to have traveled much in Europe as did the writer of *Poesie*, George apparently never traveled much.

General Israel Putnam
practitioner of "epigrammatic laconicism"

The author of *Poesie*, whether George or Richard, was impressed with the literary talents of Edward de Vere (1550-1604), 17th Earl of Oxford, an ancient relative (page 245, above). The author of *Poesie* stated that de Vere ought to be ranked "first among noblemen-poets if their doings could be made public." This contemporary Elizabethan's opinion is suggestive of the idea (among much other data) that Edward de Vere wrote under the pseudonym, "William Shake-speare," perhaps in occasional collaboration with his young, unlettered associate from Stratford-upon-Avon, Wil Shaksper. If we could only ask the old Puttenhams for details about their pal, the 17th Earl of Oxford. And did they happen to know Wil Shaksper?

The Puttenham who wrote *Poesie*, seems to have tried his own hand at poetry. The results suggest he may have been better at assessing the works of others than of creating his own. George Puttenham is believed to have written, of Queen Elizabeth:

> *Her cheeke, her chinne, her neck, her nose*
> *This was a lillye, that was a rose.*

And so on. This stuff did not keep George out of trouble at Court, as we shall see.

The parents of George and Richard were **Robert Puttenham** (?-?) and **Margaret Elyot** (?-?) a sister (daughter?) of Sir **Thomas Elyot** (1490?-1546), himself the writer of books. Sir Thomas wrote concerning the proper education of a statesman, *The Book Named the Governour* (1531) as well as the first known Latin-English dictionary (1538). Sir Thomas also wrote, for the benefit of Margaret's sons, *the Education or Bringing up of Children*. Sir Thomas' example as a scholar and writer may have been more useful to Richard (or George) than his advice to their mother about how best to bring up these boys. Both George and Richard Puttenham were often in prison and/or in disgrace. Richard was jailed when *Poesie* was licensed to the printer. In 1597, he made his will from debtor's prison, King's Bench Prison (re-named Queens

Bench in the 1840s). Richard was buried on July 2nd 1601 at ancient St. Clement Danes on the Strand in London. Brother George was said to have been implicated in a plot against the powerful Lord Burghley (William Cecil) in 1570; in December 1578 George is found in prison. George was also involved in litigation against his relatives and won reparations ordered by the Privy Council for wrongs done to him by them. George's will was made Sept 1, 1590.

"Puttenham" is said to be a compound of the Flemish PUTTE (*well*) and HAM (*hamlet*), thus, the lands of a village with its well. Land transfer records connect the Puttenhams to one Anachitil, an associate of William the Norman conqueror of England (1066). Roger, a son of Anachitil, was recorded tenant and holder of the lands of Puttenham in 1088. The extraordinarily comprehensive land census of that year – the Doomsday Book - identifies Roger as overlord and holder of the lands for Odo, Bishop of Bayeaux and half-brother to William the Conqueror. When last names began to be used in England we find mention of William of Puttenham in the mid 1100s. His daughter, Matilda married Richard Fitz-Wale of Puttenham. The proper names Puttenham (Pottenham) and Fitz-Wale (sometimes, Filius Wales) leap frog through the later Middle Ages as owners of this land, which is some forty miles north of London, near the ancient village of Tring in Buckinghamshire. But consecutive ownership does not necessarily mean common lineage.

John Putnam (?-1662), a near descendent (believed but not proved) of the star-crossed and imprisoned George Puttenham, immigrated from Aston Abbots, Buckinghamshire, to Salem Village in 1634. There he took possession of a land grant he had received by 1641, and left lands to his three sons, **Thomas**, Nathaniel and John.

John's son **Thomas Putnam** (?-1686) married twice. After his first wife, Anne Holyoke died in 1665, Thomas married **Mary Veren** (?-1695). In 1690, their son **Joseph Putnam** (1669-1724), married **Elizabeth Porter** (?-1746), and moved her into the Putnam House, built by Thomas Putnam in 1648. The house may still stand at the foot of Hawthorne Hill in Salem. Here was born **Israel Putnam** (1717/18-1790), the famous future General, the youngest, but one, of the thirteen children of Joseph and Elizabeth Porter Putnam.

The marriage of Thomas Putnam and Mary Veren brought severe consequences to Thomas' children by his first wife Ann Holyoke. In his will, Thomas favored young Joseph, to the injury of Ann's children, with the result that the Holyoke branch of the Putnam family was disbursed from Salem, while Joseph and his progeny enjoyed the accumulated wealth of at least three prior American generations of Putnams.

Joseph's wife, Elizabeth Porter Putnam, came from relative wealth. Her father, **Israel Porter** (1643-1706) was a merchant and holder of extensive lands. Israel's parents were **Mary** _____ and **John Porter** (?-abt 1673) Israel Porter's wife (and so Elizabeth Porter Putnam's mother) was **Elizabeth Hathorne** (1649-?), daughter of **Anne (Smith ?)** (abt 1612-aft 1681) and the prominent Puritan magistrate **William Hathorn(e)** (1606/07-1681), who became famous as a persecutor of all enemies in the eyes of the state and heretics in the eyes of the church.

WILLIAM HATHORNE: "NARROW AND BIGOTED IN HIS RELIGIOUS THEORIES . . . ARBITRARY AND INTOLERANT IN THE ADMINISTRATION OF AFFAIRS, BOTH IN CHURCH AND STATE"

William James wrote of this William Hathorne:

He was one of the band of companions of the virtuous and exemplary John Winthrop, the almost lifelong royal Governor of the young colony, and the brightest and most amiable figure in the early Puritan annals. How amiable William Hathorne may have been I know not, but he was evidently of the stuff of which the citizens of the Commonwealth were best advised to be made. He was a sturdy fighting man, doing solid execution upon both the inward and outward enemies of the State. The latter were the savages, the former the Quakers; the energy expended by the early Puritans in resistance to the tomahawk not weakening their disposition to deal with spiritual dangers. They employed the same--or almost the same--weapons in both directions; the flintlock and the halberd against the Indians, and the cat-o'-nine-tails against the heretics. One of the longest, though by no means one of the most successful, of Hawthorne's shorter tales (The Gentle Boy) deals with this pitiful persecution of the least aggressive of all schismatic bodies.

William Hathorne, who had been made a magistrate of the town of Salem, where a grant of land had been offered him as an inducement to residence, figures in New England history as having given orders that "Anne Coleman and four of her friends" should be whipped through Salem, Boston, and Dedham. This Anne Coleman, I suppose, is the woman alluded to in that fine passage in the Introduction to The Scarlet Letter, in which Hawthorne pays a qualified tribute to the founder of the American branch of his race.

William Hathorne, who so stirred the sensibilities of William James, was the double great-grandfather of Nathaniel Hawthorne (1804-1864), who wrote broodingly of him (Introduction to **The Scarlet Letter**),

The figure of that first ancestor, invested by family tradition with a dim and dusky grandeur, was present to my boyish imagination as far back as I can remember. It still haunts me, and induces a sort of home-feeling with the past, which I scarcely claim in reference to the present, phase of the town. I seem to have a stronger claim to a residence here on account of this grave, bearded, sable-cloaked and steeple-crowned progenitor-- who came so early, with his Bible and his sword, and trod the unworn street with such a stately port, and made so large a figure as a man of war and peace--a stronger claim than for myself, whose name is seldom heard and my face hardly known. He was a soldier, legislator, judge; he was a ruler in the church; he had all the Puritanic traits, both good and evil. He was likewise a bitter persecutor, as witness the Quakers, who have remembered him in their histories, and relate an incident of his hard severity towards a woman of their sect which will last longer, it is to be feared, than any of his better deeds, though these were many.

One should not mistakenly conclude that either William James or Nathaniel Hawthorne was viewing seventeenth century Salem through the lens of the *enlightened* nineteenth century. William Hathorne was indeed the serious, devout, energetic and intolerant leader of men Nathaniel Hawthorne and William James were at pains to describe. But James may have confused the military expeditions of Captain William the son with Major William the father. James also misstated Hathorne's role in important matters with John Winthrop; the two were sometimes on opposite sides of disputed public questions.

Even before Nathaniel Hawthorne made the name of his double great-grandfather a byword for Puritan cruelty and excess, our William Hathorne was viewed harshly by contemporaries. Called "Hathorn" in the Journal of John Winthrop, the Major was known as mean spirited and excessively harsh in his judgments. At a session of colonial Deputies in 1641, Hathorn, then a deputy (legislator) from Salem, urged the removal of two of the "ancienest magistrates because they were grown poor." This provoked John Cotton in his next sermon "to confute and sharply (in his mild manner) to reprove such miscarriage, which he termed a slighting or dishonoring of parents." Cotton went on, according to Winthrop in his Journal, to say "that such as were decayed in their estates by attending the service of the country ought to be maintained by the country and not [be] set aside for their poverty." Winthrop himself criticized Hathorn for moving to criminalize "lying, swearing, etc." Hathorn lost both these initiatives because of the stout resistance of a majority of the deputies and magistrates. Winthrop wrote in his journal that it was "a great error" when Hathorn was selected a commissioner for the United Colonies (1644: Massachusetts, Connecticut, New Haven, and Plymouth).

William Hathorn was son of **Sara** (?-?) and **William Hathorn** (?-?) of Binfield, Birkshire County, England. The younger William and his wife Anne sailed to Plymouth in 1630 on the *Arbella*. They arrived with John Winthrop and the flotilla that initiated the Great Migration of the 1630s. The Hathorn(e)s settled in Dorchester, a community organized under the leadership of another of Betty Taylor Cook's ancestors, the Rev. **John Maverick** (1578-1635/6). (See page 201.) By 1636 William and Anne were living in Salem, having received a grant of land. William was thereafter often selected from Salem as a deputy (legislator). He was the first speaker of the House of Deputies in 1644. George M. Bodge, our source, wrote, in 1891, that Hathorn's forcefulness in defense of the personal rights of "freemen" (landowners) made him popular, but that Hathorn "was evidently narrow and bigoted in his religious theories and arbitrary and intolerant in the administration of affairs, both in church and state."

William and Anne Hathorn were the parents of eight children: a daughter (name not remembered), then Sarah (1634-?), Eleazer (1637-?), Nathaniel (1639-?), John (1641-?), Anne (1643-?), William (1645-78/9) and **Elizabeth** (1649-?), wife of **Israel Porter** (1643-1706) and mother of **Elizabeth Porter Putnam** (1649-1746).

KING PHILIP'S WAR AND THE HA(W)THORNE LINE

William Hathorn (husband of **Anne**) was a leader among the citizen-soldiers, who volunteered to protect the settlements. In 1646, he held a Captain's commission in Salem Company and was a Major by 1656. William's son, William III (the two have been confused in some of the annals of colonial times) was also a soldier, protecting the colonists in their wars against the native peoples. The most powerful of the local clans were the Narragansett. William Hathorn III was a Captain in the campaign against Wampanoag and Narragansett towns during King Philip's War, 1675-77. ("King Philip" was the English name given by the settlers to the Wampanoag leader, Metacomb.) These assaults on residents in their communities, first by one side and then the other, was one of the most savage encounters between indigenous and immigrant peoples in US history, colonial and national.

The war was triggered by the execution by Plymouth Colony officials of several Wampanoag tribal members for the 1674 murder of John Sassamon (also a Wampanoag) who had informed Colony authorities that the Wampanoag, under the leadership of Metacomb, were arming themselves for a planned attack upon the colonists. The truth of this accusation was disputed at the time by Metacomb. After the clan was accused of making preparations for war on the English-speaking settlers, there is no question that both sides began then (if not sooner) to ready themselves for warfare.

For two generations prior to the war, the Plymouth Colony Wampanoag (Algonquians of southern New England) and the English-speaking settlers had been living as neighbors. Matacomb, leader of the Wampanoag was a son (or grandson) of Massasoit, the Wampanoag chief, whose welcome of the first Europeans had occasioned the first Thanksgiving. By 1660, many Wampanoag had moved into "praying towns" where their conversion to Christianity was encouraged – though they were mostly refused baptism. In Rhode Island in 1675, attempts were made to avoid bloodshed. This more accommodating environment was fostered by Roger Williams, who had been banished from Plymouth Colony, and who thus knew a victim of persecution when he saw one. Metacomb, who resided in Rhode Island and made a living as a pig farmer, was invited to meet with the Lieutenant Governor of that Colony. Metacomb complained that a once mutually respectful relationship had been subverted by the raw and biased use of the Plymouth colonial legal system to criminalize the Wampanoag who refused to live in praying towns. The objective of colonial policy, Metacomb asserted, was to deprive the tribe of their remaining lands, so that now "they had no hopes left of keeping any land."

After the June 1675 executions of the supposed killers of John Sassamon, the Wampanoag began to attack English-speaking settlements in Plymouth Colony. Before long they were joined by many other Algonquin tribes in southern New England, including the powerful Narragansett. Of almost one hundred English-speaking Plymouth towns, fifty were attacked and twelve were destroyed. Dozens of colonists were killed. In December 1675, Captain Hathorne (William Hathorn III) assumed leadership of the Salem foot company of ninety-five men. His elevation occurred after commander, William Gardiner had been killed during an assault on the Narragansett's fortified town. Others of Betty Taylor Cook's ancestors figured in this war. **Jeremy/Jeremiah Swayne** (1643-1710), Betty's great grandfather x 7, was a Lieutenant under Capt. Samuel Appleton and was wounded at Narragansett Fort. (See page 187.)

By the winter of 1675-76, the tide of battle had turned against the native peoples. Their towns had been destroyed and they were living in makeshift winter settlements in New York, where they were attacked by colonists and Mohawk clansmen. Disease and famine completed the annihilation, which losses in battle had begun. By the summer of 1676, surviving Wampanoag, including Metacomb, were hunted down and killed. Wampanoag children and women, including Metacomb's nine-year-old son, were sold into slavery, either in Barbados or Massachusetts. In truth, the Wampanoag and their allies never had much of a chance. By 1660, the native population, which numbered perhaps 15,000 in 1620, had declined to half that number. When war came, they found themselves living among some 60,000 colonists, who could also draw on the aid of other native peoples (the Mohawk) to exterminate the Wampanoag.

"HELLISH CONJURERS, SUCH AS CONVERSED WITH DEMONS"

A sometimes overlooked justification for the extermination of the native peoples of New England was their allegiance to Satan. Congregational ministers denounced the Indians for being in blatant and unforgivable opposition to the God of the Puritan and Pilgrim colonizers. In 1699, Cotton Mather, in his **Decennium Luctuosum**, equated warfare against native people with the will of God, much as the just-concluded witch trials were so characterized. In fact, Mather explicitly linked the two campaigns, holding that witchcraft among the English might have its source among the Indians, who were well known to be "horrid sorcerers, and hellish conjurers, and such as conversed with demons."

In 1671, Puritan missionary John Eliot created a fanciful dialogue between himself and the recently killed Wampanoag leader, Metacomb ("King Philip"). Massasoit, the Wampanoag chief at the time of the first English settlement had welcomed the English and celebrated with them (it is supposed) that first Thanksgiving. However, in the view of the pious missionary John Eliot, there was nothing for the Pilgrims to be thankful for in Massasoit's son (or grandson), Chief Metacomb.

Eliot, in his imaginary dialogue, has Metacomb reject Christian belief, because, as the missionary has him confess, should Metacomb pray to the God of the English Pilgrims "I shall be empty and weak." Eliot imagines Metacomb, Rhode Island pig farmer, to concede that his rejection of God will cause his own damnation. "Oh what mountains of sin have I heaped up in my wicked life!" cries Metacomb. "My heart doth loath myself to remember them. They make me abhorring to God." And so began, in print, by 1671, the invention of the SAVAGE in American rhetoric.

John Eliot and Cotton Mather were early practitioners of that venerable crisis strategy: demonize the enemy/victim. They were not the first. In the 1630s

European settlers undertook a campaign of extermination of the Pequot, after this tribe was accused of killing an English trader on Block Island. In 1637 Pequot settlements and crops on Block Island were burned and a Pequot fort at Mystic, Connecticut was attacked and set afire. Some 600 Pequot were slaughtered as they tried to escape the flames. Survivors fled west but virtually all were captured either by colonists or Mohawk Indians and killed.

Surviving Pequot men were sent in slavery to Barbados; women and children were enslaved by Mohawks and colonists, including Governor Winthrop. As few as 200 Pequot survive today. They are taking their revenge; in Ledyard, CT, the Pequot operate one of the largest casinos on the East Coast.

Without question, the colonists in 1636-7 were under a severe provocation as isolated settlers were occasionally killed or kidnapped in individual acts or by the conduct of a raiding party. Their brutal response was mimicry of the behavior of contemporary English occupiers of Ireland, where butchery was practiced against the native Irish people, and where the justification entailed the citing of Biblical narratives in which the children of Israel exterminated their enemies at the command of God. Even if it is conceded that the necessity of survival justifies an overwhelming reaction, this circumstance does not excuse the murder of a defeated and surrendered foe and the enslavement of the non-combatant mother and child. The Pequot were early victims in America of the notion that members of an opposing race are of a lower, inferior species.

In denouncing and condemning their Indian adversaries and approving their wholesale slaughter, Mather and Eliot believed they were endorsing God's will. They were persuaded that divine intentions could be discerned in the existence of the new society that pious Congregationalists of Plymouth and Massachusetts Bay colonies were inventing in the wilderness. By the nineteenth century, American sociologists would see such triumphal rhetoric as a form of *ethnocentrism*, by which ones own group is deemed superior to any other group or tribe – especially a group in opposition. The twentieth century term, *pseudo speciation*, describes the same attitude, but perhaps with a more precise recognition of the near total dismissal of the OTHER, as a justification of the many genocidal campaigns of that century.

Beginning in the earliest encounters, Aboriginal resisters such as Metacomb, were made, rhetorically and then by treaty, to justify their own removal and extermination. Notably, accused witches were also compelled to confess against themselves, thereby demonstrating the flexible hatreds of the dominant Puritans, and their willingness to cast out even their own, who were sufficiently nonconforming. Bridget Bishop, the first condemned witch to be killed in the 1691-2 hysteria, had been accused of witchcraft almost twenty years before, during Metacomb's war. These earlier accusations against her did not stick; the second set of charges did.

One of Major William's Hathorne's sons and thus **Elizabeth Hathorne Porter**'s brother was John Hathorne (1641-1717), a judge at the Salem witch trials of the 1690s. The disgrace of this affair, in which some twenty "witches" were hanged or pressed to death, may have caused the Hathorne family to change its name to "Hawthorne." (This seems doubtful; could such a small change blot out such a large dishonor? My guess is, a "w" was added by a clerk or notary.) Whether the family declined as a result, the stain and embarrassment of the legal murders in Salem contributed to the decline of godly evangelism (Puritanism, as we call it) in New England. The cruel witch trials brought lasting discredit to the Puritan vision of a resplendent city on a hill, to be seen and admired by all the world.

For these early Hathorns, the righteous founding vision required a coercive prosecutorial system. But both the vision and the system broke up on the rock of a stout American individualism, which was also imported by the founders. The weakening of an enforced consensus about how a moral society ought to conduct its affairs was abetted by the localized ethos of scattered settlements. Finding themselves on the fringe of the limitless expanse of a new continent, many of the second and third generations of English settlers, born in America, had no direct and personal experience of English society, with its classism and its King, taken to be god's agent on earth. These native born Americans saw little reason to force each other to march to church in lock step with Cotton Mather. Although revivalist fervor prompted the occasional resurgence of devotion, the passage of time increased the decay. By the Revolution, the truly devout, in the earlier rigorous Puritan style, were merely quaint. A more generous spirited "Deism" was the new self-designation of those educated Americans, who acknowledged their religious promptings.

Of the descendents of the Puritans, few who moved inland in the eighteenth and nineteenth centuries brought with them more than a mutated and mild form of their ancestors' strict religious allegiances. The serious-minded Putnams, who moved to Ohio in the 1780s and '90s, tried to plant their religious heritage in their new surroundings. They founded Congregational churches in Belpre and Marietta. But if the Putnams carried a high religious banner into Ohio, they were nevertheless marching near the end of the Puritan parade. One might even say, their form of Congregationalism, build on voluntarism and not coercion, was not a confirmation of the early purifying impulses, but rather a refutation of them.

Generally, on the Ohio and Kentucky frontier, transplanted New Englanders, Pennsylvanians, Virginians and Marylanders, too, were happy enough to enroll as Baptists and Methodists, if they enrolled in church at all. They were contented to see their children married by poorly educated, part-time preacher-farmers or itinerant evangelists, who might appear in the nearest hamlet to do the job. The unfortunate Bridget Bishop, probably more indifferent than hostile to a religious establishment, yet murdered as a witch, was born a century too soon.

"BRIDGET BISHOP BEFORE THE WORSHIPFULL JOHN HARTHON"

In Salem in the 1690s, the founding vision burned bright enough to light actual flesh-consuming fires, although the mode of execution of witches was the noose. Why did the Witch Trials happen? We might blame it on a church organization, which put violent zealots in charge of the courts. The government of the early Puritans was loosely patterned on a Reformed Church structure devised by that other Swiss reformer, Ulrich Zwingli (1484-1531), rather than by John Calvin (1509-1564). The difference is that Zwingli's Zurich was governed by the local court, whereas Calvin's Geneva and its judges and politicians were controlled by officials of the Reformed Church, sitting as a Consistory.

Would matters have gone differently in Salem if the Congregational pattern adopted in Massachusetts had followed Calvin's model rather than Zwingli's? This is doubtful. Before the Zwingli court-control model can be seen as the culprit, a case can be made that the Witch Trials were an attempt by a fading Puritan vision to reverse social fragmentation and restore the old (imaginary?) consensus. If so, the powers would have tried to keep control, whether directly through the courts or through a Calvinist-inspired hierarchy with local pastors in charge, to denounce, condemn and order executions.

Calvin's spirit seems to have been loosed in Salem even if his polity was not followed. He of course saw to the burning of people. Zwingli, in contrast, was the leading reformer most influenced by the humanist, Erasmus. While he lacked the theological depth of Luther and Calvin, Zwingli's broader reading in philosophy inclined him to ridicule rather than denounce clerical abuses. He was very much in step with a humanist spirit of tolerance, which was attractive to many (but not all) of the citizens of the free cities of Europe. In Salem, by contrast, any hint of celebration of humanity, which did not give glory to God in the prescribed Congregational forms, would have been denounced along with the alleged witchcraft.

His many descendents may find encouragement in the example of **Joseph Putnam** (1669-1724), father of the first **Israel**. Joseph has been credited with voicing strong objections to the witchcraft hysteria, which pervaded Salem and the surrounding communities in 1692. Joseph Putnam was contemptuous of the proceedings even though his wife's uncle was a prosecutor/judge at the trials and despite threats of violence directed against him by some of his own Putnam relatives. Joseph was probably too well placed to be in any real danger. The witch-accusations suffered not only from an inherent cruel absurdity but also from a class elitism, which found its victims in the lower social ranks.

Putnams, Porters and Hathorns played crucial rolls on all sides of the witch trials in Salem in 1692. **Joseph Putnam** denounced the toxic hysteria and his father-in-law **Israel Porter** held to similar opinions and worked unsuccessfully for the release of some of the accused. Meanwhile several Putnam girls and women brought early accusations and testified against the accused, some of whom were interrogated and found guilty by **Elizabeth Hathorn Porter**'s brother, John. The witnesses provided details of terrifying visitations to which they were being subjected by the "witches" among their own neighbors. Example: two children, Mercy Lewis and Ann Putnam accused Bridget Bishop of attempting to make them sign "the devil's Book." (See Supplement, below, page 412.)

The transcript of John Hathorne's April 19, 1692 examination of Bridget Bishop, before her conviction and hanging, makes for somber, sorry reading.

(The examination of Bridget Bishop before the Worshipfull John Harthon and Jonathan Curren esq'rs)

Bridget Bishop being now coming in to be examined relating to her accusation of Suspicon of sundry acts of witchcrafts the afflicted persons are now dreadfully afflicted by her as they doe say.

(Mr. Harthon) Bishop what doe you say you here stand charged with sundry acts of witchcraft by you done or committed upon the bodyes of Mercy Lews and An Putnam and others.

(Bishop) I am innocent I know nothing of it I have done no witchcraft

(Mr. Har) Looke upon this woman and see if this be the woman that you have seen hurting you. Mercy Lewes and An Putnam and others doe [doe] now charge her to her face with hurting of them.

(Mr. Harthon) What doe you say now you see they charge you to your face

(Bish) I never did hurt them in my life I did never see these persons before I am as innocent as the child unborn

(Mr. Harth) is not your coate cut

(Bish) [RECORDER's NOTE: answers no but her garment being Looked upon they find it cut or toren two wayes Jonathan walcoate saith that the sword that he strucke at goode Bishup with was not naked but was within the scabbord so that the rent may very probablie be the very same that mary walcoate did tell that she had in her coate by Jonathans stricking at her apperance The afflicted persons charge her, with having hurt them many wayes and by tempting them to sine to the devils Booke at which charge she seemed to be very angrie and shaking her head at them saying it was false they are all greatly tormented (as I conceive) by the shaking of her head]

(Mr Har) good Bishop what contract have you made with the devill

(Bish) I have made no contract with the devill I never saw

him in my life. An Putnam sayeth that shee calls the devill her God

(Mr. Har) what say you to all this that you are charged with can you not find in your heart to tell the truth

(Bish) I doe tell the truth I never hurt these persons in my life I never saw them before.

(Mercy Lewes) oh goode Bishop did you not come to our house the Last night and did you not tell me that your master made you tell mor than you were willing to tell

(Mr Har) tell us the truth in this matter how comes these persons to be thus tormented and to charge you with doing

(Bish) I am not come here to say I am a witch to take away my life

(Mr H) who is that that doth it if you doe not they say it is your likenes that comes and torments them and tempts them to write in the booke what Booke is that you tempt them with.

(Bish) I know nothing of it I am innocent.

(Mr Harth) doe you not see how they are tormented you are acting witchcraft before us what doe you say to ths why have you not an heart to confese the truth

(Bish) I am innocent I know nothing of it I am no witch I know not what a witch is.

(Mr H) have you not given consent that some evill spirit should doe this in your likeness.

(B) no I am innocent of being a witch I know no man woman or child here

(Marshall Herrik) how came you into my bed chamber one morning then and asked me whether I had any curtains to sell shee is by some of the aflicted persons charged with murder

(Mr Harth) what doe you say to these murders you are charged with

(B) I am innocent I know nothing of it now she lifts up her eyes and they are greatly tormented again

(Mr Har) what doe you say to these things here horrible acts of witch craft

(Bish) I know nothing of it I doe not know whither be any witches or no

(Mr Har) no have you not heard that some have confessed.

(Bish) no I did not.

[RECORDER's NOTE: two men told her to her face that they had told her here shee is taken in a plain lie now shee is going away they are dreadfully afflicted 5 afflicted persons doe charge this woman to be the very woman that hurts them This is a true account of what I have taken down at her examination according to best understanding and observation I have also in her examination taken notice that all her actions have great influence upon the aflicted persons and that they have been tortored by her] [signed] Ezekiel Cheever

This transcript was presented at trial, two weeks later, as evidence in itself of witchcraft. The only further evidence presented was a series of witnesses who accused Bridget Bishop of such things as appearing as a specter to them in closed rooms, of killing a pig and of causing pocket change to disappear. Beyond this was the report to the judges of an examination of the body of the accused, for marks of the devil. Bridget Bishop was searched twice, just before the first day of trial and immediately after. A committee of women stuck pins into her body and found a "witch's tet" between "ye pupendum and anus." This was said to be an unnatural orifice by which Bridget Bishop would suckle the devil as it appeared in the familiar form of a small shaggy animal. On a second examination, just three hours later, the "tet" had disappeared but the claim was then made that the devil had removed his mark to protect her. Bridget Bishop was condemned as a witch and hanged, but only after the General Court of the colony had revived a law making witchcraft a capital offense. Thus did the Salem Witch Trials become linked with "wars" against Indian towns, as legislators and judges prostrated themselves before pious hysteria in mortal combat with demons.

Some of the family, notably Nathaniel Hawthorne's cousin Ann Savage, defended their great grandfather. John Hathorne, it is contended, was simply doing his duty in posing questions to victims and the accused alike, in a time when belief in witchcraft was widespread. But the evidence presented was patently absurd and accused witches were treated with cruelty and considered condemned at the outset.

Relatives of some of the condemned and even some of the victims who were found guilty of practicing demonology, expressed the hope that God would avenge the innocent dead. May God "give you blood to drink," threatened Sarah Good. Nathaniel Hawthorne believed the curses were given effect in the century-long decline in the Hathorn(e) family fortunes. Cursed or not, Nathaniel Hawthorne worked the family's misadventures into iconic literary images. In **The House of the Seven Gables**, Matthew Maule expresses the hope that God's retribution would be directed against Colonel Pyncheon, who should be "given blood to drink."

Nathaniel Hawthorne wrote, "I know not whether these ancestors of mine bethought themselves to repent and ask pardon of Heaven for their cruelties, or whether they are now groaning under the heavy consequences of them in another state of being. At all events, I the present writer, hereby take shame upon myself for their sakes, and pray that any curse incurred by them--as I have heard, and as the dreary and unprosperous condition of the race for some time back would argue to exist--may be now and henceforth removed."

MARY PUTNAM AND DANIEL MAYO: POMFRET, CT and BOSTON to NEWPORT, KY by way of BELPRE, OHIO

If the Putnam family fortunes, as well as the Ha(w)thornes', had been blemished by the curse, these fortunes took an upward swing with the famous but eccentric round-headed General Israel and his numerous, very able Putnam relatives in the eighteenth century. Arguably, the family also ascended high on that October day in 1798, when **Mary Putnam** married **Daniel Mayo** in Belpre, Washington County, Ohio. Mary was then 25. As noted, her family had moved to southeastern Ohio shortly after the Ohio Country was opened to settlement in 1788. Her cousin, Rufus Putnam, as well as her father, **Israel Putnam Jr**, were instrumental in settling the area.

Putnam ties into Ohio grew stronger over subsequent decades. The 1820 census finds four Putnam males in Washington County (David, Israel, Rufus and William) even though (unaccountably) no Putnams were registered there in 1800. This may be an oversight in the census. Beginning as early as 1790, Putnams began to be buried in the Putnam Cemetery in Washington County, on CR 341 in Devola.

RUFUS PUTNAM

The Rufus Putnam mentioned in the 1820 Washington County census could have been the Rufus Putnam (1738-1824), originally of Sutton, Massachusetts, whose leadership in the establishment of Ohio has caused him to be seen as founder of the state. Rufus was the son of Deacon Elisha Putnam (1696-?) and Susannah Fuller (?-?). Rufus Putnam's grandfather was half-brother to the Revolutionary War General **Israel Putnam**, making Rufus second cousin to the General and second cousin, twice removed, to Israel's granddaughter **Mary Putnam Mayo**.

Rufus Putnam was a surveyor by profession. He was also a patriot and soldier, who enlisted the day after the battle of Lexington in 1775. For the revolutionary cause, Rufus built fortifications around Dorchester Heights, MA and New York City. After refusing appointment as Chief Engineer, he took a regimental command and fought at Saratoga, where the British surrendered to General Gates. After the war, Rufus Putnam rebuilt the fortifications at West Point and petitioned Congress, seeking Ohio land for veterans. This petition was granted to the organization he helped to found, the Ohio Company of Associates, in 1786. The Ohio Company purchased 1,500,000 acres of land, along the Ohio River from present-day Marietta to Huntington, West Virginia. In 1787, the Northwest Ordinance was passed by Congress, which further facilitated and regulated settlements in Ohio.

As noted, in 1788 Rufus led war veterans in the settlement of Marietta, Ohio. Under the provisions of the settlement documents, which he helped to craft, was a prohibition of slavery in Ohio. Rufus Putnam became a Supreme Court Judge for the Northwest Territory and served under General Anthony Wayne in his campaign to subdue and exterminate indigenous tribes in Ohio. In 1796, President George Washington appointed Rufus Putnam the first Surveyor General of the United States, a post he held until 1803. Rufus is buried in Marietta, Ohio, near Conus Mound, one of the many ancient burial/ceremonial mounds sprinkled across the Ohio landscape.

No doubt a number of Putnams were present at the 1798 wedding of **Mary Putnam** and **Daniel Mayo**.

NEWPORT, KY THE TERMINUS

Daniel Mayo seems to have approached life's signal events in a deliberate manner. He was 25 when he graduated from Harvard and 36 when he married. By that age, Daniel was holding the second of two federal appointments and, as stated, had acquired land in the new Commonwealth of Kentucky. Daniel's torpidity in establishing a household may be traced to a concern for security. What is known of his later life suggests a responsible, family-oriented temperament, with an eye to the future. A deed recorded on Dec 25, 1837, indicates that Daniel Mayo, near the end of his life, made a Christmas gift of a Newport city lot to each of his four children "for love and consideration of $1.00." This gesture indicates that for Daniel Mayo, family came first. Wishing to assure himself he could provide the necessities, he waited a considerable time before undertaking to found his family.

Once established in Newport, KY, Daniel Mayo took in child apprentices and orphans and apparently employed them either in his home or in one or another business venture. Local deed books record that on Sept 30 1803, Sally Wright, an orphan, age 12, was apprenticed for four years to Daniel Mayo in order to become a seamstress. In July, 1806, James Butler, age 7, and Joseph Butler, age 10, were apprenticed to Daniel Mayo to become rope makers, with the apprenticeship recorded in December, 1805. On several occasions, Daniel petitioned the local government to reimburse his expenses for taking in waifs and orphans.

Mary Putnam and Daniel Mayo had four children: Daniel Dudley, **Henry Hunt** (1810-1877), Mary Aurelia (1811-1844) and Harriet. The 1840 Newport census lists sons Daniel Dudley Mayo as a farmer, with a residence on Front Street, near Cabot St. Henry Hunt Mayo is enrolled as a dry goods merchant, with a residence on Taylor Street. But a shadow of abuse and predation hangs over the picture of an otherwise admirable family making decent, exemplary lives on the western frontier.

In October, 1802, Daniel Mayo bought a woman.

Had he remained in Ohio either as school teacher in Belpre or as Postmaster at Cincinnati, Daniel could not have done this. Slavery had been prohibited in Ohio under the terms of the charter authorizing its settlement. Mary Putnam Mayo's cousin, Rufus Putnam, had secured the charter from Congress and probably wrote it himself. But Daniel Mayo moved across the river to Kentucky, where the enslavement of human beings remained legal and was practiced vigorously until ended by the Civil War (1861-65).

In the course of Daniel's youth in Massachusetts and after the Revolution, when Massachusetts became a state, race slavery was legal and practiced widely, but was phased out in the Northeast by the end of the eighteenth century. No such peaceful transformation was to occur in Kentucky. During the first three decades of the nineteenth century, a debate raged in Kentucky and throughout the slave-holding South over the question of race slavery. Many influential and politically popular White politicians, opinion-makers, ministers and others were found on both sides of the question. But by the 1830's, the debate subsided and public opinion became fixed: race slavery was embraced throughout the White South as an essential endowment of the region's economy.

One might have expected Daniel Mayo and his wife, Mary Putnam Mayo, educated New Englanders from respected families, to have stood out publicly as opponents of slavery during their lifetimes. This was not the case.

Census and other records indicate that Daniel and Mary Putnam Mayo owned slaves throughout their lives. This means, in the absence of any contradictory evidence, one must set aside the possibility of any anti-slavery sentiment or opinion, which Mary or Daniel may have absorbed in their early youth but now only privately held. As early as 1798, Daniel is listed on the property tax roles for Newport, KY as the owner of a male slave. By 1800, he is recorded as the owner of three. In 1801, he is listed as owning no slaves but a Campbell County deed records that in October 1802 Daniel bought a woman named Becky, 20-

30 years old. In 1802, he owned a total of three slaves; 1804: four, 1805: three, 1806: four, 1807: four, 1808: six, and so on. The 1820 census for Campbell County Kentucky shows that Daniel Mayo owned five male slaves and one female slave. The census also records one free Black female in the household.

On more than one occasion, Daniel Mayo served his neighbors as the executor or appraiser of their estates. On at least one occasion Mary also served as witness to a will. These formal property transfers included the sale or bequest of slaves. In May, 1807, for example, Daniel was appointed by the court in the matter of the estate of James Smith on behalf of the widow, Sarah Smith - "to appraise in current money the slaves (if any) and personal estate of James Smith, Deed and return the appraisal to the next Court."

Late in life, former President John Quincy Adams wrote to Daniel Mayo. Adams was then (uniquely among all former Presidents) a member of Congress. In this less prestigious role Adams was a constant and vocal critic of slavery, bringing annual motions and memorials to the House of Representatives, denouncing slavery and calling for its end. But this strident and high principled activity did not interfere with Adams' sentimental attachments to a companion of his youth. In 1837, Adams penned a friendly letter to his Harvard classmate of fifty years before:

Daniel Mayo, Esqr, Newport, KY,
Washington, 22 March 1837

My good old friend and Classmate:
Sometime before the close of the late Session of Congress, Mr. Bellamy Storer shewed me a letter from you containing a notice of your kind remembrance of me, which was the more grateful to me because it came at a time when I was in great trouble for having given colour to an idea. Your letter mentioned a wish for a copy of my Eulogy upon Mr. Madison, delivered last September at Boston, and also of my Poem. I accordingly send you by

the same Mail with this a copy of each of them which I hope you will accept as a token of our ancient fellowship.

We are drawing toward the close of our career. Most of our classmates have gone before us. I think there is not one third part of our class remaining. The last departure was that of Dr. Fiske, of Worcester, who not long before had been preceded by Judge Bridge and he by Lloyd who had removed his residence to New York. Judge Cranch is yet here, and has one son, whom you may perhaps know in Cincinnati. I attended Commencement about four years hence at Cambridge, but sought In vain for one classmate but found none. I have since that time lost all taste for Commencements and have not attended another.

My Poem was an experiment. General Jackson makes experiments upon the currency and I make them upon Stanzas. I can hardly tell which of us is most successful, but I incline to think that upon the whole mine are the least mischievous. My Dennot has not made a great Fortune in the world, perhaps because he has had no credit in Bank to speculate in Public Lands. Since the publication of Dennot my wife has been chiefly occupied with Sonnets and Madrigals and Acrostics for Ladies' Albums. Pray is it the fashion for Ladies to keep Albums and for Gentlemen to deliver Lyceum Lectures and wear beards at Newport? These are among the favorite pursuits of Literature among us of the present age.

I shall be happy to hear from you always at your leisure and especially whenever you can give me good tidings of your welfare and that of your family. Being always in Memory of the days of yore, your friend and fellow student, J.Q Adams

Former President Adams' salute was timely sent. Daniel Mayo died the following year at age 76. Daniel and Mary Mayo both died in 1838, the 40th year after their marriage. Daniel died on July 22, Mary on Christmas Day. They were buried at the old Newport Cemetery on Ringgold Street. As the town grew, this cemetery was closed and all the graves, supposedly, were moved. Daniel and Mary Mayo's graves are marked today in Sec 4, lot 31-32 in the nearby Evergreen Cemetery, 5 Alexandria Pike, Southgate, Campbell County Kentucky.

SOURCES:

Mayo, Putnam and Hathorne/Hawthorne genealogy: Betty Taylor Cook's unpublished genealogy book.

John Winthrop's assessment of William Hathorn: Winthrop's **Journal**, published as **History of New England, 1630-1649**, Kendall Hosmer (editor), C. Scribners' Sons (1908), 2 vols, esp pp. 174-75, vol 2.

Hathorn(e) ancestry in England, and Anne's children: **Soldiers In King Philip's War: Being a Critical Account of that War**, George Madison Bodge, New England Historical Society, 1892, pp. 318-19.

Daniel Mayo's attendance at Harvard: "Quinquaennial Catalogue of the Officers and Graduates of Harvard University 1636 - 1915 Cambridge, Massachusetts, Harvard University Press in the Two Hundred and Seventy-Ninth Year of the College 1915." See: http://surnamesite.com/harvard/harvard1787

For Daniel Mayo at Belpre Ohio by the fall of 1789: "The first teacher in the Marietta Settlement was Daniel Mayo, a graduate of Harvard who came from Boston in the fall of 1789 and during the winter months taught the larger boys and young women in Farmer's Castle." From: "*First Schools*" **Historical Collections of Ohio** (1896, p. 799).

Battle of Bunker Hill, quote from Gen. Gage: **The Oxford History of the American People**, Samuel E Morrison (1965).

For details of George and Richard Puttenham, you might

Google George; also: nndb.com/people plus sites which argue, pro and con, the primacy of Edward de Vere as the Bard, himself. The case for a de Vere/ Wm Shaksper collaboration is made in **Who Were Shake-speare**, by Ron Allen (San Diego: Silverado, 1998); for De Vere data, see **"Shakespeare" By Another Name**, Mark Anderson (New York: Gotham Books 2005).

For Puttenham lineage back to 1088: THE EARLY PUTNAM LINEAGE, Chad Lupkes Genealogy website, which advises that not much reliance can be placed on the lineage prior to about 1350. See: seattlewebcrafters.com/ Chadlupes /genealogy/puntamstory.php

George Puttenham's poetry, printed in *Parthenides* (1579) and cited in **White and Black**, Winthrop Jordan (Norton: 1968, 1977, page 8).

King Philip's (Metacomb's) War and his confession of sin and damnation, and also the early inhabitants of the Ohio Country: **Facing East from Indian Country**, Daniel Richter (Harvard University Press, 2001), pages 90-105, 168.

A good (but dated) summary of religious events in late medieval Europe: **The Reformation**, by Owen Chadwick (Penguin, 1964).

For the early history of Belpre and the Farmer's Castle: **History of Belpre**, by C. E. Dickinson, D. D. (1920); **The History of Washington County, Ohio 1788-1881**, by H. Z. Williams.

For Daniel Mayo's government appointments, property, slave and apprentice acquisitions: notations in the county deed book, typed preserved and shared by Mayo descendent, Anne Moffett Gibbs.

William James' description of William Hathorne:

www.eldritchpress.org/nh/nhhj1.

Events from the life of Rufus Putnam: w.cr.nps.gov/museum/exhibits/revwar/image_gal/indeimg/putnam.html#Anchor-Hamilto-17608.

William Hathorne's military service: "Men and Officers who served in King Philips War," compiled by Rod Bigelow, at biglowsociety.com/rod/soldiers

Cotton Mather on Indians as witches: *Maine, Indian Land Speculation, and the Essex County Witchcraft Outbreak of 1692*, by Emerson W. Baker and also James Kences' *Maine History*, vol 40, number 3, Fall 2001 (pp. 159-189).

Details of the witchcraft trial of Bridget Bishop: **The Devil in Massachusetts. A Modern Enquiry into the Salem Witch Trials**, by Marion L. Starkey, (New York: Anchor Books, 1949), page 153. See also: "A Sketch of Bridget Bishop," by Mai-Linh Gonzales Westwood, in *The Student Historical Journal 1990-1991*, on the web at loyno.edu/history/journal/1990-1/westwood.htm

Characterizations of General Israel Putnam: *An Essay on the Life of the Honourable Major-General Israel Putnam*, by David Humphries (1788, republished 2000); the Putnam illustration was made from a photocopy in family records, identified as a portrait hanging in the Connecticut State Capitol, and containing no attribution or provenance.

Details of the divisions among Putnams and their relatives during the witch trials in Salem, MA: **Salem Possessed** (1997) by Paul Boyes and Stephen Nussbaum, especially chapters five and six, with appreciation to cousin Elizabeth Taylor Rubio for calling attention to this book.

Rufus Putnam relationship to Israel Putnam: nndb.com/people/068/000049918/

Apprentice bonds undertaken by Daniel Mayo: Deed Books, Campbell Co., KY, in the possession of the cousins, Betty Taylor Cook and Anne Moffett Gibbs.

Daniel Mayo's ownership of slaves: **Pieces of the Past**, Jim Reis, vol 3, pages 19-21; from LDS microfilm #07911 (1988).

Salem Witch Trials, incl transcript: hawthorneinsalem.org and also Margaret B. Moore's **The Salem World of Nathaniel Hawthorne** (2001).

always in Memory of the days of yore - John Quincy Adams' letter to Daniel Mayo: 1943 *Times-Star* (Cincinnati) article, which printed the letter. At that time the letter was in the possession of Helen B. Lindsey, 91, a descendent of Daniel Mayo. Where is the letter, now?

Painting Called Too Violent for Children Won't Return

New York Times, Sept. 28, 2006: Greenwich, CT. The skirmish is over and all sides are claiming victory, but a large painting deemed too violent for elementary school children will not return home.

The painting, by James Daugherty and commissioned in 1935 by the Works Progress Administration, had hung at the Hamilton Avenue School for 60 years, until about 8 years ago, when the painting — blackened by age — was removed from a wall in the gymnasium for restoration. After it was restored, the painting was hung in the town library while officials considered renovating the entire school.

Trouble broke out when officials considered a request from a school committee for the return of the painting, which measures 20 feet by 9 feet and depicts in striking detail Gen. Israel Putnam, a Connecticut resident who helped plan and then fight in the Battle of Bunker Hill. The committee wanted the painting for the school's new lobby, scheduled for completion next year.

But scrubbed of dirt, the painting became a richly colored scene of snarling animals, tomahawk-wielding American Indians and a half-naked General Putnam strapped to a burning stake.

. . . On Wednesday night, about 20 residents unanimously agreed that the painting was too violent for the school. So it will remain in the library, in the reference section, where few children are likely to see it . . . .

"PASSIONS IN OUR NATURE CANNOT BE ERADICATED"
John Adams, to "Boston Massacre" Jury, Dec 1770

Esther Kendrick
Joseph Mayo

Daniel Mayo (1762-1838)
Henry Hunt Mayo (1810-1877)
Mary Aurelia ("Rilla") Mayo Moore (1839-1901)
Mary Baldwin Moore Taylor (1863-1936)
John Oliver Taylor Jr (1891-1960)
Betty Taylor Cook (1918-2000)

Daniel Mayo (1762-1838) of Newport, KY was the son of **Esther Kendrick** (1725-1775) and **Joseph Mayo** (1720-1776). Esther, with long English and Welch lines, was named for a grandmother. She and Joseph were married on Nov 14 1745. If this date is correct, Daniel Mayo was born 17 years after his parents were married. Betty Taylor Cook has written that Esther was the daughter of Captain **Cable Kendrick** (?-?) and **Abigail Bowen** (?-?) and that Abigail's parents were **Hannah Brener** (1665-1721) and **John Bowen** (1662-1718). Hannah was the daughter of **Daniel Brewer** (?-?) and **Hannah Morrill** (1636-1717).

ESTHER KENDRICK'S ANCESTRY: BOWEN, JOHNSON, PORTER

Family genealogist and descendent Elizabeth Taylor Rubio has reported the Brener and Bowen birth and death dates and has traced the Kendrick English and the Bowen Welch lines. Cable Kendrick's parents were **John Kendrick** (1641-1721) and **Esther Green** (1653-1723). Esther's parents were **John Green** (?-?) and **Esther _____** (abt 1653-1673) of Newton, MA. Abigail Bowen Kendrick's father, **John Bowen**, was the son of **Elizabeth Johnson** (1637-1701) and **Henry Bowen**

(1633-1723), born in Woodstock, England, died in Woodstock, CT. Henry Bowen was a militiaman and took part in King Phillips War, assuming command of a company at the once-famous Great Swamp Battle (see below), after **Isaac Johnson**, his son John's father in-law, was killed.

> A SECOND NOTE REGARDING THE SHARED ANCESTRY OF MARY BALDWIN MOORE AND JOHN OLIVER TAYLOR SR (First note: Page 186):
>
> Hannah Morrill had a sister, **Catherine** (1635-1662), who died at age 27 and was the wife of **John Smith** (1621-1706), and the mother of **Mary Smith** (1648-aft 1714), the wife of **Jeremy/Jeremiah Swayne** (1643-1710). Jeremy and Mary Smith Swayne were the parents of **Benjamin Swayne** (1669-1741), the father of **Thomas Swayne** (1705-1759), father of **Mary Swayne** (Williams) (?-1781), who became the wife of her second husband **John Walton** (1709-1785). John and Mary Walton were the maternal grandparents of **Oliver Swaine Taylor** (1784-1885), who was the grandfather of **John Oliver Taylor Sr** (1862-1922). Therefore, at their 1887 marriage, John O. Taylor, descendent of Catherine Morrill Brewer, and **Mary Baldwin Moore** (1863-1936), descendent of Hannah Morrill Smith, shared a common set of ancestors: **Sarah _____** (abt 1600-1672) and **Isaac Morrill** (abt 1587-1661), the parents of sisters Hannah and Catherine. (For additional details, see Morrill in the Index.)

Henry was the son of **Margaret Fleming** (abt 1600-?) and **Griffith Bowen** (abt 1600-abt 1675) both born in Langwich, Glamorgans, Wales. Griffith, who went to America and then returned to Wales and then London, was the son of **Ellen Franklin** (abt 1759-1638) and **Francis Bowen** (abt 1576-?) of Lagwith, Glamorgans,

Wales. Francis mother was **Elizabeth Vaughn** (abt 1552-?). Through Francis' father, **Philip Bowen** (?-?) this line has been accepted by the "Descendants of the Illegitimate Sons and Daughters of the Kings of Britain (Lineage No. 156)" – from Griffith Bowen all the way back to King Henry I of England (abt 1068-1135), fourth son of William the Conqueror. (Invent your own version of this lineage, or see the *National Genealogical Society Quarterly*, Sep. 1979).

Francis Bowen's wife, Ellen was the daughter of **Jonet Delamare** (abt 1550-?) and **Thomas Franklin** (abt 1546-?). Margaret Fleming, Griffith Bowen's wife, was the child of **Alice Dawkins** (abt 1572-?) of Glamorgans and **Henry Fleming** (1568-1650), born in Gelliher, died in Llanrhidian, Wales. Alice was the child of **Elizabeth Jenkin** (abt 1542-?) and **Jenkin Dawkins** (abt 1542-?).

Elizabeth Johnson (mother of John Bowen) was the namesake daughter of **Elizabeth Porter** (1610/11-1683) and **Isaac Johnson** (1610-1675). Isaac Johnson was born in Herne Hill, London, and was killed (or died of his wounds) during Metacomb's (aka) King Philip's War. (For additional details of this war, see the Index.) Isaac mustered his soldiers (75 or so) at Dedham Plain, in preparation for the campaign against the fortified Indian village, which was located in a swamp near Kingston, Rhode Island. In command of a company of men from Roxbury, Dorchester, Milton, Braintree, and other towns, Captain Isaac Johnson was mortally wounded at the entrance of the Narragansett fort, in what became a vicious hand-to-hand struggle known as "the battle of the Great Swamp." With Isaac Johnson dead, the command of his company passed to Isaac's daughter's father-in-law, the aforementioned Ensign (Lieutenant) **Henry Bowen**. Other Taylor ancestors in the Swaine (Swayne), Hathorn(e) and Taylor lines also fought against Metacomb and in this very battle; see pages 187 and 300.

Isaac Johnson's parents were immigrants **Margaret Scudder** (1592-1655) and **John Johnson Jr** (1592-1659). John Jr was the son of **Hannah Throckmorton** (1570-?) and **John Johnson Sr** (1564-

?). Margaret's parents were **Margery** _____ (1567-?) and **William Scudder** (1565-abt 1607).

Elizabeth Porter, Isaac Johnson's wife, was the daughter of **Adrian Porter** (1585-1623) and **Elizabeth Allott** (1582-1617). Adrian was the son of **Margaret** _____ (?-?) and **Robert Porter** (1547-1623) an Anglican Priest, Rector and Vicar during a long career in Lincolnshire and perhaps elsewhere. More must be learned of Margaret and this Robert, born in the death year of Henry VIII, priest in an England ruled by the regal but suspicious Elizabeth I, and then by the vindictive, distracted, closet gay, James the First. Robert Porter ended his career as England accelerated its descent into bloody conflict over an ancient and medieval issue which has persisted to this day and thus proven to be very modern: enforced consensus in matters of faith.

The very long (for that time) span of Robert Porter's years encompassed all of Shake-speare's. Did Robert know him? Did he know Edward de Vere, the likely true playwright? Did Robert see any of the plays? With multiple theological degrees from Cambridge, did Robert Porter take an interest in the new, official translation of the Bible, the King James Version (1611)? (He was not a member of any of the translation committees.) Did the settlement of Jamestown in 1607 or at Plymouth in 1620 warrant Robert's notice?

Did Father Robert Porter harbor Catholic or Puritan convictions? Without information that might place him closer to either the Separatist or the Catholic ends of the English religious spectrum, we may assume that Father Robert was a centrist and an adherent of the Royal Supremacy ideas of Richard Hooker. A contemporary of Porter, Hooker's writings justified to English society the Tudor insistence (expressed forcefully by Henry VIII, Elizabeth I) upon the English crown as head of the English church. For Hooker, the King was God's agent on earth. In Hooker's cosmology, the King - and no other power - appoints bishops, while Parliament, in consultation with the bishops, determines articles of faith and of worship.

Hooker's formulas would be revived and modified a hundred years later, after Civil War and Cromwell, as an important rationale for the *pax anglicana* of the Restoration. But consensus in Hooker's lifetime for his pure statement of royal headship of the religious hierarchy endured just about as long as Robert Porter's career as a priest. Father Robert died as it was all falling to pieces.

There never was a *pax anglicana* in colonial America. The new world was too distant and too diverse for such late medieval English doctrinal and ecclesial pretensions, which did not take firm root. Besides, the suspicious Anglican authorities in England declined to appoint an Episcopal bishop for Colonial America. The best chance for Anglicanism was in staid and moderate Virginia Colony but even here, a population dispersed over the wide expanse of the countryside undermined a top down imposition. No sooner did the Virginia Burgesses pass laws forbidding religious variations than a boat load of Presbyterians would show up, head for the back country frontier and begin to harass the Anglican missionary priest (should any such be dispatched all the way from England) – a cleric who thought he ought to be honored for enforcing conformity upon people who had not the slightest thought to conform.

On the death in 1623 of **Adrian Porter**, Robert's son, did Father Robert console his orphaned, twelve-year-old granddaughter, Elizabeth? Robert did not. Robert had died earlier in that year. Who then did care for this child, our ancient ancestor? Who sheltered and fed our Elizabeth? Who taught her, her religion? And what flavor was it? Who helped her find within herself fortitude enough to come single on a dangerous crossing to a New World, marry **Isaac Johnson** (1636, Roxbury, MA) and there found a family? Coming down to it, we would learn what we can of Father Robert Porter, but of the two, we want many more details of Robert's grandchild, our early Betty, orphaned English girl and widowed American woman, **Elizabeth Porter Johnson** (1610/11-1683).

JOSEPH MAYO

For **Esther Kendrick**'s ancestry, see page 323. Her husband **Joseph Mayo** was born on Dec 28, 1720 and died on Feb 14 in the momentous year, 1776. James Savage, who has Joseph's birth as Feb 20, 1719, records him as the son of **Elizabeth Davis** (?-?) and **Thomas Mayo** (?-?). Thomas was the son of **John Mayo Jr** (1659-?) and **Sarah Burden** (?-?). John Jr was the son of **Hannah Graves** (1636-1699) and **John Mayo Sr** (married 1654), who, as a young boy, was brought from England to Massachusetts in 1633 by his stepfather Robert Gamblin Jr and his mother _____ (?).

Hannah Graves was a daughter of **Judith Alward /Allard** (?-1683), second wife of immigrant **John Graves** (?-1644), who arrived with his first wife and several children in May, 1634 and whom she married in Roxbury in 1635. Hannah had a brother, Isaac, but this is not the **Isaac Graves** (abt 1620-1677) who married **Mary Church** (1630-1691), and was an ancestor of **Charles Taylor** (1819-1897) by way of his mother's Parsons and Dwight lineage. (See page 164-68, esp. 167.)

Joseph Mayo was Suffolk County sheriff and a major in the First Suffolk Massachusetts Cavalry. Joseph is said by some to have served under **General Israel Putnam** (pages 292-3, 294) at the Battle of Bunker Hill in 1775. The Bunker Hill service did not occur. A roster of Massachusetts soldiers, who served during the Revolution, produces a Joseph Mayo, whose service began with his enrollment on Dec 7, 1775. This "service" terminated when he was dismissed on the day he was called to service, April 19, 1776. This date was two months after the death of our Joseph. (It is possible a clerk of the militia corrected the roster by deleting the deceased Joseph, on the date of the call-up, when he was informed of Joseph's death.) Even if the death date is incorrect and Joseph the ancestor is the same as Joseph the called-up militiaman, this roster does not document any actual military service at Bunker Hill. That battle took place six months earlier, June 17, 1775.

In 1798, Esther Kendrick and Joseph Mayo's son, **Daniel Mayo** (1762-1838), married Gen. Putnam's granddaughter, **Mary Putnam** (1773-1838), who had moved from Connecticut to Belpre, Ohio, with her parents. Most likely, it was in Belpre where Mary met the Massachusetts bred Daniel Mayo, and there married him. (Additional information is found in the Mary Putnam and Daniel Mayo sketch, beginning at page 283.)

THE BOSTON MASSACRE TRIALS

In 1770 Joseph Mayo was jury foreman at the trial of British soldiers after the event known in American history as the "Boston Massacre." Here follows a brief narrative of the *Massacre* and the legal proceedings in its aftermath. There were in fact two trials of British soldiers and a Mayo (**Joseph** and Thomas) served on each jury. The trials followed the firing by soldiers on citizens in Boston, killing five.

The background of the *Massacre* included much hostility towards the British army, the Crown and the colonial government it had installed. For two years, British soldiers had been occupying Boston as a police force, in a vain effort to keep the peace. Soldiers were being quartered in public buildings and perhaps even in private homes. Resentment against the soldiers was heightened because some were taking extra jobs in their off hours. Possibly, the soldiers were also showing interest in some of the young women of Boston, who may or may not have responded positively to their attentions.

On March 5, 1770, British Private Hugh White was standing sentry in the snowy, moonlit street before the Customs House in Boston. Private White had an exchange of words with a boy, who ran away from the sentry, crying. An angry crowd gathered and the sentry called for help. Captain Preston, with seven soldiers, responded. The crowd grew and shouted insults at the soldiers. Some in the crowd begin to throw ice and rocks. Private Hugh Montgomery was knocked down by an object thrown at him. Someone yelled "Fire!" and the soldiers fired into the crowd, killing five and wounding six.

Lt. Governor Thomas Hutchinson, Massachusetts native and the acting Royal Governor, went to the scene and waded into the unruly crowd. In the chaos he was almost thrown against the bayonets of the soldiers. Hutchinson demanded to know from Captain Preston, "How came you to fire without orders from a civil magistrate?" Hutchinson entered the building and appeared on the balcony before the furious crowd. In response to shouted demands that the soldiers be removed from the city, Hutchinson made a brief speech. He declined to remove the soldiers but agreed that they should be held accountable for any crime committed. Hutchinson shouted to the crowd from the balcony: "The law shall have its course. I will live and die by the law!" In fact, the obsessive and increasingly delusional Hutchinson, under growing pressure from what he considered a lawless cartel of determined zealots, did remove the British troops from the streets of Boston. After the Revolution, Hutchinson moved to England, where he had never lived, dying as a disgraced and banished traitor to the America in which he had been born.

After the shootings, eight soldiers and Captain Preston, their commander, were arrested and prosecuted. Loyalist Samuel Quincy was colonial Solicitor General and was appointed special prosecutor. He was the older brother of one of the defense lawyers, Josiah Quincy Jr (Samuel Quincy left for England in 1776 and died there in 1789.) The other prosecutor, this one for the City of Boston, was Robert Treat Paine, a later signer of the Declaration of Independence. Council for the defense included the above mentioned Josiah Quincy, Jr, younger brother of the prosecutor but a patriot. There was also Robert Auchmuty, Jr, for the defense, a Loyalist. He was willing to serve as attorney for Captain Preston only if John Adams, a well known lawyer and patriot, served as co-counsel. Adams agreed to be co-counsel to Preston and also represented the Privates at their trial.

The trials of Captain Preston and the eight enlisted men were delayed for months. When the trials began, they were closely followed by the public in Boston and well beyond. After seven months in jail, Captain Thomas Preston came to trial on October 24, 1770. Under the proceedings in place, Preston had to prove a negative, that he had not issued a command to fire on the citizens. The jury pool was depleted before the jury was impaneled and five onlookers had to be seated. These five were later said to be Loyalists. This, and the fact that only two of the jurors were from Boston gave rise to the accusation that the jury had been packed to favor the defendant. Preston was acquitted after the five-day trial. On this jury served one Thomas Mayo.

The second trial was that of the eight soldiers under Captain Preston's command. The soldiers had asked to be tried with the Captain but this request was turned down. **Joseph Mayo** of Roxbury served as jury foreman of the second trial. Overlooking a number of other distressing events in colonial history, such as the Salem Witch Trials, militia assaults on Indian towns, the establishment of race slavery, Crown attorney Samuel Quincy stated that the soldiers faced charges of murder in "the most melancholy event that has yet taken place on the continent of America."

The prosecutors argued that the soldiers were bullies and street fighters. The defense argued the soldiers could be judged on nothing but evidence produced against them in court. As with Captain Preston, none of the soldiers could take the stand in their own behalf.

Deathbed testimony by one of the victims, Patrick Carr, was allowed even though it was "hearsay" - a report of what *someone else heard* the absent witness *say*. The *hearsay* was admitted, because the judge concluded that no one about to face final judgment would possibly lie. However, the anti-British firebrand Samuel Adams, cousin of the defense counsel John Adams, stated publicly that Carr's testimony could not be trusted because Carr "probably died in the faith of a Roman Catholic."

John Adams concluded his summation to the jury with a widely reported speech, which added to his stature,

> *I will enlarge no more on the evidence, but submit it to you. Facts are stubborn things; and whatever may be our wishes, our inclinations, or the dictates of our passions, they cannot alter the state of facts and evidence: nor is the law less stable than the fact; if an assault was made to endanger their lives, the law is clear, they had a right to kill in their own defense; if it was not so severe as to endanger their lives, yet if they were assaulted at all, struck and abused by blows of any sort, by snow-balls, oyster-shells, cinders, clubs, or sticks of any kind; this was a provocation, for which the law reduces the offence of killing, down to manslaughter, in consideration of those passions in our nature, which cannot be eradicated. To your candour and justice I submit the prisoners and their cause. The law, in all vicissitudes of government, fluctuations of the passions, or flights of enthusiasm, will preserve a steady undeviating course; it will not bend to the uncertain wishes, imaginations, and wanton tempers of men.*

On December 5, 1770, six of the soldiers were acquitted; one of them, Kilroy, was found guilty of manslaughter for killing Samuel Gray; and another, Montgomery, was found guilty of manslaughter for killing Crispus Attucks, a free Black man of Boston.

The two convicted soldiers pleaded *benefit of clergy*, a medieval doctrine introduced originally to permit priests to be excused from proceedings in secular courts. To qualify, each soldier had to read the "neck verse" from the English Bible. The neck verse is Psalm 51, verse 1: "Have mercy upon me, O God, according to thy loving kindness: according unto the multitude of thy tender mercies blot out my transgressions." Although illiterate, Kilroy was able to claim *benefit of clergy* by simply invoking the neck verse; the actual reading requirement had been abolished by an English court in 1705. Instead of execution, the two soldiers were branded by the Suffolk County Sheriff on the right thumb with an "M" - for murderer. Apparently, **Joseph Mayo** was both jury foreman and Suffolk County sheriff. The branding was applied so a convicted defendant could not claim the benefit in the future. It has been said, these trials marked the first time the doctrine of *reasonable doubt* was invoked in an American courtroom.

MAYO ANCESTORS

Joseph Mayo's parents were **Thomas Mayo** (1673-May 26, 1750) and **Elizabeth Davis** (1678-1756). Thomas was born in Roxbury, MA on Nov 12, 1673. He and Elizabeth were married there on May 4, 1699. Thomas and Elizabeth were the parents of twelve children, Joseph being the youngest.

Joseph Mayo's mother, Elizabeth Davis, was the fourth of six children of **Mary Devotion** (1648-1683) and **John Davis** (1643-1750), John being the son of **Elizabeth** (?-?) and **William Davis** (?-?). Mary Devotion and John Davis were married on Feb 5, 1667 in Roxbury, MA, where they had been born and where they died. Mary Devotion was the daughter of **Mary Curtis** (abt 1618-abt 1713) and **Edward Devotion** (?-?). Mary Curtis, who lived to be almost 100 years old, was the daughter of **Sarah** (?-?) and **William Curtis** (?-?). Sarah and William Curtis arrived at Boston with Mary and several of their other children from London in 1632, on *The Lion*. Edward Devotion was the son of **John Devotion** (?-?) and **Hannah Pond** (?-?), who was the daughter of **Abigail Shepherd** (?-?) and **Daniel Pond** (?-?).

As stated, Joseph Mayo's father, Thomas Mayo, was the son of **John Mayo** (1630-April 28, 1688) and **Hannah Graves** (Sept 8, 1636-Oct 5, 1699). John Mayo was born in Westmalling, Kent County, England and brought to America in 1632, at the age of two. The parents of Hanna Graves, wife of John Mayo, were **John Graves** (?-1644) and **Judith Alward** (abt 1600-1683).

John and his wife Hannah are buried in an ancient cemetery in Roxbury, surrounded by other Mayos. His gravestone states that John died on April 28, 1688. Hannah died on October 5, 1699.

> Some family records mistakenly confuse **John Mayo** (1630-1688) with a Puritan cleric of the same name. John Mayo, ancestor in question, died at age 58 in 1688. He is not the Puritan minister, John Mayo (1598-1676). This other John Mayo, Puritan divine and husband of Tamisin Mayo, arrived in America from London on the *Truelove* in 1635. Our John Mayo was already in America and only five years old in 1635. In November, 1655, John Mayo the clergyman and colleague of Cotton Mather, became the first minister of the old North Church (Second Church of Boston), where he stayed too long. In 1673, he was asked to resign as his sermons were "no longer edifying." This is a sanction rarely applied to a standard seldom invoked.

SOURCES:

Genealogy generally: Betty Taylor Cook unpublished genealogy book; also James Savage **A Genealogical Dictionary of The First Settlers of New England, Before 1692 (1860-62)** *4 Volumes*, See Page 197, above.

Joseph Mayo's Revolutionary War service: "Soldiers Who Fought in the Revolutionary War," from **The Town of Roxbury** (pages 32-33), on web at: Am Local History Network (ALHN)

Boston Massacre and trial details: on the web at sjchs-history.org/massacre.html. John Adams' speech to the jury: bostonmassacre.net/trial/jury.htm.

For Thomas Hutchinson, his speech to the mob: **The Ordeal of Thomas Hutchinson**, by Bernard Bailyn (Harvard University Press: Cambridge 1974).

Mayo genealogy: Betty Taylor Cook's unpublished genealogy book; also the research of Elizabeth Taylor Rubio, niece of Betty Cook; see also the genealogical research, including a helpful and clarifying Mayo chart prepared by John Arnette, MD, of Louisville, KY, a personal and family friend. Some details concerning Puritan cleric John Mayo (not a lineal ancestor) have been taken from: murrah.com/gen/mayo.htm.

passions in our nature, which cannot be eradicated –from John Adams's courtroom speech, see page 332, above.

The Coming of our Lord and Savior made the greatest difference in the lives of women . . . Again and again we find Him dealing with women as having worth. He revealed to the woman he met at Jacob's well at high noon, hot and thirsty, the secret of the living water – the secret that God is a spirit and not confined to any one place, to any one people, to any one sex. His was the word and love for all creation.

Betty Cook

Meditation
Crescent Hill Baptist Church
Louisville KY
1980s

"BETTER TO DIE FROM A PAINLESS GUN-SHOT WOUND THAN FROM THE MERCILESS BARBARITIES OF THE SAVAGES"

Vilette/Violet [or Vallette] [or Valette] Ly(i)ttleton
Nicholas Dawson

Elinor Vallette Dawson Moore (1781-1834)
Marmaduke Moore (1808-1883)
Benjamin Moore (1837-1894)
Mary Baldwin Moore Taylor (1863-1936)
John Oliver Taylor Jr (1891-1960)
Betty Taylor Cook (1918-2000)

Elinor (Elenor) Valette (Vallette) Dawson Moore's parents were **Nicolas Dawson** (1745-1789/90) and **Vilette (Violet) Lyttleton (Littleton)** (1759-1842). Vilette Lyttleton was born on January 30 1759, at Bull Run, Virginia. Vilette's parents were **John Lyttleton** (?-abt 1764) and **Elinor Vallette** (?-?). John Lyttleton was killed under a falling tree when his daughter Vilette was five years old. Vilette Lyttleton, by the skimpy accounts we have, was a beautiful woman, whose presence at social events was much approved. Before her marriage to Nicholas Dawson, we are told Vilette was a frequent visitor in the Mount Vernon home of George and Martha Washington. Valette's great granddaughter Anna Baldwin (?-?) seems to be the source of all the details we have about Vilette. Anna wrote of Valette, "I have read letters of Martha Washington in which she mentions her friend Mrs. Dawson." The circumstances of the reading by Anna Baldwin of Martha Washington's letters is not known, and is therefore subject to question.

Other families with fine homes in the Bull Run vicinity included (we are told) a Col William Harrison, whose daughter (?), **Mary Harrison** (1761-1835), became the wife of **Thomas Moore** (1745 - 1823). Mary and Thomas' son, **William Moore**, would marry Valette's daughter, **Elinor**.

VILETTE /VIOLETTE LYTTLETON (DAWSON) (SCOTT): BULL RUN, VA – TYRONNE TOWNSHIP, PA – HARRISON COUNTY, KY – SPRINGFIELD, OH

Vilette (Violette) Lyttleton is reported to have married Nicholas Dawson in the residence of William Crawford. The fact that William Crawford gave the bride away suggests both closeness between the Crawford, Lyttleton and Dawson families and also further confirms that Vilette's father, John Lyttleton, had died before the wedding.

Did the wedding take place at a residence along Bull Run in Virginia? Probably not. William Crawford lived along the Youghiogheny River in western Pennsylvania, at Stewart's Crossing (now the borough of New Haven, Fayette County), PA. There is no reason to doubt the tradition that Vallette's girlhood home was a Potomac River residence (Bull Run) but her family seems to have moved to western Pennsylvania (Washington County) for her adolescence. The married Valette can be located with certainty, on the PA and then on the KY and Ohio frontiers. She is found in PA, married to **Nicholas Dawson** and in KY and Ohio, married to **Solomon Scott** (?-?).

Valette first married Nicholas Dawson (1745-1789), grandson of the well known first **Nicholas Dawson** (?-1728) of Maryland. Valette and Nicholas had four children, including **Elinore Valette Dawson** (1781-1834), who was named for her grandmother and her mother, and who, as noted, became the wife of **William Moore** (1780-1859) and the mother of **Marmaduke Moore** (1808-1883).

Shortly after Nicholas' untimely death in 1789, Valette married **Solomon Scott** (?-?), who soon became the father of **Sarah Scott Baldwin** (1791-1817?). After a few years in Kentucky (present day Harrison county) the family moved to Springfield, OH, where Solomon was elected the first Justice of the Peace of Pleasant Township (no date in Clark's *History*) and is listed by Clark as an elector (voting resident) of Union Township in 1811.

By way of her children, Elinore Dawson and Sarah Scott, from her two husbands (Nicholas Dawson and Solomon Scott), Valette Lyttleton Dawson/Scott became the grandmother of both **Jane Hedges Baldwin** and **Marmaduke Moore**, who thereby were half-first cousins when they married on January 18, 1834. Jane's and Marmaduke's descendants recorded this wedding date in their enormous Bibles. The date comports with the Clark County clerk's tabulations, which show the couple obtained a marriage license on January 8, 1834. Valette Lyttleton Dawson Scott outlived her daughters, Elinor and Sarah, and survived to almost the mid-point of the nineteenth century.

WILLIAM CRAWFORD: TIES TO HARRISON, MOORE AND DAWSON FAMILIES

It may be helpful to indicate that William Crawford was a leading partisan of Virginia in its dispute with Pennsylvania over the territory between Laurel Hill and the Ohio River (page 262.). In 1775, Crawford organized the first Revolutionary militia west of the Monongahela River and called it the Seventh Virginia Regiment. This militia unit marched east to fight directly against the British. Crawford, popular especially with the Virginia partisans in the land dispute, also raised the Thirteenth Virginia Regiment from the same area and commanded it with the rank of Colonel, given him by the governor of Virginia. The Thirteenth had been organized with the understanding it would remain close to home, and with the specific mission to fight Indians and any British forces combined with them. At some point, the Seventh and the Thirteenth seem to have merged into a single regiment. William and Benjamin Harrison and their brother-in-law **Thomas Moore** served in Crawford's regiment(s). Thomas Moore was father of William Moore, and thus father-in-law of Elinore Vallette, Valette Lyttleton's daughter.

Colonel Crawford's terrifying death by torture (later reported by a prisoner, who escaped) near Sandusky, in the

Ohio Territory, was a fate Nicholas Dawson only just avoided. Nicholas had accompanied Crawford when he pulled together a very irregular force of farmers and tradesmen to take on the Wyandotte and other *Originals* in 1782. (For details, see below.)

In the 1760s and 70s Crawford was a business associate of George Washington, who commissioned Crawford to scout and buy western lands for Washington. In 1767, Washington wrote to Crawford, "Look me out a tract of about fifteen hundred or two thousand or more acres somewhere in your neighborhood." On Crawford's recommendation, Washington, in 1770, secured title to 3,000 acres along Millers Run and Raccoon Creek, south of the forks of the Ohio River (apparently in both present-day Washington and Allegheny Counties, PA). These lands had been warranted to one of Washington's neighbors, John Posey, who owed Washington 2,000 pounds sterling. Later that same year Crawford surveyed 2,813 additional acres for Washington along Millers Run.

The ownership of this land was soon mired in a dispute between Washington and "squatters" who were already on the land or who entered it after the survey but before Crawford registered Washington's title. Crawford hesitated to file because of the larger dispute between Pennsylvania and Virginia, as to which colony these western lands belonged. (He may also have hesitated because of the difficulty of travelling to Jamestown, VA, to register a deed.) To meet the land improvement requirements, which Washington had to satisfy to make good his title, Crawford got someone to throw together a cabin on the land. The settlers who disputed Washington's title then put up their own cabin, close enough to the first shack to block its door.

All of this to suggest that if Valette and Nicholas were married in the Crawford residence, owing to the closeness between the Lyttleton and Dawson families, then we wish for more details before linking the Lyttleton or Dawson families with the Washingtons, along the Potomac. There are geographical hints of proximity but there are also indications of land ownership unrelated to the Potomac. Vallette Littleton (Dawson) may well have been born along Bull Run, as family historian Anna Baldwin (?-?) wrote to **Mary Baldwin Moore Taylor** (1863-1937). Vallette's first husband's family, the Dawsons, had for several generations, maintained property near or perhaps along the Potomac River, but in Maryland, not Virginia. If there was no direct association between the Dawsons and the Washington's along the Potomac, there may have been one in western Pennsylvania, based upon a mutuality of interests in adjoining tracts of land.

Nicholas Dawson is recorded as the owner of 300 acres of uncultivated land in Tyrone Township, in Bedford, (1773) Westmorland County) PA, where his father was listed as a resident, as were William Crawford, Crawford's son, Valentine, and also William Harrison. Interestingly, a David Lindsey was also a resident of Tyrone Township at this time. (For references to David Lindsey in KY: pages 255, 271.) George Washington owned 1500 acres in the same township. These ties to the same locale might have made neighbors of Nicholas Dawson and George Washington. But Washington (if not also Dawson) was an absentee owner, whose claim was disputed by settlers (squatters, Washington would have said) in the 1780s. Whether Nicholas Dawson knew Washington is speculative but the Dawson connections to Maryland and especially to western Pennsylvania, indicate where Nicholas Dawson would have met, courted and married Valette Lytteton.

With Nicholas, Vilette Lyttleton Dawson had five children: Thomas D. (Feb 22, 1779-?) **Eleanor Valette** (Jan 12 1781-1834), named for her grandmother, **Eleanor Ann Lowe** (1715-?) and her mother, and who married **William Moore** (1780-1859); George Fielding (March 22, 1783-June 16, 1871); Ann/Nancy (Oct 13, 1785-1823); and John (July 16, 1788-Jan 16, 1875). Some additional information about these Dawson children: Ann (Nancy?) married Micajah [Micah?] Phillips, in Springfield, Ohio. John married Ann Gregg Bailey, in 1846 and died in Uniontown, PA in 1875.

George Fielding Dawson married Mary Kennedy in Fayette County PA and lived in Brownsville, PA, where he died in 1871. George Fielding was given the name of an ancestor (great grandfather?), Fielding Lyttleton (?-?). Family genealogist, Anna B. Baldwin, great granddaughter of "Violette" Lyttleton and Nicholas Dawson, has recorded that Fielding Lyttleton "came to this country in disgrace as he had married the daughter of a Frenchman who had gone to London to live to save his head" and "was in trade." The idea seems to be that the Lyttleton family was of too elevated a class to tolerate George Fielding's marriage to the daughter of a French Huguenot tradesman.

Nicholas Dawson was born on April 3, 1745, in Montgomery County Maryland. He was named for his paternal grandfather. Nicholas' father was **George Dawson** (?-?), fourth son of **Mary Doyne** (?-1734) and the first **Nicholas Dawson** (?-1728). George's father, the first Nicholas, died in approximately 1728; in that year his estate in Prince George's County Maryland was distributed. The will of Mary Doyne Dawson, George's mother, is dated December 14, 1734. The mother of Nicholas Dawson (b: 1745) was, as stated, **Eleanor Ann Lowe** (1715-?). She and George were said (by Anna Baldwin) to have had a residence in the Mount Vernon neighborhood.

George and Eleanor Dawson moved their family to southwestern Pennsylvania in 1772. As stated, George owned land and was recorded a resident in Tyrone Township. It appears that Nicholas moved to Pennsylvania at that time, but he may not have remained in PA. After he married Vilette, Nicholas may have relocated to Montgomery County Maryland, where the Dawsons had considerable lands. However, by the very early 1780s, Nicholas and Valette are back in PA. Thus Nicholas came to join Crawford's ill fated march across the Ohio River, against the Shawnee.

Although several of his children lived long lives in Pennsylvania, Nicholas Dawson's loyalties seem to have been decisively with Virginia Colony. In his 1874 Dawson book (see Sources below), Charles Dawson quotes an earlier *Sketch* by Chauncey F Black (1839-1904), which states that Nicholas and his father George "were stern partisans in the boundary controversy [. . .]." This should be taken as a negative reference by Black, a prominent PA politician; Chauncey Black's father-in-law was John Dawson, grandson of Nicholas and Vilette. Black's comment relates to a dispute in colonial times between Virginia and Pennsylvania, in which our Harrison and perhaps Moore ancestors also took a part, also on the side of Virginia. (For additional details on the Boundary Controversy, see page 262, in this volume.)

George Dawson's wife, Eleanor Ann, was the daughter of Pennsylvania residents, **Mary Hawkins** (?-?) and **John Lowe** (?-?). (Lowe family members are yet found in Fayette Co PA.) With Eleanor Ann, George fathered 11 children, the second being the above mentioned Nicholas. George Dawson's parents were the first **Nicholas Dawson** (1675-1727) and **Mary Doyne** (?-1734). Nicholas and Mary were married about 1704. (Details about Mary Doyne's parents may be found in a sketch devoted to them: **Robert Doyne** and **Mary Stone**, page 357, below.)

DAWSON LINEAGE

The family of Nicholas and George Dawson has been tracked by energetic and talented genealogists. Some of these indicate this family can be followed in a line back to – you guessed it – the Norman Conquest. Some genealogists have suggested that the surname, Dawson, is of French origin: *D'Ossone*. Sounds right, I suppose. This theory dovetails (too neatly?) with the assertion that American Dawsons descend from **Sir Marmaduke D'Ossone**, associate of William the Conqueror, who invaded England from Normandy in 1066. A similar notion links early Dawsons with the Conqueror, having them hail from Osonvilla in Normandy, thus giving us the name *D'Oson (from Oson)*. Websites that want to sell you a coat of arms are full of this kind of news.

Another theory makes no mention of Sir Marmaduke, or Osonvilla but also travels lightly through time as it, too, is unburdened by documentation. By this narrative, our Dawson line reaches back to the Conqueror in the form of **Archibald Dawson**, a Saxon holder under the Normans of Greystoke estate in Cumberland County, in the north of England. Archibald is said to have maintained his status as a powerful landowner through marriage to a daughter of a Norman Knight, Thomas Neville. Might Tarzan ("Lord Graystoke"), swinging through the cinematic viney tangles, have had an English name, Archie Dawson?

From the Conquest in 1066, the Dawson name has been traced forward in a sprinkling of Knights and Lords and Bishops (Robert Dawson, Bishop of Clonfert, 1627) and others of high place. Some of these remained on their vast lands in England, some took up residency (or more lands, at least) in Ireland. By this route, we reach 17th century America. Tradition has given **Bertram Dawson** (?-?) pride of place as founder of the Dawsons of Maryland, through his sons. Bertram was holder of Greystoke in the seventh generation from Archibald. From Bertram came these four Dawsons: **John** (Prince George's County MD), **Nicholas** (son of John), Ralph (Talbot County MD) and William (Dorchester County, MD).

With the first Nicholas Dawson (son of John) there is documentation, although one always wishes for more. Nicholas may have been an immigrant or he may have been born in the county where he died and was buried, present day Prince George's County MD. This Nicholas, as stated, has been identified as the son of **John Dawson** (1650 -?) and **Rebecca Doyne** (?-circa 1712). Rebecca Doyne has been recorded as the daughter of **John Doyne** (?-?), from Ireland, who was grantee of lands along Chicamuxen Creek in Charles County. Maryland.

John Dawson, father of the first Nicholas, was Irish or, more likely, an English land holder in Ireland. He is said to have been born in 1650 in Whitehaven, Cumberland County, England. Some say this John came to America from Yorkshire, England. John Dawson is said to have lived in Goose Creek, Loudoun County VA. Mackenzie (see sources) says John Dawson had two land grants, one near Port Tobacco on the Potomac and the other in Prince George's (now Montgomery) County. Initial settlement in Virginia may have been exchanged for residency in Maryland owing to separatist hostility directed against the well connected Catholic or Anglican John Dawson.

THE BATTLE OF SANDUSKY PLAINS

In 1782, **Nicholas Dawson** took part in what was termed afterwards "the Battle of Sandusky Plains" in Ohio Territory. Family lore, if not official records, remember Nicholas as an "officer" of the Revolutionary Army. This may be true. However, Nicholas Dawson participated at Sandusky as a private. Had Nicholas served previously as an "officer" it is unlikely he would have been merely a private on this later occasion. The slim possibility exists that Nicholas had served during the Revolution and had obtained rank in some military unit. By 1782, the Revolutionary War in the east had ended, but not on the frontier. The disastrously impromptu expedition of the irregular colonial army that marched into Ohio may not have been organized with prior ranks in view. The overall commander, William Crawford, was elected on the spot.

Most likely, Sandusky was Nicholas Dawson's only connection to military activities during the Revolution. This conclusion is based on a List of Substitutes, which was created in Montgomery County in 1778 to keep track of those men who paid for replacements for themselves in lieu of their own personal military service. Such a list was required to be maintained by each county in Maryland, which had to meet a quota of soldiers, as set by the legislature. On April 24 of that year, Richard Haylip was delivered to the "German Regiment" for a three year enlistment to be served in place of Nicholas Dawson. On the question of militia service during the Revolution, our Nicholas may have been confused with another Nicholas Dawson, son of Thomas and Elizabeth Dawson. A resident of Sugar Loaf Hundred, this second Nicholas took an Oath of Allegiance on March 2, 1778 and served as a Private in the 3rd Company, Upper Battalion of the Maryland Militia.

The events at Sandusky Plains in 1782 had no bearing on the outcome of the Revolutionary War. The battle itself is important to history, but not for any military importance. Cornwallis had surrendered to Washington in 1781. A treaty would be signed in 1783. The Shawnee (Wyandotte/Wyandots), victorious at Sandusky in 1782, were ultimately defeated, forced west and virtually obliterated by the wave of European settlers who moved into Ohio and Indiana in the decades following the end of the Revolution. Sandusky proved to be but a skirmish prior to the final Wyandotte catastrophe.

The Iroquoian-speaking Wyandotte clan had allied themselves with the British during the American Revolution. Under the terms of the 1763 Peace of Paris, which formalized the French withdrawal from America following the French and Indian (Seven Years) War (1754-1763) the Iroquois and indeed all native peoples faced an ominous situation. No longer could they play off two competitive European powers in North America. Instead, they found themselves appealing to British officials to restrain land hungry colonists. No doubt the Wyandotte believed their best hope of fending off settlements was in aiding the British, who had promised that Indian lands would be secure so long as Britain won the war against the colonists. But looking to the British government proved as useless to the Indians as their earlier reliance on the French, who were fond of telling Native Americans they were "Children of their French Father." All European "fathers" proved quick to abandon "children" such as these.

Under the 1713 Treaty of Utrecht, the British had designated certain North American tribes "British subjects." A more candid title would have been "British objects." Native peoples were betrayed to the exact extent of their reliance upon agreements reached with colonial powers. Events in Ohio make this clear.

In 1758, in the "Treaty" of Easton, many different

Indian clans formally agreed to remain peaceful when Pennsylvania Colony renounced all claims to lands west of the Allegheny Mountains. In 1763, the Wyandotte around Sandusky specifically agreed to peace in what was termed a "final settlement." But after the American Revolution, the British simply walked away from any duties owed to their Indian "subjects" and allies in North America. No provision for Indians was made in negotiations between the British and the victorious colonists at the Treaty of Paris in 1783. The truth: even if written agreements had specified terms or treatment of the Indians, little of substance would have changed, because of the relentless, westward push of immigrant settlers into the wilderness.

Background to Sandusky: During the Revolution, the Wyandotte, as British allies, had been making murderous attacks on isolated White settlements all along the Allegheny frontier. This was provocation enough for townsmen living along the eastern bank of the upper Ohio to be mobilized and marched to war against the Wyandotte in May, 1782. No doubt, these colonists thought they were taking care of unfinished war business. They believed that by evicting Indians from Ohio, they were merely disposing of the last of the allies of Britain and the final obstacle to their ownership of vast new tracts. General Washington had initially ordered the sortie against the Shawnee. But he changed his mind after the new British commander in North America sent word that the British would no longer reward Indians, who took scalps. The rescinded order did not reach Crawford before he forded the Ohio River and marched on Sandusky.

The Shawnee were desperate to protect their Ohio country homes. At Sandusky, they decisively defeated a company – a disorganized crowd, really - of tradesmen and farmers. The initial day's fight at Sandusky was a draw, with only a handful of casualties. The nervous colonial leadership, in the mistaken belief they were outnumbered, decided upon a dawn retreat. But the retreat began in the nighttime, when "a strange panic seized" Crawford's men. Over the next few days, the withdrawal became a frenzied flight across unfamiliar wooded terrain.

Nicholas Dawson, at age thirty-six, probably took part as did many of the other settlers, in a sense of adventure and a strong desire to rid the countryside of all trace of the Wyandotte, who had attacked settlements in PA, and whose presence in Ohio was interfering with the Americans' plans for westward settlement.

A narrative of the events, published one hundred years after the American defeat, suggests that Nicholas Dawson may not have contributed much to the fight one way or another. In this excerpt, **emphasis** has been added to the original.

It is not to be supposed that the volunteers all reached home at once. For days they continued to struggle back. Some of the men became completely bewildered. ***Nicholas Dawson*** *had become separated from his companions, and was endeavoring to make his way home when he was discovered by two other volunteers. Dawson at that time was traveling in exactly the wrong direction, going back toward Sandusky. The men attempted to convince him of his error, but he pertinaciously insisted that he was right. At last the men told him that he would certainly be captured by the savages and tortured to death if he proceeded in his present course and that as it would be better for him to die from a painless and sudden gun-shot wound than from the merciless barbarities of the savages, they would kill him out of friendship. This argument proved successful. Dawson turned about reluctantly, and, with the others, reached home in safety.*

This vignette is found in a chapter entitled THE DOOM OF CRAWFORD (Chapter XVIII), which appeared in a work whose shorter title is **The Romance and Tragedy of Pioneer Life** by Augustus Lynch Mason (Cincinnati: 1883). Excerpts from Mason provide the context for Nicholas Dawson's participation in the Battle of Sandusky Plains and recall the tenor of the times. Mason's account incorporates a graphic depiction of the vicious encounters between Colonials and the Originals in the climactic 1780's in the Ohio Country, the region where perhaps the most desperate combat occurred in the history of North America.

Despite the illusive significance of the Sandusky engagement, the battle and its aftermath were enlisted in the ranks of eyewitness accounts of Indian atrocities. These best selling narratives, published generations after the events described, kept fresh the notion that the Wyandotte Indians and their allies had stooped to despicable and wanton savagery directed especially toward their captives. The narrative of Crawford's death was reported, supposedly, by an escapee who was, supposedly, an eyewitness. The eyewitness reported that Crawford had been horribly tortured before he was murdered.

AW-OH-AW-OH-AW-OH

The publishing and republishing of stories of Indian atrocities served a powerful impulse to purify and shape a collective identity. Readers are thereby instructed about the need to respond to alien threats. The response which was made and subsequently applauded by grateful descendents was the wholesale elimination of the foe. Extermination was justified by citing the depravity of not only the warrior-aggressor but also that of the savage woman and even the wanton child. By learning the details of the torture of Crawford, by observing for ourselves (as it were) Shawnee women poking burning sticks into the flesh of the naked and bound William Crawford, we learn to dehumanize the ENEMY. The tale of the death of Crawford, by no means the first or last of its kind, helped shape the mythic themes of the Republic under threat. Responding to the threat is a matter of self-assertion and self-preservation. Fighting with General Washington and fighting against the Shawnee was all the same thing. The tales of Indian atrocities are the bone and marrow of the national saga and are re-cycled in justification of every war. New players are merely interchanged in enduring roles.

Our ancestors became who they were to themselves and who they are to us by way of their frontier encounters and then in the telling and re-telling of these encounters. The stories of Indian outrages, kidnappings and butcheries were best sellers in their day and have only lost their explicit appeal, I believe, because they have become so deeply internalized that we *know* them without retelling them. They become, through the centuries, plot-points of identity rather than coherent narratives. We revisit these encounters in the entertainments of our own day, which sustain our image of ourselves and of our enemies in modern warfare. Our national self-definition is linked to our collective sense of participation and victory in these mythic conflicts. The image we have of ourselves as a nation reassures us that we are not simply the victorious nation but also the virtuous. We have gone to war ever since Indian Times, out of a conviction that our cause - whatever it is – is both necessary and just, and our enemies deserve to lose simply because they are our enemies.

Depravity encountered and overcome is our take on ourselves at war. This is how we see ourselves in confrontation with the Other, the alien specter. The current menace (whatever it is) to our Way of Life is the embodiment of Evil. Our Way is, inevitably if not obviously, better than the ways of the Other. The enemy of today is the blood thirsty Shawnee of yesterday. We will exterminate or at least dominate and humiliate them; we know this because we encountered and destroyed the vile Wyandotte in 1782.

J H Newton (1879) and Augustus Mason (1883) recorded the death of Col. Crawford:

Knight was present, tied and guarded, but lived to detail these particulars.

Crawford was stripped, his hands bound by a rope, fastened to the stake and to his wrists, with play sufficient to enable him to walk around the post, or sit down. He then asked, after they had beat him, if they intended to burn him, and being answered that they did, he remarked that he would bear it patiently. Pipe [Shawnee leader known as Captain Pipe] then made a speech to the Indians, who took their guns and shot powder into Crawford's flesh from his feet to his neck. They then cut off his ears, and thrust burning sticks into his body. The squaws putting burning faggots upon his feet, so that he literally walked on fire. In his pain he called on Girty to shoot him, but Girty replied laughingly that he had no gun. Heckwelder says that Crawford also called on Wingenund to save him, but the chief replied that the King of England, if on the ground, could not save him. Being almost dead he fell on his stomach, when he was scalped, and a squaw put coals on his head; then he raised upon his feet again, and began to walk around.

Knight was then taken away, but the next morning he was marched by the spot, and told by his Indian guard to look at his "big captain," which he did, and saw only his charred bones in the ashes, around which the Indians had danced all night, wildly singing the scalp song of "Aw-oh-aw-oh-aw-oh."

KENTUCKY & OHIO FAMILY TIES: MOORES, SCOTTS, BALDWINS

Nicholas Dawson survived the Battle of Sandusky Plains, but he did not live to raise his family. He died at age 44 on May 31, 1789, in route west, perhaps from Fredrick, MD. Nicholas died at Wellsville (Ohio) while he and Vilette were in the midst of moving to Kentucky. Vilette continued on to Kentucky, with some of her children. In an undated letter, Anna B. Baldwin (18?-19?) has written that her great-grandmother Vilette Dawson left two sons behind in Pennsylvania, "both half grown boys." This statement accords with the birth dates of Thomas and George Dawson, 1779 and 1783, respectively. Son John was just six months old and would have made the journey West with his mother, after his father Nicholas died.

Anna Baldwin's letter was written to **Mary Baldwin Moore Taylor** (1863-1937), a great, great granddaughter of Vilette Dawson. (See below.) The letter seems to have been written late in Anna Baldwin's life, as she stated to Mary Taylor, "Your letter came this afternoon. I knew I must get right on it as a delay might be fatal." She also commented on the eye trouble suffered by the great grandmother she called Violette. "You get your eye trouble from Violette Lyttleton. I can't tell you how many of her descendents have had the same trouble. I have gone through it but after a most successful operation I can see even more than I sometimes wish to see."

In Blue Lick Springs, Kentucky, the widow Villette Dawson married **Solomon Scott** (?-?). Mayo Taylor, family genealogist, has written (1973) that Solomon Scott's mother was _____ Wells "from Wellsville, KY near Shelbyville. Solomon Scott owned Blue Lick Springs." I believe Mayo has conflated two items of information. One is the recollection that Nicholas Dawson died in a place called Wellsville; the other is that Solomon and Vilette lived at Blue Lick Springs. These two locations are not the same. Wellsville, OH, where Nicholas is said to have died, is an Ohio River town founded by a William Wells. If Solomon Scott's mother was a Wells, Solomon may have been living near Wellsville, Ohio, and there met the just-widowed, Villette Dawson. Subsequently, Solomon and Vilette married and lived for a time at Blue Lick Springs, a spot in Kentucky, owned by Solomon Scott.

The wedding took place within a year of the death of Nicholas Dawson. Contradictory family information has Vallette and Solomon marrying in the Virginia panhandle (now, West Virginia) and not moving to Kentucky until 1793. Whether in 1790 or 1793, Solomon and Valette Scott move to Blue Lick Springs on the Licking River (present day Nicholas County) in Kentucky and live there for thirteen years or more. In 1806 Valette and Solomon Scott moved to Springfield, Ohio.

Vilette Dawson and Solomon Scott had four children: **Sarah** (1791-1817?), who became the wife of **Jonah Baldwin** (1777-1864); Mary (1798-May 18, 1877, Springfield OH, unmarried), Rebecca (1796 in KY-1848) (married Benjamin Moore, Dec 1816); and Nicholas (1801-1879, Dayton OH, unmarried). One wonders at Solomon, who married the widow Villette and named his only son after his wife's first husband and not after himself. Other slight information we have of Solomon points also to a generosity of spirit. The family recalls that Solomon Scott lead a horse 30 miles to find an Anglican priest to conduct step-daughter Elenor's wedding to **William Moore** (1780-1859) in 1804.

Also to be noted is the Moore lineage, traced back to our **Vilette Lyttleton Dawson Scott** (1759-1842) through two of her daughters **Elinor Valette Dawson Moore** (1781-1834), child of Vilette and Nicholas Dawson and **Sarah Scott** (1791-1817?), child of Vilette and Solomon Scott. Elinor became the mother of **Marmaduke Moore** (1808-1883) and Sarah became the mother of **Jane Hedges Baldwin** (1809-1993). Marmaduke and Jane, with half-sisters for mothers and thus a common grandmother, were married January 18, 1834. One of their sons was **Benjamin Moore** (1837-1894), father of **Mary Baldwin Moore Taylor** and great grandfather of **Betty Taylor Cook** (1918-2000).

In summary, in 1793, shortly after Vilette married Solomon Scott, they moved to Blue Lick Springs on the Licking River in Nicholas County Kentucky. In 1806 Solomon and Vilette moved to Clark County, Ohio, near Springfield. In later life Vilette suffered from cataracts. A member of the Church of England, Vilette died on September 19, 1842, at age 84. Vilette outlived both daughters, born of her two husbands, Nicholas and Solomon: Elenor Moore and Sarah Scott. She was probably buried in or near Springfield Ohio in a now-lost Episcopal or family plot.

SOURCES:

Birth and death dates as well as marriage dates: Betty Taylor Cook's unpublished genealogy book; Betty drew upon genealogical charts drafted by her uncle, Mayo Taylor.

Vilette Lyttleton's early life, information related to her children and her move to Springfield Ohio: a typed statement containing the recollections of her great-grandson, John Nicholas Dawson of Uniontown PA, made available by Anne M. Gibbs. The John Nicholas Dawson material has at the bottom, the name, Cass K. Shelby.

The Crawford-Washington land acquisition data may be found in **The Grand Idea: George Washington's Potomac and the Race to the West** by Joel Achenbach (New York: Simon & Schuster 2004, pages 84-87).

Dawson genealogy: Betty Taylor Cook's unpublished genealogy book; for Descendants of John Dawson as well as for Nicholas Dawson to PA: funstuffforgenealogists.com See Petersen Reproductions - 877-259-6144.

For John Dawson: see **Colonial Families of USA**, George N. Mackenzie, (1907) Vol IV, GPC, pp.115-120 – helpfully shared on the web by Mike Bailey and, from time to time, by others. (See below, for Mike Bailey.)

Dawson and Lyttleton information was collected by Anna Baldwin, great granddaughter of "Violette" Lyttleton. Anna was the daughter of Maria Dawson and Henry Baldwin. Anna's mother Maria was the daughter of John Dawson, son of Violette and Nicholas Dawson. Anna's father, Henry Baldwin, was the son of Jonah Baldwin and his second wife, Aurelia Needham.

Descendants of John Dawson: **The Monongahela of Old**, p. 204. (See below.)

For the April 24, 1788, Montgomery County, MD Substitute List, which finds Richard Haylip enlisted in place of Nicholas Dawson: *Maryland Historical Magazine* vol VI, page 256 (1911).

For the Revolutionary War service of a Nicholas Dawson: "Military Records of Rev. Patriots MD & DE 1775-1783" by FTM's Family Archives CD #133 for Montgomery County, Maryland, on a website, which also links to Mike Bailey's information on the Dawson family. See the excellent spaldinggenealogy.com/dawson

Dawson Family genealogist Wayne Dawson generously has shared an excerpt in his possession, *Bibliographical Sketches and other Memoranda of various families and Individuals bearing the name DAWSON*, compiled by Charles C Dawson (Albany: Joel Munsell, 1874).

For details of the Battle of Sandusky Plains: *THE ROMANCE AND TRAGEDY OF PIONEER LIFE. A POPULAR ACCOUNT OF THE HEROES AND ADVENTURERS WHO, BY THEIR VALOR AND WAR-CRAFT, BEAT BACK THE SAVAGES FROM THE BORDERS OF CIVILIZATION AND GAVE THE AMERICAN FORESTS TO THE PLOW AND THE SICKLE. BY AUGUSTUS LYNCH MASON, A.M. WITH AN INTRODUCTION, BY JOHN CLARK RIDPATH, LL.D. (JONES BROTHERS AND COMPANY CINCINNATI, O., CHICAGO, ILL., ST. LOUIS, MO., DALLAS,TEX. 1883)* on web at www.w3.org/TR/html4/loose.dtd.

Wyandotte and relevant treaties: **Facing East from Indian Country**, Daniel H. Richter (Harvard University Press, 2001) pages 152, 166, 187, 189-236; the statement on the next page by Buckogeahelas, page 223.

Dawson land ownership and residency in western PA is documented in James Veach's *The Monongahela of Old or*

Historical Sketches of Southwestern Pennsylvania to the Year 1800 (Pittsburgh, 1910), with excerpts at various websites.

Solomon and Vallette Lyttleton Scott residency in Springfield Ohio: *A Biographical Record of Clark County Ohio* (New York: Clark Publishing, 1902); and *The Early Settlement of Springfield, Ohio (The Ludlow Papers)*, John Ludlow (lectures delivered in 1871); Clark County Historical Society (1963).

a strange panic seized them - A description of the disastrous flight from Sandusky is found in **The Indian Wars of Pennsylvania**, C. Hale Sipe, pages 659-64.

> Sipe recorded (page 663) that the reason for the vicious torture of Crawford after Sandusky was in revenge for the slaughter of non-resisting, peaceful Delaware Indians, including women and children, at the Indian town of *Gnadenhuetten*, who had been converted to Christianity by Moravian missionaries. Their town was dangerously located between Sandusky and the English settlements to the East. A Delaware leader, *Buckongahelas*, came to the Moravian Indians to urge them to move and to warn them (Sipe, p. 651), prophetically: "*I admit that there are good white men, but they bear no proportion to the bad; the bad must be the strongest for they rule. They do what they please. They enslave those who are not of their color, although created by the same Great Sprit who created us. They would make slaves of us if they could, but as they cannot, they kill us.[. . .] And so you also will be treated by them before long. Remember that this day I have warned you to beware of such friends as these.*"

"INTO THIS PROVINCE TO INHABIT"

Mary Stone
Robert Doyne

Mary Doyne Dawson (?-1734)
George Dawson (?-?)
Nicholas Dawson (1745-1789)
Elinor Vallette Dawson Moore (1781-1834)
Marmaduke Moore (1808-1883)
Benjamin Moore (1837-1894)
Mary Baldwin Moore Taylor (1863-1936)
John Oliver Taylor Jr (1891-1960)
Betty Taylor Cook (1918-2000)

Mary Doyne (not to be confused with Rebecca Doyne, her mother-in-law) was the daughter of **Mary Stone** (?-1683/86) and **Robert Doyne** (?-1689). Robert arrived in Maryland Province in 1669-70, probably from Ireland, possibly by way of Barbados. A report has been given that Robert was born in Charles County, Maryland between 1647 and 1657. This may be correct. Robert and his brother Joshua (abt 1634-1698) were the sons of **Sarah Wharton** (?-?) and immigrant **William Doyne** (1610-?). William, of Carrichfergus, Ireland, died in Charles County, MD. Placing William, the father, in Charles County may account for the speculation that Robert was born in MD. His brother Joshua was born in County Wexford, Ireland. Possibly, Robert was born in Maryland, but was raised elsewhere, returning (from Ireland? Barbados?) when both brothers were brought in to Maryland Colony by Jesse Wharton in 1669-70.

On February 16, 1670, Jesse Wharton petitioned "the County of St Maries" for the right to take ownership of 1050 acres of land "for Transporting himself and these persons into this Province to inhabit (vis)" [20 individuals including] "Joshua Doyne" [and] "Robert Doyne." The language of the petition – "to inhabit" – implies that the

Doyne brothers arrived for the first time. Of course, the petition is meant to imply that very fact, so as to strengthen Wharton's demand for the land. Thus it is possible that Robert Doyne was born in Maryland and also arrived (again) in Maryland as a young man, "to inhabit." Sarah Wharton, mother of Joshua and Robert Doyne may have been a sibling of Jesse Wharton. The names *Jesse* as well as *Wharton* have come down the Doyne lines.

The name *Doyne* has been said to be an Irish derivative of the English *Dunn*. Perhaps. Perhaps not. *Ó Doyne* has been connected to *Ó Duinn* and *Ó Doinn*. Each one, or one or another may derive from *donn* (brown) or *hill* (dun). According to the name counters, *Ó Doyne* is rare in Ireland today while Dunn and *Ó Duinn* are more common.

Both Robert and Joshua Doyne may have been Catholic. Or perhaps Joshua was Catholic and Robert was Anglican. **Mary Stone**, Robert Doyne's wife, is believed to have been Anglican, which may have been Robert's church by his own choice and not just his wife's. It is conceivable these two brothers, arriving in Maryland together, strategically divided their religious affiliations so as to avoid making the family's fortunes too dependent on only one allegiance.

The volatility of religious identity in early Maryland would have invited a cautious approach. In 1654, **William Stone** (see Stone sketch, page 363), the first Protestant Governor of Maryland (appointed by Lord Baltimore) was removed by Commissioners sent from London by Oliver Cromwell. Lord Protector Cromwell thought he could rule Maryland personally from across the wide ocean. He and his minions, victorious in civil war and vindictive in civil peace, wanted to decrease the power of the Catholic Calvert family. They dismissed the Calvert's agent, William Stone, though Stone was himself a Protestant from neighboring Virginia. Governor Stone accepted his removal, until the arrival from the Calverts of a small, armed contingent sent to restore Stone's authority. That didn't work. In 1655, Virginia Puritans, whom Stone himself had invited to settle in Maryland, won a bloody battle that defeated Stone for good. In 1692 the pendulum swung again as the fledgling legislature decreed the establishment of the Church of England in Maryland, supported by taxes on the public and fines against non-adherents.

There is strong evidence for brother Joshua Doyne's Catholicism. In his will he left a bequest of 1,000 pounds of tobacco for the benefit of "ye poor Catholiques." Joshua also made another, odd stipulation, gifting a daughter two of his slaves should she wed a "Catholick" if she marries at all. In his Aug 16, 1698 will, this is what Joshua specified: "I Give and Bequeath unto my Daughter Jane Doyne one Mallattoe boy called Lewis and a Negroe called Mary provided she marieth a Roman Catholick if she betake herselfe to ye State of Mattrimony." The wealthy Joshua distributed half a dozen additional slaves among his children, leaving the nameless and unspecified balance of slaves to his wife. Joshua could have done none of this - owned human beings or disposed of them by devise - had he remained in Ireland or England. (For discussion of English laws concerning slavery, see the Stone sketch, below.)

Though newcomers, the Doyne brothers were accepted as persons of social position. Joshua married the stepdaughter of Lord Baltimore; Robert married the daughter of the former Governor **William Stone** (1603-1660), that is, the widow, **Mary Stone** (Thomas) (?-?). A further sign of his status is Robert Doyne's appointment as one of the Justices of Charles County and shortly thereafter, High Sheriff, a position he held until his death on July 23, 1689.

Robert Doyne and Mary Stone were married by March 3, 1674. Mary Doyne is referred to in her mother's will as "daughter Doyne." The children of Mary and Robert Doyne are: Wharton, Sarah, Verlinda, Elinor, William, and their youngest child, namesake **Mary** (?-1734) who became the wife of the first **Nicholas Dawson** (?-1728). (See page 342.) Robert Doyne married a second wife, though she bore him no children. The absence of issue is known from Robert's will, which named all of his children "from a single venture" but then also named a second wife, Ann(e) Burford. Ann(e), daughter of Anne and Thomas Burford, Maryland attorney general, subsequently married George Plater, also province attorney general; on Plater's death, Anne married John Rousby of Calvert County. By my count, the orphaned children of Mary Stone and Robert Doyne had a step-mother and two step-fathers, giving an early occasion in colonial Maryland for the playground taunt: *who's your daddy now?*

We turn aside from a weak attempt at humor in the face of rampant death, so as to acknowledge the maternal care shown to an ancestor, the little orphan, **Mary Doyne** (?-1734), who was cared for in the home of step-parents. These good-hearted (we presume) individuals did not obstruct Mary in her inheritance or in her marriage to **Nicholas Dawson** (?-1728). Their progeny survive to offer gratitude to ancient, early Americans, who raised, as their own, the children of others.

Robert Doyne acquired many thousands of acres of Maryland land, including holdings on the Eastern Shore (Somerset County). A year before his death, Robert Doyne purchased in Charles County (later, Prince George's County) a 500 acre parcel called "Saturday's Work."

Robert Doyne died suddenly in July, 1689. Struck down quickly of some unremembered cause, Robert knew of his impending death and called for a secretary to make his will. Richard Boughton, who was present on July 20, wrote down Robert's intentions. On July 23, Robert told his brother Joshua he had dictated a will and expressed the hope it would be sufficient "though it might not be informe." Robert died before the will was signed. His nuncupative (oral) will was presented in court, on July 28, 1689. The grieving family, including brother Joshua, Anne the new second wife/widow, and former brother-in-law, John Stone hurried into court with Richard Boughton, to preclude any outliers from getting their chance at intestate property. The St Mary's County Court accepted the will as proved and ordered its terms implemented.

Robert Doyne made the traditional benefactions of a wealthy man. He left to Ann(e), his childless second wife, their resident plantation. His other lands went to the children of his first wife. Robert left a tract in present day Prince George's county to his daughter, Sarah. However, this property, called "Saturday's Work" was acquired by daughter **Mary Doyne Dawson** (?-1734) and her husband, the first **Nicholas Dawson** (?-1728). They sold this property in 1712.

There may yet be standing a monument to the Dawsons of Prince George's County, which was placed years ago on the "Saturday's Work" parcel. The monument is on land which is now the entrance to Rosecroft Shopping Center off Brinkley Road in Oxon Hill, MD. Family genealogist Mike Bailey has posted these directions: "If you're driving north or south on Interstate 95 heading toward Annapolis, the Dawson Monument sits just off Exit 4 of the Capital Beltway in front of the shopping mall." Mike Bailey has also reported that many ancient Dawsons are buried in the Monocacy Cemetery in Beallsville, Md.

A partial summary: The children of Mary Doyne Dawson and the first Nicholas Dawson were John, Thomas, William, **George**, and Nicholas. **George Dawson** (?-?) and his wife **Elinor Ann Lowe** (1715- ?) were the parents of **Nicholas Dawson** (1745-1789). Nicholas married **Vilette (Violet) Lyttleton (Littleton)** (1759-1842); two of Vilette's grandchildren married each other. Vilette Lyttleton, with Nicholas Dawson, was the mother of **Elinor Valette** (1781-1834), named for her two grandmothers and wife of **William Moore** (1780-1859). William and Elinor were the parents of **Marmaduke Moore** (1808-1883). Vilette Lyttleton (Dawson), with second husband, **Solomon Scott** (?-?) was the mother of **Sarah Scott** (1791-1817?), who was thereby the half sister of Elinor Valette and who became the wife of **Jonah Baldwin** (1777-1864). Sarah and Jonah were the parents of **Jane Hedges Baldwin.** (1809-1993). On Jan 18, 1834, Jane Hedges Baldwin married **Marmaduke Moore** (1808-1883).

SOURCES:

For Dawson, Doyne, Moore, Baldwin, lineage: the unpublished genealogy book and notes of Betty Taylor Cook (1918-2000).

For Robert and Joshua Doyne and Jesse Wharton in Maryland: Hester Dorsey Richardson's 125 page report, based on original document research conducted from 1921-27, copies formerly in the possession of Betty Taylor Cook as well as Anne Moffett Gibbs, who shared this and much other information with the writer. (See Index for further details.)

into this Province to inhabit – Jesse Wharton's 1670 petition for an award of land. Taken from Hester Dorsey Richardson research paper. See page 357, above.

Doyne etymology: **Irish Families**, Edward MacLysaght, Irish Academic Press, (1991) on the web at the excellent spaldinggenealogy.com/dawson, which also links to Mike Bailey's information on the Dawson family, including his directions to the Dawson Monument in Prince George's County, MD.

A PROTESTANT GOVERNOR FOR CATHOLIC MARYLAND

William Stone
Verlinda Cotton

Mary Stone Doyne (?-before 1689)
Mary Doyne Dawson (?-abt Dec 1734)
George Dawson (?-?)
Nicholas Dawson (1745-1789)
Elinor Vallette Dawson Moore (1781-1834)
Marmaduke Moore (1808-1883)
Benjamin Moore (1837-1894)
Mary Baldwin Moore Taylor (1863-1936)
John Oliver Taylor Jr (1891-1960)
Betty Taylor Cook (1918-2000)

Mary Stone Doyne (?-before 1689), wife of **Robert Doyne** (?-?) was the daughter of Maryland Governor **William Stone** (1603-1660) and his wife **Verlinda Graves** or **Cotton** (?-c. 1675). (We opt here for *Cotton*. See page 99.) Verlinda may have been the daughter of **Joane** _____ (1580-?) and **Andrew Cotton** (1578-by 1640). Andrew has been identified as the son of **Andrew Cotton** (?-?) of Bunbury, Cheshire, England, himself the son of **Mary Mainwaring** (?-?) and **Richard Cotton** (?-1602) also of Cheshire. Mary may have been a daughter of Sir **Arthur Mainwaring** (?-?), High Sheriff of Cheshire (1563) and Knight of Ightfield.

Richard Cotton, husband of Mary Mainwaring, was the son of _____ and **George Cotton** (?-?), who was a favorite of Henry VIII, being knighted by him and given many estates: Ducote in County Salop, Cliffe and Hales in Drayton, Erdlet Grange in Staffordshire, Wincell Grange in County Cheshire and Cotes Grange in Derbyshire and a former monastery, Combermere. This Cotton line has been connected speculatively back to the eleventh century and **William**, Lord of the Manor of Cotton (Coton), in Cheshire. A daughter of Mary and Richard Cotton was

Francis, wife of George Abell (abt 1587-abt 1631), parents of immigrant Robert Abell (1589-aft 1643), who arrived in Massachusetts in the 1630 Winthrop flotilla. (See page 210.) Robert and his wife Joanna _____ (?-?), are the ancestors of countless descendents in New England and beyond.

Verlinda Cotton Stone's brother was an Anglican priest, the Rev. William Cotton (abt 1600-1640), first minister in Hunger's Parish (Accawmacke Plantation) Virginia. It is thought that Verlinda, wife of William Stone was the sister of William Cotton, and not some other Verlinda because Cotton's 1640 will (recorded in 1646) mentions Captain William Stone as his brother-in-law. However, Cotton's wife, Ann, was a daughter of immigrant **Thomas Graves** (?-by 1637), who had a daughter, Verlinda. If William Stone was married to Verlinda Graves, Cotton might have referred to William Stone as his brother-in-law. Additional Cotton family details may be found above, in a sketch of the couples **Joseph Addison** (1819-1896) and **Amanda Watts Gaines** (1821-1895) and Amanda's parents, **Virginia Watts** (1803-1882) and **James Gaines** (1798-1872).

JOHN STONE – HIMSELF A "JUST ASS"?

In 1648, Captain William Stone had come into Maryland from Virginia Colony. Born in England, William may have been the son of a notorious father, **John Stone** (?-1633). John was a privateer with a bad reputation even among that type. He was known as a drunk and a man given to angry and violent outbursts. He made a living in the transport of cargo between Virginia and Massachusetts. In 1633, he stopped over at the Dutch settlement of New Amsterdam, where, according to William Bradford, Stone attempted to seize a ship out of Plymouth Colony. Continuing on to Plymouth, Stone was arrested by Miles Standish and taken in irons to Boston. However, Stone had connections in London and was known to have made bitter complaints about the administration of the colonies. It was thought better, as Governor John Winthrop recorded, just to release him and not give him a greater forum for his grievances. Placed at liberty, Stone was soon found in Boston, drunk in bed with the wife of freeman John Bancroft. Stone was bound over yet again by the authorities, this time for adultery and drunkenness. Stone responded by abusing the magistrates, calling one of them "a just ass." The adultery indictment failed, as colonial law required two witnesses for conviction and there was but one. Stone was fined a hundred pounds and ordered to leave the colony and never return without special permission.

Out of Boston, and out of both Plymouth and Massachusetts Bay colonies, but not out of trouble, John Stone met his end at the hands of the First Families of Connecticut, the Pequot. Sailing down the coast, he puts in near Hartford where the Dutch had an outpost, and where they had gotten into conflict with the Pequot. In a trade dispute, some Dutch adventurers murdered a prominent Pequot *sachem*. Shortly after the killing, Stone appeared, invited some Pequot on board his ship, and passed bottles around. Stone, drunk, fell unconscious across a table and the Pequot clubbed him to death. Before anyone of the crew could apprehend them, the Pequot jumped overboard and the ship blew up, killing all six of the crewmen.

In a subsequent investigation by the English authorities, the Pequot claim honest mistake. They meant to take revenge on the Dutch and mistook Stone for a Dutchman. In statements to investigators from Boston, the Pequot declared, in essence: all y'all look alike. John Stone's reputation made for the easy decision by Governor Winthrop to do nothing more than report Stone's death to the authorities in Virginia Colony. The turn in events, which caused the death of John Stone, was viewed positively by pious colonial officials and their historians, who habitually described such outcomes in minor apocalyptic terms. Puritan Roger Clap recorded, "Thus God destroyed him and delivered us."

"FOUR NEGROES, ONE TURK AND ONE INDIAN"

When **William** and **Verlinda Stone** moved their home from Virginia into Maryland, they brought with them a number of indentured servants. They also brought "four Negroes and one Turk and one Indian." This accounting appears in a formal registration William Stone submitted to the land office in Maryland, demanding the right to enter lands he had been promised in exchange for bringing his family from Virginia to Maryland.

The Stone ledger indicates the dramatically different demographics of arriving immigrants in the colonies along the Chesapeake when compared with New England. One of the biggest differences was the presence of in tact families in New England as opposed to individual laborers in the more southerly colonies. English colonists, settling north of the Chesapeake Bay in the seventeenth century, reach the Colonies mostly as family groups. In but a few short years after the arrival of the *Mayflower* at Plymouth Rock in 1620, colonists landed and disbursed in a remarkable eruption of energy and zeal. However, in the tobacco colonies of Maryland and Virginia, the stream of immigrant arrivals was steady and continuous for decades after the first permanent settlement at Jamestown in 1607. The continuing influx included a large percentage of single persons, bound to labor for a term of years. These singleton drudges in Maryland and Virginia were mostly from central England by way of the slums of London or one or another port city. Male immigrants arriving in seventeenth century Maryland and Virginia outnumbered females about six to one.

The immigrants might not have come at all, had they known the fate that awaited them. Entering into a new life alone, the newly arrived were compelled to remain alone for some years. They of course could not move away from the site of their indenture nor could they take a spouse during their years of servitude. In many individual instances, the delay did not matter very much. The inhospitable climate and its attendant diseases killed off thousands of laborers shortly after they set foot on land. Put to agricultural work in a malarial environment, as Bernard Bailyn has written (see Sources, below) they "died like flies."

Those who were fortunate enough to work off their term of service, survive, find a spouse, and start a family, then witnessed a death rate of 50% among their children, who, like themselves, succumbed to the diseases of their semi-tropical environs. It was not until the end of the seventeenth century that the native born population of the tobacco colonies equaled the number of immigrants.

The demographic difference with New England of course included that other set of laborers **William Stone** had enumerated in his petition for Maryland land: his slaves. In ever increasing numbers, African men, women and children were captured and imported to the tobacco colonies. The practice accelerated towards the close of the 1600's and continued throughout the next century. The forced immigration and coerced labor of Africans was resorted to as the numbers of arriving indentured servants decreased and as those servants already in the colonies worked off their obligations and sought other work. In fact, the absence of available spouses or land near the settlements tended to create a roving class of single men, who became increasingly alienated and hopeless. Their anger boiled over in Bacon's Rebellion, in 1676. (See above, page 99, and **All of the Above II,** page 287 f.) The departure of former indentured laborers into the paid labor market - typically into one of the trades associated with construction - was an added incentive to the importation of African slaves, whose labor was needed in agriculture.

In their embrace of human slavery, our ancestors brought a social and moral malignancy upon the land of their fondest hopes - with catastrophic consequences for their progeny. For two and a half centuries the kidnapping, confinement and forced, lifelong servitude imposed upon thousands and then upon millions of human beings was initiated, sustained and expanded on economic principles and then belatedly sanctioned by legal and religious rationales.

Enslavement is an inherent debasement of both master and slave. The centuries-long degradation by the privileged and the powerful of the humiliated and the powerless, has its lingering effects. These social and psychic burdens include an irrational race consciousness, patterns of family dissolution and the corruption of legislative and legal processes that wink at the interests of the great and turn away the defenseless. We have been suffering these self-inflicted miseries for four hundred years.

Because the practice of colonial enslavement conflicted with the mythic traditions of the English yeoman farmer at peace on his own lands, new mythologies were required of English theorists to rationalize this New World custom. The new reasoning was not very late in its formation. This included notions about the elemental brutishness and innate depravity of the Black African as well as the God-given privileges and capacities of their White masters. All of this depended for its widespread acceptance upon the blessings of legal and religious authorities, which proved themselves not unready to assume this role.

The legalization of African enslavement in Maryland was formally established in 1663/4, a generation after its introduction. Note what the colonial legislature, composed of male, land owning immigrants, found of concern in 1663, sufficient to cause them to legalize slavery in their domain, thereby reversing the ancient laws and customs of England. The problem was White women: English women were "intermarrying" slaves:

> "*Divers free-born English women, forgetful of their free condition, and to the disgrace of our nation, do intermarry with negro slaves; by which, also, divers suits may arise, touching the issue of such women, and great damage doth befall the master of such negroes, &c.*"

Therefore:

> *"Whatsoever free-born woman shall intermarry with any slave, shall serve the master of such slave during the life of her husband, and that all the issue of such free born women, so married, shall be slaves, as their fathers were."*

The intent of this legislation makes clear that slavery in America was race slavery from its earliest appearance. For both commercial and social reasons, the custom of slavery was codified in Maryland in the seventeenth century, as it was in other Southern colonies, at the same time. The region made itself dependent upon a cheap and ready source of debased labor. All aspects of human striving, whether moral, commercial or carnal, were made to include the daily betrayal of the humanity of those least able to protect themselves. These included African men, women and children, as well as indentured English men and women, though of course the indentured class was not enslaved for life.

In her 1675 will, **Verlinda Cotton Stone** gave a nameless "negar woman" to John Stone, her son and executor. This donation was an altogether new feature not only in the life of an English woman born in the time of Shakespeare; it was also new to English law. Had she never set her foot in the Colonies and instead had died in England, Verlinda could not have become the owner of another human being. Nor could she have given a woman to her son.

THE CHILDREN OF SLAVES "FOLLOW THE CONDITION OF THE MOTHER" – NOT THE FATHER

The belated legal rationale for slavery achieved definitive form in the 1760's, one hundred years after Verlinda made her will, when William Blackstone commented on the subject. English air is breathed only by freemen, Blackstone acknowledged, but the African, being imported not to England but to the Colonies, is subject to the laws of the barnyard.

To slaves, Blackstone applied: *Partus sequitur ventrem* (offspring follow the condition of the mother). This was a medieval, civil (Roman law) doctrine applied to domesticated animals, never to human beings. This was, in England, the law between farmers by which the lamb is owned by the farmer who owns the ewe and the calf is owned by the owner of the cow. For Blackstone, the offspring of slaves are seen in the same legal light; such offspring retain the status of their mothers, not their fathers. The quotidian meaning of this novel application: white boys and men might do as they pleased with enslaved females. An accusation of rape or paternity could not be raised against them. (See pages 105-08, note at 111.)

The contrary doctrine, *Partus sequitur patrem* (children take the condition of the father) was the law in England as applied to human beings. This doctrine regulated such matters as the laws of inheritance. But *Partus sequitur patrem* was never applied to enslaved Black Africans in Barbados, Virginia, New England, Maryland or the Carolinas. Recognizing colonial practice, Blackstone announced that the English law of paternity was not to be applied in the English colonies to Black Africans. Blackstone in the 1760's and English law with him, was approving such acts as that of the Maryland legislators in 1664, and of Virginia, which in 1661 had decreed that infants born of female slaves were slaves for life.

The recourse to slave labor greatly influenced the size of plantations, with larger tracts of tobacco-producing lands becoming ever more practicable. The corollary, of course, was that smaller plots, typical of New England farms and early Virginia as well, became increasingly impractical along the Chesapeake. As immigrants and their children were priced out of land ownership in the coastal and lowland territory of the colonies, they looked increasingly inland, toward the mountainous western frontier, to lands still occupied by "the Originals."

"FOR PREVENTION OF THE EFFUSION OF BLOOD AND RUINE OF THE COUNTRY"

In the middle of the seventeenth century, **William** and **Verlinda Stone** were part of the leading edge of these developments. They were typical of the well-connected, ambitious, talented, assertive and miniscule colonial patrician class, who wanted large tracts and many slaves to make their lands ever more productive and profitable for themselves and their heirs.

A communicant of the Church of England, Stone became Governor of Maryland shortly before the beheading of Charles I in 1649. He was appointed by the Catholic Cecil Calvert, Second Lord Baltimore and colonizer ("proprietor") of the Province of Maryland. Cecil Calvert "hastened to secure his tenure of Maryland by showing the world that his Province was not all Roman Catholic to the prejudice of Protestants."

Maryland was intended as a refuge in America for persecuted English Catholics. But the province never at any time was Catholic in a majority of its population. In 1632 the charter had to be revised to limit its western boundary after it was discovered that Protestants from Virginia had already moved east across the Potomac River.

In 1627/8 Calvert's father had been given a charter by Charles I. This was a rental agreement. Calvert (Lord Baltimore) retained possession so long as he paid to the Crown one fifth of all gold and silver extracted, plus delivery every Easter to Windsor Castle of two native arrows. (Are we wrong to think of these people as at least a little ridiculous? John Milton somewhere wrote: "it was their loves – or perhaps their sheep - that did their silly thoughts so busy keep.") Maryland was named for the consort of Charles I, Henrietta Maria de Bourbon. Maryland residents, fondling our native arrows in the prescribed ceremony every Founders Day, give thinks that the province was not named *Henriettatucetts*.

At the time of his appointment as Governor of Maryland, **William Stone** was already prominent in

Virginia. Born in Northhamptonshire England in 1603, he was living in "the Plantation of Acchowmacke" [Accawmacke] in 1633, a commissioner, and member of the Accawmacke Court (Northampton County) that year. (Records of William Stone's appointments, land transactions and other activities in Virginia are among the oldest surviving records in that state.) In 1634, Stone was appointed High Sheriff of the county and was still living in Virginia when appointed Governor of Maryland in 1648. He moved there in 1649.

Thus Maryland's Catholic Governor Thomas Green was replaced by the Protestant Stone, who promised Cecil Calvert, the Second Lord Baltimore, he would invite many of his co-adherents in Virginia to join Stone in populating the Calvert family's proprietary colony. The appointment of a Protestant governor may have been for show. Stone, when absent from the Colony, would leave in charge the former Catholic governor. But the governing council was evenly divided Catholic and Protestant. The Catholic population was primarily in southern Maryland, around St. Mary's City, while a large group of Puritans from Virginia had settled in Ann Arundel County (named for the wife of Proprietor Cecil Calvert) at the community they called Providence, which shortly was renamed Annapolis (named for Princess Anne, daughter of English Queen Mary).

The Virginians had come into Maryland to avoid curtailments of their religious practices, as was being attempted by Virginia Governor William Berkeley. The new Marylanders proved unwilling to take an oath of allegiance to Lord Baltimore, holding the oath was "Romish" as it bound them to obey a "Popish Government." The Puritans offered to swear to be true to Baltimore's interests, but this compromise was not acceptable to the Lord Proprietary, who ordered all who refused the oath to be expelled. The impasse was compounded by continuing turbulence in England. William Stone was Protestant but not of a Separatist stripe. Unfortunately for him, many of the Virginians who joined him in Maryland, were blood and bone Puritans.

In 1635, Stone was listed as a member of the first Vestry to be organized at Hungars Episcopal Church, Eastville, in Northhampton County, Virginia Colony. Therefore, Stone was part of the religious establishment of Virginia at the time when Virginia's autocratic Governor Berkeley was harassing and fining colonists who did not attend Episcopal worship. Stone's appointment to the governorship in Maryland might have been portrayed by Lord Baltimore in London as a respectful bow to Protestantism. But in Virginia and Maryland, separatists would have seen this as no sort of recognition for themselves. Undoubtedly, some of these wrote letters and otherwise communicated to Cromwell and his agents in England, to state that an Anglican-Catholic consortium in charge in St Mary's City was no true Protestant government for Maryland.

In 1654, commissioners from England arrived in Maryland. They insisted that the province be governed directly from England by the Lord Protector, Oliver Cromwell. William Stone was compelled to resign. He stated in a proclamation that he did so "for prevention of the effusion of Blood and ruine of the Country and Inhabitants." But the risk of "ruine" soon was reassessed.

In 1655, a ship, the *Golden Fortune,* arrived with reinforcements from Lord Baltimore. The emboldened William Stone, to his misfortune, then demanded that he be restored as Governor under the terms of the original charter. Marching with his supporters toward Patuxent to reclaim official records, Stone was met by an army of Puritans, many of them recently settled asylees from Virginia Colony, whom Stone himself had invited into Maryland. These hearty, serious planters were in no mood to come once again, under the thumb of an overreaching colonial administration, and certainly not a Catholic Proprietorship. Not for this had they crossed a wide ocean and lately uprooted themselves from Virginia to Maryland.

Near present day Annapolis, at the mouth of the Severn River, the Virginia Protestants, commanded by Captain William Fuller, defeated the little army of William

Stone, agent of Lord Baltimore. Some of the defeated "Papists" were court marshaled and at least one was executed on the spot. Stone, wounded in the shoulder, only just escaped execution by firing squad.

For a time, Stone was held prisoner. His wife **Verlinda** boldly appealed to Lord Baltimore, reciting in her letter some of the details of the battle. "Not above five of our men escaped," she wrote, "which ran away before the fight was ended . . . They have sequestered my Husband's Estate, only they say they will allow a maintenance for me and my children which I do believe will be but small. They keep my husband with the rest of the Council, all other officers, still prisoners, et cetera." Stone was freed and regained possession of at least some of his lands, including his estate, Nanjemy, later called Poynton Manor. William Stone died in 1660 in his house in St. Mary's City.

William and Verlinda Stone had seven children: Thomas, Richard, John, Matthew, Elizabeth, Katherine, and **Mary Stone** (?-before 1689), who became the wife, first of _____ Thomas and then, as a widow, of **Robert Doyne** (?-1689), High Sheriff of Charles County, Maryland. Verlinda Stone, in her will, dated March 3, 1675, and probated Sept 17, 1675, left "my dearest daughter Doyne my silver salt." Mary had a place to put the silver salt as this sentimental gift had been preceded by a donation to her of considerable land from her father William Stone, in his 1659 will.

The Stone-Doyne-Dawson-Moore-Taylor line of descent is the focus of this portion of the present family history. But **Verlinda** and **William Stone** had many prominent connections and descendents collateral to this line. Mary Stone's older sister, Elizabeth married William Calvert, son of Maryland Governor Leonard Calvert and grandson of George Calvert, First Lord Baltimore. Another descendent, William Murray Stone, was the third Protestant Episcopal Bishop of Maryland. Thomas Stone, a double great grandson, was a signer of the Declaration of Independence. Descendent Michael Jennifer was a member of the Maryland Convention that ratified the Constitution of the United States in 1788. John, a brother of the signer Thomas Stone, was a governor of Maryland.

Most of our other honored ancestors were, as Emily Dickinson quietly insisted, *too intrinsic for renown.*

SOURCES:

For the descendency from Verlinda Cotton (Graves?) and William Stone and the citations to original documents, such as Verlinda Stone's letter to Lord Baltimore: Hester Dorsey Richardson's 1921-27 research and report. The creation of this document entailed the personal examination and hand written transcription of dozens of ancient and official documents in widely scattered locations in Virginia and Maryland. The notarized Richardson research was prepared to prove, as it states, eligibility in "the National Society of Colonial Dames of America." The Richardson document was typed in 1979 (125 pages) by Cotton-Stone-Doyne-Dawson-Moore-Taylor descendent Anne M. Gibbs, whose generosity, helpfulness, invaluable research and custodianship of priceless documents merits the heartfelt thanks of the present writer, and all who read this work.

Interesting speculations as to Cotton Family origins in England, based on both documentary research, family traditions and genetic testing has been posted on the web at: cottondna.family.nf. See also Cotton information at genealogy.com and roadhometofl.com

For Mainwearing descent, linked to the Cottons, see **Medieval English Ancestors of Robert Abell** by Carl Boyer (2001); Todmar.net/Ancestry/Mainwaring_main

The escapades and the death of John Stone: **John Winthrop, America's Forgotten Founding Father**, Francis Bremer (Oxford University Press, 2003) pages 237-8, 265.

Establishment of Maryland Province: **George Calvert and Cecilius Calvert: Barons Baltimore of Baltimore**, William Hand Browne (New York, Dodd Mead, 1890), available at google/com/books.

showing the world that his Province was not all Roman Catholic to the prejudice of Protestants - Quotation giving Cecil Calvert's motivation in naming William Stone Governor of Maryland: **Narratives of Early Maryland**, C.C. Hall ed. (1910), page 163.

they died like flies - The description of demographic developments in the colonies: the brilliant and above cited **The Peopling of British North America, An Introduction** by Bernard Bailyn (1985, esp. pages 99-102; quotation from page 100).

For Blackstone's discussion of slavery, his *Commentary*, at 295.

For *partus sequitur ventrem,* Justinian: *Dig.* 6, 1, 5, 2; *Inst.* 2, 1, 9.

> *Lay this Laurel on the one*
> *Too intrinsic for renown.*
> *Laurel! veil your deathless tree, -*
> *Him you chasten, that is he.*
>
> Emily Dickinson
> (Time and Eternity, LXXXII)

ILLUSTRATIONS

Elizabeth Huey Taylor – Betty Cook   10

Elizabeth Huey Taylor Cook   28

Nan Elizabeth Huey   29

Nan Elizabeth Huey   32

Nan Elizabeth Huey Taylor   36

Nan Elizabeth Huey Taylor, baby Betty   38

John Oliver Taylor Jr   42

John Oliver Taylor Jr with banjo & baby Betty   46

John Oliver Taylor Jr   51

Sara Huey Crouch   54, 60

James Addison Huey   58

John Crouch   63

Sara Huey Crouch Huey – Sally   77

James Addison Huey - "Boss"   82

Amanda Watts Gaines Huey   90

James Gaines   95

Mary Baldwin Moore   114

John Oliver Taylor Sr   116

Benjamin Moore   *120*

Mary Baldwin Moore Taylor   *123*

Mary Aurelia Mayo Moore   *126*

Mary and John Taylor   *132*

"Minnie" Moore   *134*

Charles Taylor   *140*

Delilah Booth Gamewell   *147*

Charles Taylor   *152*

Charlotte Jane Gamewell   *160*

Charlotte Jane Gamewell Taylor   *169*

Jane Hedges Baldwin   *214*

Marmaduke Moore   *217*

Jane Hedges Baldwin Moore   *221*

Jonah Baldwin   *226*

Jonah Baldwin, suffering with cataracts   *234*

Louisa Winston   *276*

Mary Aurelia Mayo Moore   *280*

General Israel Putnam   *294*

Myrix Josiah Williams   *394*

INDEX

(For ancestral proper names, please consult the Table of Contents as well as the Index)

_____, Asa and Rachel, Graves and then Gaines slaves, 94, 96
_____, Becky, Mayo slave, 317
_____, Domingo, Cotton slave, 100
_____, female, Maverick slave, 205
_____, female, Stone slave, 369
_____, Gemima, Craig slave, 78
_____, Harry, Mayo slave, 278
_____, male, Doyne slave, 359
_____, male, Maverick slave, 205
_____, Mary, Doyne slave, 359
_____, Naomi, Dwight slave, 170, 172, 177
_____, Sambo, Cotton slave, 100
_____, six Mayo slaves, 278
_____, Stone slave, 66
_____, two females, Moore slaves, ages 25 & 8, 216
_____, Williams slave, 66
_____, Winston slaves, 279

Abell, George & Francis, 364
Abell, Robert & Joanna, 364
Adams, John (1735-1826), 176, 290, 292, 323, 330, 331, 332, 335
Adams, John Quincy (1767-1848), 283, 317, 322
Alpaida (Elfide, Chalpaida), 203
American Board of Commissions for Foreign Missions (A.B.C.F.M.), 192
Amsterdam, 73, 364
Anabaptists, 71, 73
Anglican Church (Ch of England), 181, 201, 206, 353, 359
anti-slavery opinion, 92, 165, 170, 171, 194, 195, 316
Arcadia Plantation, MD, 257, 258, 264
Asbury, Francis (1745-1816), 145, 146
Auburn, New York, 113, 139, 161, 165, 179, 193, 194, 195, 196, 197, 198, 199
Auchmuty, 186, 330
Awliscombe, Devonshire, England, 201
Bacon's Rebellion (1676), VA, 99

379

Bailey, Mike, Dawson genealogist, 354, 355, 361, 362
Baldwin, 1, 2, 3, 19, 41, 49, 112, 113, 114, 115, 121, 123, 133, 137, 153, 161, 178, 186, 212, 213, 214, 215, 216, 218, 221, 222, 223, 225, 226, 227, 228, 229, 230, 231, 232, 233, 234, 235, 236, 237, 239, 242, 243, 244, 246, 247, 248, 249, 250, 251, 252, 253, 257, 258, 260, 264, 275, 277, 283, 323, 324, 337, 338, 339, 341, 342, 351, 352, 353, 354, 357, 361, 362, 363, 377, 378
Baldwin, Anna B., 232, 248, 260, 337, 341, 342, 351, 354
Baptist Hymnody, 86
Baptist, Baptists, 13, 14, 16, 21, 25, 31, 34, 48, 49, 53, 55, 56, 65, 66, 67, 69, 70, 71, 72, 74, 75, 76, 79, 80, 81, 86, 88, 94, 96, 103, 111, 153, 336
Baptist, General, 70, 72
Baptist, Particular, 69, 70, 71, 72
Barbados, 146, 175, 302, 304, 357, 370
Bardstown, KY, 80
Battaile, 260, 269
Battaille, 260
Battle of Blue Licks (1782), 75, 81
Battle of Bunker Hill (1775), 5, 292, 293, 319, 328
Battle of Kings Mountain (1780), 30, 279

Battle of Lexington (1775), 314
Battle of Piqua (1780), 235, 239
Battle of Sandusky Plains (1782), 345, 348, 351, 355
Battle of Saratoga (1777), 314
Battle of Tippecanoe (1811), 239, 261
Battle of Tours (732), 203
Battle, Great Swamp (1675), 325
Bellefontaine, Ohio, 216
Belmont County, Ohio, 269
Belpre, Ohio, 275, 284, 286, 287, 289, 290, 291, 292, 306, 313, 316, 319, 320, 329
Besançon, Hugues, 84
Big Bone Lick, KY, 57, 62, 81, 83, 84, 105
Big Bottom settlement, Belpre, Ohio, 289
Bishop, Bridget, 305, 306, 307, 308, 311, 321
Blackstone, William (1723-1780), 369
Blue Lick Springs, KY, 253, 352
Bluefield, WV, 21, 22
Boone County KY, 48, 57, 59, 62, 80, 81, 94, 96, 101, 105, 106, 110, 111, 277
Boone, Daniel (1734-1820), 80, 81
Booth, 145, 146, 147, 151, 378
Booth, Newell, Methodist Bishop, 145
Boston Massacre, 5, 177, 323, 329, 335

Boston, MA, 5, 139, 148, 177, 187, 192, 193, 204, 209, 210, 283, 298, 313, 317, 319, 323, 329, 330, 331, 332, 333, 334, 335, 364, 365
Boundary Controversy, VA-PA, 251, 265, 343
Bourbon County KY, 68, 151, 246, 268
Bowen, 186, 188, 323, 324, 325
Boxer Rebellion, 149
Boyle, Jeremiah (Union General), 219
Bracken County, KY, 275
Bradbury, William (1816-1868), 56
Browne, 376
Buckogeahelas, a Delaware, 355
Bunbury, Cheshire, England, 363
Burke, Lindsey, 102
Calvert, Cecil (1605-1675), 371
Calvert, Geo. (1580-1632) 1st Baron Baltimore, 374, 376
Calvert, Leonard, 374
Calvin, John (1509-1564), 70, 73, 88, 202, 307
Calvinism, 73, 201
Campbell, Alexander (1788-1866), 53
Capers, William (1790-1855), 141, 176
Carlisle, PA, 149
Caroline County VA, 104
Carrichfergus, Ireland, 357
Castleman, Henry Clay, 65
Castleman, Louisiana Williams, 30, 65

Catholic Church, 21, 73, 84, 202, 208, 246, 257, 268, 326, 331, 358, 363, 371, 372, 373, 376
Cemeteries, 27, 50, 64, 67, 79, 81, 88, 94, 105, 135, 159, 166, 193, 196, 199, 222, 254, 255, 256, 271, 272, 313, 318, 361
Charitas, the Ship, 244
Charles County, MD, 357, 374
Charles I, King of England, 97, 98, 182, 207, 208, 209, 245, 371
Charleston, SC, 149
Chesapeake Bay, 97, 366, 370
Cheshire, 100, 223, 363
Chicago, IL, 212, 227, 228, 229, 248, 249
China, 48, 138, 141, 142, 144, 149, 151, 153, 154, 155, 158, 159, 161, 162, 163, 164, 172, 176, 196, 199
Church, 167
Church, Beaworthy, Devonshire, Eng, 206
Church, Benjamin, 167, 188, 198
Church, Buffalo Ridge Baptist, Washington County, NC (now, TN), 79
Church, Bullittsburg Baptist, 94
Church, Congregational, Charlestown, MA, 184
Church, Crescent Hill Baptist, Louisville, KY, 13, 25, 33, 34, 65, 336

Church, Dry Ridge Baptist, Grant Co KY, 69, 71
Church, Episcopal Parish of All Souls (Christ Church), Springfield, Ohio, 231
Church, Fork Lick Old Baptist, Grant Co KY, 69
Church, Great Crossings Baptist, Scott County, KY, 74
Church, Hungars Episcopal Church, Eastville, Northhampton County, VA, 99, 373
Church, Methodist Episcopal, Warsaw, KY, 80
Church, Napoleon Avenue Baptist Church, New Orleans, LA, 16
Church, Oakland Baptist, Warsaw KY, 53
Church, Old Falls Branch Baptist, Washington County TN., 79
Church, old North Church (Second Church) of Boston, 334
Church, Rainbow Methodist, Snow Hill, Green County, N C, 145
Church, Sand Run Baptist, Hebron, KY, 94
Church, St. Paul's Parish, Kent County MD, 258
Church, Ten Mile Baptist, Napoleon, KY, 67
Church, Union Baptist Church, Union KY, 53
Church, Williamstown Church of Christ, (Particular Baptist) Grant Co KY, 72

Churchtown, Lancaster County PA, 83, 84
Cincinnati, Ohio, 11, 53, 59, 87, 92, 93, 106, 107, 108, 176, 225, 232, 290, 316, 318, 322, 348
Civil War (US), 5, 44, 52, 61, 89, 104, 108, 109, 113, 142, 146, 148, 149, 158, 159, 161, 165, 170, 171, 172, 194, 195, 205, 219, 220, 225, 278, 279, 316, 327
Clark County Ohio, 213, 225, 229, 232, 233, 235, 236, 248, 249, 252, 253, 256, 339, 353, 356
Cokesbury, SC, 141
Colonial Militia Company, described, 189, 198
Combermere Monastery, 363
Concord, MA, 179, 180, 197
Congo, Belgium, 102, 145
Connecticut, 167, 170, 171, 188, 275, 284, 300, 304, 321, 329, 365
Cook, 16, 17, 18, 19, 21, 22, 23, 24, 27, 34, 35, 37, 39, 65, 70, 75, 103, 240, 247, 296, 371, 372, 376
Cook, Barbara G., M.D., 26
Cook's Tour thru Taylor Genealogy, 247
Cotes Grange, Derbyshire, Eng, 363
Cotton, 4, 99, 100, 363, 364, 369, 374, 375
Cotton, Andrew, 363
Cotton, Ann (An), 100
Cotton, Joane, 100, 363
Cotton, John (1585-1652), 208, 299

Courtland, AL, 139, 146, 159
Covington, KY, 50, 115, 216, 222
Craig, 73, 74, 75, 76, 78, 80, 87, 260
Craig, Lewis (1737-1828), 75
Cranbrook, Kent, England, 167
Crawford, William, 262, 263, 273, 338, 339, 340, 341, 342, 349, 350, 354
Cromwell, Oliver (1599-1658), 182, 245, 327, 358, 373
Crouch, 1, 3, 12, 14, 30, 34, 50, 53, 54, 55, 59, 60, 62, 63, 64, 65, 67, 68, 77, 78, 79, 80, 86, 87, 88, 110, 377
Cruttenden, 166, 167
Culpeper County VA, 96, 101
Curtis, 333
Cynthiana, KY, 122, 213, 215, 255, 261, 263, 270, 271, 272
DAR, Paris, KY, 74
Dartmouth College, 179, 191
Davis, 94, 104, 187, 328, 333
Davis, Jefferson, 104
Dawkins, 325
Dawson, 3, 4, 99, 213, 215, 222, 229, 231, 232, 251, 252, 253, 255, 256, 258, 337, 338, 339, 340, 341, 342, 343, 344, 345, 347, 348, 351, 352, 353, 354, 355, 357, 359, 361, 362, 363, 374, 375
Dawson, Wayne, Dawson Family genealogist, 355

De Vere, Edward (1550-1604), 245, 295, 320, 326
Dedham Plain, 188, 325
Dedham, MA, 168, 188, 298, 325
Delamare, 325
Detroit, MI, 227, 228, 229, 249
Devotion, 333
Dicken Family, 94, 96
Dickinson, Emily (1830-1886), 5, 133, 375, 376
Doddridge, Joseph (1769-1826), 273, 274
Doland (Dowland), 258
Donaldson, 67
Dorchester, MA, 184, 197, 201, 204, 209, 210, 211, 212, 300, 314
Doughty, Francis (c. 1610-aft 1665), 99
Doyne, 4, 99, 110, 342, 343, 344, 357, 358, 359, 360, 361, 362, 363, 374, 375
Draper, Lyman (1815-1891), 250, 272
Ducote, County Salop, Eng, 363
Dumfrieshire, Scotland, 258
Dunstable, MA, 179, 180
Dwight, 11, 122, 125, 131, 165, 167, 168, 170, 171, 172, 173, 177, 192, 328
Dwight, Timothy (1752-1817), 168, 170, 171, 177, 192
Ecton, Mary Taylor, 52, 250
Edict of Nantes, 73, 83
Edwards, Jonathan (1703-1758), 168
Elizabeth I (1533-1603), 209, 326
Elyot, 295

Episcopal Church, 72, 74, 80, 99, 113, 122, 141, 159, 181, 196, 199, 206, 227, 229, 231, 249, 253, 326, 327, 353, 358, 364, 373, 374
Erdlet Grange, Staffordshire, 363
Erickson, 258
Erlanger, KY, 15, 45, 47, 57, 122, 124, 125, 127, 135
Evarts, Jeremiah, 192
Farmer's Castle (Belpre OH), 289
Fayette County PA, 75, 251, 252, 261, 264, 272, 338, 342
Fleming, 324, 325
Frankfort, KY, 34, 57, 80, 240
Franklin, 325
Fredrick, MD, 351
French and Indian War (1754-1763), 165, 262, 346
Frost, Robert (1874-1963), 47, 52, 251, 256, 337
Fugitive Slave Act (Law), 91, 93
Gabriel's Plot (1800), 171
Gaines, 3, 14, 30, 53, 57, 59, 65, 80, 89, 90, 91, 94, 95, 96, 99, 101, 102, 103, 105, 106, 107, 108, 110, 111, 364, 377
Gaines, Archibald, 91, 101, 105, 106, 107, 111, 344
Gaines, John P (1795-1857), 102, 106
Gallatin County KY, 53, 62, 64, 66, 67
Gamewell, 3, 48, 113, 131, 139, 145, 146, 147, 148, 149, 150, 160, 161, 169, 175, 176, 192, 378
Gamewell Fire Alarm Telegraph Company, 148
Gamewell, Mary Porter, 149, 176
Gamewell, Whatcoat (1814-1869), 146, 149, 176
Gardiner, William, 188, 302
Garner, Margaret (?-?), 91, 106, 107, 108, 111
Geneva, Switzerland, 201, 202, 307
Gibbs, Anne Moffett, 52, 110, 118, 125, 133, 137, 175, 176, 223, 248, 256, 281, 282, 320, 322, 354, 362, 375
Gilford, CT, 166, 167
Glamorgans, Wales, 324
Godwin, 168
Gouge, 3, 62, 65, 67, 68, 69, 70, 71, 72, 73, 74, 86, 88
Gould, 3, 139, 165, 166, 176, 179, 192
Grant County KY, 62, 65, 66, 67, 68, 69, 71, 87, 88
Graves, 94, 96, 101, 167
Great Awakening (the 2nd), 162, 165, 192
Green, 111, 145, 177, 323, 372
Gregory, 104
Gregson, 167
Gye, 1, 3, 184, 201, 203, 211, 212
Ha(w)thorne, 297, 298, 299, 302, 305, 308, 312, 319, 320, 321
Hackensack, NJ, 148
Hales, Drayton, England, 363
Hame(s)town, PA, 263

Hanover County VA, 281
Harrison, 4, 72, 102, 213, 216, 233, 239, 248, 251, 252, 253, 254, 256, 257, 259, 260, 261, 262, 263, 267, 268, 269, 270, 271, 272, 273, 337, 338, 339, 341, 343
Harrison County KY, 213, 216, 233, 252, 253, 254, 257, 259, 261, 269, 270, 271, 272
Harrison, William Henry (1773-1841), 239
Harvard College, 99, 283
Hatfield, Hampshire, MA., 167, 168
Hathorn(e), William, 187, 297, 298, 299, 300, 301, 302, 319, 320, 321
Hawkins, Edward W., 113
Hawthorne, Nathaniel (1804-1864), 188, 298, 299, 312, 322
Haylip, Richard, 345, 355
Hedges, 3, 213, 214, 221, 224, 225, 229, 230, 233, 243, 244, 245, 246, 247, 248, 249, 250, 252, 258, 264, 339, 353, 361, 378
Henrietta Maria de Bourbon (1609-1669), 371
Henry VIII (1491-1547), 206, 208, 212, 326, 363
Henry, Patrick (1736-1799), 102, 103, 281
Hepbourne, 258
Herne Hill, London, 325
Hinkson, 167, 262, 272, 273
Hooker, Richard, 326, 327
Huey, 1, 3, 8, 10, 11, 12, 13, 14, 15, 19, 24, 28, 29, 30, 31, 32, 33, 34, 35, 36, 38, 47, 50, 52, 53, 54, 55, 57, 58, 59, 60, 61, 62, 64, 65, 67, 68, 76, 77, 80, 81, 82, 83, 84, 85, 86, 87, 89, 90, 94, 99, 101, 103, 105, 108, 110, 133, 145, 247, 377
Huguenot, 7, 73, 83, 87, 342
Hunt (Harp), 105
Hutchinson, Thomas, 330, 335
Hutchinson, Thomas, Gov (1711-1780), 330, 335
Indiana, 53, 94, 193, 225, 227, 238, 239, 338
Indians, 187, 301, 302, 303
Indians (Originals), 290
Jackson, Andrew (1767-(1845), 236
James I (1566-1625), 97, 209
James, William (1842-1910), 297, 298, 299, 320
Jamestown, VA, 96, 97, 111, 326, 340, 366
Jefferson, Thomas (1743-1826), 68, 72, 73, 81, 102, 103, 292
Jennifer, Michael, 374
Jewett, 3, 68, 69, 72, 73, 74, 83, 87
John Hathorne, 305, 308, 312
John of Topsham, The Ship, 258
Johnson, 188, 323, 325, 326
Johnson, Nancy Collier Taylor, 15, 52, 115, 121, 122, 124, 137, 215, 216, 277, 281, 282
Jouett, Matthew Harris (1788-1827), 73
Juett, 68, 69, 72, 73, 74

Justinian, Emperor (482-565), 376
Kendrick, 4, 186, 283, 323, 328, 329
Kent County, England, 333
Kent County, Maryland, 257
Kent Island, MD, 258, 259
Kenton County KY, 279
Kentucky, 7, 11, 16, 24, 41, 45, 53, 57, 62, 64, 67, 68, 70, 71, 72, 74, 75, 76, 83, 84, 87, 88, 89, 91, 92, 93, 96, 105, 107, 108, 110, 113, 118, 125, 127, 142, 144, 151, 154, 159, 161, 173, 175, 195, 215, 216, 219, 220, 229, 233, 246, 248, 251, 252, 253, 256, 258, 259, 261, 262, 263, 264, 266, 267, 268, 269, 272, 273, 278, 279, 282, 288, 290, 291, 306, 315, 316, 317, 319, 338, 351, 352
Kentucky Wesleyan College, 113, 142, 175
Kilworth Plantation, MD, 259
King George County, Virginia, 79
King Philip's War, 187, 301
King William County VA, 74
Lancaster County PA, 83
Laud, Archbishop William, 181, 182, 207
Lawrence County AL, 159
Lexington, KY, 73
Lilburne, John, 206
Lincoln, Abraham (1809-1865), 102, 228
Lion, The ship, 186
Little Turtle, the Miami Chief, 242
London, 73, 97, 98, 137, 167, 198, 204, 207, 208, 212, 245, 246, 265, 267, 270, 293, 295, 296, 324, 325, 333, 334, 342, 358, 364, 366, 373
Lord Baltimore, 246, 358, 359, 371, 372, 373, 374, 375
Louisville, KY, 11, 12, 13, 16, 17, 23, 24, 25, 27, 33, 34, 35, 37, 45, 59, 65, 67, 104, 159, 194, 219, 277, 335, 336
Lowe, 1, 252, 258, 341, 342, 343, 361
Lyman, 167, 168, 250, 272
Mackall, 258
Madison, James (1751-1836), 104
Mainwaring, 1, 363, 375
Marblehead, MA, 180, 183
Marietta, Ohio, 68, 283, 286, 287, 289, 291, 306, 314, 319
Marmaduke, 1, 3, 41, 121, 122, 125, 213, 215, 216, 217, 218, 219, 223, 224, 233, 251, 252, 253, 257, 258, 259, 264, 269, 337, 338, 339, 343, 353, 357, 361, 363, 378
Marsh, 167
Martel, Charles, 201, 203, 212
Maryland, 72, 87, 88, 98, 99, 100, 110, 195, 205, 244, 246, 247, 252, 257, 258, 259, 263, 264, 265, 272, 338, 341, 342, 344, 345, 355, 357, 358, 360, 362, 363, 364, 366, 367,

368, 369, 370, 371, 372,
   373, 374, 375, 376
Mason, 76, 80, 81, 105
Mason, Grant Co KY, 69
Mason, Lowell (1792-1872),
   55, 56, 86
Massachusetts, 7, 148, 158,
   167, 173, 188, 192, 204,
   205, 208, 209, 210, 212,
   275, 293, 300, 302, 304,
   307, 313, 316, 319, 321,
   328, 329, 330, 364, 365
Mather, 168, 170, 303, 304,
   306, 321, 334
Mather, Cotton (1663-1728),
   303, 306, 321, 334
Maverick, 3, 181, 184, 185,
   197, 201, 202, 203, 204,
   205, 206, 207, 208, 209,
   210, 211, 212, 300
Mayo, i, 1, 4, 11, 12, 15, 44,
   45, 48, 49, 50, 52, 112,
   122, 124, 125, 126, 131,
   133, 145, 178, 179, 186,
   188, 218, 223, 256, 275,
   277, 278, 279, 280, 281,
   282, 283, 284, 290, 291,
   292, 313, 314, 315, 316,
   317, 318, 319, 320, 322,
   323, 328, 329, 331, 333,
   335, 犭352, 354, 378
Medford (Mitford), 215, 258
Metacomb, 187, 301, 302,
   303, 305, 320, 325
Methodist Church, 14, 15,
   48, 80, 113, 129, 139, 141,
   142, 144, 145, 146, 149,
   159, 161, 173, 176, 196,
   199, 278
Methodist Church South,
   Wadesborough District,
   142

Miller, Katharine, Betty
   Taylor Cook's sister, 12,
   13, 19, 21, 25, 30, 37, 39,
   47, 59, 141, 145, 176
Miller, Paul Lathrup, Jr., 21,
   25, 141
Millersburg, KY, 142
Milton, John (1608-1674),
   182, 371
Miro, Esteban Rodriguez,
   Governor of Louisiana,
   17, 268
Missouri, 31, 47, 59, 268,
   269, 273
Moore, 1, 3, 4, 20, 41, 43,
   49, 50, 73, 99, 112, 113,
   114, 115, 118, 119, 120,
   121, 122, 123, 124, 125,
   126, 127, 129, 131, 133,
   134, 135, 137, 142, 153,
   161, 178, 186, 188, 213,
   215, 216, 217, 218, 219,
   220, 221, 222, 223, 224,
   225, 228, 229, 231, 232,
   233, 237, 246, 248, 250,
   251, 252, 253, 254, 255,
   256, 257, 258, 259, 260,
   261, 262, 263, 264, 267,
   269, 270, 271, 272, 273,
   275, 277, 278, 280, 281,
   283, 322, 323, 324, 337,
   338, 339, 341, 343, 351,
   352, 353, 357, 361, 362,
   363, 375, 377, 378
Morgan, Edmund S., 110
Morpeth, Northumberland
   shire, England, 258
Morrill, 115, 185, 186, 187,
   189, 198, 323, 324
Morrison, Toni, 107
Morse, Samuel (1791-1872),
   139, 148, 173, 193
Munn, 165

Muskingum River, 283
Nanjemy Estate, MD, 374
Naragansett, 188
Narraganset fortress, 187, 188, 302
Nassau, Bahamas, 145, 146
New England, 48, 55, 98, 164, 165, 167, 170, 172, 173, 176, 180, 183, 189, 197, 198, 202, 204, 205, 206, 207, 208, 209, 210, 212, 275, 283, 284, 293, 298, 301, 302, 303, 305, 306, 316, 319, 335, 364, 366, 367, 370
New Ipswich, NH, 179, 190, 191
New Kent County VA, 281
New Moorefield, OH, 225, 230, 233
New Orleans, LA, 13, 17, 18, 21, 33, 268
New York, 16, 33, 35, 52, 88, 110, 111, 113, 121, 139, 148, 154, 158, 164, 165, 172, 173, 176, 177, 179, 193, 194, 195, 196, 198, 199, 247, 248, 278, 302, 314, 318, 321, 354, 356, 376
Newport, KY, 113, 129, 144, 275, 278, 290, 291, 292, 313, 315, 316, 317, 318, 323
Noble, 279
North Carolina, 29, 34, 142, 145, 279
Norwich, England, 105
Oates, Wayne, 26
Oates, Wayne (1917-1999), 26
Ohio, 7, 11, 24, 35, 48, 53, 81, 83, 91, 92, 93, 94, 96, 107, 193, 213, 215, 216, 219, 225, 230, 231, 232, 233, 236, 238, 239, 240, 242, 248, 249, 252, 253, 261, 262, 264, 266, 269, 273, 275, 277, 278, 283, 285, 287, 288, 289, 290, 291, 292, 306, 313, 314, 316, 319, 320, 329, 338, 339, 340, 341, 342, 345, 346, 347, 348, 351, 352, 353, 354, 356
Ohio River, 91, 92, 96, 107, 232, 233, 262, 264, 277, 283, 287, 289, 290, 292, 314, 339, 340, 342, 352
Oldham County KY, 115
Oregon Territory, 102
Panoplist, the (publication), 192
Parsons, 3, 122, 125, 139, 151, 153, 165, 166, 167, 171, 176, 179, 192, 197, 328
Partus sequitur patrem, 370
Partus sequitur ventrem, 370
Pendleton, 101, 102, 103, 105, 110, 111
Pendleton, Edmund (1721-1803), 101, 102, 111
Pennsylvania, 83, 225, 228, 236, 237, 244, 251, 252, 255, 262, 263, 264, 267, 268, 273, 274, 288, 338, 339, 340, 341, 342, 343, 345, 346, 347, 351, 356
Pequot Tribe, War, 304, 365
Philadelphia, 102, 139, 141, 142, 145, 154, 158, 172, 230, 265

Pippin the Middle (635/40-714), 203
Pittsburgh, 263, 285, 288, 293, 356
Pleasant Township, Ohio, 229, 232, 338
Plymouth Colony, 188, 301, 302, 364
Poindexter, KY, 255, 259, 270, 271
Pond, 333
Porter, 149, 176, 227, 249, 296, 297, 300, 305, 308, 325, 326, 327
Poynton Manor, MD, 374
Presbytery of Monroe, NY, 193
Prince George's County MD, 342, 344, 360
Providence, The Ship, 258
Puritans, 183, 185, 205, 207, 208, 209, 210, 212, 297, 299, 303, 305, 306, 307, 326, 334, 335, 372
Putnam (Puttenham), 4, 48, 188, 210, 275, 283, 284, 287, 290, 291, 292, 293, 294, 296, 297, 300, 308, 309, 313, 314, 315, 316, 319, 321, 328, 329, 378
Putnam, Israel, General (1718-1790), 275, 292, 294, 314, 321, 378
Quakers, 92, 195, 208, 298, 299
Rangers of the Frontiers, 255
Reading, MA, 180, 181, 184, 185
Revolutionary War, 73, 108, 165, 193, 198, 233, 251, 252, 255, 257, 262, 263, 267, 279, 283, 314, 335, 345, 355
Rhode Island, 188, 301, 303, 325
Rice, 96
Richardson, Hester Dorsey, 110, 362, 375
Roxbury MA, 115, 186, 187, 188, 199, 283, 325, 327, 328, 331, 333, 334, 335
Rubio, Elizabeth Taylor, 79, 87, 110, 133, 224, 251, 252, 321, 323, 335
Rush, Benjamin, 139
Salem Witch Trials, 5, 305, 312, 321, 322, 331
Salem, MA, 5, 24, 25, 29, 39, 188, 279, 293, 296, 297, 298, 299, 300, 302, 305, 307, 308, 312, 321, 322, 331
Sandys, Edwin, Treas, Virginia Company, 97, 98
Savage, James, New England genealogist, 181, 183, 186, 197, 198, 328
Schultz, Eric B., 198
Scott, 3, 74, 99, 213, 218, 222, 223, 225, 229, 230, 231, 236, 248, 252, 253, 338, 339, 352, 353, 356, 361
Scott County KY, 74
Scudder, 325
Seward, William H (1801-1872), 165, 194, 195, 197
Shakespeare, Wm (1564-1616), 119, 121, 203, 295, 326, 369
Shanghai, China, 141, 144, 150, 151, 153, 154, 155, 156, 159, 173

Shawnee, 235, 236, 238, 239, 262, 273, 288, 342, 349, 350
Shelby County KY, 70
Shepherd, 31, 333
Slavery, 5, 66, 78, 87, 91, 92, 93, 94, 96, 105, 106, 107, 108, 109, 110, 111, 113, 158, 162, 164, 170, 171, 172, 177, 195, 216, 219, 263, 282, 316, 320, 368, 369, 370
Smith, 168, 185, 324
Smith, Nathan (1762-1829), 192
Smythe Hundred (Southampton) VA, 97
Somerset County, MD, 360
South Carolina, 45, 48, 113, 141, 145, 146, 148, 149, 154, 155, 158, 159, 161, 162, 164, 165, 173, 175, 176, 193, 195, 196
Spartanburg Female College, 113, 142, 172
Spartanburg, SC, 113, 142, 151, 159, 172
Spotsylvania County Virginia, 75
Spring, Samuel, 193
Springfield, MA, 165, 166
Springfield, Ohio, 215, 231, 248, 249, 252, 341, 352, 356
St Mary's County MD, 259, 360
St. Mary's City, MD, 374
Stone, 4, 66, 86, 98, 99, 100, 101, 110, 270, 343, 357, 358, 359, 360, 363, 364, 365, 366, 367, 369, 371, 372, 373, 374, 375, 376

Stone, John, MD Gov., 375
Stone, Thomas, 374
Stony Point, KY, 216
Suffolk County MA, 184, 185, 328, 333
Sugar Loaf Hundred, MD, 345
Surrey County VA, 279
Swaine, 3, 113, 139, 165, 179, 180, 181, 184, 185, 189, 190, 191, 196, 197, 201, 324, 325
Swayne, 165, 179, 180, 181, 184, 185, 187, 188, 189, 191, 192, 196, 197, 198, 201, 206, 302, 325
Synagogue, Charleston, SC (1835), 149
Taiping Rebellion, 155, 176
Taylor, 1, 3, 6, 7, 8, 10, 11, 12, 13, 14, 15, 19, 20, 21, 23, 24, 25, 28, 29, 30, 31, 33, 34, 35, 36, 38, 39, 41, 42, 43, 44, 45, 46, 47, 48, 50, 51, 52, 53, 55, 57, 59, 67, 68, 70, 79, 80, 86, 87, 89, 94, 99, 100, 101, 103, 104, 110, 111, 112, 113, 115, 116, 117, 118, 121, 122, 123, 124, 125, 127, 128, 129, 131, 132, 133, 135, 137, 138, 139, 140, 141, 142, 143, 144, 145, 149, 150, 152, 153, 154, 158, 159, 161, 163, 164, 165, 166, 167, 169, 170, 171, 173, 174, 175, 176, 178, 179, 180, 181, 184, 186, 187, 188, 189, 190, 191, 192, 193, 194, 195, 196, 197, 199, 201, 206, 210, 213, 216, 222, 223, 224, 225, 240, 247, 248,

250, 251, 256, 257, 258, 259, 260, 272, 275, 277, 278, 281, 282, 283, 300, 302, 315, 319, 321, 322, 323, 324, 325, 328, 335, 337, 341, 351, 352, 353, 354, 357, 362, 363, 375, 377, 378
Taylor, David Reade, 13, 35, 39, 52
Taylor, Henry Anderson, 21, 24, 25
Taylor, James (1609/15-1698), 103, 104
Taylor, Jean Valette, Betty Taylor Cook's sister, 12, 13, 19, 21, 24, 30, 37, 39, 59, 67, 87, 137, 222, 282
Taylor, Mary Alice Stevenson, 52, 145
Taylor, Mayo Moore (1893-1982), 11, 15, 48, 52, 112, 133, 145, 178, 354
Taylor, Zachary (1784-1850), 104
Tecumseh (1777?-1813), 233, 237, 238, 239, 242, 248
Tennessee, 79, 88
Tenskwatawa, 239, 248
The Great Depression, 33
Thomson, Virgil, 40
Throckmorton, 325
Tocqueville, Alexis de (1805-1859), 194
Tougias, Michael J., 198
Tournier, Paul (1898-1986), 26
Traveling Church, the (1781), 75
Treaty of Easton (1758), 265, 267, 273, 346

Treaty of Greenville (1795), 239
Treaty of Paris (1763), 266
Treaty of Paris (1783), 347
Treaty of Union (1706), 257
Treaty of Utrecht (1713), 346
Truelove, The Ship, 179, 334
Tubman, Harriet (1820-1913), 165, 195, 197
Turley, 67, 68, 87
Union Township, Ohio, 338
Union, KY, 11, 23, 29, 31, 34, 47, 53, 57, 62, 68, 80, 105, 111
Uniontown, PA, 341
Vallette, 3, 222, 229, 231, 248, 251, 252, 253, 337, 338, 339, 341, 352, 356, 357, 363
Vaughn, 325
Virginia, 3, 7, 21, 65, 66, 68, 72, 73, 74, 75, 79, 83, 86, 87, 89, 94, 96, 97, 98, 99, 100, 102, 103, 104, 105, 110, 111, 171, 205, 208, 223, 225, 227, 230, 236, 243, 244, 247, 251, 252, 253, 254, 257, 260, 262, 263, 264, 267, 270, 272, 274, 281, 288, 314, 327, 337, 338, 339, 340, 341, 342, 345, 352, 358, 364, 365, 366, 370, 371, 372, 373, 375
Wales, 223, 296, 324, 325
Walton, 101, 179, 180, 181, 182, 183, 184, 185, 190, 191, 193, 197, 198, 201, 205, 324
Walton, KY, 101
Wampanoag Tribe, 187, 188, 301, 302, 303

War of 1812, 240
Washington County, Ohio, 313, 320
Washington, George (1732-1799), 102, 263, 265, 290, 293, 314, 340, 341, 354
Washington, Martha (1731-1802), 64, 252, 337
Watson, 88, 258
Watts, 3, 30, 80, 89, 90, 94, 105, 106, 111, 364, 377
Wayne, Anthony (1745-96) Gen., 233, 239, 314
Webster, Daniel (1782-1852), 191
Wellsville, Virginia, 351
Wesley, John (1703-1791), 173, 174, 175, 177
West Virginia, 21, 223, 225, 243, 244, 288, 314, 352
Wharton, 357, 359, 362
Whatcoat, Richard (?-1806), 146
Wheeler, AL, 11
Whestone, 258
Whiting, 166
Whitman, Walt (1819-1892), 112, 175, 177, 178

William, Lord of Coton Manor, 363
Williams, 3, 12, 30, 59, 62, 65, 66, 67, 68, 78, 86, 87, 180, 184, 283, 301, 320, 324
Wilson, Lizzie (servant, 1880), 115
Wincell Grange, County Cheshire, Eng, 363
Winchester, VA, 225
Winston, 4, 24, 25, 29, 39, 218, 275, 276, 277, 279, 281, 282, 378
Winston-Salem, NC, 24, 25, 29, 39, 279
Winthrop, John (1588-1649), 202, 204, 206, 210, 212, 297, 299, 300, 319, 365, 375
Witch Trial, Salem, 5, 305, 307, 312, 321, 322, 331
Worcester, MA, 166
Wyandotte Indians, 340, 346, 347, 349, 350, 355
Zurich, Switzerland, 84, 307
Zwingli, Ulrich (1484-1531), 307

SUPPLEMENT TO ALL OF THE ABOVE I

WILIAMS – ABOVE I Pages 65-6

Welshman **William Myrix Williams** (c 1735-1814) is believed to have been the first Williams immigrant in this line. A note in the KY State Historical Society *Register* (1904, 05) suggests a connection between William Myrix Williams and **Thomas Cromwell** (c 1485-1540), a principal advisor of Henry VIII – whom Henry beheaded. Other research shows a connection a century later, with Lord Protector **Oliver Cromwell** (1599-1658), born Oliver *Williams,* son of Elizabeth Stewart and Robert Williams *Cromwell.* See: tudorplace.com. Apparently, one or more English Williams took his mother's more prominent family name, *Cromwell,* as a last name. This maneuver would have appealed to many during the tumultuous rule of the Tudors, who were much taken with genealogy and the advantages of inherited high place.

Levi Williams (1794-1860) is remembered in a 1907 *Biographical Review* of Hancock County, Illinois as a war veteran (1812, and the Black Hawk War) and militia commander. In Mormon history he is "a drunken, ignorant, illiterate brute" for having murdered Mormon Prophet Joseph Smith and his brother Hyrum. Both had been imprisoned in Carthage, Il, where, on June 27, 1844, some 200 men charged the jail and killed the Smiths. Levi Williams and four others were tried for murder. All were acquitted – but not until after the jury was dismissed and a new jury was chosen from among the spectators. For the Mormon quote: Vol 5 *Improvement Era,* No 12, (Oct 1902, p 934).

Levi Williams was the oldest brother of **Myrix Josiah Williams** (1811-1897) (photo below). Other Williams siblings were: William (c 1796-?), John (c 1798-?), Mary (c 1800-?), Sally (c 1802-?), Kavanaugh (c 1804-?) and Nancy (c 1806-?). This Williams sibling information has been made available by Williams descendent Sally Black, cited by Byrnefamily.net. *Family History.*

Betsy Collins Williams (1777-1833) was a daughter of **Nancy Anne** (not *Sally*) **Garland** (1755-1780) and **Thomas Collins II** (1740-1820), of Albemarle County, VA. Thomas' parents were **Thomas Collins I** (1707-1752) and widow **Elizabeth Barbee** (Redd), of Spotsylvania Co VA. In addition to Thomas II, Elizabeth and Thomas I were the parents of: William, Richard (married Joyeus), and Joseph Collins (1685-1748) (married Catherine Robertson, c 1714). Thomas Collins I was the son of **John Collins** (c 1655- 1748) and **Mary Wyatt** (c 1683-?). John's parents were English immigrant **William Collins** (1612-?) and widow **Ann King** (Wildes).

Nancy Anne Garland was one of thirteen children born to **Mary Rice** (1732- by 1812) and **James Garland Sr** (1722-1812). James was one of ten children of **John Garland** (1680-1734) of Hanover County, VA and **Anne Cosby** (1698-1734). The parents of Anne Cosby Garland are unknown. John Garland was the son of **Martha Jane Hensley** (1665-?) and **Edward Garland Sr** (c 1664-1720/21) of New Kent and Hanover Counties, VA. Edward parents were Welch immigrant **Ann Philip** (1634-?) and **Peter Garland** (1628-?) of Petworth, Sussex, England.

Mary Rice (mother of Nancy Anne Garland) was the daughter of **Susannah Searcy** (?-?) and **David Rice Sr** (1704-?), New Kent County, VA, the son of **Marce (Marie?) King** (?-?) and immigrant **Thomas Rice** (1650/60-1711), born in Shiremonton, Bristol England. (Sources: for Garland ancestry: Byrnefamily.net Family History; for Collins: Williams descendent, Sally Black, in a private communication.)

A number of records state that Thomas Rice, returning from England in 1711, "died at sea" However, in a memoir by his grandson (dictated in 1814/5, published in 1824), the Rev. David Rice (1733-1816) states (page 13) that Thomas was murdered on shipboard by sailors, who robbed him of the property which had prompted his return to England. The Rice memoir and *Genealogical & Historical Notes on Culpeper County Virginia* by Raleigh Travers Green (1900, page 132.) state that the Rice family produced many prominent Presbyterians through several generations. Our memoirist David Rice was himself active in the establishment of both Hampton-Sidney and Transylvania Universities. These sources also record that immigrant Thomas Rice (or *Rhys*) was of Welch descent, though born in England.

David Rice's comments (Memoir, p. 83) on the subject of slavery, made by way of a confession at the end of his life, are worthy of preservation: "I have too much participated in the criminal and great neglect of the souls of slaves. Though we live at the expense of these unfortunate creatures, yet we withhold from them a great part of the means of instruction and grace. Many indeed deprive them of all so far as they can. This, added to that of depriving them of their unalienable rights of liberty, is the crying sin of our country; and for this I believe our country is now bleeding at a thousand veins." A member of the constitutional convention of Kentucky in 1792, Rice condemned slavery. His speech was published in 1812: *Slavery Inconsistent with Justice and Good Policy, Proved by a Speech, Delivered in the Convention, Held at Danville, Kentucky.*

GOUGE – ABOVE I Page 69

James Gouge (1777-1858/60) operated a tavern near Mason in Grant County, KY. His son, Thomas Jefferson Gouge reported this to the Williamstown *Courier* in 1881, which described James as a "caterer for the entertainment of the public." T.J. Gouge also said that James became the owner of "some 3,000 acres of land and 30 slaves, who were very much attached to him."

DWIGHT – ABOVE I Page 167

A volume recently in my possession is Benjamin W. Dwight's **History of the Descendents of John Dwight** (1874) Vol 1 (New York: John F. Trow and Sons "printed for the author"). Benjamin Dwight of course drew upon earlier sources, and cites, among others, **The History of Dedham, Mass, from the beginning of its settlement in September 1635 to May 1827** by Erastus Worthington (1827). This data confirms the records **Betty Taylor Cook** had gathered and preserved, namely that her great-grandfather, **Charles Taylor** was a descendent of **John Dwight** of Dedham MA. The following information supplements the Dwight genealogy, which appears on page 168 of **ABOVE I**.

JOHN DWIGHT & HANNAH _____

John Dwight (?-?) came from Dedham England to Watertown, MAs in 1634 or 1635, bringing with him his wife, **Hannah** _____ (?-Sept 5, 1656), daughter, Hannah and two sons, John and **Timothy.** John and Hannah arrived wealthy, although he had been a wool-comber in England – or at least the son of a wool-comber. Maybe the money was Hannah's.

"He came not," (Ben Dwight's **History** p. 92) "like many in long after years, to better his fortune, but, like the first originators of American ideas and institutions, to found a church without a bishop and a government without a king." Perhaps we owe a duty to *nuance* as a principle of historical understanding to suggest, with respect to the ancient archivists, that the motives of these immigrants were, mixed. Ancestor **John Beauchamp** (see **All of the Above II** p. 87), a financial backer of the ship *Mayflower* was likely to have joined with other backers, who expressed unhappiness with the founding and leading colonists, who attempted to enforce religious and political conformity on everyone, at the risk of the backers' profits. The backers wanted a return more than a "church without a bishop" and most likely had little or no interest in sponsoring the founding, in America, of "'a government without a king."

On Sept 1, 1635, John Dwight took part in the first town meeting in Dedham, MA. He was among the original 12 and then the original 19, who received grants of land formed the town. Ben Dwight, following Worthington, lay emphasis upon the precedent established in this granting of land, as marking a very early local government initiative in taking charge of important local affairs, to the neglect of any preserved monarchical powers to retain control over the disposition of lands. Ben Dwight cites (p. 94) Hutchinson, British loyalist, who would seek exile in England after the Revolution, to confirm the vigorous novelty of the earliest settlers, "who thought themselves at full liberty without any charter from the crown." (Hutchinson's **Hist. Mass**, vol 1, p. 45).

John Dwight established the first water-mill in Dedham (1635) and appears on the tax rolls as the second wealthiest man of Dedham. He was a founder in 1638 of the first Church of Christ in Dedham and was eulogized as "having been publicly useful," serving the town as a select-man for 16 years (1639-55). He was described as "a great peacemaker." After Hannah died in 1656, John married Elizabeth Ripley (?-July 17, 1660), widow of John Ripley, on Jan 20, 1657.

The first school building in Dedham was built in 1648, when son **Timothy** was nineteen. Since Timothy Dwight was accomplished, his mother Hannah Dwight must have been both literate and motivated to instruct her children. The school was an innovation, being (1644) the first free school in America supported by a tax upon the public. John Dwight was recorded as voting for the tax and then serving on the first committee of five "feoffees" (trustees) to manage the school.

Another trustee of the Dedham school was Michael Powell, father of Sarah Powell (?-?) who would be the 2nd wife of John's son. **Timothy Dwight**. The children of John and Hannah Dwight: Hannah (1625, in England-Nov 4 1714, in Dedham) m. Nathaniel Whiting; **Timothy** (1629, in Eng-Jan 31, 1717/18); John (1632, in Eng-March 24, 1638 "lost in the woods"); Mary (July 25, 1635, in Dedham, MA-?) "first child born in Dedham" m. Henry Philips; Sarah (June 17, 1638-Jan 24, 1664), m. Nathaniel Reynolds.

TIMOTHY DWIGHT & ANNA FLINT

Timothy Dwight (1628-1718), son of Hannah and John Dwight, was Dedham town clerk for ten years, selectman for twenty-five (1664-89) and a representative to the General Court (legislature) for at least one session (1691-92). Our source, Benjamin Dwight, quotes *his* source (Worthington) with approval, stating that Timothy "inherited the estate and virtues of his father and added to both." As a young man Timothy was "a coronet of a troop" and later" a captain of foot." His handwritten reports of the ten sorties he participated in against the aboriginal clans "still stand clear" according to Ben Dwight. Timothy Dwight was made an agent (one of two) to represent Dedham colonists in their efforts to secure a treaty to lands, which were "subject to the Indian Title" and therefore "bound by law of the colony to extinguish by equitable contract."

In 1662, Timothy reported he had obtained a treaty with "King Philip" for certain lands. The practice of obtaining treaties from certain "Sachems" was a decades-long process, which resulted in acute discomfort on the part of the nomadic and semi-nomadic hunter-gatherers, who had to show, in proceedings with which they were entirely unfamiliar that they *owned* lands when the very notion of land ownership was as newly imported to the continent as were the English themselves. See **ALL OF THE ABOVE I**, PP. 187-89, 300-302.) In 1681, the town voted that all treaties and other documents be collected and saved. Captain Dwight came forward with Capt. Fisher to present seven deeds and receipts from the Indians, which purported to show the town's rights to lands which had been acquired from the now-dead King Philip, and others. The documents were not recorded or preserved.

Timothy Dwight was husband of six and father of fourteen, ten with his third wife, **Anna Flint** (?-?). Sarah Sibley (Perman) was his first wife. They married on Nov 11, 1651. Sarah died in childbirth May 29, 1652. Anna is believed to have been known as "Perman," widow of a man of that surname. She was named Sarah Sibley in her father's will. On May 3, 1653, Timothy married Sarah Powell, daughter of Michael Powell, who was a representative from Dedham town to the General Court (legislature) in 1641 and '48. Timothy and Sarah Powell Dwight were the parents of four children; she died June 27, 1664.

Timothy married **Anna Flint/Flynt** (Sept 11, 1643-Jan 9, 1685, daughter of **Margery Hoar** (?-Mar 10, 1687) and the Rev. **Henry Flynt** (?-April 17, 1668) of Briantree (now Quincy), MA, who arrived from Derbyshire, England in 1635 and was ordained a teacher in the church at Braintree on Mar 17, 1639. Henry received an 80 acres grant "at the mount by the town of Boston" in 1639. In 1644, Henry suffered a serious loss of property by fire and apparently had to sell land to recover from the catastrophe; payment was to be made "in corn or cattle within one month into the hands of Henry Flynt, of Braintry, for his own use, in consideration of his great loss, through the hands of God's providence, by fire." Henry Flynt was credited, along with the Rev. William Thompson of opposing heresy in Braintree, that is, people "were purged by their industry from the sour leaven of those sinful opinions, that began to spread under Mr. Wheelwright's influence; and if any remain among them it is very covert." Margery Hoar was the sister of President Hoar of Harvard College (1672-75). Margery and Henry were the parents of ten children, with Anna the second child. Anna seems to have been the widow of John Dassett when she married Timothy Dwight on Jan 9, 1665.

Timothy's fourth wife was the widow, Mrs Mary Edwind of Reading, MA, who died August 3, 1688. On July 31, 1690, Timothy married his fifth bride, Ether Fisher, daughter of Hon. Daniel Fisher. Esther died Jan 30, 1690 or 1691. Timothy then married Bethiah Moss on Feb 1, 1691/92. Bethiah is credited, equally with Anna Flynt, as seeing to the care and upbringing of Timothy's fourteen children. Timothy died "full of honors and age" on Jan 31, 1717/18 at age 88. Bethiah died a week later, on Feb 6, 1717/18. It has been passed down through the family, Ben Dwight wroe, that Tim and Beth were buried together on the same day in the family vault in Dedham. The four children of Timothy Dwight and Sarah Powell: Timothy Jr (Nov 26, 1654-Jan 2, 1692); Sarah (April 2, 1657-Feb 8, 1659/60); John (May 31, 1662-?); Sarah 2nd (June 25, 1664-July 10, 1664). The ten children of Timothy Dwight and Anna Flint: Josiah (Oct 8, 1665-by Feb 8, 1670); **Nathaniel** (Nov 20, 1666-Nov 7, 1711); Samuel (Dec 2, 1668- ? but soon) (Feb 8, 1670-1748); Josiah 2nd (Feb 8, 1670-1748); Seth (July 9, 1673-Jan 22, 1731); Anna (Aug 12, 1675-Oct 15, 1675); Henry (Dec 19, 1676-Mar 26, 1732); Michael (Jan 10, 1679/80-1761); Daniel (Sept 23, 1681-? but soon); Jabez (Sept 1, 1683-June 15, 1785).

NATHANIEL DWIGHT & MEHITABLE PARTRIDGE

Nathaniel Dwight (1666-1711), son of Sarah Powell and Timothy Dwight, was a farmer, trader, surveyor and justice of the peace. After growing up in Dedham, he moved to Hatfield, MA, where he and **Mehitable Partridge** (1676-1756) were married on Dec 9, 1693. Mehitable's ancestors are recorded in my **ALL OF THE ABOVE I**, at page 168. Ben Dwight states that her grandfather, immigrant **William Partridge**, wrote his surname as Partrigg, perhaps a variation upon *Patrick*. Mehitable's father, **Samuel Partridge,** (1645-1740) was a merchant and a long-tenured Common Pleas judge in Hatfield, MA and its chief judge from 1706-1736. Samuel was also a judge of probate and a colonel of a regiment as well as member of "his Majesty's Council." Samuel lived to be 95, outliving his wife, **Mehitable Crowe** by 15 years. Early histories of Connecticut describe him as one of the wealthiest and most influential men in the western portion of the province. Samuel and Mehitable were the parents of ten children.

Mehitable Crowe was the daughter of **Elizabeth Goodwin** and **John Crowe**, early and wealthy settlers of Hartford, CT. Of their ten children, the four sons (John, Samuel, Daniel, Nathaniel) were said to have dissipated their inherited wealth but the daughters (Esther, Hannah, Elizabeth, **Mehitable**, Mary, Ruth) married well and did well by both their parents and their husbands.

Nathaniel and Mehitable Dwight moved (c. 1695) to Northampton, MA. In Nov. 1711, Nathaniel was stricken and died and was buried in West Springfield, MA. His grave is the oldest in the oldest cemetery. Mehitable continued to live in Northampton, for 45 years, and died there on October 19, 1756, age 81.Nathaniel Dwight and Mehitable Partridge were the parents of eleven children: Timothy (Oct 19, 1694-April 30, 1771); Samuel (June 28, 1696-Oct 3, 1763; Mehitable (Nov 11, 1697-Dec 22, 1697); Daniel Dwight (April 28, 1699- Mar 28, 1748; Seth Dwight (Mar 3, 1702-Sept 12, 1703); Elihu (Feb 17, 1704-June 8, 1727); Abiah (Feb 17, 1704-Feb 23, 1748); Mehitable Dwight 2nd (Nov 2, 1705-Nov 20,1767); Jonathan Dwight (Mar 14, 1707-?); Anna Dwight (July 2, 1710- ?); **Nathaniel Dwight** (June 20, 1712-Mar 30, 1784).

NATHANIEL DWIGHT & HANNAH LYMAN

Nathaniel Dwight (1712-1784) moved to Cold Spring (now Belchertown), MA in 1734. He was a propertied farmer and surveyor and also kept an inn. He was a Captain during the French and Indian (the Seven Years') War. He and **Hannah Lyman** (July 14, 1709-Dec 25, 1792) were married on Jan 2, 1735. Nathaniel kept a journal in which his religious devotion is prominently in evidence. He was remembered as serious, public spirited and devout, with little sense of humor. Nathaniel died on March 30, 1784, Hannah on Christmas Day, 1792. The children of Hannah Lyman and Nathaniel Dwight are: Elijah (Nov 30, 1735-Jan 10, 1736); Elihu (Mar 31, 1737-Mar 22, 1760); Justice (Jan 123, 1739-July 27, 1824); **Eunice** (May 28, 1742-Sept 26, 1807); Jonathan (April 3, 1744-Sept 27, 1766); Susannah (Oct 20, 1746-Sept 6, 1785); Elijah (Jan 4, 1749-Sept 13, 1795); Josiah (Jan 5, 1750-Mar 19, 1767); Pliny (Aug 11, 1753-Mar 15, 1783).

EUNICE DWIGHT & JOSEPH GRAVES

Eunice (1742-1807) and Joseph Graves (?-?) lived in Bangor, Maine. Their children: Electa (Nov 19-1762-June 27, 1776); Perez (May 9, 1764-Feb 9, 1827); Margaret (Feb 28, 1766-Dec 19, 1795); Electa 2nd (Jan 9, 1768-?); **Susannah** (Dec 13, 1769-1859); Josiah Dwight (Jan 30, 1772-?); Jonathan (Mar 30, 1774-?); Elijah (April 9, 1775-?); Elijah 2nd (Sept 12, 1779-Jan 12, 1799); Penelope (Aug 1, 1781-?); Joseph Jr (Aug 19, 1783-?); Jeremiah (April 9, 1786-?).

TAYLOR – ABOVE I Pages 165, 179 f., 189 f.

Benjamin Dwight (at page 470) has details about the career of **Oliver Swaine Taylor**, born Dec 17, 1784. Dwight specifies that Oliver taught school for 27 years "in such places" as Hadley, MA, Homer, Auburn and "Prattsburgh" NY, and at Tecumseh, Michigan. Ben Dwight's list of the teaching posts is not exhaustive (see **ABOVE I**, page 189 f). Oliver's son, Charles, wrote (**ABOVE I**, page 193) that Oliver also taught in Indiana, Ohio and South Carolina. Ben Dwight suggests that Oliver kept in touch with his former students; Dwight has written. "Of his pupils, several have been mayors of cities; three: judges of county courts; three: judges of the supreme court; six: members of Congress; two, generals in the Union army; seven: foreign missionaries; twelve: tutors and professors in college; and five, presidents of colleges. One of these was the first US ambassador to Japan; and several of them have been eminent as physicians and ministers of the Gospel." The children of Catherine and Oliver S. Taylor are: Catherine Gould (Dec 16, 1817-?) m. Delos Milton Keeler; **Charles** (Sept 15, 1819-1897); Henry Martyn (May 9, 1825-?) m. Augusta Earle, Auburn, NY; Edward Payson (Sept 27, 1827-?). Ben Dwight has supplied details of the lives of these children. Catherine Gould Taylor married Delos Milton Keeler (Sept 24, 1815-Oct 1, 1868). Delos was the son of Rebecca Baldwin (Nov 30, 1794-Oct 16, 1835) and Dr. Silas Keeler (April 11, 1793- April 13, 1867) of Sipio, NY. Delos and Catherine Keeler lived in Auburn NY where he was Sec-Tres of the Tuttle Mfgr Co (agricultural implements). Catherine and Delos Keeler were the parents of four children: Henry (Oct 26, 1857-?), Catherine (Sept 23, 1859-?), infant (b/d Feb 21, 1861) , and Charles (Jan 9, 1863-?).

TAYLOR, GAMEWELL – ABOVE I Page 139 f.

Ben Dwight has recorded (p. 471) that **Charles Taylor's** father-in-law,

John Gamewell, was born in Maryland, Sept 12, 1766. John's wife **Delilah Booth Gamewell** was born in South Carolina on April 12, 1792. Charles was a professor at the Spartanburg South Carolina Female College from 1855-58, General Superintendent of Sunday Schools of the Methodist Episcopal Church, South, 1858-61, Presiding Elder of the Wadesboro District, South Carolina Conference, 1861-65. Ben Dwight confirms **John Oliver Taylor Sr** (b. Sept 12, 1862) as the seventh child of Charles and Charlotte Taylor, placing John Oliver in the ninth generation from immigrants **Hannah** and **John Dwight**.

In contrast to Charles Taylor's allegiance (**ABOVE I**, pp. 171-72) to the southern rebellion (1861-65), Ben Dwight's 1874 book includes many details about the service of Dwight family members during the American Civil War (1861-65): Robert Watson Huntington (1840-?) was present during the 1st Battle of Bull Run. He was shipwrecked while on Admiral Dupont's expedition to Hilton Head SC and remained in the marine Corps after the war (Ben Dwight's book, p.555). Parker Swan (1842-1863) died of dysentery after seeing action at Gainesville, 2nd Bull Run 2, Popes Retreat, South Mountain, Antietam, and Fredericksburg (p. 559). Francis Jewett Parker (1825-?) was at Antietam, Shephardstown, Leestown, and was aide de camp to Gen Franklin (p. 573). Heinrich Aaron Clough (1842-?) was a soldier w 3rd MD Vol Reg Cavalry(p. 596). William Dana McCracken (1842-?) was at Antietam, South Mountain, and with Gen. Rosencrantz in TN (p. 660). Charles Tillinghast (1828-1862) died under arms at New Burn NC (p. 636). Philander Packer Foster (1823-1864) died in uniform at Raleigh, NC (page 552). Edward Richardson Dale (1844-?) was Quartermaster Sergeant with 77th Ohio Regiment (p. 667).

Daniel Green Dana (1845-1867) was with Co F, 4th Iowa Cavalry (p. 668). Joseph Bushwell Dwight was under arms (p. 706) as was Walton Dwight (1837-?), who raised recruits and served as captain, 149 PA Regiment, which he drilled; Daniel fought at Chancellorsville, Fredericksburg, Gettysburg, and 15 other engagements and was severely mounded at Gettysburg (p. 710). Harry Hopkins Watson (1844-1863) died from disease incurred while under arms (p. 742). Robert Watson Webb (1834-?) enlisted with 147th NY Regiment, was promoted to 2nd Lt, and served a total of 3 years; he moved to SC after the war, to raise cotton (p. 743). Edwin Dwight Partridge (1815-?) served in both the Mexican War and as a 2nd Lt in the Civil War; Gen. Hooker said of him: "he did not know what fear was" (p. 765). Eleazer Wilber (1824-1864) enlisted and died a prisoner of war at the notorious Andersonville (GA) Prison (p. 817). Jonathan Dwight Whitney (1823-1873) served under Gen. Sherman, in the Commissary Dept, in the 4th Iowa Regiment (p. 840). William Dwight Sedgwick (1831-1862) joined immediately (May 25, 1861) and served with 2nd MA Regiment; he was promoted to Major and died from his wounds at Antietam. William wrote in his pocket diary while dying, wounded at Antietam on Sept 17 1862 (p. 854). Charles Sedgwick Dwight (1840-?) served for 3 years with "Chicago Board of Trade Battery" and was present at Stone River, Lookout Mountain and a total of 30 battles and skirmishes (p. 862). Oliver Howard Chapin (1832-?) was a civil engineer on the staff of Gen. George McClellan (p. 866). William Orne Chapin (1837-?) served with the 4th Vermont Regiment and was taken prisoner by JEB Stuart at White House VA (p. 866). James Dwight Orne joined Sept 1861 and served for four years. Wounded several times, James Orne was in 36 battles, including second Bull Run, Chancellorsville and Gettysburg (p. 867).

George Bliss (1830-?) served as Paymaster General of NY State, with the rank of Major Gen, in command of all military operations in NY State. These operations included supervision of the payment of bounties, the organization of three "colored" regiments in NY (the 20th 26th and 31st) and responsibility for the

Park Barracks in NYC, through which 17,000 sick and wounded passed during the war. Bliss was also responsible for transit of all troops who passed through NY State during the war. After the war, he became attorney for the state Board of Health and in 1873, was appointed by President Grant to be US attorney for the Southern District of NY (p. 883). Wilder Dwight (1833-1862) was with the 2nd MA Regiment of Infantry Vols; he became a prisoner of war in 1861, captured while looking after some wounded. Wilder Dwight was exchanged, promoted to Lt Colonel and returned to active duty in time for Antietam. He died on Sept 19, 1862 of wounds received at Antietam. Wilder left many dying notes and final words and was eulogized and remembered with high regard (p. 887).

Charles James Mills (1841-1865) enlisted Aug 14, 1862 in the 2nd MA Regular Infantry Volunteers, was made a 2nd Lt and rose through the ranks to Asst Adj Gen. He was shot through both legs at Antietam and discharged. Charles re-enlisted when able to walk and was present at the battles of Wilderness, North Anna, Shady Grove, Bethesda, the siege of Fredericksburg and was killed at Hatcher's Run VA (p. 899). Charles Carroll Dwight (1832-1862) died at Ft Lookout, James Island, SC June 16, 1862 (p. 919). William Hersez (1835-1863) enlisted as a private and was commissioned a Lt; William died at Baton Rouge, LA, in 1863 (p. 970). William Wood (1848-1862) was a drummer boy from Purnam, Michigan and died at Corinth MS, June 27, 1862, age 13 (P. 985).

Albert Smith Hurd (1836-1864) was killed at the Battle of Cold Harbor, June 3, 1864 (p. 987). James McLain Elledge (1843-?) joined the US Army of Vols in Texas July 10, 1861, was mustered out on Dec 8, 1865. He was part of "the Army of the Cumberland" (the 59th Ill Regt) and was in uncounted battles. He was wounded, and was made at prisoner at the Battle of Stone River, Murfreesboro TN. Albert returned to his unit in time for the battle of Resaca in GA, then promoted to Quartermaster Sergeant (p. 990). Sereno Benedict Dwight (1837-?) enlisted in the 10th Missouri Cavalry and served for 3 years, as did his brother Francis (p. 1024). Cyrus Dwight of Raymond, NH, was a soldier in the war (p. 1026). William Nelson Elliot (1807-?) had been a doctor in White Pigeon, Michigan for 29 years, when the war began in 1861. He then became a surgeon in the 11th Michigan Regiment of Infantry, which was part of the Army of the Cumberland. Doctor Elliot served for 3 years (p. 992). William, did you leave a memoir? Did you make a record of the unqualified good that you did and the absolute horrors that you undoubtedly witnessed?

PARSONS – ABOVE I Page 165

Susannah Graves (1769-1859) was the second wife of **Nathan Parsons** (Mar 22, 1752-Oct 23, 1823), described by family historian Benjamin Dwight as a merchant and farmer, first at Belchertown, MA and then Thomaston, ME (1796-1806) and Bangor, ME (1806-1823). Nathan was under arms during the Revolutionary War "from the beginning to the end" (Ben Dwight, p. 468); he was at Bunker Hill, Saratoga, and quartered with Washington at Morristown, NJ. The children of Susannah and Nathan Parsons: Bud (Sept 8, 1787-1854, in Oconomowoc, Wisc); Sparhawk (July 14, 1789-Aug 13, 1861); **Catherine Gould** (Nov 17, 1791-July 7, 1865) (**Above I**, pp. 166, 179); Sherlock (Oct 17, 1793-?); Susan Graves (Aug 27, 1795-?); Electa Lyman (Aug 6, 1797-?); Elijah Graves (Mar 10, 1799-?); Pliny Dwight (Feb 1, 1801-?); Penolope Graves (Jan 13, 1803-?); Fidelis Parsons (Mar 2, 1805-Jan 2, 1851); Mary Vose (Mar 7, 1807-?); Park Holland (Mar 7, 1809-?); Emma Gould (Nov 2, 1812-?).

CORNET JOSEPH PARSONS & MARY BLISS

Catherine Gould Parsons (Nathan Jr, Nathan Sr, the Rev. David) was the double great granddaughter of **Joseph Parsons Jr.** whose father was **Cornet Joseph Parsons** (1620-1683). **Joseph Parsons,** known in many subsequent records by his military title, **Cornet Joseph Parsons,** came to America as a boy but earned prominence as public servant and founder of towns, which grew into cities. Much has been written about him. (See SOURCES, below). Joseph was the child of **Margaret Hoskins** (c. 1584-?) and **William Parsons** (?-?). His maternal grandparents were **Robert** and **Margret Hoskins**, one of two couples of that name in Beanminster, England, both of whom had a daughter named Margaret.

Joseph Parsons was born in Beanminster about 1620 and came to Massachusetts in 1635 (perhaps with a brother, Benjamin) aboard the *Transport* (Edward Walker, Master) out of Gravesend, County Kent. Joseph Parsons received many notations in colonial town records. Joseph is mentioned as a witness to a deed on July 15, 1636 in Springfield, MA. The deed was between Joseph Pyncheon and local Indians. In 1646, Joseph was appointed highway surveyor of Springfield, holding this position in 1653. In 1652, Joseph was elected a Springfield Selectman but was living in Northampton, MA by 1655. In December of 1656 in Northampton, Joseph Parsons was elected to the Board of Selectmen. He served as Selectman in 1659, 1664, 1667, and 1670. Joseph served frequently as a juror.

On Nov 26, 1646, he married **Mary Bliss** (?-?) in Hartford, CT, and became the parents of 13 children, 5 girls and 8 boys. It seems probable their first three children (**Joseph Jr**, Benjamin, John) were born in Hartford, as their births were not recorded in Springfield. Joseph Jr. was the father of four sons, Ebenezer, Daniel, Moses and **David**, great grandfather of Catherine Gould Parsons (**ABOVE I**, p. 166). NOTE: Catherine (**ABOVE I** p. 167), is connected further back to the same Parsons family through her Graves and Dwight lineage.

In 1656, almost 40 years before the witchcraft travesty in Salem, MA, Joseph Parsons filed a lawsuit for slander, seeking damages against Sarah Bridgman, wife of James Bridgman. The suit accused Sarah Bridgeman of calling Mary Biss Parsons a witch. In 1664, Joseph Parsons was charged with unlawfully resisting a constable in his lawful duties. The charge was not denied and Joseph paid a fine of 20 shillings. Joseph was the plaintiff and defendant is several suits over money owed. Some of these were settled out of court; in some cases, payment was made through the court or a parcel of land would be sold to satisfy the debt. Joseph Parson's business records are deposited in the Springfield, MA, Library.

On the 7th of October 1678, the General Court appointed Joseph Parsons, Sr. to be "Cornet of the Troop of Hoarse," Hampshire Co. (Maj. John Pynchon, commander). With this appointment, Joseph was third in command and the color-bearer of the Hampshire Cavalry. It is unlikely that Joseph Parsons would have received this appointment had he not been active in "King Philip's War" of a few years before. (See **ABOVE I**, pp, 187, 301.) Joseph Parsons died on October 9, 1683. He was probably buried in the Elm Street cemetery (Northampton?), and reburied in a mass grave near the Pine Street entrance, when land within the cemetery was needed for a railroad.

JOSEPH PARSONS JR & ELIZABETH STRONG

Joseph Parsons (1647-1729) was a lawyer in western Massachusetts, serving as Justice of the Peace for Northampton and for 23 years Judge of the Hampton County Court. He also served as a deputy of the General Court (legislature) for 14 years (1693-1707) and in 1696 and 1718, was "Commissioner of Oyer and Terminer." In 1711, he was commissioned captain of a company of foot soldiers in the New Hampshire regiment (command by Colonel **Samuel Partridge**, see **ABOVE** I pp. 167-68). **Elizabeth Strong Parsons** (1648-1736) was born Feb 24, 1648. Her father was Elder John Strong (see **ABOVE I**, p. 175). John Strong had come to Massachusetts on the ship *Mary & John* in 1630, the same vessel which brought **John Maverick** and **Mary Gye Maverick** (**ABOVE I**, p. 201 f.) Elizabeth and Joseph were married for more than fifty years. She died on May 12, 1736. The ten children of Joseph and Elizabeth Parsons were: Joseph, John, Ebenezer, Elizabeth, **David**, Josiah, Daniel, Moses, Abigail, Noah. David and **Sarah Stebbens** Parsons were the parents of **Nathan Parsons Sr.** (**Above I**, page 165.) See: **CORNET JOSEPH PARSONS: One of the Founders of Springfield and Northamptom, Massachusetts**, by Henry M. Burt (Albert Ross Parsons, Garden City, Long Island, NY 1898); **GENEALOGICAL GUIDE TO THE EARLY SETTLERS OF AMERICA**, by Henry Whittemore, (Genealogical Publishing Co., 1967, p 404). **IMMIGRANT ANCESTORS**, Ed. Frederick Adams Virkus, 1986, p 52; **PARSONS FAMILY, Descendants of Cornet Joseph Parsons**, by Henry Parsons, Vol 1 1912, Vol 2, 1920.

SWAYNE – ABOVE I Page 185

The father of **Jeremiah Swayne** (1643-1710) was immigrant **Jeremiah Swain I:** "Jeremiah Swain, first of the family known in America, was in Charlestown, Mass, in 1638, and soon after moved to Redding, Mass." See **History of the Town of Antrim, NH** (Cochrane, 1880).

BALDWIN – ABOVE I Pages 225, 229

Jonah Baldwin and **Sarah Scott** were married on January 31, 1809 in Champaign County Ohio. The ceremony was conducted by Justice of the Peace, Nathaniel Pinckard. See *The History of Champaign and Logan Counties: From Their First Settlement*, By Joshua Antrim, Western Ohio Pioneer Association (Press Printing Co. 1872, p. 261)

MOORE – ABOVE I Pages 258-9

Thomas Moore, husband of **Elizabeth Browne** was not the son of Richard Moore, Sr. or Jr. See: **Early Families of Southern Maryland**, by Elise Greenup Jourdan (Heritage Books, 2007, page 201). The ancestry of this Thomas is as yet undiscovered.

PUTNAM – ABOVE I Pages 293, 296

A century ago, the Putnam ancestry in England was published in *New England Families*, Third Series, Vol II, William Richard Cutter, ed. (Lewis: New York, 1915, pp. 1075-76). This book shows no connection between the Putnams of Salem, MA and the Puttenhams who were the writers of books in Tudor

England. (See **ABOVE I**, pp. 293, 295.) Many of the Putnam links in *New England Families*, especially the earlier ones, appear with the caveat *believed to be*. The *New England Families* ancestry appears as follows: **Simon** de Puttenham (?-aft 1199), who held the Puttenham Manor, followed by **Sir Ralph** (?-aft 1217), **Richard** (?-aft 1273), **John** (?-aft 1291). **Thomas Puttenham I** (?-?), married **Helen**, daughter of _____ **Spigornell**. Thomas and Helen were the parents of Henry and older brother **Roger Puttenham** (b/f 1300-aft 1322). Roger was sheriff of Hertfordshire in 1322 and husband of **Aliva** _____; their son was **Henry I** (1300-1350), father of **Sir Roger** Puttenham (abt 1320-abt 1380). Sir Roger was the father of **William Puttenham I** (?-?) of Puttenham Pen, Sherfield, Warbelton; William's wife was **Margaret de Warbelton**. Margaret was the daughter of **John de Warbelton** (?-?) seated at Warbelton, Sussex, Sherfield on London. Margaret's mother was **Katherine**, daughter of **Sir John de Fokle**, of Foxle, Bramshel and Apuldrefield.

William and Margaret were the parents of **Henry Puttenham II** (b/f 1408-July 6, 1473), husband of **Elizabeth**, widow of Geoffry Goodluck. Elizabeth's will is dated Dec 25, 1485; in it she asked to be buried at the Chapel of St Mary the Virgin in All Saints of Istleworth. Henry and Elizabeth were the parents of **William Puttenham II** (abt 1430-1492), husband of **Anne**, daughter of **John Hampden** (?-?) of Hampden, County Bucks. William's will was dated July 10, 1492 and proved at Lambeth. William directed that he be buried before the image of the Blessed Virgin Mary in the chapel within the church of the Hospital of the Blessed Mary, known as Elsingspytell, London. The children of William and Anne Puttenham were Sir George (heir and knight), Edmund of Puttenham, **Nicholas**, Frideswide, Elizabeth, Alionore, Brigide, and Agnes.

Nicholas Puttenham (abt 1460-abt 1526) of Putnam Place, was the father of John and **Henry III** (1460/75-aft 1526), who probably lived at Eddlesborough; Henry's three sons were **Richard**, John of Slapton and Hawridge and Thomas of Eddlesborough. **Richard Putnam** (1490/1500-1556/7) lived at Eddlesborough and Woughton. His will is dated Dec 12, 1556, proved Feb 26, 1557. In it he directed that he be buried at the church in Woughton. Richard was the father of **John II**, Harry of Woughton and Joan. **John Putnam II** (1520/25-1568) lived at Rowsham in Wingrave, where he was buried on Jan 27, 1568. John II was the father of **Nicholas II**, Richard of Wingrave, Thomas of Rowsham, and Margaret, who married Godfrey Johnson on June 14, 1573 at Wingrave.

Nicholas Putnam II (1540/50-1598), son of **John II** lived at Wingrave and, after about 1585, at Stewkeley. Nicholas' will was dated Jan 1, 1597 and proved Sept 27, 1598. Nicholas married **Margaret Goodspeed** (1556-1618/19) on Jan 30, 1577 at Wingrave. Margaret was the daughter of **John** and **Elizabeth Goodspeed**. Margaret was baptized, Aug 16, 1556 at Wingrave and buried at Ashton Abbots Jan 8, 1618/19. Her second husband was William Huxley. The children of Elizabeth and Nicholas Putnam (all baptized at Wingrave) were Anne (Oct 12, 1578), **John** (Jan 17, 1579), Elizabeth (Feb 11, 1581), Thomas (Sept 20, 1584) and Richard.

John Putnam (1579-1662), 12th Putnam (Puttenham) in this line, son of **Nicholas** and **Margaret Putnam**, was the immigrant ancestor. John lived on his inherited estates at Ashton Abbots until he immigrated to Massachusetts by 1640/41, when he received a grant of land and where his wife **Priscilla Deacon** (?-?) was enrolled in the church in Salem, MA. John was enrolled on April 4, 1647. John and Priscilla were the parents of Elizabeth, **Thomas II** (1614-1686), John, Nathaniel, Phoebe, and John. **Thomas Putnam II** was the father of **Joseph** (1669-1724) and grandfather of the famous **Israel Putnam** (1717/18-

1790) (See **ABOVE I**, p. 297.) Three generations of Putnams (John, Thomas, Joseph) were among the few prominent, wealthy families in tiny Salem Villege, MA in the 17th century.

New England Families, our source, states (p. 1077) that Ann Putnam, 12, a granddaughter of **Thomas II** (daughter of Thomas III) "was the most prominent child" among prosecution witnesses during the Salem Witch Trials of 1692 and "was the cause of more of the imprisonments than was any other one person." (For some Trial details and the conduct of Putnam family members, see **ABOVE I**, page 307-13). *New England Families* states that in 1706 Ann Putnam "made a pubic confession" of her regretted role as an accuser of witches in Salem fifteen years before. Ann stood while her apology was read before the congregation. Her confession came very late for two dozen people, who were executed because of the hysterical accusations of "weak and excitable" witnesses. There is some likelihood that young Ann Putnam was manipulated by her parents, Thomas and Ann Putnam, who were active in prodding her and other young girls into making denunciations. After both her parents died in 1699, Ann, age 19, became responsible for raising her siblings, who ranged in age from 7 months to 18 years. Ann never married and died in 1716 at 37 years of age.

DOYNE – ABOVE I Page 359

According to Maryland State archives (St. Mary's City Men's Career Files, MSA SC 5094), **Robert Doyne**'s brother Joshua was married to Barbara (?-?) and the father of Ethelbert, Jesse, William, Joshua, Ignatius, Edward Aloysius, Mary (who married Ignatius Matthews), and Dennis. With 2nd wife Jane, Joshua Doyne was the father of Jane. Joshua held the following local offices: justice of peace, 1675, 1677, 1679, 1680, 1685; coroner, 1676; sheriff, 1682-1685, 1688-1689. In addition, Joshua held a number of provincial offices: grand juror, Provincial Court, 1673; juror, Provincial Court, 1673, 1674, 1675. He also served as captain of the militia and owned at death, 3,946 acres.

STONE – ABOVE I Pages 363, 364

William Maximillan Stone (1603-1660) was born 1595/1596 in Northamptonshire, England and christened Oct 7, 1603, Twiston, Lancashire, England. His parents were **Dorothy Jennett** (1581-?) and Capt **John Carr Stone** (b: 1578 in Croston, Bretherton, Lancaster, England). (See *Stephen's Ancestors & Cousins* at freepages.genealogy. rootsweb.ancestry.com; this source lists Captain Stone's death date "8 Aug 1616 in Bay Colony, Connecticut," but there was no "Bay Colony" at that date.) The Maryland State archives (*St. Mary's City Men's Career Files*, MSA SC 5094) list William Stone's public offices: justice of peace (Accomack County, Virginia), 1633, 1635-1639, 1641-1645, 1647-1648; Hungars Parish Vestry (Accomack County, Virginia), 1635; sheriff (Accomack County, Virginia), 1634, 1640, 1646; and Burgess (Accomack County, Virginia), 1642.

William Stone was a member of the Provincial Council, 1656-1660, justice of the Provincial Court, 1658-1660, and a member of the Upper House of the legislature, 1658 (though he did not attend). He also was a captain of militia in 1659. At his death in 1660, Stone owned over 3000 acres, in addition to Nangemy Manor, and lands at Bustards Island. See his will: *The Maryland Calendar of Wills*, Volume I Wills from 1635 (Earliest Probated) to 1685 (Pages 1-13). (Compiled in 1904 by Jane Baldwin; Edited and Annotated by Rhoda Fone and Carol Hammett, 2001).

www.ingramcontent.com/pod-product-compliance
Lightning Source LLC
Chambersburg PA
CBHW031641170426
43195CB00035B/172